It's all About Showing Up

THE POWER IS IN THE ASKING

Vol. 2

Lady Dr. Robbie Motter

HAVANA BOOK GROUP LLC.
HAVANABOOKGROUP.COM

Testimonials

"It's All About Showing Up" by Robbie Motter is a thought-provoking and insightful read that explores the significance of being present in one's life. The book highlights the power of intentional presence and its impact on personal growth, relationships, and overall well-being. It offers practical strategies and techniques to help readers cultivate a deeper sense of presence in their daily lives, encouraging them to live in the moment, and to fully engage with the world around them. This book is a must-read for anyone looking to live a more fulfilling and meaningful life and to strengthen their connections with others.

-Melissa Hull
Global Media CEO • International Speaker • Story Coach • Show Host • Author on Child Loss • Podcast Host • Public Figure

Opportunities will happen when you SHOW UP, ASK and TAKE ACTION. It may not be right away, or it may be the time when you least expected it. Lady Dr. Robbie Motter has proven that over and over again in the chapter of her second book, "It's All About Showing Up". I was given the opportunity to write a chapter in her first book. What she described in this chapter is real, inspiring, and powerful. I am one of the 26 nominees who received the Honorary Humanitarian Doctorate degree in December 2022, and I was there to experience several of the great opportunities live in London! It was an experience of a lifetime. Also, as she said, we need to be intentional. In this chapter, Dr. Robbie Motter gave examples with a message that just SHOWING UP is not good enough, but it is a good start. SHOWING UP with the intention creates attention from others. Then when we ASK, we get noticed. Then when we TAKE ACTION, opportunities follow! Another point I would like to stress with Dr. Robbie Motter's examples, she has always paid forward with the opportunities she received. She always takes action and is grateful for every single event she is given the opportunity to attend/participate in. This is one of the important keys to why this happens to her. She focuses on the possibilities rather than disappointment! She always focuses on the positive of every experience rather than the negative. Another important lesson I would like to share is that she does not use her age as an excuse for why we can't do it. Again, she does it with intention. Thank you, Dr. Robbie, for your mentorship and tireless leadership. I am proud and grateful to be your student.

Dr. Angeline Benjamin
Action Coach with Results, Speaker, Author
Director of GSFE Virtual Thursday Network

Robbie is beyond inspirational. Robbie's life's philosophy, "Just show up!" is who Robbie is. I know this first-hand. I met Robbie for the first time 16 years ago when she was awarded the Office Depot Businesswoman of the Year Award on behalf of NAFE. When I met Robbie, I was instantly drawn to her energy and knew that she had a beautiful and giving heart. She showed up in a big way in my life. She helped me "kickstart" my first PR consultancy practice and recommended me for a large PR project for NAFE's national conference. Robbie means what she says. We should all be more "like Robbie." She not only shows up every day in the lives of so many women, but she also makes others want to "show up." Her story will blow you away and inspire you to "show up."

Lauren Raguzin
Author, Women Standing Strong Together Volume II
Change Management and Communications Leader

I have had the pleasure of knowing Robbie Motter for over 35 years and I have watched her work her magic ever since. Her magic began when she was starting her work career as a young woman and was told by her woman supervisor, she would not spend a minute helping her. That she must make her own way through life and never ask for help. She vowed from that day until now, 70 years later, that she, Robbie would always "ask", always encourage others to "ask," and to respond to all "asks" in some way. She vowed that she would listen to every "ask" and respond with help, connections, and encourage everyone to do the same to become the best we could all be by "showing up" and "asking."

This book is a testament to her magic. She has "asked" others for their stories of impact and inspiration to include in her second book.

Read all these stories, be impacted, be inspired, and see how the Robbie Magic of "Showing up" and "Asking" has propelled others and can propel you towards your best self as you then help others.

Share these stories with women of all ages. These lessons of "Asking" and "Showing up" should be learned at a young age and can become an integral part of who they are well beyond their 87th year, "ask" Robbie about that!!!

Gillian Larson
Public speaker
CBS Contestant on Survivor
Founder, Creator, and Producer of Reality Rally Inc

"It's All About SHOWING Up and the POWER is in the ASKING 2 is an invaluable guide to inspire woman entrepreneurs to be authentic and use your skills for success in your business to improve your local, national, or global market.

Ed Burtnette CLA I Vice President National Liability Claims
CorVel Corporation

It is an honor to be a co-author in Robbie Motter's first collaboration, It's All About Showing Up, The Power is in the Asking, Volume 1, along with so many inspiring entrepreneurs. I have great respect and admiration for Robbie's dedication to providing opportunities to empower and motivate women to rise to new heights. For 40+ years she has devoted her life to helping women discover and achieve their purpose, and to be recognized for their gifts and talents, which she often sees in others before they see in themselves.

Caprice Crebar CEO, Heart Link Network Worldwide for Entrepenreurial Women

It is a fascinating and an informational read. A must for anyone investing in themselves or just adapting the "ASK" and "SHOW UP" in their vocabulary.

A delightful account of Lady Dr Robbie Motter Mantra -Ask and Show Up. Each co-author's story is amazing.

It's a 5* + Read.

Jean Olexa, "The Organizer"

"Robbie Motter is THE International business icon to follow if you are ready to and willing to become the MOST VISIBLE and INPSIRING version of yourself! Robbie doesn't just walk her talk, she runs circles around the globe motivating and inspiring women to SHOW UP and ASK for what they desire. I've known Robbie for almost twenty years, and she never ceases to amaze me or stretch me to become the best I can one "ask" at a time. Don't wait, grab a copy of this book for yourself and all your girlfriends and be prepared to be amazed by the incredible stories shared in this book!"

Ursula Mentjes, USA Today Bestselling Author and founder of Ursula, Inc., and the CEO Table

Lady Dr Robbie Motter has demonstrated through her work and her word, that showing up and asking is the road to success and unimaginable experiences. A good habit she has encouraged in her GSFE members to adopt. She has graciously written a number 1 bestselling book that focuses on relevant, real time successful results. She beautifully illustrates the power taking action and showing up and asking for what you need.

It is one of the most powerful tools an entrepreneur can develop, master, and make a habit.

Lady Dr Robbie has such an altruistic spirit, she not only shows up for herself as the founder of GSFE, but she also uplifts her directors and members to other leaders from around the world. Many of the world leaders have been instrumental in helping GSFE members to expand their individual platforms.

She has been diligent in nominating, celebrating and decorating her GSFE members with honors and awards based on their accomplishments and innate abilities.

She uses her influence to secure life changing events for her most deserving members.

She has offered us a chance to speak on international stages, become first time authors and co-authors. She has even nominated some entrepreneurs to receive an honorary doctorate degree.

Lady Dr Robbie opens doors for women all over the world through mentoring and inspiring by example.

I am thankful to be the director of Northern California GSFE. I am so very proud to be a recipient of an honorary doctorate for who I am.
Dr. Stone Love Faure

Dr (h.c.) Stone Love Fauré is the premier award-winning international speaker, writer and mentor for women entrepreneurs and the go-to expert for Decision-Making. She is the recipient of the Presidential Award and an Honorary Doctorate in Humarianism Award. Dr Stone is an international retreat leader and certified coach with over 20 years of coaching experience. She is the author of Decision Time & Now, I Am Her.

Preface

Dear Reader,

Thank you for purchasing our book. My dynamic 64 co-authors and I hope you will enjoy each story as they were written from the heart.

The three greatest words are SHOW UP and ASK. I have been sharing the power of those words with women all over the world since 1975. Each day I hear more and more people use those words and that fills my heart. I keep sharing this mantra with every woman I meet along my life's path. I get great responses back when they do start SHOWING UP and ASKING about how great those two things really are.

The book was designed and created to share the impact these philosophies have had on so many, and you can have also in your life, once you implement them into your life.

I would love to connect with you and hear your thoughts on your SHOW UP and ASK experiences.

Lady Dr. Robbie Motter
Founder/CEO Global Society for Female Entrepreneurs (GSFE) a 501(c)
(3) global nonprofit.

GSFEUS.com

HAVANA BOOK GROUP LLC
2173 SALK AVE, SUITE 250
CARLSBAD, CA. 92008

COPYRIGHT 2021 All rights reserved.
ISBN: 979-8-9862-6477-6

FOREWORD

Lady Dr. ROBBIE MOTTER   the Visionary and a Game Changer

My name is Lady Ambassador Dr. Peterson PhD. I am presently the official Global Goodwill Ambassador Chief Executive Director for USA & UK Global International Alliance Program Corporation for National Volunteer Community Service Online Honorary Advocate Leadership; People of Choice Program of Uniting in Humanitarianisms Non-Profit Organization Program 501(c)(3) the Global of International Alliance Online School was established in 2016 and is an accredited program under IACET Standards for Lifelong Learning program.

Let me tell you why I learned to love and adore Dr. Robbie Motter

I have been following Ms. Robbie for many years and I have learned she is a woman that always shows tenacity, when it comes to handling her business. She is very persistent in maintaining any assignment she is involved with.

When I think of Dr. Robbie Mottor there are two words comes to mind: Visionary and Game Changer. What is a visionary?

Dr. Robbie as a visionary she has the astute ability to look into the future and know how to find innovative and imaginative ways to help others realize their dreams and then push them in to their success.

Dr. Robbie always looks at the big picture while focusing on the details in developing programs with new and creative ways in order to provide opportunities to help meet the challenges many may be facing individually and in her community. She knows how to set the bar to meet your goals, by developing and strategies that address these challenges, such as helping many to develop new talent ideals and she counsels many others by being the mastermind behind the problem.

She has worked with many top entrepreneurs from all over the world. Dr. Robbie knows how to solidify the needs of others and remains focused, never giving up in pursuit of fulfilling her dreams and that of others. As a visionary, she is confident in her own efforts to help others realize their dreams; her efforts are only measured by the depth of her own success.

When I think of Dr. Robbie Motter. I also see her as a tough and bold thinker who empowers others to help themselves to reach their full potential for success. She is a game changer.

She knows how to think outside of the box with many other organizations no matter who they are. This is why she is so very special to me.

Congratulations!

To you, my dear friend, and my sister,
Lady Amb. Dr. Lenora Peterson-Maclin.Ph.D.

Chapter Overview

It's all
About
Showing
Up

Stepped Out: Met the Calls to Action!

Mary Aurtrey

A section of my chapter in this book is dedicated to my friend (who is now deceased) and my organization (Women In Networking).

First, I am so thankful to the Lord for allowing this book opportunity to come my way and for blessing me as I bless others.

Second, I am so honored and grateful to Robbie Motter, Director for GSFE, for allowing me to add a chapter (of my own story) to her Book, "It's All About Showing Up", Volume II! Special Thanks to you, Robbie!

Third, I am also grateful to members of my organization (Women In Networking) (WIN) for encouraging me to share with others their stories about WIN and am very grateful that I have this opportunity to share other areas of my life over the years.

On November 4, 2022, I was inducted into the Indiana Military Veterans Hall of Fame for honorable military and community volunteer service at The Garrison, (Old Fort Harrison), Indianapolis, IN! Being nominated and selected is a great honor. Not so long ago, another Indiana honor was bestowed upon me which was the Indiana Governor's Torchbearer Award for Outstanding Community Service for military and civilian service.

Through many efforts and pursuits, I was able to attain financial donations and obtained matching funds that assisted women and families to improve their quality of life to have a better place to live and work. I saw the need and stepped out and helped meet the need. My Lord and Savior guided me, as He is still doing, and watched me accomplish that particular goal at the time. My words are "To Him be the Glory"!

September 2, 2011 was a day of shock for me! Out of at least 30 antonyms and synonyms for shocked, the best description for my being was "stunned". I was stunned from the devastating news of the death of the Director for Women In Networking (WIN) Organization! My friend and business associate went to be with the Lord on that day. Now, I'm left alone to run the organization that she and I co-founded in 1994 known as NAFE/Women In Networking (WIN)! This was a Network of NAFE (National Association for Female Executives) with members across the country! She was not only the Co-founder but was also Director of NAFE/WIN. She was the "brain" of the Network organization and valued it very close to her heart. As the Co-founder and Co-Director, I also felt the same way and wanted the same goals for WIN members. To keep the organization going and retain all the hard work we put into it and the members since 1994, and until the time of her passing and beyond, I knew I had to step up and show out! I knew how important it is to continue the membership and network, help women and their families, and build community relations.

My next thought was "What am I going to do?" I remembered notifying Robbie Motter, NAFE's Global Regional Coordinator at that time, whom I earlier met through the Director at NAFE's 2000 Annual Women's Conference in New York. Robbie informed me to get the announcement out as quickly as I could to NAFE and let them put it on the NAFE website since our business partner was one of NAFE's Network Directors and Co-

Founder and Director for WIN. I sent the announcement to NAFE, and they captured a portion of it and had it shown on their website.

During this time, I "stepped up" temporarily and assumed the Director's duties and maintained my responsibilities. Later, the new election of officers (WIN Board of Directors) and members voted me as their new leader and Network Director for Women In Networking (WIN).

Currently, WIN is a 501 (c) (3) Nonprofit Organization located at the Defense Finance and Accounting Service (DFAS) Center, Indianapolis, IN. This is where the majority of WIN members are based; however, there are members who are located in other states (California, Florida, Ohio, and Texas). The organization is comprised of civilians, military personnel, Veterans, and retirees. Communications are done through teleconferences, texts, Zoom, and our website (https://nafewin-indy.com).

Until WIN got a Co-Director, I ensured WIN had tax restoration, a revised Board of Directors, an updated business plan, regular monthly Knowledge Sharing Events, Annual Conferences, and other Networking opportunities for members of WIN in place. I ensured all annual filing of taxes and Business Entity Reports (BER), Department of Revenue Reporting, and official documents establishing the organization were done.

As a U.S. Army Veteran (retired) and Advocate for Veterans issues, I have contact with other Veterans and access to Veterans programs, organizations/businesses, VA benefits, and Veterans service organizations that are beneficial. Other women from WIN organization were not only inspired by my leadership and membership in this organization and Veterans organizations but also became a member: Indianapolis American Legion Women's Post #438, where I am Chaplain; American Veterans (AMVETS) Post 99, Indianapolis, IN, and Sister Soldier Network. My membership is also in other organizations such as Woman's Life Insurance

Society Chapter 703 Indianapolis, where I am president and the National Council of Negro Women, Indianapolis. I am also a Charter member for the Women's Memorial Organization in Washington, DC as a result of my honorable military service.

During my years in the military, there were several times when I had to "step up and show out". Prior to retiring from the military, I was promoted and held top positions such as Sergeant Major, E-9 (Top Enlisted Rank), First Sergeant, Master Sergeant, Sergeant First Class, and Military Occupational Specialties as a Stenographer and an Administrative Non-commissioned Officer in Charge. Worked for General Officers, both stateside (1st Cavalry Division and Fort Hood, TX), and overseas (Headquarters 19th Support Brigade, Taegu, South Korea, and the Supreme Headquarters Allied Powers, Europe (S.H.A.P.E.) in Mons, Belgium). A major portion of my job was working with highly classified and sensitive compartmental information. As a First Sergeant of a company with a 5-person staff and two attached schools of Soldiers (Master Fitness Training and the U.S. Army Recruiting School), there were many times when I had to personally fill in for certain duties because the soldiers were unavailable! I had to "show up and show out" to accomplish the mission. As the leading Noncommissioned Officer in Charge (NCOIC) with the Defense Intelligence Agency (DIA) in the Defense Attache' Branch, I worked with highly classified information and had to ensure proper handling and processing of classified information. There were times/incidents that I had to "step up and ensure everything was properly documented.

After retiring from the U.S. Army, July 1991, I traveled stateside and overseas for about a year. Later, I went to work for the Federal Government, and stayed there for 25 years before retiring. In the workplace, employees were inspired by my teamwork and leadership of running a women's organization, networking, and conducting community volunteer services.

Other women showed up, joined, and volunteered their services in the community with our organizations.

Subsequently, we voted and elected an Executive Director for WIN who is currently serving in her role, and at times, in the Network Director's absence.

There are other areas of my life where I had to "step out and show up". Chaplain for the Indianapolis American Legion Women's Post 438.

I joined the Indianapolis American Legion Women's Post in 2003, and three years later, they no longer had a Chaplain. They were looking for a spiritual advisor, but did not find one, therefore, they asked me if I would be their Chaplain. I gave it some consideration. I stepped up and met the call to serve as Chaplain for the Indianapolis American Legion Women's Post #438. Currently serving as Chaplain since 2003. As Chaplain, I conduct funeral and memorial services, provide weekly and monthly inspirations, and participate in the annual Four Chaplain's Service and other ceremonials. Whenever there's a death in one of the member's family, I volunteer to assist them.

A friend who was a U.S. Army Veteran in South Carolina passed away. The funeral director was not that adept on what to do for military funerals. I had to "step up and assist" with the proper protocol, flag presentation, color guard, and honor guard.

In 2021, Robbie Motter did not have enough judges for her Lady In Blue Sapphire Awards & Fashion Show in California. She called me in Indianapolis, IN, and asked if I would be a Celebrity Judge for her. I stepped up to help her and said "Yes", not knowing what my responsibilities would be. Because of the faith and confidence that I have in Robbie's

professionalism and business sense, I wanted to assist in this fantastic award show. This was an honor, and the show was a great success!

The Director of the Women's Memorial of Washington, DC contacted hundreds of female Veterans and military personnel to join the Women's Memorial Organization. As a Veteran, I felt as if I had to "step up and show out" and became a part of this piece of history for women. I contacted them and later submitted my information, and now I am a Charter Member.

The Women's Memorial Organization may use my induction into the Indiana Military Veterans Hall of Fame on November 4, 2022, as an inspiring patriotic story/legacy. This, along with my BIO and photos (attached with history), would be an example for military, veteran, and civilian women to emulate presently and in future. My voice can be heard on Audio in an interview for the Veterans History Project at the Library of Congress: https://memory.loc.gov/diglib/vhp-stories/loc.natlib.afc2001001.17795/. Also, since I am a Charter Member (#521274) of WIMSA, the Military Women's Memorial Organization could make my information part of its History in the Memorial. That would be an honor, not only to me, but also to military and veteran women, and to the United States of America.

In 2020, when the National Association for Female Executives (NAFE) resolved, the WIN Board of Directors and members decided to remove NAFE's abbreviation from WIN's title and documentation associated with it. Therefore, Women In Networking (WIN) revised its mission, vision, and goals, and moved the organization forward into the present.

Overall, special thanks to Robbie Motter again for encouraging me and giving me this opportunity to share my store with the world! I pledged to continue helping women, families, and those in need.

It's all
About
Showing
Up

Show up, Be Bold, and Say Yes!

Mary "MobileMary" Barnett

The Vietnam War just ended, and my mom, Gloria Alexander, was reading about the first wave of refugees. They were doctors, lawyers, teachers... and they were going to land in America without any credentials and would be forced to take welfare. She thought that these people needed help!

My mom went to the president of a local college to see what could be done. "These proud people will need to know how to apply for jobs and citizenship, and they won't accept welfare!" she said.

He agreed and said, "You have a teaching credential. Why don't you create a curriculum to help them, and I'll give you a warehouse to teach it in!"

She hadn't worked since she got married and had 6 kids, but she worried if she didn't do something, who would? So, Mom said "Yes...I can do that!" She would always remind me to Show up, be bold, and say YES, and that's exactly what she did!

I was in elementary school at the time. So, during summer while my friends were playing in the pool, I was helping my mom turn her dirty, steamy hot warehouse into a functioning classroom... and I loved every minute of it!

When the students needed to learn how to interview, Mom let me hold the giant video camera which was bigger than me, and I tracked them walking into the room and shaking hands with Mom. Afterwards, she'd privately coach them on firm handshakes and eye contact!

The state of California then asked her to do the same thing for the "hardcore unemployed" as they called them. These people were generational welfare recipients who couldn't remember anyone in their family ever having a job. She changed their lives, too, because she taught them to look for challenges disguised as opportunities! This is all because she Showed up and said YES.

As a Los Angeles Times reporter in a 1980 article, said "Gloria is an outgoing, dynamic espouser of positive thinking."

My mom was quoted to say "Enthusiasm is tremendously powerful. I get my students speaking positively and enthusiastically about what they can do and where they want to go with their lives."

My mom is still the voice in my head, and even though things change, history keeps repeating itself... and her words keep ringing true! Thinking back, it is her guiding principles that continue to help me steer the rudder of my life. I didn't really understand that as a child, but as life hit me hard, both personally and professionally, her wisdom continued to speak to me.

When I graduated college in 1988, I got a corporate job in marketing and my main task was to format the company's newsletter the "old fashioned way". But I had another brilliant idea! I brought my wedding present, a little Mac Plus computer, to work each day and proceeded to save a multi-national company $10,000 per month by using Pagemaker to lay it out digitally. I was pretty proud of myself!

After the third month, my little Mac died. My Mac+ didn't have an internal fan; heck, there wasn't even a hard drive!

When I asked the VP of Marketing to pay $300 to have it fixed, he refused and said, "It's not OUR machine."

I protested: "But I've already saved you $30,000, don't you want me to save you 40,000?" I guess he didn't!

I left his office feeling defeated, I couldn't believe it. I poured A LOT of time into this project, and he didn't even appreciate it or me, obviously. But Mom would say: God only closes doors when He's about to open a window.

The next week, God opened a window. One of my college counselors called my office and asked if I wanted to join the Loaned Executive Program, and my corporate job would PAY me to go raise money for the United Way for three months! I said...." HECK YES, I can do that!"

I had lots of experience with fundraising, and this opportunity heightened my skills and helped me create more professional relationships. As the United Way program was ending, I didn't want to go back to my "real" job...so one day, as I was leaving my last fundraiser for TRW, the Director of Marketing asked if I'd consider a consulting gig... I looked around and thought "Are you talking to Me?" ...but I played it cool of course, and said, "Well, let me check my calendar!" ...the elevator doors closed, and I started to jump up and down!

When I got home, my brilliant husband said, "Don't look too eager, wait a couple hours before you call her back." So, when I called, I said, "You know what? I think I can make some arrangements and squeeze you in!" She told me to come in two weeks and bring a contract and a P.O., and we could get started...I said, "Yes, I can do that!"

I had NO IDEA what a P.O. was? I drove to our local library (yes, Uncle Google wasn't born yet) and asked the librarian to use P.O. in a sentence. She laughed and handed me a giant book of corporate documents. I copied

a sample contract and Purchase Order, word for word...and my little company was born!

Zig Ziglar once said that it's not how far you fall, but how high you bounce that counts.... Well, in the first few years in business, we were blessed to attract and retain some pretty big hitters to our little marketing firm; from large corporations to public events and various industry trade shows, we were doing pretty well in the event marketing industry! So, I hired my husband and around year 4 or 5, we got this crazy idea to produce our OWN public events!

I wanted to do something for the WHOLE family since Steve and I were thinking of starting our own! So, I started meeting with potential sponsors. I'll never forget the day I was standing in the office of the Chrysler Corporation. I was so nervous, standing there in my little '80's suit, big shoulder pads, hair in a bun...but I kept hearing Mom in my head: "Be Bold and Push forward!" The VP of Marketing said he loved our concept, but they couldn't sponsor us until we were "big enough to fill a Convention Center."

I took that as a challenge....and went home and told my husband something sure to freak him out. "Honey, we need to rent a Convention Center!" After he stopped laughing...and it took a while, we did the math and figured that if our team could attract an exhibitor or sponsor to one event, we could just as easily sell them on three, right? So, I rented the Los Angeles, the Long Beach and the Anaheim Convention Center, all within 5 weeks of each other...and went back to Chrysler!

As I slid the contract over to Chrysler's VP, I said, "Alright, you asked for it; you've got it! We have now booked 3 Convention Centers, and we are excited to partner with you so you can give away a Chrysler automobile to a lucky event attendee!" He sat there in shock!

I reached out my hand to seal the deal. He just laughed and said, "OK, you got yourself a car!" I said, "Just ONE? Well, now we need three, one for each event, or..." I said tongue in cheek, "Should I award the hood at the first one, the doors at the second and the trunk at the third?" I think he agreed to 3 cars just to get me out of his office.

During the years of planning, I gave birth to our first child, Haley, and this event felt like a second one! We sold out the exhibit halls; most of our sponsors were promoting it like crazy...but I didn't see our Presenting Sponsor, the LA Times' advertisements in the paper, per their sponsorship agreement.

After numerous phone calls, I drove up to LA and walked up to their huge glass building, and as I cupped my hands around my eyes to look into the office windows, it was like the rapture happened! Overturned chairs and file cabinets, papers strewn all over the ground, but there was no one in sight! Long story short, I found out that the entire LA Times promotion department was FIRED a month before our event, and no one let us know!

My heart sank. What would our other sponsors do or say? How would we draw a crowd? ...but as Mom always said: "The show must go on!", so we were Bold and Showed up!

The first weekend came, and the show was a little low on attendance, but our attending families loved it! As we were packing up to move to the next Convention Center, the show decorator handed me a new bill for $35,000 in unapproved overages. We had paid IN FULL upfront, so we didn't have the money for that. ... but someone had to say it...they were Union, so we were screwed...I tried to NOT freak out as the show must go on, so we were Bold and pushed forward.

A few days before the second show weekend, my grandmother had a massive stroke and my mom asked us to step in to care for her. I had previously agreed to care for my grandmother if that ever happened as I was the only grandchild without a "real job". Since we didn't have money to pay our rent anyway, I guess God opened another window.

While my husband moved us out of our beautiful rental house, (sigh)...I was changing the diapers of my almost 98-year-old grandmother and my almost 2-year-old daughter and running the business and our team remotely from my grandmother's kitchen. Yes, it was a lot to handle!

We had to borrow money to pay the bills for the next two weekend events. But praise God, everything came together, and the attendees loved the events, I only wished there were more of them...and so did our exhibitors, so they, in turn, emptied our bank account overnight.

We had maxed out every credit card, owed money to family and friends, and had no way to pay our bills, so we had to file bankruptcy. I felt like a big fat, broke loser.

I sank into a deep depression as my grandmother got weaker and weaker. I was afraid that people were out to kill me because I was such a failure, so I kept the shades drawn, and I only took my daughter out in her stroller in the cover of night. One day my mom stopped by, and she sharply told me to open up the window shades as it looked like someone had died inside...I didn't have the heart to tell her that it was ME. I had died inside.

I had never been in a state of depression before, so I didn't know why dark thoughts kept creeping in. I tried to be bold and push forward...but it felt as if I was walking in a pool of jello. The fact that Haley and Gram, both needed me kept me alive to struggle another day.

I knew God MUST have bigger plans for me, for all of us. I just needed to figure out what they were... because I couldn't seem to hear Him anymore. In fact, it was getting harder to believe He was still with me.

A few months later, I had finally caught my breath when Gram passed away in my arms. It felt as if the Holy Spirit had filled the room to bring her home. That renewed my faith, realizing that God had really never left me! And even though I thought that experience would kill me, it didn't. It just made me stronger and more motivated to LIVE a legacy for MY children, just as Mom had done for me.

We went on to bigger projects, and the Lord blessed me with two more wonderful children! Speaking of children, If I hadn't told you yet, I'm the youngest of 6 kids, so my mantra has always been: "You're not the boss of me!"

So, one day in 2007, I was sitting with the Kawasaki Motors marketing team after an event, and they were saying that the dealers were whining about a lack of customers. Keep in mind that the iPhone had just come out that year, and it seemed as if everyone was carrying at least a flip phone. So, I simply asked, "How DO you drive traffic to your dealerships?"

They said their agencies were doing "all the things" like TV ads, mailers, and the new media, Email. I said, "Oh, but aren't YOUR customers mobile? They are literally out riding motorcycles!"

I simply suggested they could reach their MOBILE customers directly on their MOBILE phone with a Text Message. I know it had never been done before, but again, Mom always said to look for opportunities to let God show up!

Kawasaki actually liked my "brilliant" idea but wanted ME to convince their agencies that it could work. It took two years of the agencies telling

me "You can't do THIS or You can't do THAT" and I'd think "You're not the boss of me!" then I'd jump on a call with my engineers and say, "OK, now the software has to do THIS!"

When we finally launched it in the summer of 2009, it was the first national mobile marketing campaign, and it drove over 93,000 New Customers to Kawasaki's 1500 dealerships! WOW, that was the best return on any marketing campaign I had done in 20 years...

Needless to say, I dove head-first into the world of mobile marketing. Hello, I'm "MobileMary" ... by launching our Brilliant Mobile software!!!

The road forward was bumpy as it was during the Great Recession and people thought mobile marketing and text messaging was a fad, but God eventually showed up again big time, and we were blessed with an opportunity to work with the U.S. Military; in fact, we still have the U.S. Air Force and the U.S. Marines as clients today!

That opportunity opened doors to more and more companies, and today we are blessed with work... from retail stores to restaurants, from schools to city governments, from associations to coaches and industry experts, we help our brilliant clients get results.

Since 1988, through every stage of business, I've continued to look for opportunities to let God show up and to live the legacy that my mom planted in me. She would say if you want to accomplish anything, make an impact and change people's lives. Just Show up, Be Bold, and say Yes!

You can find more about Mary "MobileMary" Barnett on her website: AnotherBrilliantIdea.com as she offers Brilliant Marketing Strategy, Courses, Roadmaps, Group Coaching Programs, Content Creation Retreats as well as providing 1:1 consulting with full-service Content Creation and Implementation as an outsourced CMO.

It's all
About
Showing
Up

Show up for yourself in life every day.

Dr. Barbara A. Berg, L.C.S.W.

As this is a time in my life where I believe I need to retrieve some old wisdoms I used when I was in my twenties, and I still haven't quite articulated my asks at this time, I will begin with what happened when I was in grave need not only to pay for my entire graduate program to become an MSW, but to just pay bills.

The article will start with remembering that showing up and asking sometimes begins with realizing you have an undeniable feeling that recognizes you are truly unhappy in your circumstances! Also, you feel welling up inside that YOU TRULY DESERVE BETTER! And that somehow you BELIEVE INSIDE THAT YOU BELONG IN A DIFFERENT CIRCUMSTANCE THAT YOU TRULY BELIEVE BELONGS to YOU!

And along with that, you feel a small tingle inside- small at first- that you have a feeling it is going to happen! You may not know how, and you may not know when- BUT YOU JUST KNOW SOMEHOW IT WILL BECAUSE YOUR SOUL TOLD YOU SO!

That's how it felt for me when I was 24 years old, and I just knew I needed to get my Master's in Social Work to go any further with the work and life I wanted to do. I vividly remember in late Spring of 1977, after having

owned and operated my very own Child Care Program held at the Snow King Village in Jackson Hole, Wyoming, and then having to let it go when it didn't snow enough to have a decent ski season that, that the tourist money just marched out of town.

I had moved back East into my husband Allan's parents' house, (what a mistake that was, but then they offered, and we had no money). Then, after trying to work at someone else's childcare center and trying out waitressing, it all occurred to me quite quickly that something had to give! And something did.

Especially after my father-in-law at the time ran over my little kitten, "Shnookie Uggums", I said "That was just enough!". I've had it and I'm out of here!

So, I moved into an old farmhouse somewhere in Arlington, Virginia, with two other women in their 20's, trying to make some sense of it all! On one warm and blossoming day, I went outside all by myself in the afternoon. I looked up to a tree that I remember had only very small buds on it. After that I then sat on a quilt outside and cried for a while before I pulled it together somewhat and went inside and sat down at the old metal and linoleum kitchen table. There my two roommates had converged at the end of the day, and I found myself asking them when I should go to get a job that would get me enough money to get into and pay for Graduate school.

Right off the bat, one of my roommates said to go apply at this particular employment agency downtown in Washington, D.C. At first, I looked at her and almost went into some rage about how "over-educated" I was for all that, but then I thought this would be as good a try as anything else as I hadn't tried it yet and it was downtown where that would probably be more jobs. Besides, this was no time to be uppity! I needed their help, and it felt as if God himself sent her to me.

So, I called for an appointment and got one the next day. I remembered to put gas in my car early and peruse the area for a place to park as it isn't easy to find one there! I had dressed in my best outfit, and when I walked in through the door, I had decided to walk all the way down to the center area where I saw the nameplate of the lady I was appointed to see. When I got there, I simply sat down, expecting she would look over all the transcripts and pictures of my wonderful childcare center classes. However, she didn't do any of that.

Instead, she brought me back to an area where it looked like 50 women were typing and maybe two men. They were all taking typing tests, and she asked me to sit down and do the same. I took a gulp of water and proceeded to sort of type as fast as I could, a little here and a little there, a few words a minute. The lady semi-smiled and proceeded to tell me "I'm sorry to say, my dear, you have a very nice personality, but you really can't DO anything! You only typed 37 words a minute!!!!

With my head down, I began leaving the building as quickly as I could. However, when I was just about to open the front door and make a quick exit, I heard my interviewer add (almost as if the sound came from an old-fashioned cheerleader's megaphone,) "But wait! Come back! I just noticed on this post that a large and well-known business school is looking for 4 counselors/salespeople to help get potential students to apply, stay in, and graduate from the school. The pay is excellent!"

With that, I stopped in my tracks and made a relatively smooth "about-face". As I was walking somewhat hopefully back to my interviewer's desk, it struck me that perhaps this is how God works. You just never know for sure where your helpful connections are going to come from. If you don't show up to make your presence known and ask for something remotely close to what you REALLY need or desire at a place that just might have some connection for you, the chances of positive manifestations in life become more frustrating.

Sitting down at her desk for the second time went much better. Irene and I (we found ourselves becoming more relaxed and personable), went over my resume and discussed a few other jobs, interests, and experiences I had had along the way, that well suited my chances of getting a call for an interview. After Irene sent over my materials to the school the next day, I promptly got a call the next morning after that and was given an interview with a pleasant and "seemingly easy to talk to guy" named Harry.

Dressing again in my best business outfit, I got to my interview a little early, and Harry asked me to sit down. He told me he had a lot of applicants and was looking for personable people who cared and could stay in touch with the students. When he asked me to quickly tell him why I thought I should get the job I smiled, leaned forward, and said, "Harry, I need the job." With that, I was hired.

So, there I was, working in an amazing atmosphere, helping inner city students get in and make their way through business college and graduate. Recognizing I would have a good amount of money to help me get through grad school, I took the next step toward accomplishing my dream of obtaining a master's in social work. I had to actually GET INTO THE PROGRAM. I had often heard the saying "God is in the details", but it wasn't until this whole get this particular job and actually get into grad school segment of my life that I really saw how that is true. Even when I was going through it, I don't think it fully occurred to me, but when I look back at it now, I see how this is true all along the way.

I don't want to belabor the point too much about how I "almost miraculously got into Grad school" because I want to get to the part about something I did learn after getting my MSW about charting out how we feel in different

circumstances in our lives and how that directly affects where and how we show up and what we need to ask for.

So, with no further ado, I'll give the relatively short version of how I applied and got in. First of all, (and I think this is important, at least looking back), it NEVER OCCURRED TO ME THAT I WOULDN'T GET IN. In fact, that was the only place I applied to! I just kept picturing myself going to Virginia Commonwealth University Graduate School of Social Work in Richmond, Virginia. Even though I had never been there before, it was approximately two hours from where I was living at the time, already in Virginia, and by the time I got in, it was well over a year. I liked how it was near Washington, D.C., and I just kept hearing in my "inner ear" to apply.

I knew I would have to take the GRE's. These are The Graduate Record Examinations for getting into Grad School and I knew they were important. I also knew that I wasn't very good at this sort of multiple-choice test and practiced some, but I didn't do great on the English, and I really didn't understand the Math. However, I did have the idea to write a two-page letter to the "powers that be" at VCU and tell them why I should be considered to be a student in their social work program.

THIS HELPED. I told them about my whole running a childcare program in Wyoming and wanting to do more for some of the families that came through. (Looking back, when I think of this, whether you are sure of yourself or you almost have no idea what you are doing, ASK. Miracles are in the asking, and for all you know, you could actually be what someone has been looking for, and you are a miracle to them, too!)

In every equation of the human experience, there is someone who needs to ask and someone who needs to give. Asking is a two-way street, and you are walking on it right now!!!!!

When I found out I was accepted, I was beyond thrilled! I majored in "group work" and did intern with some individual and family clients, and somehow this all prepared me to be a grief counselor years later, which is still one of my favorite aspects of my life's work even up to right now and beyond.

In the training I had after I became a therapist majoring in grief and trauma (along with other aspects of life's dilemmas).

I learned to make a grid with those I worked with as psychotherapy clients and other circumstances that helped us see what was going well in their lives and what needs special mentoring, help, direction, and major changes. With each type of situation, there are a number of ways to show up and a number of ways to ask. Below is a way the grid works:

Let's say you could place your life on a scale of 5 to 1. Each number represents how you feel about certain aspects of your life and what you are in a position to ask for and at times give. You may notice that parts of your life can feel like a 5 and parts can feel like a 3. You may choose which number you want to focus on at this time. Let's start with number 5.

At a 5: You may have feelings that you would continue to be very happy if a majority of aspects in your life always go this way.

You may have a wonderful and fulfilling home life, job, and or an amazing community/group affiliation that helps sustain you, and you feel your spirit is uplifted and you happily belong. You love how you spend your time and your days, and you have lots to look forward to.

At a 5 you could feel joyous, thankful, and appreciative among other words.

You may be desiring some new activities to get into and want to ask about who is a good remodeler for your home or who you could play pickle ball

with. You could have asks such as new places to show up and join a group with others or volunteer your strengths. You could be needing to make sure your finances are in good shape so you can continue a good life. You could be investigating new work and new charities to support with a positive sense that you will find them. The deal is you can speak up for what you want and need and aren't afraid to ask for things to go differently, if need be, because you see this as a negotiable world and you can get to the "Yes I can have that" and probably "so can you".

You could request of others to possibly join in some project you are into, take a trip with you, or help reorganize your house as your needs for things are changing. You are happy. You like what you are creating in life.

4. Life is going quite well. Things are "good". You are well connected and have a list of people and services you can call upon if you need them, and you often say yes to others when they need you.

You often feel willing, open to new ideas, generally sure that things will work out, and you are a valued person in this world at large and to those you know.

You could ask for a mentor or professional or dear friend to help you with something, you feel close to the spirit within you, you can admit when you need help, and you ask those who are inclined to say "Yes" and will come through with what you need. You don't "beat around the bush". If you feel isolated at times and are not always quick to jump into something new, you give it a try as a four because you know the importance of being well connected.

3. Three is an interesting place to be. You may be hoping some issue will "blow over" and life will return to copasetic and sort of doable again, but you just know it won't---not this time. You could feel stifled, angry, torn,

and/or nervous here to name a few. This is no time to "have no asks". Even if you don't know what you are asking for, show up at a group meeting, perhaps Alanon for spouses and adult and sometimes teen children of alcoholics, call friends and be real, get a therapist, reach out to a person and or place where you can get help and support before things get worse. And above all, be proud of yourself for facing that "something has to give" before a crisis shows up to take things out of your own ability to make your own choices and decisions.

2. Every day feels like a crisis is about to happen. You definitely feel a sense of urgency is with you and take ten deep breaths and take a walk. This is no time to make drastic changes or do something that might make you feel good in the moment but could "blow up in your face" and make matters even worse in the long run. Frankly, most of us have been in a position like this some time or another in our lives. This is often where you can finally make that call to get help that you have been thinking about but haven't done in a long time. Call those who have been there for you and don't tend to "talk behind your back". Go to a meeting such as GSFE or a 12-step program or a wise friend and TELL YOUR STORY and ASK for help, support, and someone to be there. Maybe a night on their couch can help. At any rate, show up as you are. The world is getting stranger every day. People are having issues they never dreamt they had and even issues they didn't know existed. Make a call. Let someone visit you. ASK. We need and love you.

1. I have been here. While I wasn't actively suicidal, I couldn't bear to have my life go on the way it did. I had left my daughter's father in 1997, and I not only hadn't planned it out very well, but I didn't realize how I was still attached to my husband even though I couldn't stay another day. I didn't realize how much my relationship with my 9-year-old daughter at the time would drastically change. However, when I began to get honest about it and got real help with the right people and ASKED for help in

ways I never did before----miracles did happen, and they can for you. It did not happen overnight. It takes either having or borrowing self-worth to have the courage to even believe you have the right to ask. I remember reading Ken Keye's book "Handbook to Higher Consciousness" and then, I started to ASK. And I received help in ways I never dreamt could happen. But you have to keep living to find out what miracles can occur when you "ask anyway". And joy will come. Namaste`

"It's All About Showing Up & The Power Is In The Asking"

Dr. (h.c.) Alesheia Randolph Bush

I decided to ask two of my closest friends, what is the first thing that comes to mind when they think of me showing up? Davia said, "You're always willing to step up and give of yourself."

Angela's response was, "You have such a busy life, but even if every single thing in your life is coming at you at once, you still somehow manage to support everyone around you.

We ask and the answer is always 'What do you need? I've got you!'...".

It's funny that they had similar responses because I never really thought about it until I was asked to contribute to this project. But when I think back over my life, there have been several pivotal moments where just showing up or asking changed everything in life and love for me.

I met my husband, Robert in October 2010 in Philadelphia during a very stressful and emotionally charged time in my life. You see my mother, Diane Randolph, who was the warmest, most beautiful person you ever met – my rock – had just been admitted to the hospital after having her sixth stroke in a ten-year timeframe. It was a Sunday afternoon, and I decided to go to Ross Dress for Less (my favorite place to shop!) to clear my

mind and decompress. As I was walking down the home accessory aisle, I encountered a handsome, tall, dark, well-dressed gentleman. "Hello," he said. I responded in kind and kept moving through the aisles. It was one of those instant attraction moments, but really, who meets a man at Ross? So, I pushed those little butterflies aside and kept on shopping. A few minutes later, the same gentleman approached me as I was looking through the dresses. He said, "I left the store, and God told me to turn around come back and introduce myself to you." At first, I thought he was crazy! He gave me his business card and asked me to call him. If I'm being honest, I had no intention of calling him.

Later that afternoon, I went to the hospital and shared the story with my mother. She started asking me questions like, "What did he look like? What does he do for a living? What type of shoes did he have on? What type of car did he drive?" I couldn't believe my ears! My mother was in the hospital after suffering a stroke and all she could think about was me and this guy that I met. So, at my mother's request I called him, and we scheduled our first date one week later. Talk about showing up!

We went out a few times over a six-month period. In April, he told me he got a job offer in Los Angeles and was moving back. I figured that I had not invested too much time in the relationship, so it would be easy to walk away and end it. Less than a week before Robert was to leave, my mother suffered another stroke and was admitted to the hospital. Robert rushed to be with me and prayed for my mother's healing and recovery. I knew he was a loving, caring, patient, God-fearing man the minute my mother's old bed pan fell over and splattered down his pant leg. He didn't even flinch.

Robert moved to LA, but he would call my mother and pray for her while she was in the hospital. My beloved mother passed away a few weeks later on May 3, 2011. Robert came back for the funeral, and he remained in constant

contact with me months later. I was the only child, only grandchild, and only niece with an extremely small family nucleus. My mother was my best friend and number one cheerleader. Robert knew that I really didn't have anyone else, and he quickly became one of my closest friends.

Fast forward seven months, I received a call from a recruiter at Allergan in Irvine, California, asking if I was interested in applying for a job to head a new and innovative department. I was born and raised in Philadelphia and had just celebrated my 10-year work anniversary at GlaxoSmithKline. I had no intention of leaving let alone moving 3,000 miles away Orange County, California, where I knew absolutely no one. But once again, I decided to just show up!

I decided to interview for the position, and I got the job. I moved to beautiful sunny California in July 2012. Moving to California opened an entire new world for me filled with hope and endless possibilities. It allowed me time to discover myself, to face my fears, and to heal my grieving heart. It also allowed me to see Robert on a regular basis and we began to solidify our relationship and plan for our future together. I ended up falling madly in love with the man that I believed God had created just for me; my Boaz had found me, and we were married in 2015. If he hadn't had the guts to ask, and if I hadn't been brave enough to show up and respond to that ask, we would have passed each other by.

In 2016, a position managing international business opened in a newly acquired entity of Allergan. In the beginning, I wasn't even being considered for the job, so I decided to ask for the position. I put together a compelling presentation and all the stars aligned. I got the job as international business manager. One of my favorite scriptures is, "Ask, and it shall be given you; seek, and you shall find; knock, and it shall be opened unto you..." (Matthew 7:7) This scripture is a reminder that anything is possible! It is all about

hope and we can truly have whatever we believe as long as it is in God's will.

In 2018, I sought out another opportunity to lead the Americas for one of the leading skin care companies in the world, ZO Skin Health. I have been blessed with so many wonderful and amazing opportunities in my life but I either had to show up or ask for the chance. I still feel like the world is my oyster and filled with even more wonderful professional opportunities for me if I just show up! I am nowhere near done; this is just the beginning!

My life changed again in 2020 when I showed up for a beautiful stray Siamese that I named Princess Coco. I have always been an animal lover, but Coco and her kitties led me to one of my life's passions: animal rescue and advocacy. Coco began coming around in February 2020. After several weeks we noticed her belly and suspected that she might be pregnant. I enlisted the help of my friend, Mrs. Debbie Eskow, Founder & President of Save a Kitty California, who was there every step of the way to walk us through how to trap Coco and her kittens as well as how to socialize feral kitties. Coco was extremely illusive and disappeared for a while. My husband and I were sick with worry not knowing if she was hurt or worse. Then, to our surprise she brought all five of her babies to our backyard on June 9, 2020. It was such a magical experience watching her call and seeing them appear one by one. We believe that Coco gave birth to the five fabulous kittens on or around April 21. Coco and her 5 babies were a challenge to trap; however, we managed to trap Zoe and her brother Gabriel. They were approximately 12 weeks old. We trapped Tabitha a week later. Under the advisement of Debbie, we began looking for a local Vegas rescue to help us find wonderful forever homes for Coco's babies. The wonderful rescue that committed to helping us place all of Coco's babies was Vets for Abandoned Pets in Las Vegas.

In the midst of dealing with Coco and her fabulous five, we had another four-legged feline visitor show up in our backyard on August 30, 2020. We had never seen her before but somehow, she knew we would feed her and make sure she was safe. She was a beautiful, sweet, and talkative four-year-old Ticked Torti Tabby. We named her Sheba. We posted on a couple of local lost pet sites, but no one reported her missing. She had been dumped. We trapped her on Tuesday, September 8, and we took her to Heaven Can Wait to be fixed the next day. They scanned her for a chip, but unfortunately, she didn't have one. Not knowing if she was feral or not, the plan was to Trap-Neuter-Return (TNR) her, and we were prepared to continue providing food and water. TNR is successfully practiced in hundreds of communities and in every landscape and setting. It is exactly what it sounds like: cats are humanely trapped and taken to a veterinarian to be neutered and vaccinated. After recovery, the cats are returned to their home or colony outdoors. The staff also confirmed that she was a sweet girl and not feral. She was in heat, so we got her just in time! When we picked her up after surgery, we knew that we could not place this sweet girl out on the streets to fend for herself. So, we got a larger crate to make her comfortable in our garage! We began calling the list local resources provided by Heaven Can Wait. This time, Rescue Treasures Cat Cafe answered our plea, and Sheba was adopted on September 13, 2020.

We were finally able to trap Coco two weeks after we trapped the last of the five kittens. She was tired and ready to escape the Vegas heat. You see, Coco was pregnant again. We had planned to transport her to the Save a Kitty Sanctuary in California, but when Debbie saw the videos, she communicated how risky that would be for Coco and the babies. We prepared a room for her to safely deliver the kittens. Coco gave birth to the second litter of seven beautiful and healthy kittens. I have never been blessed to have children of my own so watching this beautiful creature give

birth, nurse, and care for the life she created was one of the most rewarding experiences in my life. While Coco was quite feral, she allowed me to help care for her and the kittens. We tended to them until they were 10 weeks old and then transported Coco and her babies to Save a Kitty. All of the seven kittens were adopted to loving homes, and Coco will live out the rest of her life loved, safe, and cared for in the beautiful surroundings of the Save a Kitty Sanctuary. Coco's kittens from the first litter were trapped at an advanced age and needed extra love and time to get used to humans. Greyson was the first to be adopted on December 5th, Zoe on December 10th, and Tabitha on December 27, 2020. The final two kittens Gabriel and Chloe approximately 9 months old were adopted on January 10, 2021. Showing up for them was a commitment that I was honored to make!

I guess God really wanted me to show up for the kitties in our Las Vegas community because He continued to send them to us. On August 8, 2021, we noticed another kitty wearing a pink collar come to visit. We started placing food out for a couple of days in hopes that the kitty would come back so that we could trap, find the owner, or foster until a spot in a rescue opened. Lady Duchess was trapped on September 1. We took her to the vet the next day, and she was not microchipped. We got her fixed and prepared to foster her until she was adopted. Lady Duchess was adopted in October 2021.

I must say that this was one of the most rewarding times in my entire life. Being able to love and care for God's creation was an honor and privilege. My experience showing up for these kitties gave me a new sense of the power of unconditional love.

God is not through with me showing up for kitties. On September 15, 2022, while working in Orange County, California, another kitty in need crossed my path. A beautiful Lynx Point Siamese mix who was apparently

dumped too. He needed urgent medical care and after he was treated for an eye condition, we were Vegas bound. We are currently fostering Duke; however, we are 99% sure that he will be a foster fail and will become a permanent member of the Bush family. And, as long as there are kitties in need, I will continue to show up!

Showing up in love and life has blessed me abundantly. Showing up for that first date with Robert led me to marry my soulmate and partner for life. Showing up for all the kitties allowed me to discover a passion for animal rescue and advocacy. The simple act of showing up has created life-changing moments, cherished memories, and opportunities beyond my wildest imagination including being asked to contribute to the book. God only knows what is next...I can only say that I promise to keep showing up!

Take A Shot on Yourself

Dr. (h.c.) AnGéle Cade

Have you ever had a moment where you heard that voice inside of you say to be quiet and shrink. I remember a time when I didn't think that my voice mattered, and that caused me to never ask. I remember a time when I didn't think that my presence mattered and that caused me to never show up. I want to take a moment to thank the strong examples in my life that reminded that showing up wasn't for others, but that it actually meant showing up for myself. I want to share with you my mindset during these seasons in my life.

Because of my back story, I felt unwanted, rejected, and in constant state of not feeling like enough. There is a lot of pain in the past. I faced abuse both physical and emotional. As a little girl I moved from country to country not quite fitting in where I landed. I searched for belonging in the wrong places and ended up in a gang in the late 80s, at the height of the gang wars in Los Angeles, CA was at an all-time high causing senseless killings throughout the city. One week before my 14th birthday I was shot in the chest during a drive by that would halt my activities in going down a path of sure death. The life that I was living was filled with violence and drugs so that by the time I ended middle school I statistically only had a 2% chance of graduating from high school. After overcoming the odds of my

childhood, it felt as if life dealt me cards from what appeared to be from the same unfortunate pack. So many things could be pulled from the hurt of my past, but I was fortunate enough to meet my high school sweetheart, change my school, change my friends, moved to a different city, and even got a counselor that believed in me more than I believed in myself. After a series of events, I was able to not only graduate from high school but go on to the college of my choice.

Sometimes I think that life is a race that I will wake up one day and say I finished or even I won or sometimes sulk in the thought that I lost. I am here to share with you that life is not a race that ends but a series of races, placed in a marathon that continues on multiple levels physically and spiritually.

In this next season in my life, I married the love of my life. We were faced with multiple pregnancy losses and one of them was so devasting that it took me into a 3-year arbitration with the hospital following the next 10 years of extreme depression. In the midst of this I started a business because I had lost everything else and didn't know what else to do.

Someone that I did some work for through my last employer called me and asked if I would do some work for them directly. I didn't realize on my own that someone else would see enough value to compensate me. This began to shift my attitude towards showing up. This potential client didn't know how to contact me, and they reached out to a vendor that emailed me in hopes of a response.

Prior to this I worked for an accounting firm, and I thought that this job was everything. I was an administrator and the controller on staff supervising a team of bookkeepers and accountants. One of my dear friends actually got me this job. She was referred to this accountant and while in his office noticed that there was some disarray and a few administrative things

seemed out of order. She immediately told him that if he needed help, she had the perfect person to work with him; that was me. He notified his office manager to reach out and get an interview to see how I could contribute to his practice. I remember walking into the offices; there was three different office spaces, one of the office managers, another for the owner and another office down the hall for the staff. The only office that had the semblance of organization was in the office of the manager. After a pleasant interview I was excited to be offered a job that got me off the 405 freeway. If you know anything about Los Angeles, I was asking to get out of that commute route that caused me to lose hours of my life in some of the worst traffic in the world. I quickly said 'yes' to the job and started my career in business clean up and didn't realize it. Every day I showed up with a mission to make things better. I had an autonomy that I never experienced before to enlist systems, programs, and staff in a way that I saw fit. I began developing relationships with vendors, contractors. and clients that allowed me to start to find my voice while developing my opinion. My opinions became perspectives toward growth, scalability, and the pursuit of success for the firm. I began spending late nights toiling over the issues and giving my early working years to this business that wasn't mine. I struggled as to why I cared more than the owner and manager that was there before me. Why wasn't I able to find my voice, my reason or my purpose as the work became more stressful.

A change occurred as my boss at the time started to host meetings for a new start up business. A production that totted Hollywood assets and content that would be worth millions of dollars. They wanted to raise money, bring heavy hitters on board, and needed a Chief Financial Officer. So, my boss decided that this was the best move for him, and he jumped right it. There we were with no experience with initial public offerings, public placement memorandums, or the running of a production's studio. Because of this

choice money was coming in from investors and I was working a triple shift. I found myself literally working for two different companies 7 days a week. It was a very stressful time in my life, but as the investor funds came in, it seemed possible that this was a path to increase income, position, and freedom. During the next 6 months, over 9 million dollars crossed my desk, and the principals acted as if it would never stop. When I refer to this time period, I remember seeing that the executives changed the keys to their cars and keys to their homes. They upgraded in ways I could only imagine; they were taking trips to Thailand and throughout Europe. They were instructing us to open offices in Hollywood and Burbank; the spending was faster than anything I have ever seen.

After those 6 months the investor had lessened, and the expenses were outpacing their ability to keep up. I was left in an office fielding calls by disgruntled investors and collectors. Mornings were coming earlier, and the nights were longer. Even my husband began to question my commitment to work. I felt as if everything was hanging on by a thread, and if I didn't step up, it wouldn't work or maybe more specifically I wouldn't have a job. At this point I was trying to focus on the primary practice and keep those clients happy, but the owner our head CPA was no longer coming into his office. He was no longer doing the work for the office; he was no longer showing up. He was running from the confrontation; he was running from the truths that what he and his partners have started they in no way could finish.

Weeks would go forward and no response, no infusion of cash, no answers, and no business model that promised to make millions. I found myself in the office alone and crying, thinking how I made this decision to end up here at the whim of someone else's mistakes. I came home and began to make some calls. I called the office manager who was AWOL. I called the owner who was dodging me, and I even called his wife to question the upcoming

payroll for the staff. It was one of those moments in your life when you feel the pressure from a world of situations that you didn't create.

I decided the next morning that I was going to use my authority and let everyone go while they could still be paid, and the situation became worse. So, the next morning I spoke with each person one by one and presented them with their last check as to not create additional issues with the labor board. I recall the moment without even being clear of my own position but knowing that I wanted to communicate with others with the same respect that I would want. It was a Tuesday afternoon in the office; now this office was different then the disjointed one that I had walked into years prior. This was one complete office with multiple spaces for the departments, a server room that housed our server racks; it was a space that any firm would be proud of, and I was proud of it. I sat down at my desk and called the owner to tell him that I did my very best to hold things at bay, to ward off the wolves to steady the break. I wanted to let him know that I did the best I could to protect what he had started including his reputation. but I could do no more. I was sacrificing my 3rd payroll cycle, and this was causing detriment in my own home. I began to slowly write a letter that would inform the owner that I could no longer work for free and that his lack of communication has forced no other option but for me to leave his company and pursue the funds owed through the local labor board. We were losing everything and could no longer afford our apartment and had to move in with my in-laws. I was embarrassed and overwhelmed at the idea that I was an adult married woman that couldn't cut it out on my own.

This event fed into that voice in my head that echoed that I wasn't enough and that whatever is wrong is because of me. It was a tortuous time of my life. I was preparing myself to go back out in the job market, and then all of sudden, I got a communication that a client of the firm was looking for me. I was extremely nervous because I was no longer with the firm and

wondering if I had done something wrong, wondering about the lawsuits that were piling up that I wanted to stay away from. I began to just ignore the outreach from the client thinking that it is not for me because I couldn't be who they really wanted to speak with. After a night of tossing and turning, I woke up with a different thought, just SHOW UP!! Just take the meeting and see what happens, just see what they have to say. I reached out to the client and scheduled a morning to go by their office. I went not knowing what to expect other than knowing that I am a hard worker, good person and great administrator. I showed up and the client was so happy to find me and received me with open arms. He said that he knew that I was behind all the good service and work while at the firm and didn't want any of it to stop. My body language changed. I felt comfortable and confident that it was me and that "me" was more than enough. He wanted to talk about the rate that I would charge to take care of him. You see my business started at that moment when I showed up, every hurt, disappointment and loss culminated to this moment when I went home and scurried to create a logo, estimate, email, and rate sheet. I asked for more than what I was being paid knowing the value that I would bring to the table. I showed up, and when I did, the opportunity presented itself to ask and 'ask' I did. That occurrence was in the fall of 2002, and I have never looked back. I find myself looking up these days and taking the opportunity to SHOW UP and ASK with great anticipation for the amazing things that are destined for me.

I began to attract others that live and embody this methodology such as Lady Robbie Motter, Doris Johnson, Shirley Henry, Denise Jackson, Roselyn Ralph, and Jacqueline Goldberg (aka Pink Lady). My heart is filled with examples of women that walk in the confidence to know their worth. Because of these examples in my life, I have a successful business, loving marriage, and a wonderful son and have received my honorary doctorate

and many awards over the years from my community reminding me that I am more than enough.

Showing Up
Tina Casen

Showing up opens the possibility of creativity and not only to allow others to notice you but for you to notice others and help them to achieve their goals. You cannot help yourself or anyone else without showing up. It was 2014, and I had just spent 4 years being stationed at Fairchild Air Force Base in Washington. For the first 29-years of my career, besides working for NASA, I worked in the medical field, performing surgery or supervising in the hospital. My position was ending, so, without my knowledge, some of my old supervisors put in packages for me to transfer to a different base. Apparently, there was a board, which was made up of five Generals and Colonels to choose the best candidate, out of many. They chose me, to be an E9/Command Chief Master Sergeant, for Space and Missile Systems Center (SMC) at Los Angeles Air Force Base. At the end of one of my very first meetings, I stood confused. I told the rest of the officers that I did not understand any of it, and that coming from the surgical side, an LR meant a lactated ringer (LR in the space realm means launch and range). I told them that I only knew RN to mean registered nurse, but for space it means range and network. When I apologized for not understanding, they told me that that was the very reason that they chose me. They said that Space and Missile Systems Center was a strange bird that did not act like the Air

Force, so, they wanted someone (me) to come in and teach them how to be more like the Air Force.

After working at SMC for a couple years, some of my colleagues brought me another colleague who wasn't feeling well. They asked if he could rest in my office. Most of our military bases have gone through reductions and no longer have hospitals. They do not even have emergency departments. They have clinics and do not have any devices or medications for lifesaving. Being the only one with medical experience, I began assessing him medically and doing first aid. The entire time, he was telling me, "Thank you, God bless you." Every time I took his pulse or blood pressure, he said the same thing. He did not want us to call 911. He wanted to rest and then drive home when he felt better. However, after no relief, I asked another colleague to call 911 anyway. The paramedics kept getting lost, and while we waited for them, my dear colleague collapsed. We contacted the clinic and got two of their best medics to come to our building even though it was not allowed. I began performing cardiopulmonary resuscitation (CPR). You see, I did not just show up. I was led to be there and show up when I had not planned it. I was the only one with medical experience at a Space and Missile Systems Center unit. What are the chances of that? What if I hadn't been there, and he drove home to rest? What if he passed away while driving? Would other people in other cars have been injured or lost their lives? The paramedics finally came and sadly they did not know how to perform life-saving procedures. The two medics and I did CPR for a very long time, and we finally took him down 4 stories. Then one of the Airmen and I loaded him into the ambulance. I was with my colleague for his last hour and a half. He was the kindest man that I had ever worked with, and I still envision him shaking my hand and greeting me as I went into classified meetings. This was a Friday. The Monday after was the anniversary of my father's death. He also died at work.

When I went to the funeral, I was trying to decide if I should go up to his wife and daughters since I had been with their father until the end. I decided to "show up." I spoke to the daughters, and I told them that their dad was gentle and kind till the end, thanking me and asking for God to bless me. I told them that my father died the same way at work, and I never got to say goodbye, nor did I know if my father suffered. I wanted them to know that their father went very quickly and did not feel pain. I told them that their father was very calm. In my own way, I wanted them to feel some relief, knowing that their father died peacefully and quickly. So, you see, sometimes you purposely show up, expecting or not, and sometimes God shows you where you need to be. I felt very comforted and hopeful that the family had some sort of peace and comfort as they didn't have to wonder and let their minds wander. They were very thankful.

I served four years there and retired with 33 years, 1 week, and 4 days of Air Force Service. I am now 100% disabled but would gladly show up again and again for my country if I could.

When you show up, you are making the commitment and opening the possibilities for being the best you that you can be. There is a difference in being present and in showing up. Showing up requires a commitment to being dedicated and consistent. Don't wait for success or inspiration to come to you. You must actively show up and expect the blessings or expect to bless others, but you cannot do this if you do not have the motivation to go out and get it! You cannot expect to reach your goals if you aren't showing up and reaching for them.

The Power Of Showing Up And Asking

Lady Dr. (h.c.) Amanda Coleman

I am grateful for this opportunity to speak about the power of showing up and asking. When I look over my life, I have many stories of all the ways God has blessed me when I took the first steps in this journey of life, and I showed up. I believe that God created each one of us for a purpose and we are gifted with life.

I have met several key people that have turned into family and been great mentors to me because I have been at the right place at the right time. It has been about a year since I was first invited to come to an event with GSFE (Global Society for Female Entrepreneurs). My friend highly recommended that I took some time for myself and visited California in March 2022. I joined GSFE and booked my ticket for the tea party and unbeknownst to me I met one of the wisest women that was and still is a MENTOR to me---Lady Dr. Robbie Motter. While on the car ride to the event, Lady Dr. Robbie shared so much wisdom on life with each one of us. She spoke about parenting and being a mother and woman in corporate America, relationships, and community through GSFE along with some of her personal stories. I was able to hear her story that I could relate to, and it was exactly what I needed. I had to get my phone out and take notes. I've been told that success leaves clues so because I showed up and made a decision to take this trip out to California when finances were rough and when things weren't going as smoothly as I wanted to, but I still moved forward. That is the key when you show up despite what you may be going through whether circumstances, whether financial hardship whether it's grief or any other life challenge the key, is to show up. Show up when you don't feel like it. Show up---especially when everything around you makes you want to just stay home and stay to yourself. I have always been an introvert in case you didn't know although I am still a friendly, outgoing young lady. There are lots of times I like to be by myself, but I have realized that it is more powerful to be around other women and men that are successful, have goals, BIG dreams, and are like-minded so that you do not get washed away in this thing called life. Loneliness is not good. As a single mother, I learned very fast that I needed to have a good circle not just for myself but for my daughter. As the saying goes, it takes a community to raise a child. For example, a few years back I was invited to go to church and because I decided to show up that Sunday, I met a very dear lady named Ms. Kathy Langley. Ms. Kathy became like an aunt to me. She was the family that I wished for, and she would always be there for me and my daughter. If I had not shown up to church on that Sunday, I would have never met a lady that has been a great support system for me and my daughter. When I fell on hard times, she opened up her home to me and my daughter; Ms. Kathy invited us to all of her family functions and invited us to go out to eat at unique restaurants. One day her niece had a birthday party at her apartment complex, and because I showed up, I was introduced to several members of her family that are still like family today. Aunt Kathy also taught me that I needed to be consistent in prayer and with my faith. I am so grateful that I showed up that day to church. Even though Sis Kathy is no longer with us, and her death was very hard for me to deal with, meeting her changed my life for the better. I also decided to go to grief share, and I am glad I showed up there as it helped me to deal with

some emotions I had buried and needed to heal to grow.

I hope that the next time someone invites you somewhere whether it's to church, a coffee shop, an in-person meeting, a zoom meeting, or toastmasters meeting that you will show up because you will never know who you're going to meet. You never know who those lifelong friends will be. When you show up, you meet new people and form new relationships. A few years before that I went to a prayer conference in Orlando, FL, Pastor Sam Oye. That is where I also met my mentor and friend Dr. Omenesa. I wanted Pastor to pray for me, and I had purchased his book about prayer and wanted him to sign it. I decided to not leave empty-handed and without this powerful man of God praying with me as I had a very major request. I followed my spirit and went to the room he was in, and I asked Dr. Omenesa if he was able to spare a moment. She didn't make any promises, and I waited for a while. Pastor Sam was able to pray for me and sign the book. If I never asked that day for what I needed, I would have left unfulfilled and with regret. I asked and my request was granted. I am overjoyed today because the prayers sent up to heaven came through. Thank you, Jesus! If I never spoke up and asked Dr. Omenesa, I would never have formed a friendship. I would have missed out on a mentor that has led me to meet so many Blessed and genuine people. I am grateful.

I met one of my closest friends Shadae and her mother and sister because I showed up at a young adults' meeting at church. My friend has also become CLOSER than family. What you may not know is that for 10+ years I was in the U.S. without family. I was lonely and depressed and struggled as a single mother. One night I prayed, cried, and asked GOD to send good, godly people my way and he did. Recently, Shadae showed up at a major medical appointment and had she not been there I may have not made it home safely. Thank you, Friend.

I know it's human nature to turn down invitations, and I'm a true believer that not every invitation needs to be accepted. God will guide you if you ask him; we just never know what door he has prepared for us to walk through. Now more than ever before I choose to be obedient and show up like never before because you never know whose life you are going to change because you showed up and were obedient. Ponder the fact that you never know who you are meant to meet, that can help to bring you to your next level.

Let's talk about one of the biggest reasons why we choose not to show up in life and ASK for what we want. Fear. Fear of the unknown, fear of missing out, and fear of meeting new people because society has taught us not to speak to strangers. I can't count the numerous amounts of times whilst traveling, in my daily commute, or at a GSFE or P2 meeting and I have met someone and ASKED if we can keep in touch. I have met so many amazing and powerful people. I am grateful. I am not afraid to ASK because I love to make new friends and build relationships. My grandmother says "if you don't ask, you won't get" in her Jamaican voice- meaning if you don't ASK for what you want in life and DEMAND Greatness, you won't get it. There is so much POWER in ASKING.

I was asked recently to compete in the area contest for table topics for Toastmasters. I woke up that morning of competition in a lot of pain. I showed up and did my best despite the circumstances and came 3rd place. If I never showed up, 1) I would have let down my fellow toastmasters, our club, my president and area director 2) I would not have placed, and 3) I would not have a story to share about the POWER of SHOWING UP.

The first week of January 2023, I traveled back to California to compete in the woman of achievement national's pageant representing my home state Florida. I showed up. I had fun and met so many powerful women that are passionate about their purpose in life and choose to make a positive impact

on others. I showed up and competed. I asked individuals and businesses for sponsorship. I received sponsors because I was brave enough to Ask. If I didn't, I would not have advanced to the next step. This has been a major accomplishment in my life in more ways than one. Thank you to my sponsors. The biggest surprise was that I was crowned as M.S. U.S. Woman of Achievement 2023. I showed up, took a leap of faith, and competed. I will continue to SHOW UP for those no longer here. This is a part of my legacy! This platform is important to me because so many lives have been lost; Sadly, I have had friends lose their lives due to domestic violence, and they are not here to fight. Why do I continue to SHOW up? It's important to help End Domestic Violence. Showing up is half the battle.

Ask your friend if they are okay. Ask, "Have you eaten today?" When was the last time you asked someone how they are doing today? Ask your child(ren) if there is anything they would like to discuss. Make ASKING the new norm on ALL LEVELS.

On the other hand, I would like to highlight that when we don't SHOW UP, it affects others. Please don't be Selfish and only show up when you feel like it and when it is convenient for you. My mother taught me that as a leader you MUST show up. As a mother I must show up; if I don't, it affects my daughter. I want to be a good role model. As a manager, I SHOW UP for my team even on my WORST days. There is something that grows inside when you take the step to show up. Resilience is built when you show up. Faith increases when you show up. Joy is restored. Peace is gained when you show up. Clarity is obtained when you show up. Respect is earnt when you show up. Will you decide to SHOW up? Or will you let another year go by full of excuses and allow life to pass you by?

I Want to encourage you not to let fear hold you back. Continue to ask the questions that are inside your brain, ask for referrals, ask for business

partners, ask a smart question, ask if you want to learn new information, ask, ask, ask, and don't stop asking. Book that flight, cruise, and hotel resort stay. Purchase tickets to that event you know you need to go to grow. Show up for YOU. Show up at that appointment. Show up at graduation. Support and show up for your friends and family.

Keep Showing up. There are times when your mind is overworked, and you are just tired but SHOW UP anyway. There are times when you are ILL with a headache or back pain; take some medicine and show up anyway. Stick to your commitments and be consistent and SHOW UP! I believe that sometimes we miss our miracle when we don't show up. Show up for the person that feels as if he/she is drowning in life because of debt, family issues, or mental health because you make a difference and sometimes you can be the light in a dark world. Be cognizant that when you show up you help another individual to continue to live and continue to thrive. Show up for your children, show up for your family, coworkers, friends, and even your haters. Show up and when all is said and donel, you will look over your life and have numerous amounts of examples, testimonies, and stories that will give hope because you showed up.

Quotes I CHOOSE to live by:

- You miss 100%of the shots that you don't take.

- "It's never too late to be what you might have been"-George Elliot

- Associate yourself with people of good quality if you esteem your reputation for tis' better to be alone than in bad company,' -George Washington

- "People are like dirt, they can either nourish you and help you grow as

a person, or they can stunt your growth and make you wilt and die."
-Plato

- "One Should never stop being trained. That is a victory.' -Sun Tzu (pg. 33)

- "You cannot solve a problem with the same level of thinking that created it"-Albert Einstein

- "A hero is an ordinary individual who finds the strength to persevere and endure in spite of overwhelming obstacles"- Christopher Reeve

- The journey of 1000 miles starts with a single step- Chinese Proverb

I want to thank EVERYONE who has ever SHOWED UP for me. I often invite friends and family to events whether for Toastmasters, GSFE and Pearls and Paul International. Thank you for your support. To my mother, Lady Sandra Burton thank you for ALWAYS showing up. There are not many events she doesn't show up at even when she was halfway across the world, thank God for ZOOM! My mother is a prime example of the POWER of ASKING as she asked me to become a business partner and that is one of the BEST decisions I ever made. Thank you to my beautiful daughter Le'Aisha Marie. I pray as you read this that you gain CONFIDENCE to ask. Thank you to my father Gauntlett Clive Burton for showing up to my events, my first book launch, the Talent competition for the National Woman of achievement Pageant 2023 and thank you for showing up when I needed you the most. I am grateful to my father for SHOWING UP as a stable male figure for me and my daughter.

Show up anyways
Dr. (h.c.) Angela Covany

In life it doesn't matter why we show up, sometimes we just need to show up not knowing the reason. It could be we were just invited. Involuntarily or voluntarily. I would like to add showing up doesn't necessarily mean in person. Sometimes A simple phone call to reach out and let someone know you are thinking about them or a text to express gratitude can lead to nurtured friendships and open doors to new experiences and invites to more show up opportunities. When I joined NAFE, I was going through a lot of uncharted territory trying to promote my newly published #1 Best Seller. Attending my first meeting was an opportunity to share my book and my business. I had no idea I would become connected to a network of like-minded women that would later become the family and sisterhood I now call GSFE. The friends I have met over the last 7 years have been closer to me than some family members I have known my whole life, that truly want and desire to help me become the best version of myself I can become. I aspire to inspire my own children to become their best as well. I never thought I would be given a leadership role within the network, but I am grateful to be a director of a local chapter. It makes my heart happy to be part of a community of women that are not caddy or in competition, but rather part of a collective of women who truly want to help other women succeed

in their talents, strengths, and to guide one another's highest potential to come to fruition. GSFE sets the bar for true camaraderie. I am so grateful to Robbie Motter who as one individual has seen the true potential in all of her members and as a heart centered leader has pushed and continues to push each member to try new things, to show up, to own the ask, to continue to believe in their selves and to never stop growing. Since I've been a part of this group, I have seen an exponential growth in the members personally and professionally. The speakers who speak monthly share real hard-earned lessons in business to help other female entrepreneurs avoid the pitfalls of entrepreneurship with no sales pitch and nothing to gain. There are not many individuals who do that despite fear of sharing well-earned secrets. Yet alone worrying about competitors in their field of expertise. One thing I learned is that competition doesn't stand in the way of honest servitude. There is plenty of success and abundance to go around. Too many people never begin to go for their passions in spite of talent or skill because of fear of competition, a lack of a support system or lack of proper knowledge. I am forever grateful to the precious GEM of Robbie Motter for her friendship, love, light, mentorship and wonderful quality time we share and have shared for many years. She continues to inspire me daily. Since the expansion of GSFE internationally, I have been honored to meet some of the most wonderful women with the most beautiful kindred spirits I now call my sisters. I am excited to keep showing up in life and look forward to where I will show up in the future for others as well.

Show Up Today

Recently my father transitioned, and I realized the feeling of not having parents with me in this life anymore. At least not on the physical plane. My mother transitioned when I was 21. It was a tragic loss that no young

adult should have to bear at such an early age in development. I was able to process it a lot easier knowing that I still had a loving father. Now at 43yrs old, I am realizing what this process feels like for myself and the importance of showing up for family. There are so many times in life especially with toxic family members that we tell ourselves we are just too busy to spend time with our parents, but when they are gone, it is time you can not get back. I want to encourage you to work through differences and realize **the only thing in this life that is permanent is family**. Strengthen those bonds while you still have the opportunity. I know some people are very difficult or needy in their later years and caring for them can be exhausting on many levels. They require much more patience, understanding, and forgiveness but at the end of their life's journey you will be glad you took the time to spend. They say friends are the family you choose and I do believe that is true as well. Friendship is also a two-way street. I encourage you to show up for your friends, even if at times it may feel inconvenient. Life is truly fragile, and **life is** as John Lennon said it best **what happens when we are busy making other plans**. Please value the people in your life with your presence and show up fully present in life for those that you care about as much as you can. We get so caught up in life's daily demands with work and our own families that we try our best. Sometimes, we just need to pause and put out more effort into the things that are truly important. Family is at a core level the most important asset we will ever have. The only thing I wish at this point, is that I would have made more time in person with both parents. As nice as the phone conversations are and social media help us connect, nothing replaces the joy that is felt by your loved ones simply with your presence.

How "Just Showing Up" Created Two High Tech Companies

Dr. (h.c.) Verlaine Crawford

There are many times that I have Just Shown Up, and that action has changed my life. Those moments in time have given me the opportunity to create lasting relationships, advance my career, develop my business, and create new opportunities that I could not have imagined. This story is about how my "showing up" made a huge difference in two businesses that I had the good fortune to help grow and develop.

In my twenties and thirties, my career revolved around communications, marketing, advertising, and public relations for several organizations, including the AT&T, the International Paper Company, the Queen Mary Project, Capital Records "Keynote Magazine", The San Gabriel Sun Newspapers, Jack Lawler Advertising, and the Lodge at Pebble Beach.

In 1982, I decided to become an independent marketing consultant in Silicon Valley at the time Apple was going public. Bill Gates of Microsoft had made his deal with IBM, and the personal computer had just arrived on the scene. The tech world was off and running.

Learning About the Computer Industry

For a full year, I attended all the meetings where software and hardware techies got together, and venture capitalists circled like hawks around the

potential millions of dollars to be born. I finally landed a software engineer as a client, representing his program to new hardware companies. Even though I secured a contract with the first portable computer company, Osborne, working with this developer was a nightmare. He continuously threatened to commit suicide because "no one truly understood how beautifully he had written his computer code."

Finally, I prayed to God and said, "Look, God, you have the highest level of sales capability in the Universe. Please find me a client who is easy to work with and can afford to pay me!"

I had forgotten my prayer when a couple of weeks later, in mid-December, I received a phone call. A man named Dan told me he had seen my small ad in the phone book about being a marketing consultant. (Showing up can be an ad, brochure, website, or social media post.). Dan asked if I could help him, and his friends write a business plan for their venture capitalists.

"You already have VC's funding you?" I asked. (It was very unusual for a startup to have venture capital. Many entrepreneurs had asked me to work for free with the possibility of stock in their company. I needed an income, so I had said no and waited.)

Dan replied, "Yes, we have money and are prepared to pay you to help us write the business plan over the holidays." I agreed and began work the next day.

Using "The Information" (Intuition) in Business

It was my first day on the job. The book that I carried with me everywhere, "A Course in Miracles", was sitting on the desk staring at me. Ever since I was twenty-two years old and a man in an elevator handed me the book, "As a Man Thinketh", I had been studying how our thoughts create our reality. It is my understanding that beliefs are the seeds out of which grow thoughts that generate emotions (energy in motion), which lead to action and then manifestation. This knowledge had been my secret weapon to magnetize and manifest the desires of my heart into my life.

It was "The Information" (as I like to call it), which is based on intuition and inner guidance, that helped me when I met with the founders and venture capitalists of the newly formed company. It seemed that I was effortlessly able to answer their questions about where to place ads for their software, which trade shows to attend, and the type of marketing that was needed to succeed. I helped write the business plan, and we named the company, "Intelligent Technologies" with offices in Palo Alto, CA. They offered me 5% of the company and a large salary plus commission, I was totally excited about the opportunity to participate.

In a Little Over a Year, I Sold the Company

With advertising, public relations, personal meetings, and trade shows, I promoted our software package, PC Express, and was able to take the company from zero to a multimillion-dollar company in one year. I sold it to a high-tech company from London called Logica. I liked that name. It made sense to me that the company I had helped to create, "Intelligent Technologies", would merge with Logica.

I wish the process of creating, funding, promoting, and selling Intelligent Technologies was as simple as those few sentences sound, but it wasn't. Working in a startup is for the young and crazy. There were twenty-four-hour days and so many trips to New York, Washington, DC, Florida, Texas, and to Europe for trade shows and sales meetings that I felt I could see myself coming and going.

We had only ten employees, which meant that each person did many jobs, and we kept waiting for the developers to make the software work. PC

Express was a PC to mainframe communications package. In the beginning, you could send only a small document through the internet to the central computer.

Except you couldn't. It didn't work. Everything we take for granted today—sending photos, documents, videos, and movies through the air---was just not possible. It was the beginning of creating the World Wide Web.

So Many Things Went Wrong Along the Way

There were many fiascos, such as when I arranged for the developers to demonstrate the capabilities of "PC Express" at Bank of America corporate offices in San Francisco. I watched the techies hook up the modem to the PC with the IT executives of the bank standing around the room.

Our software engineers stood like statues staring at the modem, which slowly began to blink back at them. Then they walked across the room to see if the signal had reached the other computer hooked to its modem. They stood for the longest time, bending down to look closely at the modem. Nothing. Then they walked back across the room to stare again at the other PC with the modem. Nothing.

I thought I was going to die. I wished I could fall through a trap door in the floor and disappear. We did not sign a contract that day. But because I showed up, we eventually signed a great contract with Bank of America, Wells Fargo, American Express and many more. In fact, Bank of America wouldn't bring in new computers until their salespeople had come to Palo Alto to be certain that PC Express worked on their machines.

I created a brochure to promote PC Express and sent them to the decision makers of the Fortune 500 companies. We had an overwhelming response!

At the same time, we found ourselves in the middle of an unfriendly

takeover attempt by a rather unethical company from New Jersey. And then, I learned that Logica, a high-tech company located in London, was interested in acquiring our company.

Our CFO and I arranged to meet with the Logica CEO at our offices in Palo Alto; and unexpectedly on the same day, the CEO from New Jersey arrived at our offices with our investors. So, we moved the Logica meeting to a hotel. It took some major maneuvering to stop the bad guys and get the million dollars down payment check from the good guys. We won the day, and I happily received my "Golden Parachute".

Celebration Time Followed by another Startup.

After an exciting trip to Europe (the subject of another story), and before I knew it, I was working at my second start-up where I was once again co-owner and Vice President of Marketing. The only thing crazier than working at a startup company is to go to work for a second startup.

Syntactics was a small company that had been in business for five years and had developed a word processor running on UNIX. Only huge companies like AT&T and governmental agencies such as NASA and the IRS used UNIX. The owner of the company had only made $25,000 in five years.

So why did I join this company. Because the name of the word processor was CrystalWriter. I kid you not. I love crystals, and so I went to work to promote CrystalWriter.

How to Show Up to Save a Company

It was early on the second day at Syntactics, and I had only one question on my mind, "What new product can we develop that will take this small, software company from obscurity to fame and riches?"

I closed the door to my private office and settled back into the large, black

leather chair. I stared at the desk where my book, "The Course in Miracles", proudly displayed its blue textured cover with gold type. I didn't have a clue about what to do.

So, I asked for help from the Universe and opened a magazine. I gazed at the page in front of me. Suddenly, three words, located in different places on the page, lit up. I know it sounds strange, but it was as if the words glowed on the page. Those three words were "Document", "Management", and "System". Document Management System. "That sounds good!" I thought. "Everyone would like an efficient way to manage their documents."

So, I quickly went to the VP of Development and asked if it was possible to create an application to organize documents. He stared at me and then peered off into the distance for a few minutes and answered, "Sure, why not?" I went to Ernest, the President, and he thought it was a great idea.

Ernest Said We Didn't Need to Go to the AT&T Meeting

A few days passed as I began learning more about UNIX when I received a brochure from AT&T inviting us to a meeting in Santa Clara to announce their new computers. I told Ernest we needed to attend. He responded with the statement, "Oh, no. It is just a public relations event where they'll try to sell us their computers."

"That may be true," I replied, "but we still need to show up." He looked at me as if I were slightly crazy, but then he nodded and said under his breath, "Okay, we'll go."

A week later Ernest and I sat together in an audience of over three hundred people. He was right. The presentation was all about purchasing their new, desktop computers that ran on UNIX software. There was a lot of razzamatazz and a dramatic sales pitch saying these were the best personal computers ever created.

Looking for the Person with Light

Finally, the presentation was over, and Ernest looked at me and said, "Now, we can go. Right?"

I said, "No. I need to look for a person with light around them."

He stared at me as if I were crazy but appeared to bite his tongue and didn't say anything. I could see that he did because I had successfully promoted and sold the previous company. He thought perhaps I knew what I was doing.

I gazed around the room, and there onstage I saw a man who seemed to have a light around him.

What do you mean "Light?" You might ask. Well, maybe it is a gift that I have, and maybe everyone can do it, but they just don't know they can. All people and things in nature have an energy field around them called an aura or the new phrase is "a body energy field." Sometimes I can see an aura. You may have felt or sensed energy around certain people or have experienced negative or positive energy in a room. You are feeling that energy field.

Regardless, that's what I see—a light or a glow out of the corner of my eye—and I said out loud, "Oh, there he is." The CEO stared at me as I pointed to the man standing on the stage who was dressed in a light blue suit and tie (men wore suits and ties in those days) with a bright face and sandy-colored hair.

I led the way through the crowd and up to the stage and came face-to-face with the gentleman who seemed to be lighted from within. I introduced myself, "Hello, I am Verlaine Crawford, VP Marketing for Syntactics, and we have a great word processor called CrystalWriter that runs on Unix! And this is the president of our company."

He smiled and responded, "Welcome. I am Bob Whitecotton (I loved that a man named Whitecotton would have light around him.) I am here from AT&T corporate offices in New Jersey. How can I help you?"

"I think we can help you," I responded. "We are developing a Document Management System."

A huge smile spread over Bob's face as he called out loudly, "A Document Management System! I have always wanted a Document Management System!"

I looked down at Ernest (he was shorter than me) and noted that his mouth had dropped open.

Bob continued, "Here is my card. Call me as soon as possible, and we'll arrange for you to come to headquarters in New Jersey to discuss how we can work together."

A Flight to AT&T in New Jersey Starts a New Chapter

That was the beginning of an amazingly smooth and easy relationship with AT&T. They paid for my flight to corporate headquarters and for the limo to pick me up at the airport. (The driver was an Italian fellow who proudly announced that his last name was "Capone.)

I was escorted through the enormous facility into the office of a lovely, older lady who was the contract negotiator. She and I both sat on the same side of the table as we put together the contract, which changed the fate of Syntactics. We received $350,000 up front to develop the product. (No company was paying upfront money at that time.) The executive team decided to make CrystalWriter the "Word Processor of Choice for AT&T". They requested that I become a member of their software council as an advisor, which meant there was a great meeting in Fort Lauderdale on a

large yacht to talk about the advertising and software for AT&T.

Syntactics grew and I secured contracts with government agencies and Olivetti in Italy. It was an extraordinary time of experiencing the flow of energy that moves through all things and on occasion can be a wild ride that takes you to new heights.

So Why Was I Called for the First Software Company?

What trick of fate started this journey? A few months after landing AT&T, I happened to meet Dan at a coffee shop. Dan was the technical wizard who helped to create PC Express and finally made it work. We had coffee together, and I asked him about his call to me that December almost two years before.

"What made you decide to call my marketing consulting company to help write the business plan for Intelligent Technologies," I asked.

"Oh, that was easy," he responded. "It may sound strange, but I opened the phone book to marketing consultants, and your name lit up on the page. It had light around it so I knew I should call."

How Do You Know When to Show Up?

How do we know when to show up? It starts as a feeling, a sense of well-being. I often pretend that there is a TV screen in the middle of my forehead, and I ask my guides to project a picture or video of what will happen if I make that move, if I attend that event, or if I post that announcement. If the picture is blank, I do nothing. If a vision starts to move on the screen on my forehead, I watch and see what is happening. If it looks good, I move forward.

Is that wishful thinking? I don't think so. I feel that I am watching a probable reality that something good will happen and the story will continue.

Does it always happen? No. Sometimes the screen stays blank. Other times the picture will show up only if I am patient and aware. If it does not, I let that thought, that idea, that concept float away to make room for my next adventure.

It's all
About
Showing
Up

It Takes Guts to Leave the Ruts

Dr. (h.c.) Laurie Davis

The first time in my life that I showed up and asked for anything that I can remember was in 1962. I was twelve. My Dad had lost his big paying job with the steel company he worked for as a payroll clerk and accountant. The company went bankrupt. Happily, I can say that it had nothing to do with my dad's brilliant mind or honest character.

What happened next was the lack of income. For the first time, I seen my family struggling to put food on the table. Back then there was no severance package or compensation, so Dad went on Unemployment Insurance that paid 36.00 every two weeks. I decided to ask my dad for a meeting. He agreed and the next day we sat down. I shared that I wanted to know if he would allow me to help the family. I will admit I was nervous not knowing what reaction I might get.

Dad was a proud man, so initially this was not well received. He had no idea what I had planned. I proceeded to share my idea, to at the very least pay for the groceries each week. I could see how much stress that was causing my mom and the other kids in the family.

It is a scary feeling not knowing where our next meal might be coming from in that moment.

We lived on a street that was sprinkled with those war time prefabricated houses inhabited mostly with young couples and kids just like us. Once Dad got over himself, he received my project and became my encourager. We got out colored paper and crayons and created handmade flyers. I placed one in each person's mailbox up and down the street.

The flyer read the following: babysitting, housework, lawn mowing, and dog walking. Reasonable rates call Laurie at xxx xxx xxxx. In case of emergency parents are nearby at 35 Symonds St. Dad being a numbers man helped me with the pricing and I was about to launch my first business. The phone started ringing and soon I was working every day after school and on weekends. I remember how excited Mom was to now be able to get back to shopping for food again and not be worrying about it. Dad helped me to manage the finances and we were partners from that day forward.

All because I showed up and asked for what I wanted to do. It left me feeling proud of myself and my family and not long after Dad got a new job, and we were back to never worrying about anything ever again.

Memory number two of showing up and asking.

The next phase of my life would see me showing up for an appointment with my Guidance Counselor at school. I was in Grade nine preparing to enter high school and we were to be evaluated to see which program we would be best suited for in high school. There were two ways to go. One was a general curriculum that prepared us to enter a blue-collar position, secretarial, hairstylist and the other was the Academic which prepared us for university. I will never forget that day. I even remember what I was wearing: a lime green Banlon sweater set that I was so proud of as it made me feel like a woman.

In the sixties as a woman if we wanted to go professional, we became a nurse, a teacher, or a hair stylist. The expectation was we got married had a family and stayed home to take care of them. I remember marching down the hallway to enter the office of Ms. Brown.

As I entered, she had her face looking down on my records. She immediately advised me that I would be placed in the General program as my marks were not reflective of someone who would make it for higher learning. I was devasted. Secretly I had hoped to one day having a professional life, a teacher.

The way that I retaliated to her review was that I wanted to become an archeologist just to get her attention. She looked up at me and said that girls cannot be archeologists. It was then I realized if I want something I needed to be more vocal, so I asked her what she meant by that.

She back paddled slightly and said that she then supposed girls could be that, but I certainly did not have the brains or the marks to pull that off and I should reconsider the general program and get a job as a secretary.

I stood up and let her know in no way was that acceptable and I asked that she place me in the Academic stream because in the end I would have more options. After some more discussion she relented based on my persistence not on my marks. I also walked away that day realizing that having breasts can be a career blocker.

The first day of high school was a joy and now I am on the path I knew was in my best interest. My experience as a young entrepreneur was beginning to influence my boldness that would prove to be of great benefit further down the road of my personal and professional life.

"Knock and the door shall be open, seek and you will find, ask and it shall be given, the key to this heart of mine." Sung by Jim Reeves

Memory number three of showing up and asking.

I had graduated with a scholarship to the Nova Scotia Teachers College where I would spend two years taking my initial teacher training. I excelled here and my marks were higher than they had ever been. I loved everything about it.

We were informed that Superintendents from across the province would be coming to interview us. At that time there was a shortage of teachers back in 1970 and we could pick whatever grade and school we wanted as there would be positions. The going annual income was 2500.00 per year.

The employers each had a space where we could present our self and get all our questions answered. What did the benefit package look like, how large is the student body, things like that.

I of course always had business on my mind so the extra question I asked was is the provincial rate the most I can expect for earnings? I kept hearing yes that is all we can do.

However, a turn in the road was about to happen. I asked this of the Superintendent of the largest school board in the province and he smile at me and said you are the only person I have spoken with today who has asked that question. In fact, we do have a couple of communities that offer an extra 1000.00 per year.

They are marginalized communities where the risks are higher and outside of the city, so travel is involved. Without any further ado I jumped in and shared that I would have no problem going there. Most of my fellow colleagues were shocked and amazed that this opportunity was available. They showed up but failed to ask for what they needed. In the end I

would be earning that extra 1000.00 which came in handy to pay off my student loan.

I remained in the community for the next 6 years.

Memory number four of showing up and asking.

I was ambitious for a woman of my age in 1970. As soon as I was in the classroom teaching my next move was to become an administrator in the role of a vice principal. Each time an opportunity showed up I applied. I was told how arrogant of me to think as a brand-new teacher without any experience I could take on this leadership role.

When in grade seven at the age of 12 I was presented with a silver dollar and a certificate for exhibiting leadership skills. I was already convinced I could do this.

In those days in our neighborhood east coast Canada school boards were not elected they were appointed so you could have someone there for years holding down their chair. The trail of applications and interviews began. Each time a position came up we of course were notified as they hired from within. For seven consecutive years I continued to show and present myself before the board to be interviewed. I had three strikes against me. I was young still in my twenties. I was a female wanting a position that was dominantly held by males at the time. I was ambitious in a slow-moving system.

Finally, year number eight rolled around, and another position showed up for me to apply. I was quite discouraged by now thinking I would never get promoted. My husband encouraged me offering to drive me there and

support my desires. So, I got dressed and we headed out to meet the board for the eighth year in a row.

One of the board members was an aging farmer whom I had met on every interview before this one. I sat next to him at the board room table while he at the same time gave me an eye roll that would sink the strongest of hearts. I was armoring up to face rejection once again.

To my surprise he stood up and started a speech that I was not prepared for at all. He declared there would be no interview. Based on my consecutive appearances before the board he advised the board that they just needed to give me the darn job at once. He shared that he had no doubt that if they did not give me the job, they would continue to face me for on God knows how long. I practically flew myself all the way home. Yes!

There are times when showing up and asking for what we want can be extremely stressful and frustrating. I know persistence is one of the greatest keys to getting what we want.

Memory number five of showing up and asking.

Driving by on a rural highway I saw it shining red with white trim under a myriad of huge trees, my first home. There was a for sale sign. I stopped and wrote down the number of the real estate agent. Upon returning home I called to make an appointment for a viewing. We were married just a year and knew we wanted to start off owning our very own house.

The house was listed for 21, 000.00. My husband was skeptical because according to him our limit would be 18.000.00. I negotiated with him on this and insisted we should purchase the house as an investment. That made total sense to me. Of course, we would need to get a mortgage. Now here

is the kicker. In 1972 in Nova Scotia Canada when applying for a mortgage they did not include the woman's earnings in the calculations. What? I was the one making the most money in my teaching job remember.

I was furious. I made an appointment with the mortgage company and demanded to me the manager to discuss this whole issue. I could not believe it. I entered his office by myself to have a discussion as to why this was the case. His response was that they could not rely on that income because I would only be working a year or two and then the babies would be coming, and I would be at home. I made it very clear that this was not the case and even if babies did arrive, I planned to pursue promotions and advances in my chosen career which by now you my reader learned that is exactly what transpired.

He also let me know my timing was impeccable because there were some policies under scrutiny in this very area of allowing the woman's salary to be included. I explained this was discriminatory and unacceptable. I remember the look on his face when I shared that if our mortgage would not be approved and I was to lose out on my pretty little house among the trees I would go higher up in the company, I would go to the press etc. and then I left.

Once I got into my car, I was shaking like a leaf on one of those towering trees, and the tears flowed. I had scared myself thinking I could march in there and face that challenge.

One week later to the day the phone rang, and it was the manager from the mortgage company. Laurie I am excited to share with you that your mortgage has been approved and we only needed to add in half of your salary to make it all work. Thank you for coming in and helping me to see how unfair those policies were, and we need to make changes. As a company moving forward, we will now always calculate in at least 50% of

the woman's income as part of our process.

I know I helped to make history. Two years later we flipped the property for 45, 000.00.

We purchased a more expensive second home and guess where we went to get our next mortgage?

I have many other stories of showing up and asking, however I wish to conclude with some thought-provoking questions for our readers to explore some of the obstacles we face when wanting to show up and particularly ask anything of anybody.

In the early days of my career as an entrepreneur I found it difficult some of the time to ask for the money once I had made the sale. I wonder how much money we have all left on the table because we were afraid to ask. Please check out the questions get some paper and start journaling.

1. How many times have I made excuses and not shown up or accepted an invitation?

2. Why have I been afraid to ask for help?

3. Do I understand that burdens shared lighten the burdens?

4. Am I willing to increase my level of participation in life by showing up for life more often? How will I do that?

5. When we do not ask, we are actually stealing joy from others by not allowing others the opportunity to give. How many times have I done that?

In our world where independence is highly overrated and validated, we have become fearful to actually admit we need help. We perceive that to be a sign of weakness or not able to handle our own problems. Hogwash I say.

I cannot even begin to imagine where I would be today without my ability to show up and ask. Thank you to each and every person I have met who supported me, validated me and most of all challenged me. For without any of that I would be lost!

She is A Pivot Woman
Dr. (h.c.) Yolanda Davis

She pivots to live what she dreamed of and created. She gathered her dreams, then structured all her plans. She stepped back into her dream and then stepped out again. When she stepped out of her dream she stepped out with a vision. Her vision included what she needed to pivot emotionally, physically, financially, spiritually, and financially. She studied women who had pivoted. She put each woman in a season based on color. She gave the pivot woman a journal and a journey as she became her own best version of being.

A Pivot Woman

She pivots to discover the what of who she is and her journey. She pivots alone and sometimes she pivots with her tribe who has her back.

She pivots to fulfill and feel who she is in this very moment of her life.

She pivots to align with her yearning, her calling, her hopes, and even her passion. She pivots to her right to discover a new sight and to be a rebel.

She pivots to her left and saw so much beauty and had to catch her breath.

She pivots to her right and into her yearnings and dreams.

She just knows that it is time to pivot to

Find her what, her who, and herself.

She made pivoting necessary, crucial, and a strategic plan.

She evoked that you must.

Pivot until you arrive at your destination.

She made pivoting about winning.

She made pivoting about letting go

of the noise, the drama, and the untruths.

Pivoting is about embracing your life, your change, your growth, and your uncompromising necessities.

She chose to pivot to discover, to change the rules, to make new rules, and to enter the new seasons of her life.

She chose to pivot to connect with her energy and essence.

She chose to pivot to become one with her soul.

A Pivot woman Pivots

She pivots to fulfill the dreams and desires she holds in her heart. She pivots to have freedom, exposure, clarity, and new possibilities for her life. She pivots to connect to and ignite her warrior spirit. She pivots to create her legacy and to leave her very best in the world. She is A Pivot Woman

She pivots in life for the comfort of peace. She pivots to open herself up to give love and to be loved.

She pivots again to have her own path which reflects her vision, her wisdom, and destiny. She pivots away from her sad moments to create her happy moments. She pivots again to be in alignment with her calling. She pivots to become enlightened and to enlighten others around her.

She pivots to give her life a wink, a smile, and a hug for some of her most amazing and indescribable moments.

Skye Adams had always been a trailblazer, yet after decades of being married, she found herself sitting across from her close friend Lisa Alexander chatting about what was next in her life after her divorce. She shared with Lisa how she wanted more out of life for herself than just another relationship. The two women continued to chat for several more hours sharing their life stories until they each had their own plan for what was next.

Skye was the most outgoing of the two women and shared how she had this vision of becoming a pivot woman; the persona of a woman who would pivot graciously in and out of every season of her life that was presented to her. She became very passionate about pivoting into the best version of herself that she could possibly have. Skye was ready for the road out in front of her and was leaving dust on the road behind her; she was ready to pivot to experience having it all.

Skye and Lisa continued to talk and laugh into the early morning hours until they each made their own blueprint on how they would pivot, evolve, and grow. They both committed to pivoting in every way possible to discover and fulfill pivoting to become the best version of themselves.

Skye discovered that many people took personal and professional development courses to gain knowledge on how to pivot. For the next

several years, Skye took personal and professional development courses on a regular basis. In her personal development, she learned how to get what was in her way out of her way to create the life that she wanted. She learned how the use of language, coaches, and accountability could help her expedite and achieve what she desired. She was committed to her self-growth and development and would drive two hours one way, three times a week to her courses. She became a leader and coached during her time in her programs. She developed a new community of friends, and accountability partners and began to grow in ways that she could only imagine were possible.

As she continued to grow personally and professionally, she also began to grow spiritually. She was able to let go of old hurts, old memories, and even some of her old "habits" She pivoted to explore her desire to travel. She expressed feelings of gratitude for this moment and time in her life. She believed that she was the persona of a pivot woman. She went on to travel to Italy, Rome, Paris, Greece, Spain, Portugal, London, Germany, Amsterdam, Morocco, Egypt, Dubai, Hawaii, Miami, Jamaica, and Cancun. She took financial literacy courses, rebuilt her credit, and took self-esteem and empowerment courses to rebuild her confidence. She was beginning to taste her version of what being a pivot woman felt like. As she continued to pivot, she expanded her knowledge and real estate portfolio. She began investing in Joint Venture large housing community projects, luxury-style properties out of the country, built Assisted Dwelling Units (ADUs), mentored and coached women on how to invest in real estate, and purchased a property near the beach for herself.

Her friend Lisa decided to go a more traditional route and spoke with counselors and therapists to heal from her past experiences. Lisa focused on her experience of feeling betrayed and abandoned by her former spouse. It was during an intense therapy session that she acknowledged and

embraced that her feelings did not have to rule over or ruin her life. It was at this moment that she began to have an uncontrollable cry. The therapist allowed her to cry far past her allotted time. After her therapy session, she expressed to Skye how free and light she felt. With continued support from her counselor, Brooklyn began using color as her form of therapy.

She was encouraged to select up to six colors that resonated with her healing and her pivot into the new seasons of life. Lisa carefully chose green, yellow, red, brown, black, and purple to begin her color therapy. As she wrote in her journal, she described each of her pivoting moments and the impact using color. She also described each season with color as if she had pivoted to that exact moment and time.

She describes how the season of green allows her to feel alive with growth and expansion like plants. She explained that growing like a plant allowed her to reach new heights and feel emotionally watered and nurtured during this season. This is the season when she experienced being hopeful because of the opportunities to grow, expand, and experience being lovingly mentored.

She describes the season of yellow as the season of glowing and feeling radiant and reaping rewards from having made good decisions. This is the season when she receives lots of compliments because she seems to be glowing.

She described that in the season of red is when she feels emboldened, and filled with love, power, and passion. This is the season that stretches her and builds her self-confidence beyond her standard boundaries.

She explains that this season of brown is when she was guided back to her basics to be grounded with the earth (God); the soil and to get centered with her life. This season reminds her that being grounded can be rich and

replenishing to feeding your spirit.

She explains that in the season of purple how she feels connected to her spiritual royalty. It is during this season that she takes time to remember her royal history, to be restored, and feel empowered.

She describes how the season of black is the season that draws her to feel like a woman of eloquence and elegance. This is the season that reminds her that being a woman; wearing a black gown with black gloves is a black eloquent moment in time to proudly pivot.

Upon finishing her own therapy, Lisa was asked if she would consider doing peer support with others who were facing challenges. After accepting the opportunity to provide peer support, Lisa went on to speak at groups and agencies throughout her state. As the word got out about how passionate, she was about having women embrace moments of life using colors as a way to heal and feel, she began to get paid speaking opportunities. From this moment on, Lisa hit the ground speaking all over the United States and eventually the world about using colors to embrace your seasons of life! Lisa's simple message not only changed her life, but it also changed and impacted the lives of women all over the world. Feeling so pleased with her life, Lisa felt as if she needed a long sister to sister conversation with her friend Skye to update her on her new opportunities. She wanted to let Skye know how she had used color to heal and pivot into her quite amazing life. Lisa shared with Skye about her new platform called "My Sister; My Sister; I See You" which she developed after meeting so many beautiful and amazing women. She explained to her how she uses colors, pivoting, and positive words with sisters all over the world to bring the experience of feeling heard and even healed.

Like Skye, she had grown in her confidence to know that she was indeed her own version of a pivot woman. The two women spoke for more than

three hours and set up their train ride to Napa Valley California to unwind and celebrate for ten days. During their stay in Napa Valley, the ladies enjoyed several spa days and sat by the poolside. They rode in the hot air balloons, rode the Napa Valley Wine Train, and visited Napa, Art Walk, the famous Oxbow Public Market, Napa Valley Opera House, and Blue Note Napa. Skye and Lisa relaxed, played, and celebrated being friends, sisters, and most of all being "A Pivot Woman" respectfully!

A pivot woman she is...

She is you, she is me, and she is us; She is we.

She is the persona of a woman who dares and yet cares for herself and others.

She is okay with being number 1, number 2, or even number 3.

She is a source and resource.

She is Godly and godlike. She is full of spirit, resiliency, purpose, and passion.

She is the alpha and the omega.

She is prudent and whole.

She is grateful and vibrant.

She is filled with love.

She is a revelation; she is the center and the end.

She is at peace.

She is my sister.

She is forgiveness. She is reflection. She is fruitful, friendly, and given favor.

She is strong and abundant.

She is mature. She is seasoned.

She is a trailblazer. She is learned and with purpose.

She is the violin, harp, and flute. She is melody.

She is the trumpet. She is a dancer. She is heart and an inspiration.

She is essence and divine. She is a lady. She is a woman of strength.

She is you. She is me. She is eloquent. She is legacy.

She pivots to create her own space in the world.

She pivoted to let go of her losses, she pivoted to open up and celebrate her wins.

She pivoted fully naked and authentic with herself.

She pivoted to see herself in the mirror without a mask.

She pivoted fully to embrace her journey of pivoting.

She pivoted to rebel against the status quo.

A Pivot Woman

She is a mom, a sister, and a friend.

She pivots to having a winning spirit.

She pivots to forgive.

She pivots to cry.

She pivots to embrace and enjoy it all. She pivots to define as well as redefine her purpose and destiny.

She is here to preserve her intention and her legacy.

She pivots to be present with presence and confidence.

She also **"shows up"** for herself.

And so, I pivot.

We are all one decision away from creating a whole different life.

Think about that for a minute.

On days like today, that truth rings with a harsh tenor.

But there is a softer cadence there too, no matter how hard we have to squint in order to hear it sometimes. You can always pivot. You can change directions. You can change your mind. You can change your brain. You can change your habits.

It is not simple.

It is not easy.

It will not be linear.

But it is possible.

If you feel suicidal, I'd ask you to consider a pivot.

It can be life changing.

Chebra Dorsey International ICONIC Celebrity Designer Loves Showing Up!

Dr. (h.c.) Chebra "O'chea" Dorsey

Showing up is so important to your success. It leads the way to greatness! For instance, I remember when I went to Los Angeles for a red-carpet event that I was invited to I didn't really want to go, but I attended anyways. I met so many wonderful people there, like actress/singer, Wendy Lynn Adams, and Jarvee Hutcherson, a big name in Beverly Hills and Hollywood. The President of the Multicultural Motion Picture Association (MMPA). He was such a sweet person. He was having a birthday party, and he invited me to his party in Beverly Hills and I met a lot of great entertainers. Jarvee and I stayed in touch afterwards. I remember him asking me what I did for a living, and I said I was a designer. He said, "Wow!" I told him I have a boutique in San. Diego. He asked to see my designs and said he had heard about the great things I was doing for women and my community by having fashion shows. I was so honored when he told me that I was going to receive a high honor award from his motion picture association in Beverly Hills called The Lady in Red. I was so happy and amazed with so many celebrities also receiving awards. After I received this award and gave my acceptance speech, it was like a dream come true. It is a night I will never forget. Dreams come true by showing up!

After that, many wonderful things began to happen for me. I was asked by Jarvee Hutcherson about having a fashion show together in San Diego. I said, "Hey, that would be nice. O'Chea Fashions with Motion Pictures. Wow! Let's do this." Jarvee said, "Okay, we'll announce this at the pre-Oscar's event coming up that we are collaborating and putting on a fashion show." I'm so glad I showed up because this beautiful and amazing lady named, Robbie Motter came up to me and introduced herself. She said, "I would love to come to your show in San Diego." I said, "Yes! Please come. I can't wait for us to connect." Wow! The day of the show arrived, and there she was. Robbie came with Joan Wakeland. It was a fantastic show with wall-to-wall people enjoying themselves at the "Jarvee Hutcherson of the Motion Pictures Association and Chebra Dorsey's O'Chea's fashion show". It was a hit, and I received another award, the Iconic Designer Award. I was overjoyed!

After the show, Robbie said, "I'll call you." When Robbie called, she told me about her organization GSFE, and she asked me if I would like to join. "Of course," I said. Since I joined her Global Society of Female Entrepreneurs, I've been amazed at what I've seen her do with so many powerful women. Since showing up as a GSFE member, along with doing more fashion shows, I've received numerous awards, like the President's Call to Service Award, from two Presidents, Humanitarian Awards, She Inspires Me International Award, etc.---so many I don't have room to list all of them. GSFE is now international! I just received my Honorary Doctorate Humanitarian Award December 2022 in London, England. It was the best thing and most exciting thing I've ever done in my life. I had never traveled out of the U.S. and had to get my first passport. I attended numerous Galas in London and received more awards including a beautiful gold Eagle award, and I got to meet so many dynamic international women from a variety of countries, I got to travel and to interact with 26 amazing women from GSFE. who made the

trip with me. Without showing up, none of this would have happened. Like I said, "Showing up is a success story in your life." God is so good always!

Another great thing that has happened by showing up is that I have been meeting people in the motion picture business in Hollywood. In 2017, I had started my own radio show called Testimonial Thursday, and one of the people I interviewed was entertainment veteran, Marneen Fields. She was a stunt woman turned actress/singer who worked with Clint Eastwood on The Gauntlet, and she's done a lot of movies. She showed up at my studio, and we had a blast. She even wore a black and grey sparkling O'Chea gown I picked out for her to receive her Legendary Stunt Woman Award at a huge Las Vegas event. We stayed in touch. I didn't know that she was producing her own movie titled, "Who's Gonna Take Care of Me?". When I heard about it, I called Robbie and then called Marneen. She said I could play Aunt Muggs (her mom's sister in the movie). What I did not know was that because I had a speaking part in a movie I could now have an IMBD page like all Actors and Actresses have here is my link, https://m.imdb.com/name/nm7684996/?ref_=ext_shr_em

In setting up the page it brought back memories of things I had done in the past that I had forgotten, like I used to be in plays like A Christmas Carol, and Hair where I opened the shows singing and acting. Guess what? It all came back to me. Wow! I can't believe it! The film is going to be submitted to Academy award qualifying film festivals once completed. Marneen has praised my performance in the film, and I can't wait to see it. It's so important to show up and know that showing up is so important. Always remember, showing up is your success story! It certainly has been mine. I have donated over the years thousands of hours to volunteer for community events and have been blessed to have been interviewed in numerous U.S. and International magazines; two recent ones were an LA California newspaper that said "Ochea fashion designs are beautiful and

influence a woman to step out in her beauty as her designs show confidence and beauty for women,"

I have been honored to design for many celebrities like stellar award winner Lady Shaunte who wore my designs and one of them ended up in Ebony Magazine. Actress Karole Freeman, Katrin Williams and R and B singer Nyaira Collins are just a few of the celebrities I have designed for Corazon Ugaldo Yellen, a top model globally, was a model at my 2022 Fashion show and fell in love with the items she modeled so purchased them. She models all over the world and is not only a top international model but also a well-known beauty pageant winner. She has worn a few of my designed gowns at several international shows, and they have been featured on the covers of Paris and Thailand top magazines. One of my clients referred someone that was going to the White House to my Boutique, and she fell in love with my fashions and wore one of the dresses to the White House. Michelle Obama the President's wife commented on how beautiful it was. So, you never know when you show up where your products, services, and talents will be displayed. I have had many exciting moments that have happened that I never dreamed would happen. One I am very proud of was getting an award in December 2022 in London, England, and having the opportunity to speak at Parliament as well.

Another amazing "Show Up" time was showing up at the Connected Women of Influence annual awards and luncheon and hearing my name being called to go to the stage was exciting. Three of the finalists in this category were called, and then like the academy awards, the winner is called out and my name was called as the winner of the "Woman Breaking Barriers: award. I could not believe it, as the other two women were amazing. I am grateful to Robbie Motter and GSFE for nominating me and for the judges that seen I was worthy of this prestigious award. None of us do the work we do for awards, we do it because it is our passion. However,

when someone recognizes your work and presents you with an award, it's such a great feeling of accomplishment for being of service to others.

Also, recently I was notified that I am in the "Expert World Leaders, Volume 2" book. that has individuals from all over the world featured. In 2022, I was asked to MC the SIMA (She Inspires Me) an International Gala with individuals from all over the globe attending... I also was asked to MC the GSFE Extravaganza 7 day of entertainment and desserts. This was a fundraiser for GSFE and also for a Veterans group Milvet. I loved doing it, and the audience loved having me there so in 2023, I will be stepping out and doing more events as their MC.

Everybody has a story and so do I. My life was not always perfect. I had many hurdles I had to get through. I was a single mom with a son, so I had to be a great mom and be the breadwinner, and during the 2009 economic hurdle I lost my house and found myself homeless. It was tough but I was not going to let that stop my dreams as I am a woman of determination, and I looked at it as just a way to give me more knowledge, and because I have great determination and faith, I knew I could bring myself back, and now you can see where I am today with faith, perseverance and ambition.

So, remember you are in charge of your destiny, and you can do and be anything you want to be. You need to SHOW UP and ASK, and don't let anything or anyone stop your dreams and goals. It was not easy, but I am resilient, and I worked hard. Have belief in yourself and you can accomplish anything. I had a purpose in life and knew I could fulfill it. I learned to Show Up and ASK. It was not easy at first but the more I did it the easier it was. It is now 2023, and I am writing my first book, titled "What Are You Wearing, the Spiritual Inspirational Side of Fashion" This book is also opening doors for others in the fashion world to join me with their stories as one of my co-authors so if you are interested in knowing how you can be a part of this book call me my number is listed below. We are planning on launching the book December of 2023.

Each day I am exploring more International Connections from many countries outside the US as well as expanding my US contacts. My passion and goal in life is to help more women look and feel beautiful not only outside but inside as well. I will do a collaboration with the Global Society for Female Entrepreneurs GSFE a 501(c)(3) for their annual fund-raising fashion show in May of 2023. I am a member of this organization, and this is the 4th year I have been a part of doing fashions for them. They have honored me with two "Call to Service Awards" from two Presidents of the United States. I will continue to serve my community and to SHOW UP and ASK.

It's all
About
Showing
Up

Anecdotes of life
Dr. (h.c.) Viola Edward

Your personal story is full of anecdotes that have changed the course of your life in the blink of an eye. Our day-to-day existence is full of unexpected events that have played and continue to play with your destiny.

Together we could write great murals, as in ancient Egypt, recounting the casual sequence of anecdotes, those episodes uniting our births and deaths, the two most important events framing our lives.

Treasured by our eternal life-souls, what we call coincidences are actually meeting points completing the web of the cosmos that we all form. A web that, without our part, would be impossible to co-create.

Accepting the weakness of our intentional power and seeing with inner integrity, the vanity of believing ourselves to be independent actors with divine grace is as important to our enlightened growth as for one who, after much struggle, gives up and allows herself to be carried off at the mercy of the seas only to find herself appropriately abandoned on safe shores.

In Yoga, that age-old philosophy, it is said that the mat where the Asanas are performed represents one's world. Extending this concept, we could also say that the place we find ourselves in at any given moment will also

be our world. This understanding generates a certain peace in our hearts. At least one of our struggles or states of suffering would dissipate when we accept that we are living out what corresponds to our world. Judgments that we generate around the lived experience will be more or less clouded to the extent that we allow our fluidity to show its graceful way.

It is often said that everything begins and ceases in a dependent way. The law of cause and effect is easier to understand after the events have passed and we are re-threading, one by one, the fateful stitches, threaded like shadows in the water, which allow us to live out what corresponds to us. We are but puppets in the hands of the great maker of the blue seas and the sky.

I could tell stories of love that began in the innocence of a gaze that met my eyes. My inner child could narrate the aroma of my native lands or the embrace we gave each other, three generations in a farewell that came as quickly as the crimson of an early morning. The adolescent who dwells in my memories could return to laugh at the moving adventures of my passage towards womanhood, that hormonal bustle that erupts like smoking lava from ancient volcanoes, reminding my mother that I had already grown up with my hair flying against winds and tides. Ah, what a lot of stories...

The truth is that if we take a good look at the accounts of our experiences, we could, as we do with tangled hair, go from strand to strand unveiling who we are and what our dreams contain, some lost, others treasured and alive, waiting for good winds to hoist sails and make way.

There are so many incentives to live with, finding paths, meeting people, groups, families, achieving goals, acquiring knowledge, and learning of all kinds. In truth, we are all heroes and heroines on a journey in search of our destiny, which we will discover step-by-step, overcoming our dragons or silencing fears in the caves, but always knowing that our destiny is made to

our measure; that there will be nothing and no one who is not at our height and disposition.

We all belong even if we have forgotten our names. Beyond any judgment we were begotten by divine grace and therefore have a father and a mother who gave us life, the greatest possible gift and that if so disposed, we will ourselves be givers of life to the descendants of all the human species on these lands.

Now when we shake hands with someone who by "chance" appeared in our history, let us feel grateful to be at one with everyone, to be part of a great network of encounters and mis-encounters, that when we look back, as the poet says, we will see the path that will never be trodden again, but thanks to those experiences, we are living our stories, the ones that make us the beings we are in the inextinguishable existence of vital energy.

When destiny knocks on our doors, it is called "serendipity" which means a fortunate, valuable, and unexpected discovery or finding in an accidental, casual, or causal way that can occur when one is looking for something and without realizing it, discovers something else. In the history of science there are many examples of important discoveries where luck played a major role.

Some examples that appear on Wikipedia about multiple serendipities are the discovery of penicillin in 1922 when Alexander Fleming was contaminated with a fungus on a bacterial plate, later discovered that no other bacteria grew around the fungus and concluded that something killed them.

The French chemist Benedictus in 1903 discovered laminated glass when he accidentally dropped a glass jar on the floor without breaking it because

it contained the remains of a celluloid solution that made it resistant to shocks.

And I could name other examples of how coincidences and even dreams can open doors to unimaginable benefits. Yet our academic upbringing leads us to look only for what can be proven with certainty, and this is often a very valid truth, but it can also close our senses to other possibilities.

In the course of our stories, when we are planning every millimeter of our projects, it is always good to be open to the unusual of chance, to those opportunities that link our destinies to the folds in time and space that have the power to transform our future.

Magic exists!

A piece of the intuition and magic of my love story

When I was 40 years old, I met Michael in Almeria, Spain, during a Global Inspiration Conference (GIC). On the closing day of that week of workshops and conferences, organized by the International Breathwork Foundation (IBF), when I entered the big tent set up for the day's general meeting, there were about 130 people present, I felt a strong call of energy.

I glanced about to the right and to the left looking for the source who was detonating my feminine waters and maybe about four meters to my left. There was this man sitting in lotus position who didn't even look at me, but I, feeling that force so direct towards him, without thinking or organizing, just letting myself go by intuition. I took a paper and pencil and wrote to him: "Dear sir, (because I didn't know his name), thank you very much for sharing your energy with me. I regret not having met you yet." I remember writing to him about this inexplicable but genuine connection I was experiencing that had moved my gaze and my invisible bodies towards

him. I wrote quickly as if receiving an astral dictation that crossed all time about the true and pure surprise I was feeling.

That little piece of paper was then passed from hand to hand until it reached his person. When he read it, I could feel his surprise at receiving this kind of confession, but he looked at me and smiled. I levitated with that look that made me feel pure heart at that moment, like the inner blush that miracles produce when they run through the torrent of my intimate life.

Michael confessed to me afterwards that he felt almost desperate with the slow pendulum swing of time that morning, trying to focus his mind on the lectures of the speakers. He said that his heart was running on excited fast, yearning for the meeting with me that from that moment he felt part of his history.

When the break came, we looked for each other, each taking a few steps towards the other. When I told him what I could put into words of the strong connection I had felt, he told me that although it was not easy to generate this kind of connection, he had also felt the magic when he laid his eyes on my smile.

From that moment on, we were never separated again. That was on 10 June 1999.

Later that day, in the sunny afternoon, we went down to a beautiful lake, a corner of heaven on earth, where he invited me for a swim. Radiant and confident, I said yes, even though I didn't know how to swim. Just like that, I got naked with my truth, I believe that showing strengths and limitations from the beginning of a relationship is essential.

Michael tenderly and understandingly assured me that he would take care of me, so I put my hands on his hips, and he towed me behind his back like a small, happy, and confident dolphin across the lake. Years later he taught me to swim with gentleness and dedication for which I am always grateful. Overcoming trauma, finally trusting, and swimming was one more step towards my freedom in the water of life.

Right then and there, after this first meeting, we both changed our plans and decided to make an overland journey together in Michael's van, equipped with kitchen and bed. We travelled from Almeria up into the mountains of the Sierra Granada, an emblematic road full of human traces.

Previous steps...

To tell you the truth, in my thirties I was a woman who did not trust myself enough to start a stable love relationship. However, I wanted to. So, I entered into a series of short-lived relationships because at the slightest sign of conflict, I would run away like a frightened cat. But there came a time when I calmed down and understood that to share a real bond, I needed to heal my own conflicts first.

I got down to work and worked deeply on the subject of loving relationships. I decided that first of all I would marry me, myself. I harmonized head and heart to relate emotionally and rationally with my body. I went to work in solitude on my inner disorders that are always reflected in others. I rearranged my spaces and confusions, entering more deeply into the clarity where I could see and hear, where I could feel my alignment with myself.

With this certainty of being ready, willing, and with love for myself, I left on a trip to participate in that meeting of professionals Breathworkers that would take place on "the other side of the pond" as we say in Venezuela to the sea that separates us from Europe.

I think the connections are like that. If we are healthy and actually ready to share, we can see the relationship. That's what happened with Michael. I was ready. I had worked with me for many years. I had freed myself from

a lot of negativities, from victimization, guilt, and shame---all those things that we accumulate over time.

Space for dreams

In September 1999, Michael came from France to visit me in Venezuela. As lovers, since the beginning, we discovered that we had and still have such a beautiful physical synchronicity, simply being in tune with each other. We also had many more incentives to keep on building a long-distance relationship that lasted almost four years and led us to meet in different parts of the world until we married and settled in Cyprus.

For me, falling in love with a man who was so different was a strong complication. What helped me the most was that our relationship was always intoxicated with truth.

In those first four years of being in love, we had several break-ups, but I remember that when we broke up, I was always grateful to have met and love such a person. I think that when such encounters happen, it is already a blessing of life, no matter how long it lasts.

In one of these separations and re-encounters, when he saw one of my photos, he wrote me this poem:

Love's Song

How spins your morning world?

as I feel you, across your ocean,

distant in that peaceful self-made safe space,

dimmed down, protected by high mirrored walls,

sheltering from the heat of your desire, cool and alone,

far from my brown body, the wind of change in your rich chestnut hair.

It scares me to see you withdrawn from longing,

Your loving arms folded across your soft breasts,

Molding the hurt and the ecstasy into a stifled memory,

Dusty and unused, pushed away, unwelcome, and dry.

your brown eyes too sad to feel, choked beyond tears.

your heart abandoned and beyond expectation,

too tight to open, unwilling to cry.

Vivid image and solitaire,

not one you might choose to sing about.

But listen to this, hear my song.

Viola, you are beloved of God,

Mo' mina, the one who believes.

I have known you from within,

In so close, your breath warm in my ear.

I have felt your core upon me, squeezed you here to my heart.

Come, mix with my longing, tumble in these thoughts,

tousled and relaxed among the words spilling from my lips,

be showered with the love flowing from my heart.

your body wet and alive, pulsing with quiet acceptance,

hope and belonging deep in your dark eyes.

I know how you love me,

and how I adore to love you,

For you have uncovered my soul

laid bare my wounds and bathed them in your soul.

My spirit is learning to sing again,

healed and respected, open and vulnerable.

Hear my song, for I trust you with my heart.

Michael, 8th Feb. 2002

I had doubts because I am a very free person with grit. From a very young age I became the breadwinner in my family. I exercised leadership in my jobs. I am a therapist, I mentored and taught large groups, and I was very independent and free-spirited. So, for me, my life partner would have to be a free person of heart and mind with his own story and his own glory.

And so, time went by, the relationship grew stronger, love grew bigger.

We dream of loving and caring for our partner and of being loved, cared for, and appreciated for who we really are. The conscious relationship is one that is filled with sincere acts of love and care. It is about giving and knowing how to receive. This attitude develops from the conscious intention to bring joy and satisfaction to the other and also to let love come into our lives with everything.

When this dynamic works both ways, giving and receiving flow in a progressive, nurturing, and harmonious intimacy. Above all, two variants occur: 1- knowing that we have our own responsibility to be happy and 2- that the other one should have everything you want for yourself. These two variants are very important to nourish the consciousness and the greatness of the loving partnership.

So, we did, and we keep in this mode...

It's all
About
Showing
Up

Ask the Universe
Dharlene Marie Fahl

Be careful what you ask for—meaning, ask with care, ask with intention, set out a purposeful yearning into the Universe and then let the magic happen—or so we've been told. We are also cautioned to be careful what we wish for—just in case it comes true. Are wishing, asking, and setting intentions all the same things? Could a random thought unleashed into the ethers be just as powerful as a desire with calculated forethought? It is—if the timing is right. Keep in mind that the Universe is on its own schedule and that it just may not align with ours. Even the most passionate, heartfelt intentions and aspirations may not line up with what the Universe has in store for us. Usually, this is when people get discouraged, quit, stop believing, or even get angry. Trust that there is always a Greater Wisdom at work on our behalf—especially when things happen NOT to be happening when we want them to.

Twenty years ago, I asked two questions. I did not give either of them much thought. I was just curious. The Universe either thought I was ready or simply waiting on me. The questions I asked were, what is tea, anyway? And why did it seem that tea was associated with spirituality and tranquility? As a Canadian, I had consumed tea for much of my life but never once thought about what it was and how it ended up in my cup. As a

spiritual seeker, I discovered that tea was interconnected with inner peace and meditation, and I wanted to know how that came to be.

The majority of the business "gurus" I followed at the time stated that one must have a plan—that a goal without a plan was just a wish. We were to write out our goals and every step required to attain each one. Create a business plan. Figure out how. Do market research. Decide a target market. Calculate costs. Find a way to fund a business. Look for investors. Set up a line of credit. Yada. Yada. Yada. Nothing spiritual or enlightened about any of that!

Nowhere did anyone say, Ask the Universe. I did have one mentor who stated—know your WHY and the how will take care of itself. If your why is big enough—the how will be easy enough. That was a much better fit for me.

As I continued my spiritual learning journey and put starting another business on the back burner, I encountered a particular church of New Thought. We gathered weekly for twelve weeks—twelve of us—asking questions and looking for answers. In one of our deep discussions, one woman expressed her frustration with her two teenage sons and how at a loss she was for dealing with them—without destroying them. Her solution was to remove herself from the situation, make herself a cup of tea, sit in her rocking chair in another room of the house, and sip in silent prayer. I joked about her having a cup of sereni-tea, or perhaps tranquili-tea, to soothe herself before losing herself. At the end of the class, I gave my eleven close and now dear friends, each a teacup with three teabags in it, along with a healing prayer. Of course, the first one I wrote was:

Sereni-Tea.

In peaceful repose, I breathe in all that I am.

I marvel at the simplicity and purity of divine serenity.

From this place of perfection, I am undisturbed.

I am calm and refreshed, most unperturbed.

I see God. I feel God. I hear the word.

Clearly and calmly, I am one with this Force.

I am intact. I am whole, pure, and good.

I see the reflection of my own perfection.

No defects and no deficiencies.

Nothing can diminish the goodness and God-ness of me.

In serenity, with deep gratitude,

And along with each sip of tea,

I realize God is all of me from within me.

This is my place of bliss—from here I can do and be anything.

So, with ease and grace, I surrender my pace.

I have nothing to fear, there is no race, no rush, no hurry, no finish line.

Every day I know victory in the arms of the Divine.

My giver, my deliverer, the provider of bliss.

I need for nothing. The aches are all gone.

My soul is free to be all that it is—love is all it can be,

And that's good enough for me. Amen.

Because we had all shared deeply personal stories about our lives, I wrote the prayers as a form of release for them. They were, Sereni-Tea, Tranquili-Tea, Tenaci-Tea, Sobrie-tea, Reciproci-Tea, Compatibili-Tea, Festivi-Tea, Liber-Tea, Anxie-Tea, Longevi-Tea, and Infini-Tea. As I presented each teacup, I read the prayer for the individual aloud, and everyone cried. I was stunned. Before long, others in the church asked me to write specific prayers for things they were challenged by—I soon had over fifty prayers. It was at this time that I asked my two questions, and the Universe answered.

Within weeks, I learned of The World Tea Expo in Las Vegas. I showed up—and the world of tea opened for me. Two months later, I was taking classes with the Specialty Tea Institute of America to become a certified tea specialist. A few years after that, I was invited to speak at international tea forums and events. The community of tea producers, growers, shippers, wholesalers, and retailers is a very spiritual, sociable, and supportive bunch. I took trips to tea fields and factories in China, Japan, and India—I was offered accommodations, learned tea production first-hand, and made tea friends all over the globe.

In short, I will explain what tea is—it all comes from one plant—if it does not come from that plant—it is not tea. The plant is Camellia Sinensis—from its leaves comes white tea, green tea, oolong tea, pu-erh tea, and black tea. Everything else is an herbal infusion, of which there are thousands, with numerous health benefits, but they should not be called tea. These can be from berries, bark, flowers, seeds, leaves, roots, etc. We infuse them like tea but should not confuse them—the tea plant has its own unique and powerful health benefits.

Tea is associated with calmness because the Buddhist monks who discovered the plant and, upon chewing the leaves, found themselves relaxed—yet stimulated enough to sustain hours of meditation. The monks also learned how to propagate, dry, store the leaves, and eventually infuse the dried leaves in hot water and drink the steeped beverage. The quieting of the mind is how we tune in to our own inner wisdom. My two questions led to the discovery of the world's number one beverage, next to water, and how tea shaped many aspects of our global history.

I took the concept of calming one's mind while sipping a cup of tea and created a seven-sip guided tea meditation. The next question I asked was can you love yourself for the entire time it takes you to sip a cup of tea? It does not sound that hard, does it? For the precious moments it takes you to sip a cup of tea mindfully, all you need to do is think loving thoughts, talk kindly to yourself, forgive yourself and others, pray, ask for clarity, release, and relax. None of this is difficult, but surprisingly, it does take practice. Each sip serves as a reminder to let go, breathe, and return to thinking good things. In that short time, your mind is going to wonder. Use each sip to bring you back into a positive state. This type of rumination becomes a full-sensory, kinetic meditation. It is aromatic, flavorful, warm, and soothing; you are listening to good thoughts, visualizing yourself happy, whole, healed, and feeling inner peace. I promise you—for a culture that does not meditate—this is an ideal way to start.

When I was asked to put my healing tea prayers in a book to share with the world, I panicked. I was not a writer. Who was I that anyone would want to listen to? Self-doubt can leave one frozen in their tracks, and I was just about there when my senior minister and good friend asked her parishioners, if not you, then who? If not now, then when? Tears streamed down my face as the Universe answered those questions. Me—now! I heeded the message and finished my first book, which eventually became an Amazon best seller. The journey took a few twists and turns, but I got there. I listened. I asked more questions. I continued to show up. I came to be a writer. I became a poet. I went back to school. I earned degrees in

English and Creative Writing and am now pursuing an MFA in Poetry.

Ask the Universe. Know what you want. Ask for it. Share your vision with others—even if it is wild and out there—you never know who can help you. If your dream does not scare you—it is not big enough. Yes, dream big. Dare yourself instead of doubting yourself. Show up at events—someone you need to meet will be there—someone there needs to meet you—even if both of you are unaware. Ask for help. Oh, my, that is a big one, isn't it? There is no such thing as a "self-made millionaire or billionaire." No one gets there all by themselves. They were self-determined. They had help.

Perhaps you are still searching—still asking questions—still unaware—longing for something you cannot name. Please do not let this stop you from showing up. When you put yourself in a new environment—change happens—shift happens—life happens. Allow it to happen.

Upon moving to the Inland Empire from San Diego, I was content to just be—for a while—to settle in. I allowed myself time. We all need that—we all deserve that. When an article appeared in a local newspaper about a woman from my new area hosting an event—I decided it was time—that I was ready to get back out there. Sometimes we show up thinking it is for a particular reason and then discover it was for something entirely different. That event was where I met Robbie Motter. She was not the woman hosting the event, but she was the woman it was time for me to meet. I loved her energy—her sincere desire to see women succeed—her message to ask for what you desire and to show up.

I joined her group NAFE, and when she formed her own non-profit group, GSFE—the Global Society For Female Entrepreneurs—I became a charter member. As she continues to amaze me and inspire me, I am honored to witness so many other women claiming their power and achieving their desires, as well as the many others who are willing to help. Yes, many women

attend events to grow their businesses, but this should not be the primary goal, and one should not get discouraged about numbers, income, or added sales. All of this will happen, but showing up and offering to help others is much more powerful. Showing up for only one reason is too limiting—think bigger—open to new possibilities. As Joseph Campbell stated,

"We must be willing to let go of the life we planned so as to have the life that is waiting for us."

While loving yourself and sipping a delightful cup of tea, ask the Universe about the life that is waiting for you—no more playing small. Ask to be shown. Show up to be shown. The possibilities are infinite.

Infini-Tea

So great are the gifts of God.

That they cannot be measured.

Absolute, boundless perfection is the God I know,

And I know God is all there is.

The Force is infinite.

There is no space between God and me—we are one.

This Oneness is immeasurable and immutable.

Infinite love is given to me free of all boundaries.

I am good enough to accept and embody God's love just as I am.

A love for eternity from Divine Infinity,

Is the greatest treasure of all.

For this gift, I feel from the core of my being.

A love and appreciation beyond words.

God knows the home of love and gratitude,

This place that defies borders and

This place where words do not exist.

This is the birthplace of infinity.

From here, from within, while sipping tea,

I release all limits, all fears, and all smallness.

I completely trust this Infinite Wisdom.

It guides me always, guards me always,

And governs me—all ways.

For all of my days. Amen.

Life is about believing in yourself and believing in something greater than yourself. I use many terms for God in my healing tea prayers—please use one that feels right for you. I am at peace with the God I have come to know—from within—not the God taught to me. Also, from my spiritual group experience, one of the twelve members stated that he must be praying "wrong" because none of what he prayed for happened. I was deeply affected by that and discovered that most of us pray from a place of disconnect—myself included. A place where we are separate from God—detached from our Higher Self—perhaps this is where the problem arises. Prayer is said to be us talking to God, and meditation is us listening to God—both are extremely powerful—especially from a place of oneness. Pleading, begging, or bargaining is not praying. Praying from a place of gratitude and thanking

this Infinite Wisdom for every one of our dreams and desires—our ASKS—yes, before they happen—is where our true power lies. Take yourself to this infinite place while sipping a cup of tea—your real life is waiting for you.

Could I have put any of my tea adventures and spiritual awakening in a business plan? Did I map it all out to make it all happen? No. I allowed it to unfold. Does it continue to evolve? Yes, it does, and I am extremely grateful for all that has manifested and what is yet to come. Keep sipping. Keep dreaming. Keep being your best and beautiful self.

The Benefit Of Showing Up
Nicole Farrell

Here I am here in my new town. Sun City in 2006 was the name of our quaint little town.

POPULATION 79,000 people! Now in 2022 it has increased to 100,000 residents with the new name Menifee.

I have to take you back to 1992 when we lived in Vista, California. John, my husband of 10 months, decided to take me on a nice drive in the countryside on his day off from working as a general Manager of Toyota dealership in San Diego.   It was a beautiful sunny Wednesday afternoon.   We went on the back road taking it easy for about an hour; then we came upon Valley Center. He said I sold a truck to someone here I wonder if he still has the truck. He remembered he had a restaurant. We drove in and out of little country roads. We saw an old-fashioned hardware store and a feed store and some old houses with porches. I loved everything about our drive. Then we drove around the corner. John said, "That's it." He noticed Fat Ivor's Rib Rack Restaurant.

Yes, it was right there. He said, "That was a few years ago, but I think that's the place, I sold him a pickup truck about 8 years ago. Let' s see if he still owns the restaurant." We stopped and got out of the car. It was really hot

in July. We entered the restaurant and sat at the little bar. It was pretty empty---actually there was no one there. We ordered a cold beer. The bartender was a lovely young lady named Vickie about 35 years old with 2 young kids.

We conversed and then asked by the way, "Who is the owner of this lovely place?"

She answered, "Oh ... Tom is. He's in the back. Let me get him".

John waited anxiously and here came Tom the owner saying, "Hi, I think I know you. You look so familiar."

John said, "Well, hello Tom. I sold you a pickup truck about 8 years ago."

Tom replied, "Yes, you did, and I still have it. It's working very well."

While John and Tom were talking about the good old time, I chit chatted with Vickie the bartender. I then asked her if she had kids' parties sometime at her house or in her neighborhood. I said I can do small parties with my karaoke machine. I was using karaoke cassettes then, and the words were printed on pages in a 3-ring binder. My idea was to bring my small karaoke machine and play songs for the kids, like 6 to 14 or so, dance, etc. She said "Well, I don't, but Tom my boss needs some music this Friday night, and this coming Saturday we're having an honorary Mayor celebration; we need a microphone and speakers and music. She asked me if I could accommodate them; we replied we could make it happen. I don't know how we did it, but we went on home and asked ourselves what are we doing?

John disconnected our four-foot-high mahogany living room speakers, loaded them into our van, and used our laser machine karaoke player. We also brought a few discs and lots of music CDS.

We drove back to Valley Center 20 miles away to Fat Ivor's Rib Rack. We set up outdoors by the big fire pit with lots of cowboys. They were cute, too, and so were the country girls. Well, at the end of the event, the owner of the restaurant offered us a weekly Karaoke job. Lordee, were we ready for this? John was working full time as a general manager of Cadillac dealership in San Diego, so I was on my own loading and unloading my karaoke set up of big 4-foot speakers and everything. Yes, sirry! I have to admit I never asked for help, but someone always helped me load and unload. Dear Rudy, what a nice helpful person he was.

Just by SHOWING UP to see if an old friend who was still the owner of a restaurant in Valley Center, now, I had my first karaoke job. This is how it all started! Two weeks later we celebrated our one-year wedding anniversary. At Fat Iver's John joined me at the end of his shift. I even brought my wedding veil and wore it. That was very special.

By SHOWING UP at the special event because john wanted to find out if his old acquaintance still had the truck that he sold him 8 years prior, we then were hired to do a karaoke show on a weekly basis. The word got out and another bar owner approached us and offered us a karaoke job at his bar at Sunset Lounge in Escondido. It was so successful. It was full capacity! Then we got booked at the Mission in San Marcos 3 nights a week. The owner of another restaurant bar and grill, The Comstock in Escondido asked a couple of ladies to give me his phone number to please call the owner. He wanted me to work for them. I eventually did call them even though I didn't think it was important. I had no idea he wanted to hire me for a couple of nights. I was working 5 nights a week by then 8 to 1 am. What was I thinking? Well after a few years it allowed us to have a down payment for a rental. Yeah! Moving forward.

We purchased our home Sun City home in 2005 and totally remodeled it and moved in in 2006. We moved here to retire after 16 years working as a Karaoke Host in San Diego Co.

I won several prestigious Awards as the best Hostess and most Entertaining in San Diego Co. between 1992 and 2006. it was a lot of fun for years until I was diagnosed with Breast cancer and then a year later with a brain tumor. That put a stop in my career. I put everything in storage. I had no idea that someday later I'd have to take my sound system out of storage to I SHOW UP. And that's a good thing.

While living in Sun City I was getting my treatments for health issues surgeries, skin graft, etc.. My husband and I would frequently go to our local restaurant Boston Billie about 5 minutes away. We loved our quiet little life while still remodeling our home. We didn't know anyone here. One day we were having the best bowl of vegetable soup and a tuna melt. What a good combo that was. It was a delicious lunch. There we were eating and talking over this and that. We could not help but hearing hustle and bustle in the adjoining room with nice archway openings in the walls. We could see something, but it was subdued. My curiosity got the best of me, and I kind of walked slowly to the room and quietly asked, "What is going on? Are you planning a party? What are all of these decorations for." it was filled with flowers and balloons; it was just lovely.

This very pleasant looking lady was being really nice even though she was really busy. The lady said, "Oh. we 're having a Fundraiser for Child Against Child Trafficking. We're going to have a karaoke tomorrow night. Please do come by; it will be fun."

I said, "I can't promise because we really don't go anywhere. We don't know anybody; I'll think about it. Thank you for the invite."

I didn't let them know that it was my passion. I love Karaoke. I left the room with a big smile and sat right down next to my husband John. and I said, "Guess what. They're going to have karaoke here tomorrow."

He said, "Really? How nice!"

My singing spirit woke up. I couldn't believe it. They will have karaoke in this little sleepy town. Oh my God, I am so happy!

So, guess what, the next day, my husband dropped me off at Boston Billie since we live 5 minutes away; it was so convenient. I joined everyone in the big room next to the dining room and took a seat. I expected to sit by myself not knowing anybody. I really didn't want to mingle; I wasn't ready for that. To my surprise some longtime friends of mine were there as well to sing Karaoke. I hadn't t seen them in 10 years from San Diego Co. What a pleasant surprise that was. We hugged and kissed and talked about what had transpired in the last few years trying to catch up on the good old karaoke days.

Yes, they were astounded about my cancer with complications!

My mastectomy had gone wrong. I had to have several skin grafts all over my chest. Then in the middle of my treatment a for skin graft, I was diagnosed with a brain tumor which delayed skin graft surgery (before reconstruction) so I was ready to just sit. Let it be one day at a time, and whatever will be will be in Sun City with a population of barely 79,000. I really came to Sun city to die and finish my life here---no ambition--- nothing to strive for.

Well, I was doing ok in this sleepy little town I thought---not too sleepy after all. I came to realize that later that little sleepy town had so much to offer; people were active, busy with Fundraisers, Christmas events playing golf, etc.

At my first visit for karaoke at Boston Billie I signed up to sing. I was quite nervous because I hadn't been in public for a couple of years or sung at all. I was out of practice plus having some old Karaoke friends right there at our local restaurant who knew all about me made me uncomfortable. They knew me, but no one else did.

I sang "La Vie En Rose", a song from Edith Piaf. I had a nice round of applause which made me feel really good. It took my worries about my health issues away for a minute.

Then to my surprise a nice lady approached me and praised me about my singing ability, and she went on to say, 'Hello, Nicole. My name is Joan, I am with the Sun City Woman's Club, and we're having a fashion show in a few months; the theme is An Evening in Paris, and we loved your song tonight. It was so beautiful." She went on to say, "Would you do us the honor and sing that song at our event. It would be perfect".

I was taken back. I said, "Me singing in public for a Fashion show! I don't know. I only sing karaoke sometime."

The following week I went to sing again at the Karaoke show which was a Fundraiser for Woman against Child Trafficking. A few ladies came and talked to me. I sat at my table with my friends of long ago. They were telling me that they were with Sun City Woman's Club and invited me to their monthly luncheon. It was so interesting. I ended up joining a Club the first one in my whole life. All because I SHOWED UP to the very first KARAOKE show at Boston Billie.

I'd like to share that after we moved to Sun City to start a new life and recoup from my breast cancer mastectomy gone wrong is when they discovered that I had a brain tumor. We had several second opinion appointments with all my doctors in San Diego and after several visits, consultation with different neurologists and doctors, it was decided to have 30 sessions of radiation in San Diego Cancer Center. During my radiation I had to wear a form fitted plastic mask that was so tight I had waffle marks all over my face for about an hour after leaving the cancer center.. I would also get panic attack in the radiation machine like "get me out of here. I can't breathe."

Thank God for my family taking care of me That was a long drive for us so my brother Yves and his wife Nancy living in Oceanside had me spend a week at their house for my treatment. Then my daughter Ginette and her husband Chris with 2 young daughters living in Poway took me in for another week. That lasted for over 6 weeks, from one house to another.

During that time, I was watching my sister-in-law Nancy and my brother Yves knit. I was watching my brother and thought "if he can knit so could I. While sitting around at night, they taught me how to knit. Then I'd bring my knitting to my radiation waiting room sessions and I would knit away. It made the time go by quickly there while waiting for my turn to get zapped. I just could not put it down. I even knitted scarves for the staff. I didn't know it would mean so much to them. Some cried tears of joy and compassion.

I eventually made knitted dolls, I stuffed the body with cotton balls, and then sewed the knitted parts together in the back. They became complete dolls that you could hold and cuddle.

Back at the Women s Club there was an Arts and Craft contest. I entered my Hand knitted dolls. I would give those dolls to the home shelter for the Abused children from Child trafficking. The kids could cuddle them and share their most intimate secrets. The Dolls had no mouths so they could not repeat what they heard from the children sharing their secrets. It was a comforting doll to them.

I won first place I was thrilled and so surprised. I still have my Blue Ribbons to prove it. All of that originated from SHOWING UP at my brother's house for my radiation treatments to be closer to the Cancer Center.

Then came the Fashion Show. I was the most nervous person one could ever see. It all worked out ok. I then was asked to perform at more events all because I first showed up at the Karaoke show; then the moment of truth arrived. I had never sung in public other than at a karaoke show. So, after a show at Boston Billie, I was asked, "You must have sung before?"

I said, "Well, ... I never sang /performed in public before, but I had my own karaoke show. So that helped a little. I had 25 to 30 singers a night, so I never sang. My job was to let the singers that signed up sing!" I confessed to Robbie that I had my sound system locked up in storage.

Robbie said, "Well, we need you here; we need your talent. Get your sound system out of storage." All of this for SHOWING UP

Here came the big one. One day Robbie approached me and said, "Nicole, I gave your name to Sun City Core president. She is looking for a DJ for their Christmas dinner dance in December."

I laughed, "No, no, not me. I don't know how to do big events. I am just a Karaoke DJ."

She said, "I know you can do it. Just tell them yes."

I was thinking no way. I'm not a ready for that. Well guess what? I did it. There was dinner, dancing, about 14 performers, a children's choir, and hula dancers. It was a big success; they even hired me for the following year.

I would have never gained that confidence and experience had I not SHOWED UP that night at a restaurant Fundraiser and to sing at their karaoke show.

I've done a lot of shows since then, and I am a coordinator of performers and DJ for several events and perform as well, it's a marvelous feeling. I thank God for my many blessings.

I was invited to participate for Menifee's got Talent in 2013. I turned them down to sing in a talent competition, but they convinced me to sing as a guest; they said that would be fine. So in between my doctors and neurologist's appointments, I made it on time. I almost cancelled singing for the Menifee's talent as a "guest". I was so tired, so they requested that I sing" La Vie En Rose". While singing my song, I handed out fresh roses to the people walking up to the stage. I had 18 roses so there was a lot going on while singing. That made me smile!

THERE WERE ABOUT 20 PERFORMERS FOR THE CONTEST time to announce the winner. THEY CALLED MY NAME AS THE WINNER! SAY WHAT??? I was stressed from my neurologist appointment blood test that day I started crying I couldn't help it; the staff had played a trick on me to make me sing for the contest. Oh my God! That was the biggest surprise of all from just SHOWING UP.

I did shows for Menifee Arts Council where we have performers in all genres coming to sing for 30 minutes outdoors as a soloist. I was in charge of them and was coordinating the rotation of singers. It's all about SHOWING UP. We have a lot of those singers being discovered and are now performing at other events.

What warms my heart is that I feel instrumental in people coming out of their comfort zone by coming to our show and I am sure at other shows to sing for the first time and over the months and years they are now performing as soloist in public. They are very appreciative, but I let them know that they had it in them all along. The talent was just waiting to blossom, and it did because they "SHOWED UP".

I will always be indebted to Robbie for pushing me to the extreme level--to push me to where I didn't know I could reach top limit. It happened because I "SHOWED UP".

It's all
About
Showing
Up

Journey Home To Sierra Leone
Dr. (h.c.) Stone Love Faure

One of the most important times in my life, I showed up and asked for what I wanted was when I was speaking at the Luxe Sunset Boulevard Hotel in Los Angeles, California, for the Amazing Woman platform. I met a lady named Robbie Motter. She was the director of NAFE. She was actually our global director. She told me that she loved my speech and that I was one of the most dynamic speakers she had ever heard.

She then asked me if I would be interested in being a part of NAFE. I asked her, "What is NAFE?," and thanked her for her compliments. NAFE was the National Association for Female Executives. I was intrigued. I immediately said, "Yes," and, in time, I became the Northern California Director of NAFE. That was back in 2012.

Today, I am Dr. Stone Love. I was awarded my honorary doctor degree in London in 2023. I knew this was quite the honor to be recognized for my humanitarian work, but what I didn't know is that I would meet Queen Dr. Imambay. She is the founder and president of the Disabled International Foundation out of the UK and Sierra Leone.

She didn't know that I had taken my DNA test with African Ancestry back in 2013. I knew that she would be surprised, so when I ordered my sash, I ordered USA and Sierra Leone since I was from both places.

I had found this out through the DNA test that I was a hundred percent Sierra Leonean from the Mende tribe, and so was she.

We met and we immediately embraced. There was a sisterhood that we could not explain. That, coupled with the knowledge that we were both from Sierra Leone, I could not wait to sit down and talk to her. I was very curious about the country, and I knew that if you could prove your citizenship in Sierra Leone, that the president would grant you citizenship.

I told her about this knowledge, and she was ecstatic. She said that last month, they had just had Americans gaining their citizenships in Sierra Leone, and that she would introduce me to the ambassador and also the president and arrange for me to receive my own.

I was over the moon. All this for showing up and asking for what I wanted. I knew that I wanted my Sierra Leonean citizenship, but I had no idea how to get it. In 2022, I found out.

We were both happy. We talked about our family. We both had six children that are now grown adults. We have so much in common. She even resembles my Aunt Lola. The connection was apparent.

We were to be recognized at another event the following evening. That evening, she presented me with a royal, traditional gown from Sierra Leone. It was cobalt blue, and it fit perfectly. I wore the gown to the event, and I felt glamorous.

I was to give a speech on stage that night, and I could not begin my speech without sharing the story of my beautiful outfit. I recognized Queen Dr.

Imambay, and everyone praised the gown. It was the first time I was able to explain, internationally, who I was and where I was from. Dr. Imambay applauded enthusiastically as I recounted our story of kinship.

That is just one excellent example of showing up and asking for what you want. When I was presented with the opportunity to be in this book, this was the story I thought of. This is a very real and important story of my lifetime.

Choosing to allow African Ancestry to analyze mtDNA and make the discovery of where I was from was not a hard one at all. But what was hard for me is when I received the results in the mail, and I read where I was from, I bursted into tears. That was something that I did not expect. Sure, I thought it would be fun to know where I was from, but I did not know that the moment I found out would bring such heart wrenching tears. I still do not understand the full depth of those tears, but I know that I know where my home is.

I am very excited that this year, 2023, I will travel to Sierra Leone, Africa, and receive my citizenship. They have a wonderful time planned for us. This will open many doors. I want to bring gifts and make my presence felt. I do not know exactly what the future holds or exactly what I want from Sierra Leone, but I know I want to give.

Since Dr. Imambay is the founder and president of the Disabled International Foundation. I will certainly give to that organization, and I would also like to build a well in my mother's name. I think that bringing a well of living water to the villages will be my sincerest form of gratitude for the country, my country.

My children are very excited, and so are my nieces and nephews. We all hope to travel to Sierra Leone together one day, and we will. I dream of

building a house there and getting to know people, bringing the expertise of what I teach to women and girls. The reason I received the honorary doctorate in humanitarianism is for my work in this field. I will bring my books and my teaching and my love to the country.

Sierra Leone is also known as Freetown, which means they fought off the colonizers that would enslave their people. They did not allow their people to be taken, and they earned the name of Freetown. This makes me extremely proud of my ancestors and what they have done. It is my sincere hope to be a credit to the people there and all their accomplishments.

All this for showing up. "Showing up" is a phrase coined by Robbie Motter, the CEO of Global Society for Female Entrepreneurs, which she created when NAFE decided to go in a different direction.

I have gotten so much from this organization of women. We offer mentoring, trainings, and community and uplift female entrepreneurs around the world. We are currently in Canada, in the UK, and, of course, the United States.

Showing up is certainly a practice all entrepreneurs want to master. You never know what may happen when you show up and ask for what you want. It may not be at that particular event, it may not be that particular group of people, but someone can be a resource to you.

It has happened every time I have shown up. The magnitude goes up to finding out what is your country of origin all the way down to your next client. Keeping promises to yourself will yield these kinds of results. And what do I mean by "keeping promises to yourself"? It is not telling a promise; it is completing the action of the promise to yourself.

I have kept the promise of my health and fitness by going to Pilates, and what I did not know is I would establish a community there, a community of clients, people that would hire me to speak, and friends.

This concept of showing up can permeate throughout your life. It is the single best lesson I have learned from being around and under the tutelage of Robbie Motter. It just reminded me of what an asset I am to myself, simply by showing up and asking for what I want.

Another transformational instance of showing up was when I showed up to a wisdom forest in Chartres, France. I have told this story before, but it is such a powerful story that it is worth repeating.

I did a seven sexy city tour for my book, Decision Time. The last date was to be in Toronto. My girlfriend at the time invited me to come out to her retreat and speak with her guests about the principles of my book. Three weeks before I was to arrive in Toronto, she had to cancel. She told me that she had to cancel because she was going to take a wisdom course in France. I had never been to France and, at the time, had not intended to go to France. But she said, "I think you should come with me instead of speaking at the retreat," because the retreat was to still go on, just without her.

I thought about her invitation for a minute. And although I did not intend to visit France, the idea flourished in my mind. I thought, I could go to Paris, and my book will become international.

So, I showed up. I, too, took the course in Chartres, France. There, one of the instructors was Jean Houston, which is a good friend of Oprah's. She suggested that I be a guest on Super Soul Sunday, and it just snowballed, all because I showed up.

Showing up has certainly become part of my life. I no longer just say "no" to an invitation at face value. I have learned to show up intentionally with the idea that something great is going to happen and also having the courage to ask for what I want.

Someone will be a resource or referral for me. I have learned how to show up and make it work for everyone concerned. I know my value, so when I show up, my presence is a gift. I, myself, can be a resource or a referral to someone else. So now I know that showing up and saying "yes" to someone else is also saying "yes" to myself.

This is just one of the things that I have learned to master by being the Northern California Director of the Global Society for Female Entrepreneurs. It has opened many doors for me, and I have walked in and opened windows and invited in the spirit of prosperity for all.

One more instance of me showing up is showing up for myself in thought. Being the mother of six children is the greatest accomplishment of my lifetime. What I have come to realize is I am not just a mother, but I also am a listener, and that my children have taught me.

I have one view of their childhood and raising them, and they have a totally different one, which is often funny, sometimes disappointing, but mostly sobering. I have to take into account what my five daughters and my son have to say about their rearing, so I have shown up in my own thoughts with respect to what they have had to say. I realize, through doing that, that I see better their point of view.

I understand now that they have gotten only one side of me: the mother, the teacher, the disciplinarian, the referee, the encourager, but there is a completely different side of me with respect to my clients, my fans, and my followers. It is almost like the difference between your self talk and how

you would speak to another person. With my kids, it is closer to my self talk.

They have also gotten the sterner part of me, the meaner part of me, something that I would never show to outsiders, such as my clients, my fans, and friends. I only learned that from showing up in my thoughts for myself in an effort to understand my children better---specifically, the difference in what they say about their childhood and what I think about their childhood and how different those two things are.

I have learned to show my children the same respect in listening to them as individuals, in honoring them as women and men on their own journey, as opposed to just my kids. I have uncovered many lessons. Those lessons will be different for everyone, but there are lessons to learn from showing up in your own thoughts with respect to what your children have to say, and that just may be the greater showing up I have ever done.

I am honored to be on this exploratory journey of my mind and action. It has yielded a knowing of myself that could not have been attained without the ability to be present and show up with the idea concept or action.

I have laid this over every aspect of my life. As I had suggested earlier, you can, too. You may not find a country. You may not understand yourself and your children better, but the gifts of showing up will be abundant. I can guarantee this much. They will be as different and as individual as your own heart and mind.

I encourage you to show up and ask for what you want, and you will get something even better, because that which you seek is also looking for you. And the you that you are becoming is also seeking you, and what better way to find it than by showing up for yourself.

I have asked for many things, but the abundance of the things that have shown up have been the things that I am ready for and my heart desires the most. This, I wish for you as well.

I can tell you from experience that showing up makes this life so very interesting, so very rewarding, and full of surprises, surprises about your actions and their results.

Submitting a chapter in this book is also part of showing up for myself. I have been asked to be in many anthologies, but I have only said "yes" to this one and two others although I realize that being in an anthology expands your reach and takes your name to places that you could not have gone alone, but I wanted to focus on my craft of writing, and that, too, is part of showing up for myself.

I also learned through my mtDNA test with African Ancestry that Dr. Maya Angelou is also a hundred percent Mende tribe from Sierra Leone. I am pleased to know that my favorite writer and I share the same ancestry.

She is another reason I am committed to my writing, so I not only show up for myself, but I show up for my ancestors as well. So, look for me in the literary world. Hopefully, I will make it to your bookshelf.

It's all
About
Showing
Up

Showing Up Takes Courage

Marneen L. Fields

With all my might, I've swung for the fence in life, danced like no one was watching, soared on the wings of eagles, and climbed the jagged Hollywood Mountain peak to reach the highest pentacle---all because of my soul's intense desire to nourish my entertainer's spirit and have my talent recognized with thundering applause.

Because my talent showed up, brave and courageous, I became one of the top pioneering Hollywood stuntwomen in the world in the 1970s and 1980s, once coined Hollywood's Original Fall Girl and awarded a Fall Girl license plate in 1985. Again, I was awarded the Legendary Stunt Award, a lifetime achievement award for my contributions as a stunt woman, a stunt actress, and an actress in 2018 from the International Action on Film Festival.

Excerpt from Rolling with the Punches with a Hollywood Fall Girl publishing worldwide by Briton Publishing Spring of 2023.

The stunt I'm most famous for (because I showed up) is being punched backward off a moving train by Clint Eastwood in The Gauntlet.

In the summer of 1977, I packed my travel bags and headed for the dry air and sunny climate of the Arizona desert to film the stunt I've become most

famous for within the industry, getting punched off a moving train by Clint Eastwood in his classic action thriller, "The Gauntlet." I landed the job after receiving a call from Clint's stunt double and stunt coordinator, the great, Stuntman's Hall of Fame stuntman and stunt coordinator, Buddy Van Horn. I remember showing up for this life changing day as if it were yesterday.

I was just hanging out in my small studio apartment when my land line phone rang. When I picked it up, I heard a soft-spoken man with a Southern accent introduced himself saying, "Hi. I'm Buddy Van Horn. We're shooting a movie in Arizona and Paul Stader gave me your name saying you're a champion gymnast and you could easily do a jump off a moving train." Though I was quite apprehensive about it, I accepted the job without hesitation and was hired by Buddy, on the spot, over the phone just because of Paul Stader's belief in me and reference saying I could do the dangerous jump. It was far too good an opportunity thrown into my lap to turn down because it allowed me the luxury to prove myself as a stunt woman, something I was determined to do.

I had about two weeks to get ready before I was due on location in Arizona, so I spent time practicing on the swings at the playground at the local beach because Buddy mentioned I'd be landing in some sand after my jump. I felt on top of the world standing and swinging on the moving swings, then leaping off them while they were still in motion to roll across the sand as I practiced over and over.

Clint directed the movie and starred alongside his future wife Sondra Locke. He plays Ben Shockley, an alcoholic, down on his heels cop from Phoenix, who is given the seemingly simple task of traveling to Las Vegas to escort a troublesome female witness named Gus Mally (Locke) back for a court case. This "nothing witness" for a "nothing trial" ends up instigating a white-knuckle fight for survival as the police officer and his witness are chased across the desert by corrupt officials who are determined to kill them both before they reach their destination.

For my big scene, I stunt doubled for actress Samantha Doane (one of the tough biker gang chicks), Shockley and Mally run into a second time when they are lifted aboard the carriage of a passing goods train. A fight breaks out in the carriage, and they tie Clint back into the corner while the three try to rape Sondra lasciviously in front of him. Clint breaks free and gets rid of the two male bikers throwing one and kicking the other one off the train. Shockley angrily approaches the female biker, who looks at him and says, "You wouldn't hit a lady, would you?" Shockley replies by slugging her (me) in the face. His punch sends me flying backwards with a half twist out of the train carriage onto the hard and hot desert floor, ending the train scene with an exclamation point! I also doubled for Samantha during the fight scene where they tie Clint up in the corner of the carriage. You see the back of me slugging Eastwood in the stomach and kicking him in the groin while he's tied up.

I had henna tattoos drawn on me by one of the make-up artists and black roses were painted onto my shin for the background scene. A heart with an arrow through it was painted onto the top cleavage of my chest, and arrows were painted onto my upper biceps for my stunt scene. The hairstylist took an hour putting my hair into pin curls to securely pin a long, thick, curly, black wig onto my head to ensure it wouldn't come off during my stunt. The wig was not only intensely uncomfortable to wear in the Arizona heat, but it gave me extra concern about the possibility of it disturbing my field of vision during the jump, but I didn't share my concerns with anyone. Each morning for over a week, I stood around as the stunt biker chick with the wig attached tightly to my head waiting for my big moment to jump off the moving train.

For the backward leap with a half twist from the moving train carriage, all I had for protection was a small, young boy's football girdle, and some knee pads strapped to my knees under a pair of seedy old blue Levi's (matching Samantha's wardrobe). All movie stunts are serious business, and each one carries its own potential risks, but this one filled me with a strong level of anxiety in the lead-up to its execution. As Mr. Eastwood blocked out the scene for me, he positioned me to be standing with my back to the open train carriage. This meant I'd be exiting the carriage, blind, going off backward, and have to perform a half twist as I leave the carriage to position my body to travel in the direction the train was moving. This made this stunt ten x's more difficult and dangerous. From the moment Clint throws the punch at my jaw, I was thrown into an awkward physical position that followed with a twisted movement throwing me high into midair.

Clint and Van Horn had blocked out my scene with me and gone over the approximate area where I was expected to fall and roll at a high speed into some tumbleweeds. I was warned by both that I must make sure my body always moved in the same direction as the train or I could be thrown back under the train's wheels and crushed to death. The way I was positioned going off blind and backwards and having to perform a half twist made this extremely hard to do. Only because I had the background as a champion gymnast was I able to pull this off.

I watched in nervous anticipation as the props department prepared the ground for my crash landing. They removed as many rocks as they could; then they rolled in a small wheel barrel full of sand. They poured the sand around the general area I'd be landing in to help cushion my fall, but there were still a few cactus plants and smaller rocks in the area. I remember them tossing an old rusty Coke can and more cactus plants and tumbleweeds onto the sand to make it look more authentic.

One thing you must bear in mind is when your body leaves an object traveling at a speed like that, the gravitational pull carries you along with the object, even after you have left it. The train was traveling steadily at around five miles per hour, which may not sound like much, but it's a whole lot more when you are the one who must make the leap and muscle your body into alignment from an awkward twisted position to align it with a huge, steel, iron horse. As I performed the half twist to align myself with the massive train and launched myself off the carriage, my body, unexpectedly, popped high up into the air, and I flew horizontally at the same speed the train was moving (carried against my will) along the side of it. All this happening within seconds prior to beginning my descent. While in mid-air, my arms, legs, and body flailed uncontrollably for what seemed like slow, terrifying minutes rather than the seconds it took to complete the fall. It was very frightening for me at that moment because there was nothing, I could do but be pulled alongside of it. In those few seconds, I had to muster all my strength to force my body to keep moving in the direction of the train and keep my equilibrium. Luckily, my powerhouse gymnast body was strong enough to keep holding on in midair. However, there were moments where I thought it was all over for me, and it crossed my mind that I was doomed for tremendous disaster where I'd lose my fight with the centrifugal force, smash into the side of the train, and be thrown back under the wheels and pulverized. I was free falling and being hauled against my will, not only by the gravitation force field, but also the powerful train's enormity that was determined to throw me back under it. It was very frightening. At the same time, I was also trying to keep a mindful eye on where I was going to land. I was terrified at that moment as I battled the speed my body was traveling. Thoughts of why I was even here doing this crossed my mind. The noise of the train and its gravitational pull had me feeling if I lost my hold at any moment I could be thrown back against the side of the carriage, or even worse, sucked under its rolling wheels, and crushed to death. All

of this added to the incredible anxiety and adrenaline that was charging through my body. I concentrated with all my might to force my flailing body to remain steady and keep going in the direction of the train, and it was extremely difficult to do.

Once the gravitational and centrifugal force fields left, the pull of the train dissipated abruptly, and my body fell like a sack of potatoes, hitting the harsh Arizona floor with a force equal to the weight of my body times the speed of the object. In other words, I hit the ground at a high speed and about a 625 pounds impact, pretty darn hard. The speed and impact caused me to flip, head over heels, wildly ten or fifteen times before slamming into a cactus of all things, which halted my roll. I was rattled and bruised, but miraculously came away without a scratch on my exposed arms and face. I went from incredible apprehension and fear to feeling like a complete champion in seconds! I had conquered the potentially deadly jump off the moving train and got to walk away without any broken or fractured bones, only a badly bruised left heel. Without my physical strength holding on for dear life during the execution of this stunt, it could have so easily taken my life.

When you watch the stunt in the film, you can see how close I came to landing on that rusty old Coke can (props threw in at the last minute), that could have cut me to Smithereens. The Coke can shows a reference point to the speed and distance I traveled alongside the train in mid-air before it dropped me like a flaming potato. It sends chills up my spine to think we all stood around watching the props department nonchalantly toss it into the sand (presumably to give a bit of variety to the barren landscape). My youth and inexperience made me ignorant to the damage it might have caused had I stepped on it or collided with my body on it upon landing. It would have most likely severed my foot. This was still the days of the hard tin Coke cans, not the easily crushable aluminum ones which became the

mainstay not long after, but even hitting an aluminum can in this dangerous circumstance could have done serious slicing damage. I hate to think what might have happened if my face landed on it, or if I had hit the back of my head on it while rolling over upon landing. I was unbaptized and was not religious back then, but looking back, I can see that a powerful angel on my shoulder was protecting me.

Despite the incredible risks and the immense terror which gripped me during its execution, my backward jump with a half twist off the moving train on "The Gauntlet" is still a stunt of which I'm incredibly proud. It's certainly one of the defining moments of my stunt career which was virtually launched overnight because of it. They put my jump in the trailer and on the press lobby cards. A still photo of my jump was shown in all the entertainment sections of the big Los Angeles newspapers like the "Los Angeles Times." My talent was the talk of Hollywood, especially within the stunt community, and everyone began taking real notice of me. It was one of the most dangerous stunts a female had performed on film in 1977 (if not the most dangerous). It looked amazing and startlingly authentic when it was seen on the big screen for the first time, and that's because it was. It continues to hold up incredibly well on home video today. People still gasp when they see my jump for the first time, because they can see that it's real! No matter how advanced cinema special effects might look today, thanks primarily to computer technology, nothing will ever match the genuine excitement of a courageous 22-year-old stunt girl with little more than a pair of knee pads, a football girdle, and a lot of heart and spirit, taking a great and dangerous backward blind leap off a moving train, into the unknown, in the name of filmmaking.

It's all
About
Showing
Up

Confidence Is Part of Showing Up

Get ready to take the initiative and transform your life!

Ada Gartenmann

I want tell you a little about you how you can use the process of gathering information and the power of asking that is within you so that you can become that person who's led by inspirations.

It is important to remember that we're all born with innate qualities and to know how and when to use them in our daily lives. I will mention some of these qualities to help you identify them, so you can take action and put them into practice in a manner that will be impactful and change your life as I have done already myself.

When I discovered that the creation of networking was a wonderful strategy to contact different people from all over the world and to learn about different cultures, I loved it. I knew what it was all about because I had traveled a lot already, and I always had this personal magnetism or natural way to communicate with people. The most important thing that I learned was to just simply be myself. This combined with my polite manners and without making any efforts, made my fellow travelers feel that I was the best at public relations because I was getting what I wanted to attract into my life.

Learning more about others became so important to me that I was happy when I realized my abilities and put them to work in my own way. I was able to gather useful information to have a secure travel experience. I always asked simple questions, such as what the most popular and inexpensive places are, like restaurants and local activities. It was easy to engage in this manner with other travelers, make new friends, take photographs, and create beautiful memories during my travel adventures.

I remember once someone said, "Traveling with you is super fun and I feel safe." It gave me a lot more confidence, and I thought to myself that this must be an ability that I could figure out how take advantage of.

During this trip I met someone who owned a hotel where they did yoga and Pilates retreats in Palma de Mallorca, Spain, for young people who wanted to lose weight. I asked the owner what it was like, and as soon as I said that I would like to go, not only did he give me the information, but he also said that if I could get two more people to go with me, that our stay would be complimentary.

Identifying your abilities is one of the many ways to help you know yourself and identify different opportunities. It's a great way to explore new horizons.

On that day I realized then that if I had not started to identify, analyze, and understand my own abilities that I would not have had the opportunity to go on that retreat.

Similarly, if I had given up on that trip because I didn't have the extra funds for a vacation, I would not have accomplished everything I did for myself, including saving money and helping others, and I would not have met this person who changed my life by helping me lose weight. So, I trusted my

intuition and after listening to my friends, we all decided to venture on the trip to this retreat in Palma de Mallorca.

Sometimes when you make a sacrifice your decision can lead up to a better place than anything you could have ever imagined. Having confidence in yourself, can bring you so many opportunities that will lead you to have options and help you make good choices.

I was glad that I did go on that trip in 1977, as I was able to transform my body into the one, I always dreamed of and wear JLO's first collection as my inspiration. As a Latin woman I want to be able to support other Latinas and wear designer clothes that's designed to flatter my Latin curves.

On another occasion, I met the representative of a cosmetics chain that sold its products through a catalog. This new business relationship opened new doors for me. It gave me the opportunity to earn money and begin to develop my leadership in business by selling slimming products.

For me speaking about slimming products was fascinating because I was struggling with my own weight, and I was able to share my own experiences. The company had a growing global presence, and I was able to build a wonderful network around the world and sell slimming products that became part of my lifestyle.

Since then, my life has been filled with collaborative opportunities. I have had the chance to collaborate in this book, thanks to Robbie Motter, the CEO and founder of GSFE, and form a friendship with very beautiful memories. I appreciate and admire her a lot as a leader and influencer.

He who cannot be a good follower cannot be a good leader.

— Aristotle —

It's important to have a human connection with people aside from just networking on the surface so as to attract the most benefits. The way you ask can create and define the outcome of any future opportunities. Being a good communicator is key for a leader because you can ask others questions and use the very same information to have connections that later on can generate opportunities for personal, spiritual or economic growth and even emotional support.

Maybe I will introduce you to a wonderful person who may one day become your husband, wife, business partner, or even an amazing forever friend, like Robbie Motter. We met during the coronavirus pandemic via Zoom and then at one of SIMA's conferences. Since then, we have had a lot of fun and we continue working together. She has also introduced me to some fantastic ladies from her networking group.

It's important to share our stories and to motivate and be an inspiration to one another, as well as to be honest, to act with integrity and decorum and to be loyal and support each other under any form of partnership.

I am glad that she came to visit me in England and that we were able to spend a few weeks in my residence in Chelsea, London. It was a life changing experience to meet a person like her. She's a very hard-working, kind lady.

I am also very glad to have met Virginia Earl, Writing Coach and Serial Entrepreneur, at the 2020 SIMA Awards in California. I am grateful that we were able to spend Christmas and New Year's Eve together in 2022 at my home in London. During her visit, we had the chance to talk about business opportunities and develop an incredible friendship.

Lead from the heart.

It is the power behind inspiration.

— Ada Gartenmann —

The power of asking is in communication. How do you ask? Do you ask direct or indirect questions? What tone do you use? Demanding, humble or even more demanding?

If we use the power of persuasion in a negative way, we will have negative results.

However, if we use it in a positive manner, we will obtain mayor supporters who will be interested in our objectives and thus become part of our dreams and the petitions that we put forth to others without being too aggressive o persistent.

The idea is not to be insistent nor manipulate others to do what we want to do, but to share goals and dreams whereby they will feel inspired to support us from their heart. It is good to have knowledge and a business strategy to be able to accept a "No" as an answer without affecting relationships negatively. We plant seeds with love and care, and we watch them grow into their full potential.

One of the tactics I use and that works very well for me is to say something like, "Wow, what you have done is incredible and I would like some day to have the opportunity to participate with you or go to that beautiful place. What you do is spectacular. You're the best at it."

As you can see, I used two potent ingredients, like recognizing an added value and respect, so that without me even realizing it the other person will be more inclined to say yes.

In communication it is as important to know how to say things as it is to know how to listen. And with regard to listening, we must take into account that an organization, and its members, not only speak with their voice, but also with their gestures, and even through their silence. The same way that silence speaks volumes, so does inaction. Inaction is a silent form of action. Everything is part of communication, whether it's verbal, non-verbal, action or inaction.

It is important that you use your education, good manners, the power of exchange, your intellect and the social decorum that hopefully you have developed throughout your career. All of this combined, will make you stand out.

Here are some tips to consider to convey a positive image, which can be achieved with minimal effort.

1. Take care of your reputation and personal image. You need to be vigilant of your actions, your choice of words and basically how you look.

2. The positive opinion that many people have about a person, or a business brand is important, and it's reflected in everything and anything we do or are a part of as this can define any future relationship in all of life's opportunities.

3. Having good qualities and habits is fundamental to maintain a good reputation, including educating oneself to be a globally influential person.

4. I would like to mention a few things that I have noticed every time that I decide to attend an event or develop future relationships.

—Be punctual when you're attending an event. Don't arrive three hours late as it's considered disrespectful to your host and guests who did arrive on time. The level of respect you put out will equal the level of respect you receive. Plan ahead the night before and research how long it will take you to get from where you are to the location of the event, especially if the event starts during rush hour. If you're late, people will notice and remember you and you may not be included in the guest list next time. Emergencies do come up, but if you do have a valid excuse for your tardiness then make sure you apologize to the host. Just don't be late due to poor planning.

—When you purchase a ticket to attend a fundraiser and if for whatever reason you're unable to attend, or you arrive late and there's no food left, or you're dissatisfied with the event's catering service or anything else, do not request a refund. It is considered in poor taste to request a refund. It's a fundraiser and people who normally attend will buy tickets to support a cause they believe in. If you didn't purchase a ticket, don't try to sneak into the event without paying. Someone always keeps a record of guests who paid and those who didn't. You don't want to be remembered as someone who takes advantage of a charity event.

—There's a time and a place for everything. There's always someone watching. So, pay attention and be aware of your actions. Avoid making a scene and being loud in front of others. Don't embarrass yourself. Always use your inside voice no matter what the circumstances are, and if you cannot control yourself, then take whatever is troubling you elsewhere, away from the event. Choose your actions and words wisely and be considerate of those around you. Remember, you're not alone in the room.

5. Public opinion matters when you're trying to create a positive image. Do the right thing and you will be remembered for your integrity and professionalism.

6. Invest in your education by hiring an experienced life coach. You might even consider hiring several life coaches with different expertise throughout your career. You want to stay up to date within your industry and technology. Things change fast these days. What worked the month before, may not work the following month.

7. Your personal brand is primordial. I recommend that you have someone who will help you elevate your image as your personal brand.

8. Developing a sense of sensibility and empathy will help your piety be a guide or serve as an inspiration to others so that everyone wins.

9. Following the latest fashion trends and colors that go with your personality, and skin tone, as well as wearing the right fragrance, will not only make you feel well but will also leave a lasting impression that will be engraved in the mind of the audience. This will give you even more opportunities to speak about different subjects with people you normally associate with.

10. A positive image is the beginning of all strategic reputation, whether at a personal, institutional. or organizational level, either a corporate or non-profit business.

11. Give from your heart and say and do things from your heart without expecting anything in return. Eventually, whatever you put out will come back to you equally and sometimes even in greater quantities. When you do things naturally from your heart, without forcing them, miracles will happen.

I love to practice reciprocity but it's difficult when others don't reply in kind, or even take advantage of you and bully you while thinking that you're not sufficiently influential or that you meet their same level of standards, which is a very common issue in the leadership or networking world.

As a social leader, I like to impose with authority and clarity what I like and above all to educate myself constantly and consistently. This law establishes that if we have already ceded to someone's previous solicitations, it is probable that we may leave the door open for that person to ask us for major favors in the future, which is why I ask that you develop your own intuition as you use the power to show up and ask.

A good leader must know how to interpret all the information that his or her team transmits. Even when it comes to the level of emotions, you must also develop or have knowledge about emotional intelligence so as not to offend anyone. Make sure that when you ask, that your message clearly conveys what you want to ask so that you get a positive answer and get what you want. It's important that you're flexible, humble and provide them with alternatives and convey your message with confidence.

I had another amazing opportunity to be part of the most innovative cosmetics brands companies worldwide that opened the door to help me grow and mature as a businesswoman. At the same time that I became passionate about cosmetics and beauty products as a consultant for L'Oréal, ELEMIS®, La Prarie®, I created my own aesthetician line, F.O.Y (Fountain of Youth) for my own salon.

F.O.Y. became a very successful formulation and I managed to sell it to one of the biggest lab groups of cosmetics based in Croatia, which in turn distributed it throughout Europe to other labs and is still in distribution today.

I also became the founder of many other salons, and a partner in beauty and fashion entertainment businesses around the world. Being featured in so many magazines like Vogue, Women's Wealth, BBC Channel 4, catapulted my career. Today, I continue to be a contributing writer for the lifestyle sections of two Latin newspapers, Express News, and Extra.

To ask the right question is already half the solution to a problem.

— C.G. Jung —

The magical key is knowing how to ask the right way. Once you're able to accomplish this, miracles will happen, and you will win all games.

Influential leadership consists of working simultaneously with people and ideas, making it possible for the efforts of the former to be coherent and aligned with the strategic actions of the organization as well as for IT.

It's important that as a leader of influence that you know how to be persuasive when you ask others in a company group or amongst friends. It must be observed that they are an integral, responsible people who provide trust, who are clear in their intentions, honest, coherent, persevering, disciplinary and constant. They must also be sure of themselves to be able to guide others by being firm in their decisions, objective, and authentic.

Another important aspect to highlight is that a leader must have an analytical capacity, a broad criteria, consideration and respect for others, and the ability to listen, among other characteristics. Exceptionally, you can have a personal magnetism to attract others, innate empathy, charisma and be a helpful person, not selfish nor envious, but kind. These qualities will stand out before any social group, as well as practicing any activity in which you are good and making positive collaborations in your community.

Persuasion is a process of social influence on the other. A process that, as we have seen, is the order of the day. We try to influence others, their options, their speeches, and their ideas. Everything that surrounds us has to do with communication and the management of the information that we emit and receive. It is very important how we use it and that we are vigilant, grounded, and present. Every time we show up, we're meeting new people and creating lasting impressions in the minds of those we meet.

Be aware and be prepared because you just never know when the next opportunity will present itself and change your life 360 degrees.

Confidence is part of showing up.

Get ready to embrace success.

— Ada Gartenmann —

....

ADA Gartenmann is the CEO and founder of SIMA Global Foundation and a bestselling author, mentor, and motivational consultant. With over 25 years of experience as a beauty, wellness, and fashion business consultant and lifestyle expert, Ada is a serial social entrepreneur and a multi-award winner.

In 2022, she was recognized for her altruistic humanitarian work by the President of the United States, Joe Biden, who awarded her the U.S. Presidential Lifetime Achievement Award. Ada also received the BAFTA Diversity Award (British Academy of Television Film) in 2022 for her efforts to promote and help Latino culture and new talent in the UK. She has been selected as one of the 50 Inspirational Women of 2021.

As an inspirational humanitarian, activist, and advocate for the rights of single mothers and child survivors of domestic violence living in extreme poverty, Ada's priority is to provide equal opportunities through education and leadership. She has won over 100 successful business awards, and her contribution to the United Nations Human Rights earned her the UNO Excellence Award (United Nations Human Rights Office) in 2022.

She is also a recipient of the Diversity Advocate Award 2022 that promotes and helps Latino culture and new talent in the UK, and she was also selected as one of the 50 Inspirational Women of 2021.

Ada is a member of more than 150 organizations around the world. Her leadership vision is very clear. She loves peace and freedom, equal opportunities for humanity, and is committed to helping people transform their lives, unite, and support each other to create a new sustainable world. As a bestselling author, mentor, philanthropist, and beauty, wellness, and fashion business consultant, Ada is a true inspiration and a role model to many around the world.

It's all
About
Showing
Up

"Get Up, Get Out, And Get A Life!"
(That You So Richly Deserve.)

Jackie Goldberg "Pink Lady"

Hi, I'm Jackie Goldberg, known to the world for the past 60 years as "The Pink Lady." Kermit the frog once said, "It's not easy being green." I say, "It is easy being Pink and looking at life through Rose-Colored Glasses!"

At this enlightened stage in my life, at 90 years young, with 5 wonderful children, 6 super grandchildren, and 11 delightful great grandchildren, I have learned how to live my life to the max with a positive attitude and lots of gratitude.

In so doing, you could well change the course of your life, as I did, because "It's All About Showing Up and Doing the Work!"

It is apparent to me that we all have a story to tell. It's not how we tell that story but how we live it that matters.

Now more than ever, I am able to enjoy my journey through life by Showing Up with energy, enthusiasm, and excitement. I've always been a survivor of life, never a victim.

You could say that my life is a continuous, exciting roller-coaster ride; at 90, it's still rolling along at break-neck speed.

To me, life is precious---every moment of every hour of every day. I intend to make the most of it and so should you!

Showing Up, no matter our age, and continuing to be vital, creative, and productive can lead to tremendous success when and if you are receptive to learning from those with greater expertise and accomplishment.

Ever since I can remember, I've had an upbeat positive outlook which has unequivocally led me to not let anything or anyone "rain on my parade." I have learned how to live longer, better, and wiser one day at a time – and so can you.

One example was when I was 25 and became a widow with 3 children under the age of 8. Instead of drowning in self-pity, my late husband had always said – "Life is for the Living – So Live It" – so, I got up, got out and got a new life by Showing Up and taking a manicure course, graduating, with the end result of a job that supported my family. When one does that, you become self-sufficient and gain self-esteem. And so, I did.

I soon met my second husband, a widower with 2 children, by Showing Up at a singles weekend. YEEEESSSS! WHY? Because when you are committed and dedicated to living life well, you soon find yourself walking taller, with that spunky bounce in your step and feeling so much better about everything you do. We should all be able to help others feel that same zest for life, that "joie de vivre" that I have.

After 39 years of marriage and working as a Women's' Wear Sales Rep, at age 71, I became a widow again. WOW! Culture Shock! I was not 25 as before. But I knew that I had a new feeling of freedom, allowing me to take chances and re-invent myself to do all the things I had only dreamed of doing. And so, I did (again.)

If you are thinking of re-inventing yourself, so that life doesn't pass you by, it can be done. Remember, life is a journey, so grab hold of it, open your mind and your heart to it, and live it, love it, before you leave it.

I hope all of you reading my story will adopt this philosophy: "It's not where you start in life that counts, it's where and how you finish."

So, I began a fabulous new journey; Showing Up soon became second nature.

I needed to decide what I wanted to do differently. So, I decided to enter SHOW BUSINESS! Once again, my positive attitude with lots of gratitude, gave me the chutzpa (intestinal fortitude) to unlock new doors. HOLLYWOOD, here I come!

To begin my new career, I needed exposure, so I entered a Ms. Senior LA County Pageant. Oh, My! What a learning experience this turned out to be!

Every entrant was age 60 to 90, and all 23 were phenomenally talented. On the other hand, there I was---not a singer or dancer. So, I took Shakespeare's soliloquy (To Be Or Not To Be) and made it my own: (To Age or Not to Age, That Was The Question.)

And guess what – I won over these fabulous ladies. I asked the judges, "Why me?"

They replied, "Pink Lady, you exemplify what a Ms. Senior is---a woman who is energetic, productive, with a zest for life and comfortable being who you are, not old but simply growing older."

My picture was in the newspaper and an agent called inviting me to his office with my "headshots." (Who knew what a headshot was?) The day came and I Showed Up in his office, excited and ready to be the next "Hollywood Star."

The agent asked for my headshot, saying "I first want to assure you that the Casting Couch days are over."

When I heard that, I grabbed my photo back and said, "But that's why I came into the business in the first place."

He started to laugh and said, "My dear, with that positive attitude and energy, you'll make it in this business." And I have.

I soon got my first film and became a member of SAG (Screen Actors Guild.) This was truly one of the best times of my life. Hopefully, these first steps in re-inventing myself will show baby-boomers and seniors that life continues after you turn 60. I always want to prove to the younger generation that you don't stop living at any age but continue to Show Up, as there is still "a lot of livin' to do."

After many auditions, I noticed how aging talent struggle to find parts. And so Senior Star Power Productions, a nonprofit corporation, became my next venture. The mission was to put those of an age to work and empower them to continue doing whatever they want in the industry we love.

During this period, I produced 10 Musicals and employed several hundred very talented senior actors, musicians, and crew. We were able to show them that there was still time to kick up their heels and live it up to enjoy the years they had left.

All my Senior Musical Shows have always had intergenerational audience appeal. After one performance, one of my cast members asked a young man of 13 who had accompanied his grandmother, what he thought about the show. The boy replied, "It was better than Spiderman! I didn't know people that age could sing and dance. And I didn't think they were still alive at that age." That made my day.

I also do Commercials (Washington National Bank, Para Eagle International Perfumes, GUCCI Watches, Equinox Fitness Clubs, and a Super Bowl Commercial for Loctite); Television (House), and the 2019 Music Video of the Year ("You Have to Calm Down" with Taylor Swift, Katy Perry, Ellen DeGeneres and RuPaul.)

In 2022, I loved playing the wild, funny, Delia, in the horror comedy podcast, "I Love Lucifer," created by Susie Singer Carter and Don Priess, and opened the martial arts/comedy Movie "Gimme My Money" directed by Bill Vigil due out in 2023. Not bad for 90.

It all started with my first Stage Play, "Grapes and Raisins", at the Stage Door Playhouse. The part required the actor to wear a sexy Victoria Secret Teddy, fishnet stockings, and a fluffy fur coat. So, I Showed Up, saying loud and clear, "You Better Believe It!" What fun it was as the audience commented on my figure and my spunk.

Twenty-four hours a day is not enough for this Pink Lady, but I make it work. I even wrote a book while doing everything you are reading about. It's called, "Get Up, Get Out, & Get A Life!" I am especially proud of the chapter called, "Senior Sexuality," where I talk about dating over the age of 60. YEEESSSS! "Senior Sexuality is alive and well – ANY TIME, ANY PLACE AND AT ANY AGE!"

LEGENDARY STAR MAE WEST SAID,

"WHEN I'M GOOD, I'M VERY GOOD,

BUT WHEN I'M BAD, I'M EVEN BETTER!"

I am now working on my next writing effort, "It Ain't Over 'Til I Say It's Over."

And, Guess What, not to be outdone by PLAYBOY, I became the COVER and CENTERFOLD in the First Published Copy of AGELESS MAGAZINE, Autumn 2022, featuring women from 40 to 90; GUESS WHO WAS 90?

The words "slowing down" have never, ever been in my vocabulary and should not be in yours.

Life, my friends, is downright fabulous when you Show Up and are ready to do the work.

To reach a world-wide audience, I created (with my partner - wait 'til you read that story) an Intergenerational Television Variety Show – "PINK LADY PRESENTS." Now, in our fifth year on television, every Sunday evening at 5 PM on the EMT MEDIA TV Network (Channel 25.1) and 24/7 on PinkLadyPresents.com.

These shows feature "lives being well lived," guests of every ethnicity, from all walks of life, and talent including actors, writers, singers, musicians, artists, magicians, civic leaders, and our most under-served and under-valued - veterans and their families.

I must confess that I love every moment of being "out there" – performing, entertaining, and continuing to be active, proving that everything is possible.

So, what else do you do? I Got Up, Got Out and Got a Life (again.) In so doing, I met a retired Vietnam War Air Force Chaplain, whose name DOV is the acronym for "Directing Opportunities to Veterans." And guess what, he is 12 years younger! OH, YES!

We had never met when he called and asked for tickets for one of my shows

for the WWII, Korean and Vietnam War Veterans. It was a 12-week run, and I offered tickets for each week. In week 12, DOV called to thank me and told me how everyone loved the shows. I asked him what he thought, and he admitted he had not seen the show; that he only got the tickets for the other veterans.

As we were closing that Friday night, I asked him to attend. My then current partner of 7 years, Arnold, had been very ill and passed away two weeks later.

I asked Chaplain DOV to conduct the Celebration of Life for my beloved Arnold. He did and the rest is history. Ten magnificent years together have brought us to the present.

It gives me pause to remember how grateful I am for all the wonderful blessings and recognitions I have received.

One of the reasons why one must Show Up was when I became a member of the Hollywood Chamber of Commerce. There, I promoted Hollywood by staging my musicals in Hollywood Theaters. The Chamber honored me with the Esteemed Heroes of Hollywood Award with one of my co-recipients, Judge Judy Sheindlin. It made me feel that my work with Senior Star Power Productions was recognized and validated by the Hollywood Community.

Receiving the Susan B. Anthony Award from the California Federation of Business and Professional Women had me reflecting that today more and more women like myself are serving in Corporate Leadership and not taking "NO" for an answer in anything they want to accomplish. That's why you must Show Up to be successful.

People are always asking me, "Hey, Pink, what do you do to keep yourself looking as good as you do?"

My answer, "EVERYTHING I CAN!"

As you can see, I believe that all of us have to love who we are; we need to feel that we are special and unique. For when we Show Up, it is the following message that counts:

Today, let's fall in love

with the person in the mirror,

the one you see every day

but seldom truly look at.

The one who gives more

than she ever takes.

Today, let's take nothing,

not this day, not this moment,

not this chance, not even

ourselves for granted.

Let's first love who we are.

That includes, keeping my hair PINK, eating a pescatarian diet (seafood), and working out at the gym 5 to 6 times every week. I forgot I do have one secret vice that keeps me in shape all the time: a scoop of Haagen-Dazs Vanilla or Pistachio Ice Cream every night!

MY ANNUAL RESOLUTIONS

To keep my independence as long as I can and curb any old-age signs.

To better pace myself in my daily life so I can accomplish more.

To always remember to say "Thank You" to the Powers that Be for giving me another day to live my life to the MAX.

To count my blessings and love my children and family, cherish my friends, and hold dear the loves in my life.

Yes, my friends, I have come a long way. I remember when a friend of mine, who is 88, said, "Life should not be a journey to the grave, with the thought of arriving in a great and wonderful body but to skid in sideways, champagne in one hand, a chocolate-covered strawberry in the other, completely used up, worn out, laughing and yelling loud and clear, "WHOA! WHAT A RIDE I'VE HAD!"

As you see, I'm a woman who knows who I am. So, here's what I did. I went to the cemetery a few months ago and bought a fabulous, you guessed it, Pink Frosted Casket and, just to be absolutely certain it would complete the ensemble, a Salisbury Pink Headstone to match; engraved on it is:

THE PINK LADY
JACQUELINE H. GOLDBERG
WIFE, MOTHER,
PINK GRANDMA AND GREAT GRANDMA
"IT AIN'T OVER 'TIL I SAY IT'S OVER"

SEPTEMBER 3, 1932 – ∞

Someone said, "Life is a succession of many moments and to live each

moment by Showing Up is to be successful. For the true spirit of life is not to try to control it but to use what happens to improve it.

My beginning years were wonderful; my middle years were full of adventure; and now, in my 91st year, the best years are yet to come. To be able to have that energy and zest for life that I had when I was 4 years old – I pray to heaven to have at 104! Then, maybe - just maybe - I'll think about slowing down BUT not altogether."

I would like you to remember that it's not the breaths we take in life that count, but what we do with the breaths we take.

And when you realize who you truly are, you'll be able to live your life the way you want – having the time of your life.

THE BOTTOM LINE IS,

"I'M NOT BUYING INTO IT'S OVER.

IT'S NOT OVER

'TIL YOU OR I SAY IT'S OVER!!!

It's all
About
Showing
Up

Showing Up + Asking = Making Spirits Bright

Mary Greene

Introduction

Am I Stuck? I felt as if I was stuck without making progress in my life. My skills and talents resembled hot soup boiling in a pot, just waiting to be served. I consistently kept myself engaged in meaningful activities and opportunities to assist others. These activities kept my skills sharp. My life was changed by a phenomenal experience demonstrated through this title: "Showing Up + Asking = Making Spirits Bright."

Here is my amazing journey when I became Executive Director of the Greater Washington Women's Network (GWWN) in Washington, DC, and complemented its mission and vision.

The chapter format "Showing Up + Asking = Making Spirits Bright" is presented in an interview style. There are topics, questions, and answers explaining how GWWN is "Showing up and Asking." The responses are addressed by highlighting GWWN accomplishments through the years. At the end is "Knowledge Sharing" that provides tips to inspire and support action. The topics:

Showing Up: Equipped – Asking: Not a Problem

Showing Up: Developing and Implementing Programs – Asking: Graciously

Showing Up: Facing Challenges – Asking: For Solutions

Showing Up: Networking Bonuses – Asking: For Perks

Showing Up: Invitation: Speaking Engagements – Asking: Greater Awareness

Showing Up: Pearls of Wisdom – Asking: Create Innovative Thinking

Showing Up: Volunteers and Supporters – Asking: What is on the Table?

Showing Up + Asking = Making Spirits Bright

Further, this chapter is also to illustrate actual educational lessons. It facilitates interests and stimulates personalized learning. GWWN's impressive and memorable history has something to offer you! Thanks for showing up!

A Clear Fresh Start

I am showing up now and cordially appealing to your question, "What's in It for Me?" The question always provokes an answer. The question provokes the title of this book: "It's All About Showing Up: The Power is in the Asking."

This Is My Story: "Showing Up + Asking = Making Spirits Bright"

Showing Up: Equipped – Asking: Not a Problem

Being passionate about encouraging and supporting others to help untap their potential has always been my purpose in life. Therefore, in June 2001, when I was nominated as Executive Director of Greater Washington

Women's Network, Washington, DC, I was excited and equipped for the position.

Sherreen Ogletree was stepping down as Executive Director. She said: "I knew you would be the Executive Director to elevate GWWN." Her words reminded me of my sister Dennie Jones's encouraging words before she transitioned. "Get actively involved in women's organizations. You are qualified and it will enhance your life!" She was correct!

Preparation: Qualifications

My professional leadership experience included Director of Counselor at St. Augustine's University (the first woman in that position), a facilitator at Shaw University, both in Raleigh, North Carolina, and a Counselor at Barber Scotia College, Concord, North Carolina. While on Barber Scotia's campus, etched in my heart was Dr. Mary McLeod Bethune's legacy, a former graduate there. Dr. Bethune was a pioneer, educator, and women's rights advocate, who served as an advisor to five United States Presidents. She is a distinguished role model whose achievements inspired us.

Also, I was equipped with knowledge, skills, and abilities transferable from other positions for services performed in private sectors, churches, and government agencies. My achievements and academic credentials are a Master of Education in Guidance and Counseling from the University of North Carolina, Charlotte, and Bachelor of Arts in Sociology from Livingstone College, Salisbury, North Carolina.

Furthermore, before coming on board with GWWN, I graduated from these organizations' training programs: Dale Carnegie Course (12 weeks) and Washington Project Program (WPP), "How to Run a Business: A-Z" (12 weeks) in Washington, DC.

I credit Migdalia Baerga-Buffler, a former co-worker, now transitioned, for sharing the WPP, "How to Run a Business" training opportunity with me. She rushed up to me excitedly and said, "Mary, here is the training opportunity we've been waiting for to start our business." She continued: "The class is free." She was interested in Jewelry, and I was interested in Etiquette. It was unbelievable we graduated three months before I became Executive Director of GWWN. Was it a coincidence? I think not, it was God's designed plan.

This additional training was an extra leadership booster. I had a leading-edge to exercise confidence, boldness, and the right attitude to ask for assistance. For example, identifying criteria to advance GWWN, meeting with directors and leaders, brainstorming and sharing ideas. Encouraging members to serve on the executive board and recruiting volunteers beyond GWWN membership.

Knowledge Sharing: When opportunities arise for training and visiting other places to expand your insight, accept the offers; show up. You may not see a current purpose, but your journey instinct says, "Go, do it!" Get all the training you can and embrace opportunities to build your confidence and resume. Your skills, qualifications, and positive attitude will take you to successful heights.

GREATER WASHINGTON WOMEN'S NETWORK

WHO WE ARE: Overview

Greater Washington Women's Network is located in Washington, DC. It is a small powerful nonprofit 501(c)(3) organization operated by members and volunteers. There is no salaried staff. Our team has a passion to serve. Serving is an honor. GWWN was established in 1995.

GWWN is an organization in which women gain valuable experience, information, business and leadership training, and recognition. It is a "Timeless Connection." GWWN was an affiliate of the National Association for Female Executives (NAFE), until its business model changed in 2021.

Mission: invest in our members, business, and professional women, through education, networking, community service, resources, and youth development.

Vision: Enhance. Advance. Give Back.

Showing Up: Developing and Implementing Programs – Asking: Graciously

How did you show up and ask graciously to support your initiatives?

Our new goal was the "Management by Objectives" (MBO) approach. Therefore, our initiatives were our guiding map. We showed up and asked graciously by partnering and collaborating with women and other organizations to extend program activities and resources such as The White House Council on Women and Girls, Healthywomen, Strengthening Partnership Program, and Women in the Boardroom.

Promoted our mission and vision to recruit professional prominent (women and men) speakers and panel members to provide pro bono services. Speakers such as TV anchors, White House staff, DC Congresswoman Eleanor Holmes Norton, and The Honorable Joan M. Pratt, CPA (elected Comptroller in November 1995) As Comptroller for the City of Baltimore, served as Chairwoman of the Baltimore Employees' and Elected Officials' Retirement. Some businesswomen included Dawn McCoy, Founder and CEO, Flourish Publishing Group, LLC, nationally recognized speaker, and author and Kristina Bouweiri, President and CEO, Reston Limousine, metropolitan area's largest limousine/shuttle service.

Scheduled a fabulous VIP tour for GWWN at the White House.

Identified benefits to encourage organizations, schools, and members to promote our Leadership Award Program, emphasizing recognition and academic scholarships for the community.

Announced our e-newsletter and a community resources newscast for communications to advertise GWWN and other organizations' events, recognition, and opportunities for career/personal and business development for women and youth.

Knowledge Sharing: No matter how much experience, education, and successes we have, it is critical to show up humble and ask graciously for assistance. Sometimes you might get special treatments.

Showing Up: Facing Challenges – Asking: For Solutions

You do encounter challenges, right? Yes. Where do you get answers? Answers to our challenges come from various sources such as members, research, networking including NAFE, professional businesses, and training.

What are some challenges you have resolved by asking?

Volunteer Staff Resources: Communicated with companies offering free recruitment to nonprofit organizations. Utilized their services to recruit volunteers for various positions.

Developed a comprehensive volunteer program to recruit volunteers.

Offered internships to students, also at colleges and universities for academic credit. Wrote an academic proposal to New York University for an intern college student to assist with projects.

Sponsorship Venues: Meetings/Events. When Adams Bank was unable to

support us to host events, we negotiated with Robert Half International (RHI) and OfficeTeam (OT) to serve as a venue hosting GWWN events. When RHI and OT downsized, we contacted the Charles Sumner School Museum & Archives, public libraries, and restaurants including the historic Mayflower Hotel, Washington Court Hotel, and Hilton Hotel.

The Navy Memorial in Washington, DC reached out to us to sponsor our networking events. We were honored and thrilled.

Quarterly Luncheons: Developed and implemented luncheon events, attracting day professional women to attend.

Joint Networking Events: Better Together. Virginia NAFE local affiliate in Alexandria, Shirley Archer, founder, and director, and GWWN consolidated resources facilitating monthly networking events on a rotating schedule. This was successfully accomplished until she relocated.

The New National Women's History Museum: Congresswoman Carolyn B. Maloney (NY-12 District) hosted a luncheon with women organization leaders to share her vision and brainstorm.

Do you have any outstanding challenges? We are always refining to improve just like companies and other nonprofit organizations. We have experienced positive results from showing up and the power of asking. Challenges are not always resolved according to our timing or when we want them done. Therefore, we believe there is a solution to every challenge/concern, and the answer will come because we asked.

Knowledge Sharing: Patience and persistence are critical characters to exhibit when challenges and problem-solving are involved. An effective leader understands that challenges strengthen, reveal unknown victories, and prove that all things are possible if we only believe. There is a season and time for everything. Therefore, never give up; just keep on asking!

Showing Up: Networking Bonuses – Asking: For Perks

How do you feel about Networking Bonuses and asking?

"Go wild without spending money!" Everyone loves "freebies" and so does GWWN. That is why we search for businesses, and companies for promotional items to use as door prizes, for activities winners, meeting packages, treats for events, and table favors.

Also, GWWN requests complimentary tickets for various events. Companies sometimes offer complimentary tickets. If GWWN is unable to get free tickets, we ask for noteworthy discounts or negotiated by "sweetening the deal." We use our marketing component to "seal the deal." While free tickets are more favorable, we are pleased to get discounts.

These are members benefit perks (rewards) that are sometimes offered to guests. Perks always spark excitement because everyone looks forward to surprise benefits.

Who has given GWWN complimentary tickets?

U.S. 44th President Barack Obama Inaugural Ball. GWWN was honored and excited to receive complimentary tickets. GWWN was represented!

Leadership and Development Champions: Events Attended for Training,

NAFE Top Companies for Executive Women, Cipriani, New York, various events

Working Mothers: National Conference Supporting Hourly Workers, McLean, Virginia

Diversity & Flexibility Alliance Annual Conference

Business Summit: Young Entrepreneurs Award Saunders Scholars Finals Competition Luncheon

Girl Scouts Gold Award Centennial Anniversary, Cannon House Office Building, Washington, DC

For 100 years, Girl Scouts have made meaningful, sustainable changes in their communities and beyond. The Girl Scouts Gold Award is the highest honor.

Knowledge Sharing: Out of the blue, a networking bonus perk opportunity is offered to you. This is an excellent volunteer benefit. Volunteering does not pay a traditional salary. However, volunteering provides exposure, networking experience, valuable skills, sense of purpose, and self-confidence.

Showing Up: Invitation: Speaking Engagements – Asking: Greater Awareness

Do you have any formal speaking training? If you do, where did you receive it?

Yes. My Toastmaster International training is a speaking bonus. I completed the CTM (Competence Training Manual) level before I became GWWN Executive Director. This is another skill set I developed that prepared me for the position.

Has GWWN received invitations for speaking engagements?

Yes. GWWN received invitations to show up as a speaker at various events and served as a panelist for trainings and conferences. A speaking engagement invitation is not only to show up, but to ask audience through

your speech to "grab the hook," for greater awareness or education. GWWN has been invited back to speak.

Would you share several of GWWN's speaking engagements?

I was honored to be chosen as the speaker on behalf my graduation class for the following:

Strengthening Partnership Initiatives non-profit (SPI) Leadership Training Program. A year's training sponsored by Office of Partnerships and Grant Development, Executive Office of the Mayor, Washington, DC. My second "How to Run a Business" graduation.

Frostburg State University in Maryland, "Career Strategies for Women" sponsored by the National Council for Negro Women Organization

The Washington Center for Internships and Academic Seminars: "Women Empowerment in The 21st Century" to strengthen and inspire the women of Sonora, Mexico, in their career (panelist).

Aspen Institute: "Women in Management and Business Seminar" (panelist)

The Homeland Security (Government Agency): "How to Break Women Barriers"

GWWN, a speaker along with Dr. Marie Savard, author of "Ask Dr. Marie", one of the most trusted voices on women's health, wellness, and patient concerns, sponsored by Healthywomen

GWWN, a speaker along with now DC Mayor Muriel Bowser, Saint Gabriel Sodality, DC Prayer Breakfast

Knowledge Sharing: You heard the phrase, Practice Makes Perfect. Prepare yourself to build confidence speaking in public. A speaking engagement may arise. You might have to show up to speak instead of key leaders who

are unable to participate. Volunteering opens numerous surprising doors.

Showing Up: Pearls of Wisdom – Asking: Create Innovative Thinking

Are there any Pearls of Wisdom takeaways you want to share?

Yes. GWWN communication includes "Pearls of Wisdom" such as motivational and positive quotes, inspiring articles, and encouraging messages from me. The purpose is to educate, create insight, and hope. Also, to energize and change our moods to take positive actions. Here are three original (quotes) "Pearls of Wisdom" cited in GWWN Newsletters and Highlights.

"Positive words generate a solid ground; negative words generate sinking sand." - Mary Greene, GWWN Executive Director, "Important Now More Than Ever," Newsletter No. 21- May 2020.

"Good manners seal the deal." - Mary Greene, GWWN Executive Director, "Mom's Viewpoint," Newsletter No. 26 - September 2021.

"There is not a big "I" or "little you" on a team. There are invisible eyes, that can see what others can't see, to get the job done." - Mary Greene, GWWN Executive Director, "GWWN + You = An Astounding Year in Review 2020-2021," April 4, 2022.

Knowledge Sharing: "Pearls of Wisdom" expand awareness and open our mind to look at life from a deeper insight to evoke creative innovative thinking. I encourage you to read and think about these messages. Then allow creative innovative thinking to flow and take actions.

Showing Up: Volunteers and Supporters – Asking: What is on the Table?

Is The Table Set for Success?

Yes. Because...

The team shows up, shares, and executes the same vision. I always say: "Success is not measured by the number of people, but what people bring to the table to make an event or organization successful."

The table is set with GWWN Volunteers and Supporters' Benefits for "Making Spirits Bright" on behalf of themselves and others. See what is on the table:

GWWN: (1) provides essential resources, training and leadership opportunities to develop your business and career, (2) showcases your business or special activities in our broadcasts: (newsletters, newscasts, and special interests express publications), and networking events/ meetings, (3) recognizes achievements, (4) offers discounts for GWWN's events, (5) receives and shares complimentary events tickets, (6) identifies untapped talents, (7) gives and receives personable touches, (8) passes it forward in the community, (9) builds relationship, learning, and growing together, and (10) explores opportunities to expand your horizon.

The table is set to **Acknowledge Volunteers and Supporters.**

This "Thank You" acknowledgment to volunteers and supporters was featured "You're a Big Deal – Awesome, Women's History Month," GWWN Newsletter No. 28 – March 2022. The heartfelt message is still applicable.

THANK YOU FROM THE BOTTOM OF OUR HEARTS!

"We honor you volunteers and supporters. You are a great asset to GWWN. In case you are unaware, GWWN is a members-operated without salaried-staff and volunteers' organization. Your talents, contributions, donations, and love connection propel us to perform with confidence, touching and changing lives."

MEET OUR TEAM

In this chapter it is an honor to include a special message to GWWN Fabulous Team – You Showed Up!

SPECIAL PERSONAL MESSAGE FROM MARY GREENE, EXECUTIVE DIRECTOR

Longevity Volunteers and Supporters – 20+ Year Stamina

Thank you GWWN's volunteers and supporters who have taken a stance supporting me and GWWN for more than 2 decades.

Supporters: Who are our supporters? They include a variety of people such as donors, subscribers, advocates, partners, friends, followers, and more. Some supporters help us in more than one capacity. Whatever your role, you are making a difference. I do not know you all by name, but my heart does and recognizes your deeds. You have been faithful and your dedication rewarding. On the outskirt you quietly attributed to GWWN's success!

Back Stage: Prayer Warriors – In my personal life, prayer is a critical spiritual component. Nothing can be accomplished without prayer. There are many women who pray for me, and I am grateful for everyone's prayers. I am a witness; we all need prayer. Also, without God we can do nothing. But with God, we can do all things through Christ which strengthens us. These women stepped forward supporting me on behalf of GWWN in this area: Elaine Brunson, Mary Foster (appointment time), JoAnn Gresham, Linda

Holz, Pearlie Isler, Geraldine Ward, Stephanie Williams, and Deborah Wright.

Service Oriented: Fitting the pieces together: GWWN consists of several different puzzles. Every piece must be angled correctly to fit into the right puzzle, at the right time, to complete tasks. There are those who stick by me like glue. I thank God, they do not let go. These are the people with the puzzle pieces: L'Tange Alexander, Ron Alexander, Gloria Blackwell, Cheryl Blount, Marilyn Dawson, Jenifer Golson, Novella Gumbs, Frederick Isler, Helen Lawson, Kevin Lawson, Sherreen Olgetree, Frances Simpson, and Samuel Whitfield.

My Family: Frederick, my husband's love empowers me, and he is a rock. He wears many hats, an angel, friend, adviser, and more. He appreciates my gifts and gives me freedom to express them, as I execute my purpose. Also, this family unit includes his mother Pearlie, a powerful prayer warrior, and his sister Helen, who is available when she is needed with a wonderful spirit. God placed Samuel in our lives and heart years ago. He is a loving, caring, and supportive brother. What a blessing! I thank God for all my family, especially my sisters (Gloria, L'Tange, and Novella) for their love, patience, support, and believing in me. They are my pillars.

Knowledge Sharing: To all volunteers and supporters, on behalf of GWWN, I cannot thank you enough for all you have done. Your investment in GWWN will yield great returns because "It is more a blessing to give than to receive."

Showing Up + Asking = Making Spirits Bright

What are some of GWWN's accomplishments and impact "Making Spirits Bright?"

Accomplishments

Record-Breaking

Our community service component reveals we are not only showing up but providing financial donations. Our record-breaking donations during 2020-2021 program year was outstanding. We contributed to 13 out of these 15 nonprofit organizations we support, and this list is not inclusive:

(1) Suited for Change, (2) Women In Networking (WIN), (3) Global Society For Female Entrepreneurs, (4) The Training Center, (5) Darfur Women Action Group, (6) Maryland New Directions, (7) VolunteerMatch, (8) We Are Family, (9) Horton's Kids, (10) Generation Hope, (11) Community Crisis Center, (12) Capital Area Food Bank, (13) American Heart Association, (14) American Red Cross, and (15) St. Ann's Center for Children, Youth, and Families

(Established 1860, oldest organization).

Hands: Better Together

We are amazed; our passion, love, and commitment touched so many people - women, men, and youth.

GWWN's accomplishments and impact "making spirit bright" on women are:

Gainful employment

Received academic scholarships for college education total: 11 awarded to women and men.

Changed careers.

Obtained higher salaries in their profession.

Returned to college for higher education.

Started businesses.

Grown professionally, enhanced their self-development.

Built long lasting relationships.

Scholarship Recipient Feedback

"One of our members was approached by a former scholarship recipient. She was ecstatic to share the impact GWWN had in her life. She said, "I remembered you from GWWN. I received a scholarship from GWWN to continue my college education when it was needed. Now I understand the importance of doing your best and keeping a good academic grade point average. It paid off for me. Thank you so much." GWWN "Passion Moves Forward to Serve" GWWN Highlights 2018-2019, page 18.

Feedback about GWWN

Comments like these confirm our impact is making a difference:

"Thanks to GWWN investing in me, I've been promoted."

"I always feel good when I am with GWWN. You make me feel special."

"GWWN helps me to keep my skills professional and sharp."

"As a small organization, you have a big heart and really care."

"You're a Big Deal – Awesome, Women's History Month"

GWWN Newsletter No. 28 – March 2022.

GWWN HONORS AND AWARDS

President Biden's Lifetime Achievement Award

President's Obama's Lifetime Achievement Awards

GWWN Board of Director Awards

Uptownscoop and the Washington Mystics (Sheila Johnson's, co-founder of Black Entertainment Television (BET) and owner of Washington Mystics Basketball Team: Leadership Service in Community Award

Women In Networking (WIN)

Certificate of Appreciation: Claudia Gillard Foundation Scholarship

Outstanding Financial and Inspiring Support: Claudia Gillard Foundation Scholarship Award

Knowledge Sharing: GWWN is a dynamic organization that exhibits compassion; it inspires and promotes women's success. The fabulous, empowered volunteer team makes it happen!

Now that you have read this chapter, did you see that I was not stuck? I was being groomed for the position. My gifts and talents were bubbling to be utilized. I am elated, now the pot is no longer boiling but is being used to "serve others!"

This chapter is just a synopsis about GWWN. I have shared my personal background, how GWWN showed up, asked, and received answers by using topics as a story line captivating GWWN's outstanding successes. It described the magnificent power of volunteering which includes benefits. Also, showing up equipped and prepared give us greater fascinating

confidence to ask. For example, asking: graciously, for solutions, perks (discounts and rewards), greater awareness, how to creative innovate thinking, and What is on the Table?

Therefore, Greater Washington Women's Network

Mission: invest in our members, business, and professional women, through education, networking, community service, resources, and youth development.

Vision: Enhance. Advance. Give Back.

Is being accomplished by "Showing Up + Asking = Making Spirit Bright!"

What's next for GWWN? It will be revealed because we asked!

Readers: Thank you for reading this chapter, now answer the question: "What's in It for Me?"

Thank you, Dr. Robbie Motter. Your love for others to succeed is breathtaking. It is building a legacy that will live forever! I am delighted NAFE connected us.

Thank you, Angela Covany, and the Havana Book Group for sharing your marvelous gift. You create magic!

A Timeless Connection!

With Love,

Mary Greene

GWWN Executive Director

"Show Up Equipped to Serve Guests at The Table."

It's all
About
Showing
Up

I Just Keep SHOWING UP....

Denise Gregory

My name is Denise Gregory and when I first showed up, I met Robbie Motter. You see it was in 2014 when I was at a Mastermind event. It was one of the first ones I did as I was still new at vendor events. This event was at the Marriott in Murietta California. I was in this group, and we had two speakers; one was Laurie Raupe and the other one was Robbie Motter. This was an annual event with the mastermind group that I belong to. I showed up, and attendees supported me by buying jewelry from me. The topic was so inspiring by both ladies that I could not wait to meet them. I spent two hours selling Premier Designs jewelry. These two ladies talked to me about their meeting group; at the time they were in Nafe. These ladies wore red dresses, and that was my favorite color. Robbie Motter invited me to be a vendor at one of her events, but I was already doing another event. I gave her my business card.

Time went on, and I was at the end of my contract with Mastermind, I wanted to go into another direction. I went to a chamber mixer and liked it, so I joined. They gave me a vendor events, and I showed up to all of them. Murrieta Chamber had a mega mixer, and Robbie Motter and Joan Wakeland showed up to my booth and talked to me about this new group she was starting called GSFE and asked if I would be interested in coming

to one of her meetings that she had at the time. She had about 15 different ones all over California. I still did not think I was ready for another group. Well, Robbie called me and asked me to be a vendor at her first GSEE event and asked me if I knew of any other vendors. I said yes. I sent her five ladies to be a vendor alongside of me. I showed up to this event, and it was an upscale event. The ladies were dressed in cobalt blue dresses. Robbie showed up in the fanciest dress I've ever seen. The food was good, the singers were awesome, and the ladies got up to dance. Again, I was not ready to be a sister of GSFE.

Robbie and I just kept showing up at events like the Queen Mary two years in a row until Covid hit, and that's when I started to slow down. I could not work could not do events. Meanwhile Robbie was building her network on zoom all over the US. Finally, when things started opening up, I went back to work, and again I showed up at another vendor event. Robbie was there and said she had been building GSFE through zoom and new networks we're opening back up. I did not sign up for the chamber again while on Covid, so I thought, well, let's go to a GSFE Meeting, so I went to the Temecula one because it fit into my schedule. The Temecula was where I finally signed up. I got my last job back three months after I signed up for GSFE which is in Menifee, and when I found out that it meets on Wednesday at lunch, it was the right time for my schedule as it was so close to my last job of the day. I switched to the Menifee Network. I kept showing up, and Robbie asked me to be the co-director of this meeting. I said 'yes'. The following year she asked me to be the meeting Director because she seen that I was showing up.

My life has grown so much, and it's all about showing up. I have seen my life change in so many ways through my will of showing up. I love to show up because you never know what God has in store for you. He has brought the best of myself out in me. Thank you, Robbie Motter, for showing me

how to be a leader and the wonderful woman I have met in my life just by showing up.

During my leadership I was able to help the Menifee network grow which brought in more dynamic women to share their stories and build relationships with.

Recently I had a new SHOW UP, and that is to be a teacher and to homeschool my wonderful grandson which meant I needed to step down from my director job and transfer back to the Temecula GSFE meeting as they meet at night. Recently I attended their meeting, and many of my Menifee GSFE members were also there. I was presented a beautiful bouquet of flowers and a card signed by the members to thank me for my leadership with the Menifee network.

Because I wear many hats, I am going to cater the Menifee meeting luncheon on March 8, 2023, which is International Women's Day and is the day that this book will be launched. I am now not only a teacher to my wonderful grandson but also a co-author in this dynamic book with my other GSFE sisters. Each story will touch a life.

So, keep SHOWING UP and ASKING it will change your life. It has mine.

How Showing Up Has Changed My Life
(And others)

Lynda J. Bergh Herring

When I was a little girl, all I wanted to do was be a ballerina. I watched the Rogers & Hammerstein version of Cinderella on television, and I was HOOKED! When I won the Little Miss Yorba Linda pageant in 1964, one of the prizes I received was 6 months of free dance lessons. I was on my way!!

For many years I focused completely on my dancing, especially ballet. Classes also included tap, jazz, Hawaiian, baton twirling, and even belly dancing, but ballet was always my favorite. I was at the dance studio every chance I got, worked as a "junior teacher" and the reception desk, and attended every dance conference I could. I lived, breathed, and dreamed dance. I even planned to major in dance in college and was accepted to the University of Irvine.

Although I loved dancing, I was painfully shy. I had no desire whatsoever to act or speak in front of anyone, not teachers, classrooms, or from any stage.

Due to some unexpected plot twists in my life, my career changed from ballet dancing to law enforcement to ultimately becoming a private investigator. My willingness to show up has changed dramatically, especially in recent years.

One of the earliest cases I worked as a private investigator involved a missing child. While I had worked on a few similar cases in law enforcement, this one was different. The child had been taken by a distant family member who, before we had a chance to rescue her, was sold to other for sex. It was not called Sex Trafficking at that point in time, but that is exactly what was going on. We were able to find the girl and get her to safety. Her family member went to prison, much too briefly, was released, and committed a similar crime. He is currently serving life without parole in another state.

That case fueled my passion for the fight against Sex and Human Trafficking, especially of children. For many years I have worked quietly in the background on missing child and trafficking cases. My work has included locating perpetrators and victims, including taking part in some rescues. Other than occasionally testifying in court, I still avoided speaking publicly about the work I was doing. Public speaking terrified me, but I have never hesitated to show up to help any missing or endangered child.

In October 2021, I was invited to a presentation given by Opal Singleton, CEO and President of MillionKids.org, a non-profit created solely for the purpose of raising awareness and providing education to assist in the fight against child exploitation, including sex/human trafficking and sextortion.

My friend introduced me to Opal as a private investigator. Opal looked me up and down, asked me a couple questions, and within two or three minutes said, "I want you on my radio show". I was pleasantly stunned ... and terrified. Even so, this topic made it well worth me showing up and stepping far out of my comfort zone. I was a nervous wreck leading up to the recording of the show, but once we got started, everything flowed. The show first aired in January 2022 and was rerun in July or August 2022, with excellent feedback (according to Opal) both times.

Since doing that radio show, Opal has provided multiple opportunities for me to speak, write, and take part in assorted activities to raise awareness regarding sex and human trafficking of children, sextortion, and online exploitation, especially involving children.

In October 2022, I wrote an article based on the information I shared during the radio show and including statistics from NCMEC (National Center for Missing & Exploited Children), the Federal Bureau of Investigation, and the Department of Homeland Security. That article begins with the three comments I most often hear from parents and children when working on missing child and trafficking cases. Those comments are, "My child would never do that", "That will never happen to me", and "I've warned my kids about the dangers of social media".

According the NCMEC, 89% of children sleep with their phone or tablet nearby, even in bed with them. According to the FBI, there are 500,000 predators online at any given time. Those are some terrifying statistics if you have, or know, children. Teenagers are being lured, groomed, trafficked, and sextorted online. That's not to say trafficking does not occur in other ways. It does. However, the majority of trafficking by a stranger starts with online contact, typically in a chat room. Young children and teens often believe that since what they are doing is taking place online, it isn't real, just like the online games they play. They do not realize how dangerous it is to follow their new "friend" from the chat room where they first interacted to a second location. If you're grabbed off the street, the last thing you want is to be taken to a second location. This is the same thing but online. The kids do not realize that once they send a photo to someone, they can never get it back. When a predator catfishes or lures a child or teen into sending illicit photos or videos and then demands money to not release them, the kids do not realize that it's already too late and impossible to get those photos and videos back. Tragically, they often cannot fathom there being any way out of what has happened other than suicide. In addition, there have been reported incidents where the kids have met with their predator, only to end up raped and/or murdered.

When speaking with children and adults regarding online dangers, as well as "stranger danger" in the real world, I often comment that the parents need to act like parents, not like their child's best friend. The parents need to know ALL their children's social media accounts, preferably including passwords, and they need to know their children's friends. Parents typically only know the app their child uses the most, not all the apps they are on. Regarding the password issue, the parents do not need those to "spy" on their children, but they should be somehow accessible in the event of an emergency. Too many cases and rescues are delayed due to issues accessing social media conversations and chats between the missing kids and their perpetrators. I also always say, "Until the individual is 18 and paying for his/her own phone, it belongs to the parents". That phone is "on loan" and the parents should have access at all times, and they should be aware how to check for dangerous applications and activity. A controversial opinion perhaps, but it is what I believe.

Another reason I am so willing to continue stepping out of my comfort zone and showing up is to help educate parents, grandparents, aunts, uncles, anyone who knows a child, etc., about how important it is for children to feel comfortable speaking with their parents or other trusted adults about uncomfortable situations. Grandparents especially make great confidants. The kids need to know their parents believe in them and that they are not going to get in trouble if they tell their parents they have gotten into a situation online that requires parental or law enforcement assistance. The predators in these cases are master manipulators, and teenagers are not capable of handling them on their own.

Most recently, I have been presenting workshops through Children's Fund and MillionKids.org regarding this topic. Preparing for that first three-and-a-half-hour workshop was challenging to say the least. Hours and hours and hours of research went into creating my PowerPoint presentation. The information is so important to help keep our children safe that it has been well worth my showing up. The workshops take place via Zoom and are free of charge and have been attended by people from around the world. In addition to investigators, I believe anyone who has a child or knows a child needs to receive training regarding how to keep them safe. Parents especially need this information, and I am more than willing to do whatever needed to show up and provide training regarding how to keep our children safe.

The issue of sex and human trafficking, as well as sextortion, is a growing concern everywhere---not just in third world countries. It is happening in your neighborhood. Since I have been volunteering in this particular field of investigation, I have received a lot of push back, threats, and abuse from perpetrators and parents who do not want to believe these crimes are happening ... until it happens to their child. Then I'm suddenly their best friend.

Instead of being afraid to show up, it is so important we do all we can to educate ourselves and every child regarding how to keep themselves safe, not only online, but also out in the real world. Kids, especially teenagers, are often not willing to able to speak to their parents about scary situations or sensitive issues. That needs to change. Kids need to know from a very early age that they have someone they can safely speak with about any topic.

I was recently contacted by a long-time fellow business owner who learned some friends of his daughter have been the targets of assorted online predators, one in particular, for five years, and they just came forward

because they did not know who they could tell. Five years!! The victimization and attempts to gain cooperation and grooming of additional victims began when the girls were in the eighth grade. Yes, the eighth grade. They are now freshmen in college. Had someone shown up and educated them about the dangers they could face online, this activity would have hopefully been reported years ago. I cannot help but wonder how many girls and boys this particular predator has interacted with during the past five or six years. He could have hundreds of victims, none of whom had reported him prior to this. The young lady who decided to show up and report the activity to law enforcement is a hero. No doubt about that!

While I do not consider myself a hero or wonder woman, I do know that by showing up, I have personally helped rescue victims, gotten predators off the street, and have educated a LOT of adults and children about online and real-world dangers children face. I will be doing more of the same and will not stop showing up, no matter the cost.

It's all
About
Showing
Up

"Showing up" for the Next Generation

Dr. (h.c.) Lauryn Hunter

Many mentors or strong female role models have guided me to be the best version of myself throughout my life. I was taught that if you don't do anything, you get nothing. To achieve my objectives, I realized I needed to act or motivate others to act with me. Many people today talk about "manifesting their dreams," but without action, it is just a thought. I struggled academically in school as a child because I had dyslexia. I was active in a variety of activities, including Girl Scouts, swim team, water polo, model UN, and leader in my church youth group. I am a natural caregiver, and I love bringing people together for a good cause. Growing up with a single mother taught me about women's equality and how to assist those less fortunate than myself. I am inspired to empower the next generation of women to be confident, successful, and strong emotionally.

My four aunts and other strong women in my life taught me the importance of "Showing up" along with the power of the "Ask". As a caregiver for people's emotional needs, I've always been eager to help and have a strong constitution. When I was in Girl Scouts and earned my Gold Award, I learned the value of belonging to a community. We gathered as a group and learned a verity of life skills I still utilize today. For my final community service project to receive the highest honor in Girl Scouts I collected

feminine hygiene products and my troop helped make drawstring bags to hold toilet items. These individual bags full of personal items were given to a women's shelter in the area. This act of kindness was simple and duplicated multiple times in my life to create a similar donation that can have a huge impact. Small gestures of love impact or enhance a person's daily levels of comfort or basic human needs. Sometimes donating cloths or providing a basic need can be easier for people to accept than directly giving money. When we ask for help and invite the community to serve, no dream is too big.

I've always aspired to be a community leader who inspires others to achieve their own personal goals and dreams. When I went to nursing school, I realized that I was more interested in people's social and emotional well-being than in medical wounds or illness treatment. My interest shifted to human behavior, child development, and neuroscience to better understand how we can heal trauma and PTSD through art therapy or other creative arts. As a mental health supervisor at Cedars-Sinai Medical Center in Los Angeles, I have been instrumental in developing the Share and Care curriculums for students, parent workshops and teacher trainings. Our art therapy groups cover a wide range of topics, including self-esteem, social skills, and anger management, in addition to school-wide programs on bullying, leadership, and acts of kindness. As the founder of Hunter Therapy Family Counseling, I employ a variety of creative therapeutic approaches with clients, including art therapy, sand tray, mindful parenting, and gardening. As a collaborative therapist, I combine art making with conversations to provide effective means of providing personal insight and emotional well-being.

Being a member of the GSFE: Global Society of Female Entrepreneurs has provided me with one of the best opportunities in my life professionally, to learn about myself and to share interests with my GSFE sisters. Our group focuses on women assisting other women in their personal lives

and businesses, all while developing beautiful friendships! When I first met Robbie Motter, she offered me the position as the West Hollywood director. These meetings began with guests sharing information about themselves, their professional backgrounds, and their "Ask" for the night. The best part about these meetings is that when the "Ask" was spoken aloud, someone in the room knew someone who could assist. I had this experience when some issues arose in my father's family, and I required the services of an inheritance lawyer. Before the meeting ended, a member gave me the contact information for a lawyer she knew. I was able to get a consultation and felt relieved after learning more about how to proceed.

After several years of connecting women in West Hollywood, I realized I had a stronger desire to help young women and teenage girls learn life skills. Working in schools with children and adolescents for the past 20 years, I've noticed that young women are not taught or encouraged to learn basic life skills such as etiquette, money management, how to fill out a job application, how to write a personal bio, what a professional photo is, verses a social media post and most importantly, how to develop a business mindset, and help find ones BLISS. Furthermore, following COVID, our youth faced a slew of social and emotional issues related to social anxiety and a of public speaking. I realized children and adolescents are now COVID kids and they all experienced the loneliness of going to school online. In my opinion the greatest concern is for the kindergarten, first and second grade children. The missed out on extremely important brain development being home during the pandemic. It is extremely important for children to socialize outside of the family. This allows for diversity to be experienced, to learn the importance of sharing and to learn how to self-regulate in uncomfortable social situations.

I "asked" Robbie how we could assist the next generation of females. I was inspired to provide opportunities for high school juniors in my

community. Family friends needed extracurricular activities and volunteer hours for their schools and college applications. Robbie suggested we start the first GSFE youth network based on my experience working with children and adolescents. Our fellow GSFE sisters reacted positively to the announcement of our new GSFE youth network. The goal of this youth leadership program is to assist high school girls in becoming active members in their community, preparing for college, and learning key life skills to become successful adults. Each month, I would interview and select GSFE speakers to present to our teens on a variety of topics such as staying organized, public speaking, women's self-defense, and marketing.

Our group focused on inspiring and educating high school girls by increasing their self-esteem, confidence speaking in front of people, learning the steps needed to succeed in high school, earning community service hours, and assisting these young women to develop a business mindset. Our monthly Zoom meetings welcomed members in other states outside of California as well as international youth from our GSFE London and Canada networks.

Every month, our group shared their "Ask" for the month. We also would discuss the highs and lows of their months and what topic they wanted for the following month. These topics of support or interest were used to select speakers. They primarily requested assistance in developing confidence, improving, and overcoming social anxiety. My goal evolved into exposing various powerful women with diverse perspectives about life and the journey of their careers. The speakers all provided useful coping skills the teens could actively use in their daily lives. The group provided enjoyable activities to help our girls stay organized and identify their priorities each day, month and throughout the year. We discussed the steps needed to achieve short-term or long-term goals along with the importance of being of service to the family, helping with chores, and maintaining academic expectations.

When the world shut down because of the pandemic the homeless numbers increased and became a very visual problem on the streets of Los Angeles. I started to become very unsettled and emotionally impacted by this crisis. My heart hurts when children lack basic needs such as food, shelter, and warm cloths. I began to hear more about women and children living in shelters when the world was on lockdown and people lost jobs then their homes. This became a global problem while we all learned how to navigate the world with COVID. I became deeply committed to giving these women an opportunity for a second chance. Our youth network decided to host a clothing swap to give back and provide these women a kiss of HOPE. This clothing drive was open to all GSFE members, and women from across the organization donated clothing. We all spent the day trying on clothes and sharing memories. The ladies all left with bags of clothes, and we donated the rest of the bags and professional dresses, shoes, make-up, and toiletries to a women's shelter in Downtown Los Angeles. The goal for collecting these clothes and toiletries was to provide these women and children with the dignity of showering with their own supplies and clean clothes. This act of service provided the teens with community service hours needed for graduation along with the fun of developing a sisterhood. Our second clothing swap was inspired to donate all items collected to our female soldiers at the VA. The best part is our GSFE sisters supported the women who supported our country.

The Youth GSFE network was proud to host a vision board workshop. As the group grew, trust was developed. These young ladies opened to each other, finding parts of their identities and passions. New questions came up when the girls started applying to college and were asked questions they had never thought of before. They had gotten to know each other and were able to point out each other's strengths. This was beautiful to watch how they inspired each other with great support and encouragement when

applying for colleges. The girls struggled with the personal questions being asked in these applications. The joy to see the girls find themselves in making art, with collage image and being able to stand up in front of each other sharing goals with the group was amazing. They were inspired to dream big and apply to any school they wanted. Images were used in these vision board workshops to represent self, family, peers', personal goals, and future dreams. With a diversity of skills, I was able to facilitate therapeutic conversations that assisted our GSFE teens in processing what they wanted and needed in life. They investigated ways to become more self-aware and consider their priorities to create future opportunities. These positive experiences provided the group to visualize and create personal connections with other GSFE members.

Inspiring our young women to be educated teaches them that knowledge is power and how our next generation of female leaders WILL lead the world. This network is a little over a year old, and I am very excited to see the power of these young ladies and how they will change the world helping one community at a time.

It's all About Showing Up

Showing Up, a Matter of Life & Death

A Prequel to 1st Vol. of "It's All About Showing Up"

Dr. (h.c.) Deborah Irish

It was a beautiful sunny day as I worked in my art studio in Menifee, CA. My home studio is my happy place with a second story view of our cul-de-sac. My workbench is below my window where I can look out to see kids playing and neighbors coming and going. On this particular afternoon in September 2016, I glanced out my window to see Val, an elderly gentleman who lives three doors down from us, mowing his lawn. Maybe 20 minutes go by when I glanced up again to see that Val was now lying on his side in his front yard unconscious. I yelled out the window to my next-door neighbor as she was getting into her car to call 911. I ran as fast as I could downstairs, grabbed a blanket, and quickly told my husband Rick that Val was unconscious, all without missing a step. I ran so fast; I don't think my feet touched the ground. Once by his side, I could see that Val didn't seem to be breathing, and his coloring was not good, and I covered him with the blanket. My neighbor had 911 on the line and handed me her cell phone. The dispatcher had me describe Val's condition. When I told her that he wasn't breathing, and there was no detectable pulse, she told me I need to roll him onto his back and perform CPR. Fortunately, I had taken a CPR course a few years before, so I knew what to do. Chest compressions to the beat of the Bee Gees song "Stayin Alive" until the paramedics gets there.

Administering CPR is no easy task, requiring strength and stamina. It was a fairly warm day, and I began feeling overheated and fatigued. By this time, Val's wife is outside with us, standing on her driveway, looking very distraught. Some neighbors had gathered around, and fortunately, one of them knew CPR. She was able to take over chest compressions until the paramedics arrived. I took Val's wife into her shady garage, out of view of her husband receiving CPR. Paramedics arrived and continued administering CPR, using the defibrillator a couple of times before putting him into the ambulance. It did not look good.

Several days went by, and I hadn't heard any news about Val's condition or if he even survived. About two weeks later, I saw Val's son in front of Val's house. Val survived! He had a heart attack but was going to be ok!

When he was well enough to come home, Val, his son and 2 granddaughters "Showed Up" on my doorstep. Val asked me, "Are you the one that saved my life?" According to the doctors, if Val hadn't received CPR when he did, he would not have survived his heart attack. Val and his family thanked me, handed me a gift with a thank you card, and gave me hugs. It's humbling knowing that I helped someone have more time on Earth with his loved ones.

That's just the beginning of the story. From that experience, I had an epiphany. Something struck me immediately after that life and death situation. I realized that there was no thinking involved, only action. I didn't know that I was capable of administering CPR and saving someone's life. In fact, I remember taking the CPR training course, hoping that I would never have to apply it in real life, in fear of not being capable. There was no time for thinking, only action. If I were to allow myself to think and analyze the situation, the outcome would have been very different. I couldn't help but wonder, "What are the possibilities if I get out of my head and trust my instincts?". This led me to my next realization. That we can think our way out of just about anything, even our hopes and dreams.

For most of my life, I had a mental list of things that I dreamt of experiencing but thought they would never happen. Such as witnessing a total solar eclipse, seeing the natural phenomena of Horsetail Fall glow like lava, witnessing aurora borealis, zip lining, skydiving, etc. As I look back, my list isn't outlandish (except for maybe skydiving). I had it in my head that these things were out of reach and weren't possible for me; therefore, I didn't pursue any of these things.

Here's where it gets interesting. Once I had the experience of saving Val's life and realized how much thinking can get in the way of action, the opportunities of fulfilling my list of impossibilities became a reality. I started seeing things as possibilities rather than impossibilities and within a fairly short period of time. I started checking things off my "Impossible List", starting with seeing the Firefall at Horsetail Fall in Yosemite, CA.

It was an impulsive 2-day 3-night trip with my dad Robert, my son Skyler and his wife Ysel and me. The weather conditions have to be perfect for the waterfall to appear to glow like flowing lava. Not to mention, the illusion is only possible during 2 weeks in February at dusk. We were there February 27 through March 1, 2017. Thinking that we missed that small window, we had no expectations of seeing the natural phenomena. But we couldn't help ourselves and had to at least try. Our first sunset there, we found a spot with a view of the waterfall. Unfortunately, the weather didn't cooperate. There was cloud cover. We weren't disappointed though. There were other tourists trying to catch a view of the glowing waterfall too. One person told us that the weather conditions weren't perfect, but that he saw the falls with a slight glow the evening before. Now we were excited for the next sunset.

The next day, we did some exploring and found an even better location to see Horsetail Fall. When the time came, we were ready in our newly found spot. There were quite a few more people at this location, making it fun because we were all there for the same thing. There's something exciting about waiting to see what nature is going to do. There were patchy clouds and it seemed like it might not happen. If the sun doesn't shine on the waterfall, there is no glow. Apparently, there are some people that have traveled to Yosemite year after year just to see the glowing waterfall with no luck due to weather. We waited patiently and to our great surprise, it happened, and it was amazing! It really looks like lava pouring down the cliff. Everyone cheered! It was so inspiring that I am now working on oil paintings depicting different natural phenomena that have a lot to do with my "Possible List".

Since then, I have checked off a few other things on my "Impossible List", which I now call my "Possible List". Within a couple of years, I would go zip lining in the Redwoods with friends and skydiving with Skyler and Ysel to celebrate her 30th birthday. I still have a lot of things on my "Possible List" to experience, and I will continue to add new things to that list. But so far, the biggest thing I have checked off my "Possible List" was seeing a solar eclipse in 2017.

My intention was to observe The Great American Total Solar Eclipse through the eyes of an artist. I knew beforehand that I didn't want to be in a festival environment or where it would be too crowded. With these things in mind, I began planning a trip with my dad and his wife Vonda, my son Reese, my youngest sister Esther, and our friend Caryn. We decided to take a road trip to Stapleton, Nebraska, in Caryn's van.

A partial solar eclipse is fun, but a total eclipse of the sun is spectacular and is the only time that the sun's corona is visible. "Showing Up" to a total

solar eclipse is the best show on earth! If you've never experienced one, you're really missing out. I highly recommend that everyone experience a total solar eclipse at least once in their life. The lighting and colors are surreal. Think Wizard of Oz when Dorothy wakes up in the land of the Munchkins.

This is a peek into what I saw...

As the moon moves into position to block the sun, things begin to change. At first, shadows become very crisp, and as daylight dims into near darkness, a cool breeze picks up. As it continues getting darker, the animals get quiet and automatic lights come on. It feels as if the sun is going down, but there it is, high in the sky being blocked by the moon. Being in the moon's shadow, which is approximately 70 miles in diameter, we see beyond the shadow, giving us what looks like a colorful 360° sunset. Observing our immediate surroundings, I noticed that everything is grayscale. It's strange to look at your skin to see gray.

All the color is in the sky.

Once the moon completely blocks the sun, you're able to take off your protective glasses. The moon is now a very deep black disc. I don't think there's a darker black on Earth. The contrast between the corona and the moon is striking. It almost looks as if someone punched a hole in the sky. Seeing it for the first time brought tears to my eyes and I just about fell to my knees. It was so magnificent and beautiful, I felt like I was looking into the face of God, seeing something I wasn't supposed to see.

The corona isn't made of flames, like I once thought. The corona is made of plasma that is bright white with almost a pearl-like quality, which is alive and moving with pops of red and purple flashes of light. You can see breaches of flame arches coming from the surface of the sun, peeking out

from the moon's edge. It's not easy to describe through words, which is why I create paintings to record what I saw.

Then I noticed that the stars came out, quickly realizing they weren't stars at all. They were planets! Yes, Mercury, Jupiter, Mars and Venus were all visible during this eclipse. Standing here on Earth with the Sun, Moon and the planets visibly in the sky all at once was an incredible feeling. I had a very strong sense of the Earth's position in our solar system, spinning through the universe and yet my feet were firmly planted on the ground. I felt like I had in some way experienced "The Overview Effect", a book by Frank White about the overwhelming emotion that astronauts feel from seeing Earth from space and having a strong sense that we are all connected. It was an awe-inspiring moment.

Frank White states that "the Overview Effect is a message from the universe to humanity. The message is that the Earth, when seen from orbit or the moon, is a whole system, where borders and boundaries disappear, and everything is interconnected. Our planet is a tiny spaceship in an enormous universe, which is itself a whole system, of which we are an important part. We are the crew of a natural spaceship called Earth, which is hurtling through the universe at a high rate of speed".

From peacetour.org/overview-effect/

Once the eclipse went through all its beautiful stages, I pulled out my sketchbook and made sketches with notes so I wouldn't forget anything about what I had just seen. I'm so glad I did (you would be amazed at how much detail we forget unless we take notes. I call taking notes "Showing Up" for my future self.) Once home, and after a good night's sleep, I woke up with such joy and excitement about the whole experience. I was so grateful for the wonderful gift that God gave me. For the first time ever, I had a very clear vision of what my art is supposed to be about. There was a voice in my

head that kept saying "All you have to do is record what you saw through your paintings." Wow! It's that simple huh? Yes, it's that simple.

Everything that led me up to that point finally seemed to make sense. I've always had a fascination with the sky and space. In fact, I remember my dad and I lying on our backs on the lawn during meteor showers to see the falling stars. I still like doing that. When I was 10, my dad took me to Mount Wilson in the San Gabriel Mountains, away from the city lights, to see Comet West. Even my art experience matches up to what I want to achieve. About 2 years before seeing the eclipse, I started painting landscapes with the moon as the focal point, embellished with gold leaf. I also have an extensive sphere collection made of different materials, such as stone, crystal, glass, metal, etc., that I started years ago. I went around counting my orbs and it turns out that I had over 50 of them scattered all over the house. Seeing the puzzle pieces of my life come together and showing me my purpose is such a gift. I could say that "Showing Up" to see the eclipse saved my life by giving me a clear vision of what my purpose is.

Update after I wrote my chapter for the 1st volume of "It's All About Showing Up". Witnessing The Great American Total Solar Eclipse sent me on an all-new trajectory with my art, switching from acrylics to oils. I continued working in oils, experimenting with new techniques, achieving the effect I want to represent the vivid colors of a solar eclipse. June 2022, Robbie Motter informed me that Aggie Kobrin was organizing the National Space Society Space Settlement Summit 2022 in LA in November. "Asking" oftentimes creates our own opportunities, so I called Aggie and "Asked" if she planned on having an art exhibit at the Space Summit. She said normally she does not have an art exhibit at this particular annual event, but then she said, "You know what? Yeah, let's do it!" So I got to work and pulled together a nice collection of my oil paintings of solar eclipses and full moon landscapes. This was my first solo art exhibit. I "Showed Up" and had a great time connecting with interesting people, talking about space and my art. It was fabulous and I can wait for the next one. Thank you for the opportunity, Aggie!

What does my future hold? "Showing up" and experiencing more solar eclipses and other natural phenomena, such as aurora borealis, erupting volcanoes, lighting, etc. Through my art, I want to help people commemorate that special moment they experienced during any natural phenomenon. When a photograph just won't do, I can create an oil painting, capturing the look and feel of that special moment in a way that no camera can. I am accepting commissions for custom oil paintings based on your experience. If you're interested, you'll find my contact info in this book.

Thank you, Robbie, for letting me ride on your coat tails while you show me how to make my own coat. I will keep "Showing Up and Asking" because these two simple things lead to possibilities that just might save a life in more ways than one.

It's all
About
Showing
Up

Showing Up In The Master's Plan

Jayne Jorden

Have you been seeking and asking, "What is my Purpose, my Calling, my Desire, my Dream or my Passion?" I've found one can become blinded in the questioning and experience called PARALYSIS of ANALYSIS. When all along it could be HIDDEN IN PLAIN SIGHT. Yet seeing one's reflection in their life's journey can reveal the answer.

For me, the past three decades (out of 6.5 of my life journey) seemed much rockier than the previous 3. The climbs much steeper and the roads much narrower and more curved and mountains and valleys to conquer with little reprieve to catch a breath. Little did I understand how my PURPOSE was IN each PRESENT being played out along the way as I would "Show Up". I was continually seeking what was HIDDEN IN PLAIN SIGHT.

I began penning poetry as a child. Later in life I experienced an inner knowing I was to publish a book.... but what topic? What did I have to offer of interest to others? Who would want to read about my life story or a book of poems and a fictional one never struck a chord. That had been a 35-year question. I am a slow reader as my imagination carries me away from the pages, and I pass through realizing I have no idea what I just read. With the

exception of the Word of God and inspirational spiritual based writings, I would I stay engaged.

With the covid challenge. It came time to dig through my heart of memories as mortality became much more realistic in the daily news. As I sheltered within the confines of home with more time of secluded activities, my attention came into writing my reflections and uncovering the gems of each challenge I had overcome. Finding the good within them became a way for me to avoid temptation of depression and hopelessness. If it aided me in a way, I thought perhaps others would benefit.

The writing began to flow with a topic covered each day for many months. Its conception began on Valentine's Day 2022. I'm still inspired from new opportunities, and the collection grows. The "book" On My ♥ Inspirational nuggets found on life's journey is in the making, and my PASSION developed in writing. I post these in social media places to share encouraging thought with hope to inspire and plant positive seeds of growth as multitudes face questionable futures.

Life's journey did and still does offer a myriad of opportunities where a lesson may be learned and passed on to help others. That's IT! That's the PURPOSE! In the

"Showing Up" to each opportunity presented it welcomes the chance to learn and grow from it. Connections made as a puzzle being formed with each piece designed to create the final masterpiece. We can merely go through life "showing up" yet miss the gained prize only to retake the lesson again and again until the lesson be learned once and for all. We can "get Bitter or we can get Better". The choice is our own. With open eyes and hearts filled with expectation, we can be the key to unlock the treasure.

The treasures once HIDDEN revealed the PURPOSE of my CALLING: to minister to dis-eased souls with the DESIRE to lift hearts and aid in overcoming obstacles. Forgotten DREAMS are revived. New DREAMS emerge, as PASSION is birthed through Divine direction.... all for The MASTERS PLAN.

Showing Up Around The World Opens Many Doors Of Opportunity And Changes Lives

Ambassador Dr. Imambay Kamara

Ambassador Dr, Imambay Kamara is the President and Founder of DISABLED INTERNATIONAL FOUNDATION UK/SIERRA LEONE, AFRICA

Dr. Imambay Kamara Global FOUNDATION supports vulnerable Women and Girls.

Dr. Imambay Kamara who has continuously dedicated and transformed lives in various communities for over 21 years. She is the International Global Humanitarian Chairperson for Ladies of All Nation International. She is a Global Multiple award winner for her groundbreaking work. She is a Philanthropist, Global Ambassador for Commonwealth Entrepreneur Club, Disability Rights Activist, Women Children Activist and also Campaigning to stop domestic VIOLENCE against Women and Girls

She is also an Inspirational Speaker. Campaigner to stop Female Genital mutilation (F.G.M) and to stop early Childhood Marriages

Dr. Imambay Kamara was born in Guinea, Her Father was a Guinean from the Susu tribe, her maiden name is Sumah. Her Mother is a Sierra Leonean from the Eku Creou tribe in Forebay the Eastern part of Freetown Sierra

Leone.

Dr. Imambay Kamara grew up in Sierra-Leone, where she did her primary and secondary education, but she escaped from the Sierra Leone Civil war in 1991 and came to the UK and continued her College and University education at the Lewisham College in London, University of London and also the GLOBA INTERNATIONAL ALLIANCES(GIA) University in Atlanta, USA, where she was awarded an Honorary Doctorate in HUMANITARIANISM by successfully completed the requisite hours to qualify by devoting, serving, and promoting human welfare.

As a Philanthropist, she continues to demonstrate extraordinarily high level of Excellence by servicing as a National Advocate of International Services that has been approved by the University Board of National Volunteers of Community Service...

She worked for the local Government in the housing department as a customer services Manager, and she also counseled people who were going through challenges in their lives.

Dr. Imambay was brought up single-handedly by her late disabled mother. As you can imagine, things were very difficult for her and her family. The constant verbal abuse, ongoing discrimination, and segregation within the community and outside the community purely because her mother was disabled was hard to take. This was the compelling reason why she decided to set up the Disabled International Foundation on the April 11, 2001, in honor of her late Mother Haja Fatima Saptieu Badara Thorpe and to Campaign around the world to stop all kind of discrimination AGAINST people with disabilities.

Her mother returned from the holy land of Mecca where all Muslims people will go for forgiveness, but unfortunately when she returned to

Sierra Leone two days later, she passed away. She is one of the 100 most Successful Women in the world and the 50 most influential Women from her Country-of-origin Sierra LEONE although she is now a BRITISH CITIZEN..

Honored with PRESIDENT Joe Biden's Global HUMANITARIAN LIFETIME ACHIEVEMENT Award in the UNITED STATES OF AMERICA, she is the director of GENDER and Equality for West Africa, Youth Empowerment member of Giving Women Switzerland, Geneva, Global Society for Female Entrepreneurs (GSFE) in the United States and also a member of so many other Women's organizations.

Dr. Imambay Kamara is a mother of six wonderful children and also blessed with four wonderful grandchildren.

Her dedication, inspiration, and hard work across the world to help disabled people is supporting so many disabled people of all categories as well as so many orphan children has made such a difference in the world as a result during the time of the Ebola epidemic in Africa.

Dr. Imambay Kamara is a Female Genital mutilation survivor and Domestic Violence Survivor.

She has been impressively recognized both locally and internationally for her work and SHOWING UP as a Disability Rights Activist/ Children Rights and Women Rights Activist which has also earned her various different Awards globally.

Having experienced first-hand the challenges that disabled people face due to having a disabled mother, she set out on a mission to priorize disabled people within Sierra Leone, Africa, and the countries around the World This was designed to help eliminate the negative stigma attached to them. In 2011, she was amongst other organization's that helped enforce the

Policy and Advocacy on the Disability Act 2011 in Sierra Leone, which lead to the appointment of a DISABLED Minister who was a blind Man at the Ministry of social WELFARE Gender and CHILDREN Affair

Also, in 2014 her campaign again continues with the Collaboration with other Disability Organization's there was a DISABILITY Commission and also, another appointment of a DISABILITY COMMISSIONER; he was also a blind Man. For the first time ever in the history of Sierra Leone there was policy in place for people with disabilities in Sierra LEONE. What a big achievement. Also, that same year her organization Collaborated with another Organization Handicap INTERNATIONAL for the Implementation of the free medical for pregnant women and Mothers.

Her Organization Collaborated again with the Handicap International to support and raising awareness Countrywide especially for people with disabilities to register and to vote for their rights during any Presidential elections in the Country so that they will have equal rights to become a Parliamentarian or any higher offices. She is also campaigning for the implementation of the Policy as she stands for DISABILITY Rights, example Employment, Accessibility, INCLUSIVENESS IN ALL ASPECTS OF LIFE as well as trying to better the lives of others internationally.

Dr. Imambay also makes an impact in her resident country, United Kingdom, supporting other charities HUMANITY AND INCLUSION UK and many more. She does volunteer work. She is a Patron and AMBASSADOR for other Charitable organizations.

As an active campaigner for Leonard Cheshire Disability UK, she has helped to put policies in place for Disabled people. She has been a guest speaker in Geneva, Switzerland, on issues of Disability, Women and Girls She has also spoken at the UK house of Parliament and at the Royal Institute of International Affairs at Chatham House during the Ebola Epidemic

in Sierra-Leone that claimed thousands of lives. She is a campaigner for Disability awareness. She is also a Signatory to the International Female Genital Mutilation (FGM) policy implementation in the UK in 2014. Her latest project includes with support from her family two schools she had constructed that are situated in Tonkolili district, Sierra Leone and an orphanage situated in Lungi, Sierra Leone.

She is also working for Disability Empowerment Centre leading towards self-reliance of people with disabilities and young people. As much as she has achieved, she continues to strive to achieve more within the upcoming years to improve the lives of those less fortunate. Every year she celebrates her birthday by putting SMILES on the faces of the under privileged by supporting them with food and non-food items and also celebrating all festive occasions including Easter and Christmas party and sending donations of Gifts. and Disability Accessories, Clothing, Shoes, bags, educational Materials, Laptops and Medical simply for the Children and adults. She has dedicated her life to these services, and this is what she promised her mother she would help to tackle discrimination, stigma, and the mistreating of disabled in Sierra Leone and beyond. This is what has kept her going no matter the challenges she faces.

Her work has been recognized around the world, and she has won so many awards around the world including America, Morocco, Egypt, India, and Africa due to her HUMANITARIAN service that has given her the opportunity to travel to so many Countries around the World meeting with wonderful and influential and Inspiring people from across the GLOBE.

Every year she hosts two a charity events and Awards dedicated in support of Education, Health & School projects and Libraries and Empowerment Centers, as well as helping the most vulnerable people, Widows and the elderly. She is currently working on another project to open a beauty Parlor

and a boutique where Women who are facing so many challenges in their lives can come and have pampering session and beauty treatments and feel good and restore dignity and respect. As she herself has been through so many challenges, these sessions helped her so much, so she wants to give other women this opportunity and also offer great job opportunity for them. She is a business owner.

October 10, 2021, which was her birthday in collaboration of the Mental Awareness' Day she launched her FOUNDATION Dr. Imambay Kamara Global HUMANITARIAN. This Foundation supports vulnerable women and Girls. She also added Dr. Imambay Kamara International Academy School and also Dr. Imambay Kamara Children ORPHANAGE Home in Sierra LEONE.

She is also working towards Agricultural projects to promote Community development.

During the Global pandemic Dr. Imambay supported the most vulnerable communities both here in the UK and in Sierra LEON she had also finished writing her autobiography Title: WALKING IN MY MOTHER' SHOE And inside the book there will be a chapter Titled: SILENCE NO MORE. THE book will be coming out very soon. She is also a Co-author in the book The Most 100 Successful Women in the World.

The benefits I have received for SHOWING UP and traveling the world is I have met interesting dynamic individuals and I have been able to make a difference in the world.

HELP US TO CONTINUE TO SUPPORT THE VULNERABLE, organized by Imambay Kamara

HELP US TO CONTINUE TO SUPPORT THE VULNERABLE, organized by Imambay Kamara

Disabled International Foundation is a non-profit organization campai... Imambay Kamara needs your support for HELP US TO CONTINUE TO SUPPORT THE VULNERABLE

The Most Unique Marriage Ask

Annmarie Kelly

Like many people, probably you, too, I saw the importance of showing up in business, in relationships, and in my own life. I also watched as friends and colleagues taught me the power of asking – for business, for help, for a need or for a want. Still, it wasn't easy for me to ask, especially when I felt the stakes were high...like in relationships...until it was too important not to show up in my own life and make the very unusual ask that changed my whole life.

It was 1986 and I'd been dating the same man for a year. We were exclusive, and I thought we were solid and didn't need to do anything else to be happy. Until...

The subject of marriage came up one beautiful Friday night at Jane and Lou's house. Their poolside deck was beautifully decorated and, before long, two more couples joined us. The light-hearted conversation flowed easily between the eight of us. So did the drinks.

At some point the topic of weddings came up. I don't know why, but it wasn't long before it got personal to Joseph and me. I cringed inside when I heard Jane ask, "What about you two? What are you waiting for?" I laughed

it off, but I could tell Joseph was paying attention to how I responded, I was non-committal.

After that night, however, Joseph started talking about marriage. He wasn't asking, so I didn't have to give him a "yes" or "no" answer. But I knew it was only a matter of time before he did ask, and I knew I didn't have an answer.

Months went by and, early in the new year of 1987, Joseph hadn't let the marriage conversation go. So, rather than join that conversation, I decided to shift the focus. I suggested another kind of commitment.

"Let's buy a house," I proposed.

What I was hoping for was that Joseph would see the long-term commitment of a thirty-year mortgage as satisfying, and the best way for us to start building a life together. At the same time, as a licensed real estate broker, I knew my ask didn't have the same legal weight of a marriage. I knew we could buy a property as partners. I also knew that, if we didn't work out as a couple, getting out of a joint house venture was way easier than getting out of a bad marriage.

My trepidation about marriage had nothing to do with Joseph. I loved him and I had confidence in Joseph and me as a couple. Joseph was – and still is – a good man. We traveled life well together. We shared many common interests, including crazy family backgrounds. So, we enjoyed each other and also had a mutual understanding about the past and a respect for how well we both survived our histories.

My marrying-reluctance also wasn't that I hated marriage. In fact, when I was younger, I really wanted to get married. My parents, my friends, and society said it was the right thing to do. The messages of my childhood were subtle. In high school, the good Notre Dame sisters were in lockstep with my Italian-Catholic parents. Together they provided solid mind-

programming for a marriage-focused future for women. I felt as though getting married and having children was my only important goal.

Yet, into my mid-twenties, I was still single. During those years, I shifted between dating and being single, a bridesmaid in several weddings, but not the bride. I was even engaged for a little while. Ending my engagement was a huge turning point. It wasn't just hard to do. It devastated me. For a long time, I wallowed in that lonely valley of confusion and depression where many women go when trying to make sense of something sad or nonsensical.

When I emerged from that valley, I was cynical about marriage. With new eyes I saw what was happening to many of my married girlfriends. It seemed like when they changed their names, they changed who they were. They were no longer the free-spirited girls I hung out with to have fun. They dutifully showed up as wives and mothers but stopped showing up for themselves.

In our conversations, they hinted that marriage wasn't all it was cracked up to be, and how the perfect guy they married wasn't so perfect. "We have nothing in common," and "he comes home and does nothing...I'm exhausted," or "I think he's having an affair."

Disillusionment turned into sour attitudes first, then into resentment. The once-youthful upward curves of their mouths began to show the first downward bends of bitterness. Some divorced, but many stayed and stuck it out, showing up for themselves only in their dreams. The marriages broke their hearts – and their spirits.

By the time I was twenty-eight, I began to think that the "until death do us part" marriage might not be such a good deal for a woman. So, I decided my best bet was to "show up" in my own life. I put more energy into a career,

bought a house, and was creating my happiness all by myself.

That's where my thinking was when I met Joseph at a Reiki share on the Sunday night before Thanksgiving. During "share breaks" we discovered that we lived about a mile from each other. At the end of the night, we exchanged phone numbers.

My first "ask" was the following Friday. I hadn't heard from him and wondered if he would call. I decided I'd stop wondering and call him. I invited him to my house the following night to exchange Reiki. He said "yes", and we set it up. It was a one-time-only ask. If we had a good night (and we did), it would be up to him to do the asking for the next time. Happily, Joseph did.

After that we became a couple, mostly just hanging out and enjoying each other's company - until that fateful poolside Friday night at Jane's, followed by my January'87 suggestion to buy a house and live together. It was a big step, but one that made good sense to both of us.

In the winter of 1987 when Joseph and I met with a mortgage broker and then began searching for a house we could afford.

In the spring, we found an eighteen-foot stone and brick row house in Drexel Hill, Pennsylvania, a small working-class neighborhood not far from Philadelphia. Throughout that summer, Joseph and I scrapped together every penny we had for the closing at the end of September. On the day we moved, we took with us whatever furniture had been in our apartments. We had to scrape together enough money to pay the movers. We barely filled up a living room, dining room and one bedroom.

Though we were financially strapped, we were happy and excited and shared a lot of love and dreams. We were among the "young kids" in the neighborhood, and we liked it.

The following summer, Joseph's August birthday was just a few weeks away. I wondered what I could get him for his special day.

I was thinking about that on the night the two of us went for an after-dinner walk. We took our usual trek on the two-mile path inside the historic Arlington cemetery, which was a popular route for walkers and bike riders. The mid-summer sun was setting, and the heat of the day was subsiding.

As we walked and talked, I found a good opening and asked, "What do you want for your birthday?"

Without hesitation, Joseph said softly, "I want to get married."

I was a little stunned by his answer. Married? I thought, "Where did that come from? We're living together. We own a house together. Isn't that enough?"

While I was thinking and adjusting to the emotional shock to my system, I wasn't answering. And then Joseph said it again.

"I want to get married," Joseph insisted, this time with a little more definiteness.

I was panicky, and a little annoyed. What can I say?

"How about a watch?" I asked. "I'll get you a really nice one."

"I want to get married," Joseph repeated, this time more firmly.

"Hmmm," I replied, still a little stupefied. "Let me think about it."

Though I didn't let Joseph know what I was thinking, I wasn't so happy to be in a decision-making state of mind – at least not about marriage.

After years of striking out on my own, I loved feeling confident in my ability to stand on my own both personally and financially. The power of financial confidence was just one way I showed up for myself, and it was really important. Emotional independence was another. I'd reached a point where I knew I'd be happy with or without a man. I wasn't interested in giving that up.

Yet I loved Joseph. My resistance to marriage wasn't about him. In my mind, the way marriage was done by everyone was a setup for failure.

With so much trepidation, I wondered what would happen if I said "no" to marriage. Would Joseph want to break up? Would he move on?

For the next couple of weeks, I said nothing more about it to Joseph. Instead, I rummaged around in my thoughts looking for answers.

At first, I rationalized that it was the right time for me. The man who wanted to marry me was a good man. We were of the same spiritual beliefs. We lived together easily. We had dreams together. We set goals and made plans. It wasn't perfect, but I could see us being together long-term.

Long-term, yes. But for forever? I couldn't see forever.

For the next few weeks, I walked for miles, sorting through my thoughts, looking for "the answer" to the problem. As I meandered through the streets of my neighborhood, I thought about the many couples I knew who had taken that fateful walk "down the aisle" thinking that they would be together for the rest of their lives. It didn't happen for them. How could we do it better?

Finally, on one of those morning hikes, the goddess of logic and creativity joined me. As I let her take over my thoughts, a new model began to form in

my head. What if Joseph and I only got married for five years? I could live with that. Then, if we still liked each other, we could get married again.

The more I tossed the idea around in my head, the more I liked it. In my heart, the idea felt freeing. In my soul I felt at peace. I wondered what Joseph would think. Would he be as comfortable with my odd idea as I was?

It was a BIG ASK.

One night, as we were having dinner, I told Joseph we needed to talk. The look on his face made me laugh. He seemed relieved when he found out that "the talk" wasn't about splitting up, but confused about what I was asking.

"We'll get married for five years," I proposed, "and if we still like each other at the end of five years, we'll get married again." I also explained that I believed it was the only way I could comfortably and optimistically marry anyone.

Once he knew I was serious, Joseph and I talked about some basic logistics. After playing around with the idea in his head, he agreed to create this new model for marriage with me. We agreed to marry – but just for five years.

A couple weeks later, for Joseph's birthday, we invited our mothers and siblings to celebrate Joseph's special day. We welcomed our guests and served up beer and wine and some snacks. After singing "Happy Birthday" and while everyone was enjoying cake and ice cream, we announced our plans to marry.

Since we didn't have any money, and there wasn't going to be a big wedding, we set the date for the following month. On September 24th, 1988, Joseph and I were married - for the first time - on that same poolside deck where the talk of marriage first started.

Since then, Joseph and I have been married SEVEN TIMES. Our renegotiation and reset conversations start in the spring...they take a lot of thinking and talking. Our ceremonies have taken place at Arlington Cemetery, Neumann University, Valley Forge Chapel, Tyler Arboretum and Faunbrook Bed and Breakfast. Marriage #3 happened just weeks after we moved into a new house. It's the only time we did not have a ceremony. Instead, we went to New York City and attended the Conan O'Brien show....so I always say we got the Conan O'Brien Blessing.

In the early days of our first marriage, some people laughed at our five-year commitment idea. They didn't take it seriously.

Joseph and I were totally serious. Joseph and I believed we were embarking on an experiment. Over time, we were proven correct. The Five-Year marriage is the ultimate exercise in showing up. Each of us must show up for ourselves first, then for each other, and finally, for the relationship.

I knew, when I first asked Joseph to do a five-year marriage, that I was taking a risk. What I didn't know then was how taking that risk and asking for a five-year commitment would shape my life, and Joseph's, and our relationship. And I didn't know then that it would influence how Joseph and I showed up with others and in the world.

We also didn't know, in 1988, how the world, and love and marriage, would evolve – and that so many young people (especially young professional women) would understand the wisdom of The Five-Year Marriage (so much faster than we did at the beginning).

When you don't show up, and when you don't ask for what you want or need, you never know what kind of amazing and life-changing experience you could be turning away.

It's all
About
Showing
Up

I Showed Up: Journey to Finding Comfort in Being Seen

Dr. (h.c.) Lynnette LaRoche

It wasn't long ago when I was reluctant to attend social events or network. It was safer in my known space and conditions. I also did not ask. I learned in my early adulthood that asking had a price attached to it. I would be expected to give something in return.

But for me, not showing up was more about not feeling comfortable around people I did not know. It was about feeling that I did not belong. I always felt different from everyone else. I felt watched but not in a good way.

If I reluctantly showed up for an event and if there was not music or dance along with it to keep me company. Usually, I would fade into the background, trying to go unnoticed.

The other safeguard for me about not showing up related to not being coaxed into helping yet someone else in "trouble". As an emotional soul, it gives me great discomfort if someone is in need, potentially painfully so. I've always been one to jump in to save them or to fix the situation. I've always been the giver.

Giving, giving, giving. I was always ripe for being taken advantage of. So, staying away, I protected myself, my emotions, and my energy. Staying

away protected me from pouring until my cup was dry.

Working from home since 2016 reinforced the reluctance to be seen and to stay in my cove of safety. It was before everyone started using video meetings during the pandemic, so I never took to showing myself. I handled everything by email or conference calls---the perfect veil of privacy and invisibility.

The COVID-19 pandemic did not change my routine much. Before the pandemic, I worked from home. I worked out daily in my home gym. I shopped for groceries during hours when most adults were busy in the office. I shopped for everything else online. Even during this time, I faded away. I got tired of the group texts about if it was too early to drink or what edible they were trying to numb their inability to be social. I was not going in to save anyone.

It was just before the pandemic that I decided to start my own business. The reality of needing to use social media was hard for me. I was concerned about privacy. I wanted to keep myself hidden. But I wanted to make an impact, so I tiptoed into the wild.

Facebook. Instagram. Twitter. Clubhouse. Now Clubhouse was perfect because it was still visually anonymous. It was just my voice and the weight of my words. Yes, there are the profile pictures, but it was really about what you had to say.

I didn't hang with Clubhouse very long – maybe 3 months – as it was becoming time intensive. I was being asked to join this club and that club, speak at this club, and collaborate with this person or group. Hey! It was supposed to be a shield to keep me behind the veil.

I built some great friendships over those initial years of the pandemic … some only for a reason and a season. Lifetime? We shall see.

I will say that Showing Up in Clubhouse brought learning experiences that were costly but also connected me with a genuine soul LSW who was on her journey to finding her business nirvana. LSW invited me to networking meetings that were held at members' home.

Since moving back to San Diego in 2021, I was on a quest for authentic connections and people I could really relate to who were also on this entrepreneur journey. So, I said 'yes' to attending the networking meeting. It was at this meeting that LSW mentioned Secret Knock, one of the few, invite-only networking events for entrepreneurs. A voice said to me that I must attend. I did!

I still struggled being around people I did not know and still felt out of place. I told myself it will get better. I have since Showed Up at three Secret Knock events. I am working with the Secret Millionaire and will publish a book under his tutelage on building high-performing teams that will have testimonials from top industry business leaders!

It was also through Secret Knock that I met a gentleman JM who seemed to be disappointed in my responses to him about my business. But he introduced me to a known business/life coach who has a different approach to helping people make money through analysis of multiple assessments he has you take that maps out your money DNA. This man, DM, is truly someone whose life exemplifies using the Law of Attraction to live abundantly. I needed this in my life!

Another person I met through Clubhouse brought me into connection with another beautiful soul KM who then introduced me to Global Society of Female Entrepreneurs (GSFE). I Showed Up at a few Chapter meetings and events and enjoyed the experience. It aligned with my intent on finding meaningful connections with likeminded souls.

However, I found myself shrinking back into my former self. But Lady Dr. Robbie has an innate way of subtly coaxing the diamond from within into the forefront. So I spoke at a chapter, drove hours through windy roads to attend meetings, and dialed into virtual meeting.

When I happened to go to meetings where Lady Dr. Robbie was speaking, it felt as if she was speaking to me directly. She encouraged me to step up and Show Up. I vowed to do so even when I felt I was reverting to old comforts.

I said Yes to Lady Dr. Robbie's invite to sit and listen to her son play guitar, witnessed the reunion of a brother and sister, and enjoyed the music and the socializing. I said Yes to putting my hat in the ring to receive the Honorary Doctorate Degree from Global International Alliance. I said Yes to speaking at a leadership conference and contributing to a book dedicated to Queen Elizabeth, driven by Dr. Pauline Long. I said Yes to speaking on World AIDS Day at the House of Parliament, London. I said Yes to receiving the Superwoman and Superhero awards. I said Yes to contributing to this book when I originally said I would not because I had not felt that I had "Showed Up" enough. I finally said Yes to being a radio host for Fabulous Lifestyles.

By showing up at a recent chapter meeting, I was able to meet one of our GSFE sisters LF who is so inspiriting and genuine, and only want the best for us all. She connected me with a well-known hypnotherapist who is mentoring me in my hypnotherapist practice as well as in business.

There is a bounty of abundance when you allow yourself to be seen. To be vulnerable. To allow people to know you. You never know who you may meet who is a link to that breakthrough that you need. My association with LSW led to contributing to an anthology that was an international bestseller, beating out two celebrities that launched the same day. It was through the LSW authoring world that I was interviewed for WOW

Warrior Magazine and TV Show as well as contributed an article to the magazine. I also said Yes to my own radio show on the network!

It didn't end there. In our chat after the interview, the owner SL, who is such a great listener and connector, then identified two or three people she will connect me with to collaborate and/or to realize the big picture of the impact I want to make in this world.

All these magnificent events and experiences would have never happened had I stayed in my home not wanting to be seen, judged, or uncomfortable. I had to trust that as long as I come from a place of integrity and confidence in who I am, I will find those who will ride along with me in my journey. Those who don't resonate with me can hitch a ride with the next vehicle!

When you decide to Show Up, you unlock a world of opportunity, people, and resources that can help you along your journey. You can connect with a mentor who can help you through challenges you face or to guide your journey as it unfolds. You will meet incredible people that will inspire you. Open yourself up to possibilities as sometimes that inspiration can lead you down an unexpected, but delicious path.

Now, not everyone you meet will be right for you. When you are searching for clarity, building your confidence, and early in your business journey, you can be a target of those who will take advantage of you under the disguise of wanting to help you, showing fake empathy ... after all, you are family.

Even with all these beautiful experiences, I still struggle with being seen, to break out of my chrysalis, and to Show Up. This is a journey and not a final destination. As long as I keep making efforts to connect, I will succeed at Showing Up and allow my inner exquisiteness to shine.

So, along this journey, I have learned that there is more positive than negative in Showing Up. When you decide to Show Up, give of yourself, encourage, and inspire others, you awake to opportunities that may not have been available had you not Shown Up---opportunities that can help you grow as individuals, and see opportunities that blossom into successes. Now, I am working on Asking.

It's all
About
Showing
Up

Ask The Father, He Will Show Up

Dr. Cherilyn Lee

The journey of my life taught me to show up for others, myself, and most especially for God. All my near-death experiences are proof that I can do all things through God. If you show up for God, God will show up for you. Matthew 7:7 ESV "Ask, and it will be given to you; seek, and you will find; knock, and it will be opened to you." Showing up for God is not just repenting on the weekend or repeating a few verses. Showing up for God is revealed by our attitude, acceptance, and inner thought life, and who we really are deep in our hearts and soul. God gave us a spirit to be filled with love, not fear, and a desire for us to spread His love.

Showing up with God is powerful! In our daily lives, without a connection with God, obstacles can seem impossible. But God has shown me all things through Him are possible. God has helped me through unbearable sorrows, such as losing many loved ones over the years and losing everything I own in one night, including my business and car, due to fires set during the Los Angeles riots. God showed me how to simply show up by living in the moment, being present, and taking one small step at a time. Even the smallest step is better than taking no step at all. Just show up. No matter what happens if you keep showing up, eventually, you will achieve your goals.

God showed me how to show up and soar even during stressful times that would normally crumble most people. God showed me setbacks would not stop me if I was dedicated to showing up and making an effort. Showing up with God enabled me to recover faster than was usually possible and helped me to swiftly move on to the next opportunity. Whenever I ask God for help and show up with profound faith, He blesses me more than I could ever imagine.

My Comprehensive Alternative Family Practice was bustling. I was confident as a Board-Certified Natural Healthcare practitioner, but I didn't have the self-esteem needed for a career in the public life. Overcoming many life-threatening situations stirred my passion for combining Eastern and Western medicine, which integrates mind, body, and spirit. With God's strength, I was showing up and healing my patients one at a time. My dream was to expand my reach to help as many people as possible. What held me back was my shyness and an agonizing self-consciousness that resulted from many painful conditions and experiences that I endured throughout my childhood.

I recognized my challenges gave me a unique perspective on life that motivated me to show up and search for ways to help others and always strive to do more. It's been almost twenty years since I was invited to a National Association of Female Executives (NAFE) meeting. I showed up and was blessed to be introduced to the incomparable Robbie Motter. In 2017, she founded the Global Society of Female Entrepreneurs (GSFE). She gave me the support I needed to step outside my comfort zone and share my astonishing story of almost having both legs amputated, surviving pulmonary embolisms, flatlining twice, fully recovering from two comas and other illnesses. Throughout these ordeals, because I learned how to show up with God, my audio autobiography, "Written Before I Was Born,"

received the "2019 Her Story Award" from the Women's Federation for World Peace USA, where I also showed up and serve as an Ambassador.

It was easy for me to speak up on behalf of my patients, but it was truly difficult for me to ask others for anything I needed, which at its core is love and acceptance. As a young girl, I always felt I was punished for being ill. I couldn't understand why I had so many health problems. My hardship with asthma landed me in the emergency room, unable to breathe countless times. I was constantly in and out of hospitals due to my eczema or asthma, where I was alone and confined to my room. The drugs didn't work well in those days and had adverse side effects. I wheezed with every breath, which sounded like an off-tune musical instrument in my head all the time. My parents' second-hand cigarette smoke contributed to my asthma. Finally, my mother quit smoking, but my stepfather continued.

My eczema was so bad that I had bloody sores from scratching all over my body and had to change my diet. Like many chronic health conditions, eczema is a skin condition linked to allergies and emotions. Along with my asthma, my eczema definitely had its roots in emotional pain. Not surprisingly, I had several food allergies that often made me sick and prevented me from eating the same food as my family and schoolmates. Watching everyone else eat delicious meals persuaded me to show up and study everything I could about nutrition.

Children are not born to be malicious and hateful, but unfortunately, they learn to persecute children who are different. Kids would throw dirt on me, push me, tease me, torment me, and call me names like "raccoon" or 'lizard girl" because the skin around my eyes and mouth was dark, scaly, and peeling. The daily treatment I endured was damaging and harsh, especially because I had no friends. Emotional healing, releasing resentment and forgiving the bullying and other injustices liberated the internalized pain weighing me down and destroying my life.

Compounded, my parents divorced when I was two months old, and my biological father was absent. My mother remarried two years later. My stepfather and I were not close. As a young girl, I recall my mother telling me that her mother-in-law did not want her son to marry a woman that already had a child, and most especially a sickly child, which left me feeling unwanted, less than, and ashamed for not being well like all the other children. Our relationship was cold and distant as he treated his biological daughter very differently than me.

I remember when I was in elementary school; I asked my stepfather for 10 cents to buy myself something at the neighborhood store. He looked down at me and said, "I don't have any money for you." The way he said it, I believed that he didn't have any money. There was not a harsh tone in his voice. I didn't feel sad at the time as I began to walk away. But before I could exit the room, my little sister walked up and asked him for 10 cents. My stepfather reached into his pocket and gave her a dime. That was a huge shock and stabbed me right down to my core. Why would he give money to her and not to me? My spirit was crushed. His behavior created deep-seated anguish and left me with feelings that I was not as good as others.

From that moment on, I was determined never to ask others for anything. It taught me that I was not worthy and not to ask people for what I wanted. So, at a very young age, I started working to earn my own money and never asked anyone for anything. The hurt, rejection, and numerous disappointments I received from my biological father and stepfather plagued me for decades and became integral parts of the fabric of my life, leaving a deep scar encrusted with layers of trust issues that made it difficult to ask for what I wanted.

On the contrary, when children are allowed a voice, empowered, and free, revolutionary change can occur. Showing up to GSFE over the years and receiving unconditional support from dynamic and sincere women gradually helped my inner child reclaim her voice. My peers saw me as successful because I consistently showed up for my studies throughout many years and created a thriving holistic family practice, the NuWellness Healthcare Clinic. The internal residue from years of abuse fueled my determination to spare others the needless pain I suffered and find the most effective ways for people to heal. For decades, I showed up to workshops, seminars, and symposiums, praying to receive knowledge so that I could shed light on debilitating diseases that plagued me and others.

Unbeknownst to me, I was going to be catapulted into the media spotlight. In 2009, I showed up and shared my gifts with the King of Pop. In turn, Michael showed up for me by teaching me a valuable lesson that enhanced my life. He showed me how he blocked out the public scrutiny since his early days as a child star. This kind gesture would eventually give meaning to my actions and assist my choice to fly with the eagles because my destiny was written before I was born.

The world knows the icon, Michael Jackson, but I knew him as the man who flew with the eagles. One night, I thought he would be a sad, nervous wreck because the news reported his cherished possessions were being auctioned off. When I showed up at his home, he was a delightful father, as usual, interacting with his children as if nothing was happening. He taught me to show up and remain in high spirits whenever there was gossip, jealousy, or resentment, which he saw as baby chicks chirping. Instead, he chose to fly with the eagles above all the chatter. He reminded me that if you're flying with eagles, you don't have time to "tweet" and lower your vibration or be concerned about those who do not appreciate you. His attitude to fly with

the eagles and raise his frequency enabled him to share his majestic music with the world.

Although I was blessed to know the real man in the mirror, when the world lost a mega superstar, the media ignited its fury at me. As Michaels's practitioner, I became a witness in a high-profile trial and lost my anonymity and privacy. I found myself pulled in many directions. When Michael died, it became difficult for me to leave the house. Because I was willing to show up and be interviewed by Nancy Grace on CNN, Robbie called Nancy and shared with her my personal story. She said I was a woman of impeccable character, compassion, and dedication to healing others.

Throughout the last decades, I have been honored to have the privilege of showing up to GSFE events. Within these organizations, I gathered many golden nuggets that spurred my growth and pushed me beyond what I thought was possible, which reassured me to lead by example, using my voice to champion the defenseless. As a holistic practitioner, I am on the cutting edge of new alternative healing modalities. My healing-oriented treatments incorporate conventional medicine with accredited, scientifically proven holistic methods and yield exceptional results. At my clinic, we use many advanced technologies and perform Free Beauty Shop Stroke Screenings. I also offer a quick three-minute Cardiovascular and Autonomic Nervous System Screening using the FDA-approved medical device Max Pulse.

For years I have been interested in offering thermography screenings for patients because it can detect diseases before symptoms occur. Typically, a thermography screening is expensive and not covered by insurance. Most practitioners who own the CRT2000 Thermographic System charge anywhere from $250 to $500 per session, which the average person can't afford. I dreamed that one day I could offer these screenings for free. I prayed for my dream to become a reality.

One day, a dear colleague called and told me about a particular company called Eidam. She said, "I found a company in Canada that manufactures the machine you've been excited about. You should contact them."

So, I called the manufacturer and shared my vision. "It is crucial to provide a service for those most vulnerable and those who cannot afford out-of-pocket services for thermography. I'm excited about your system because there's no radiation, and I would finally be able to screen pregnant women. I would like you to sponsor me and underwrite your thermography system through my nonprofit that we're currently forming."

The lady graciously said, "Well, the manufacturing costs are high, and they retail for over $20,000, so, unfortunately, we cannot give these away for free."

While she was talking, I silently thanked God for my new device and recited my favorite mantra—"I am so grateful that I am a magnet for miracles."

My self-esteem and confidence propelled my momentum to keep asking over the next few weeks. Because I learned to speak up and didn't take no for an answer, they ultimately sent it to me for free, and my nonprofit, the NuWellness Development Foundation, offers the only cost-free thermography, a Painless and Radiation Free Breast Cancer Screening to men, women, and teenagers using the CRT2000 Thermographic System. Because I overcame my insecurities and learned to ask for help, the CRT2000 Thermographic System has saved many lives, including my own granddaughter, who was diagnosed with breast cancer at 17 years old. Without this screening, her cancer would have remained undetected.

I am a highly sought-after Integrative Practitioner and global media personality. I host and produce a weekly TV/Radio Show on my YouTube channel, "NuWellness TV with Dr. Lee." The acclaimed series explores advancements in natural health, physical fitness, nutrition, integrative medicine, human rights, well-being, and self-discovery, interviewing leading experts, some of whom are referred by Robbie. She also praises me and shares my NuWellnes program with her vast networks.

I have been honored by three US Presidents, Obama, Trump, and Biden with four Lifetime Achievement Awards because I showed up for my volunteer services. I have received numerous awards and recognition from government branches at every level, from the City Council to the State Department, for the humanitarian work I provide under my NuWellness Development Foundation, Inc., a 501(c)(3) nonprofit. I couldn't have done any of this if I hadn't found my voice, believed in myself, learned to ask for help, and showed up. I became resilient and committed to showing up to receive "the treasures" and embrace the mutual support from members of GSFE, who continue to share my journey.

It's all
About
Showing
Up

It Is Joyful to Show Up

Dr. (h.c.) Jeannette LeHoullier

I am grateful for the many friends that I have--especially for my GSFE sisters who I have grown closer to over the last four years. I find myself not surprised at how willing my sisters are to provide support, encouragement, love, and compassion in all of my challenges and my joys.

Showing up is such an awesome motto that Robbie Motter thoroughly enjoys and promotes. I chose the name JOYFUL DIVA because many people have commented that my laughter brings Happiness and JOY to them. So, let us talk about the acronym.

J-O-Y-F-U-L.

J – Join In

What it means when you show up is that you are joining and you're making an effort. It is utterly amazing. The possibilities. The connections. The Dreams. All can come true. What interesting people you can meet along the way.

I have had so many experiences in the past year in showing up. They have provided opportunities that are just unbelievable. First off, I joined our local Karaoke Tuesday night as a way to start singing again. In high school

and early in my adult years, I often sang and performed. I say humbly that I have been blessed by God with a voice. Finally, I'm choosing to share it again with myself and others because other people get JOY from hearing it, and I love singing.

Our GSFE sisters, Charmaine Summers, and Nicole Farrell started Karaoke night at the Sun City Cherry Hills golf course almost 2 years ago. Honestly, I had hesitated to join in because I was feeling shy, and I was not familiar with karaoke.

My experience in singing in the past was performing without a microphone and just not following someone else's beat while seeing words. In high school, I was honored to perform solos and be the lead female in the Opera entitled "Amahl and the Night Visitors" (a children's Christmas opera about a poor disabled boy who meets the three Wise Men in the story of the birth of Jesus).

But the thing called karaoke is a whole new experience for me. Let me tell you that after doing karaoke, I began receiving encouragement mostly from my GFSE (Global Society of Female Entrepreneurs) sisters: Robbie Motter, Joan Wakeland, Charmaine Summers, Nicole Farrell, and Joanne Groch. These ladies encouraged me by saying that I sang well or just said, "wow". Their positive comments encouraged me to get out of my own protective shell that I created. Furthermore, by going to karaoke, I was given an opportunity by Robbie Motter to perform at the annual International Kindness Day awards event. Through this opportunity, Joan Wakeland, the event coordinator, connected me with a fabulous young artist named Grande Sean Coles. We did our best to prepare and sing "The Prayer," made famous by Celine Dion and Andre Bocelli. Grande's expertise and vocal training helped my operatic voice come alive again. Although it was not our best performance, we showed up. Blessedly, it was well received

by the crowd, and it was a JOY to sing for others. Of course, wearing my favorite color pink that day as part of the day's theme made the day even more special.

Another opportunity came up that same day. I was offered a duet with my new GSFE sister, Marneen Fields, for her upcoming movie "WHO'S GOING TO TAKE CARE OF ME NOW?". Wow - this is a remarkable opportunity, and I am so excited to be involved in this movie about mental illness, homelessness, physical illness, verbal abuse and aging in a dysfunctional family. I am not only going to be singing several songs, but I also have a small acting part in her movie!

O – OUTSIDE

Be JOYFUL while you are busying yourself outside each week. You must get outside your home, your office, and your environment and try different things. By "Showing Up". this means pushing yourself at times to show up even if you're not feeling like it. Through showing up for instance, I've been able to join Robbie and some of her friends for winery outings to listen to her son Ed perform. At a recent winery evening, I also enjoyed talking with our publisher, Angela Covany (GFSE sister) and her prospective client whom we shared more about the theory about showing up. Robbie had already mentioned showing up to the young gentleman and discussed the book he was writing. Being outside can lead to not only enjoyment but added participation as well.

Y – You Can Do It

Yes, absolutely! You can do it when you put forth effort. There are so many people in your lives that will come along side of you to encourage you in ways that are just unbelievable. Of course, we have some negative folks in our lives who can bring us down. Yet, just like most of you, I've learned to

remove myself from the negativity and to join myself with positivity and positive folks. You can do it if you set a goal, you can accomplish it. There is nothing stopping you but yourself. So, connect with others, events, and training that help you accomplish what you want to do. For instance, I am often taking free or low-cost trainings that enrich my life with knowledge, skills, tools, and they help me along the way to accomplish my goals and dreams. It is a positive path to accomplish and do what I set out to do.

F – Fully Engage

This means each effort that you make must be fully engaged. You must connect and follow through. Soak in the connections and engagements given to you. Engage means that you fit one cog into another cog, and it starts moving like a watch. However, if you fail to do the connection there will be no engagement.

Another example goes back to my vocal coach and singing partner Grande Sean Coles. Through engaging with him as a volunteer performer for International Kindness Day, he was able to share with me some new techniques to help my voice become healthier and my vocal cords heal from years of problems. By being fully engaged with this young professional, my life has also been changed in a positive manner. When practicing, I had an absolute fun time doing it. Grande's singing sessions were filled with training, laughter, and camaraderie – fully engaged. I took advantage of a connection and went with it even though I was at first hesitant and a little bit uncomfortable due to my own self-doubts. It ended up being a fantastic experience singing with him. Now I have a new friend who shares some of the same interests in music and business.

U - Understand

Understand is a broad word; however, it can be simplified by saying

understanding is also knowing what you want and going for it. Show Up - because life is a treasure map, just like Robbie says. Those two things are important, but you must follow through with and ASK. That ASK is another way of identifying and understanding what it is that you need help with or what type of connection with others you are looking for. Also, it is a way to understand and a way to grow.

Last year, I was a co-author in Angela Covany's book "LOVE YOUR HATERS". Wow! That was a fantastic experience and an honor to be included in her book. Each writer of the book shared a chapter defining a moment in their life of loving someone who was a hater or had a hate relationship with. The process of writing afforded us an opportunity for self-analysis, remembering incidences in our lives, and understanding what got us through the pain. We relived and then released again what turned our attitudes around to a response of love rather than hate.

Another show up moment was connecting with a GSFE sister that I become familiar with because of the LOVE YOUR HATERS book. Debbie Love and I have similar pasts. We bonded, shared, and became acquainted. Through understanding there is growth. Please pick up a copy of the book on Amazon, major book sellers, Walmart, etc. The authors share so many remarkable stories – it is really awesome!

L - Love the Possibilities

There are possibilities around each corner. Yes, it may sound like a cliché, but it really is true. My life has many examples. My GFSE sister, Nicole Farrell, was hospitalized several years ago with Covid. I got out of my comfort zone and showed up by sending her a text just wishing her good health, good days, and saying hello to encourage her. Through my friendship with Nicole, I've met another person who is beautiful both inside and out.

There is connection, understanding, support, and all kinds of wonderful JOYFUL love from sisters in GSFE. I must say that I am not partial only to GSFE sisters because I am blessed to have many friends who I connect and enjoy life with who are not connected to GSFE. This book is a wonderful opportunity to mention the GFSE sisters because I've gained so much from knowing them.

I can give a benign example of seeing my primary doctor Helen Tran, who is not only a remarkable physician, but she is also just an amazing person. She treats me with respect and provides positive comments during our visits that encourage me. I've shared my first book of Robbie's "Showing Up", and she was very supportive. I will be sharing my second book "LOVE YOUR HATERS" as well as this third book that you are reading. Love the possibilities as it refers to Dr. Tran, reminds me to enjoy my passion - which is music and singing. Her classical piano concerto performances have sparked more JOY in me, because I know it is a passion, I must continue to participate in.

About a year and a half ago I remarked at our local GSFE meeting that I wanted to get back into singing and speaking. The singing passion has been accomplished and continues to blossom. It has been a dream of mine since I was 16 years old. Speaking engagements will come when God's timing provides the best opportunity.

We must dream to accomplish and see what possibilities there are in life. Having a goal, a dream, a hope can turn out to be remarkable when you follow through. Because life is truly a treasure map just, like Robbie says.

Love possibilities – they can occur when you Show Up.

In conclusion, my name is Jeannette LeHoullier (pronounced with a French accent), and I am JOYFUL DIVA. My business is JEANNETTE'S JOY. I

help women and seniors. Servant leadership is my focus – as Jesus Christ modeled. Support others by coming alongside them life and assist or be a listener – whatever it takes.

Don't forget to SHOW UP and ASK - possibilities will happen to you as well.

Eyeing The Seat As The President Of Kenya

H.E. Ambassador Prof. Dr. Pauline Long

The assumption that leaders are elected or chosen is overrated. Many of us shy away from leadership contest for fear of being rejected by the very people we long to serve. Luckily in my teenage life I realized there was something unique in the power of stepping forward to ask for exactly what you want.

It was in the spring of 1991 in my beautiful country of birth, Kenya, that I reported to secondary school for the second term of the year. One may be confused with the term spring season when it comes to a tropical country that only resonates with heatwave. However, we are reminded that Africa as a continent goes through four seasons, too; the only difference is they are extremely mild. What I would term as winter in Kenya would be 20 degrees Celsius, the opposite of the -1 degrees I have just experienced in my city of residence London, United Kingdom. During this Kenyan spring season, the association of Girlguides, Scouts, Brownies, and Rangers tended to hold several camps in Kenya. Some of these camps were local and close to my school while most of the camps were in major cities in Kenya such as Mombasa, Nairobi, Nakuru, and Kisumu. All four cities are beautiful with natural forests surrounding them and hence provide conducive background for camping.

Subsequently as an avid die-hard member of the Girlguide movement, I followed every activity, all rules, and all regulations with keen interest. As a brownie and girlguide in primary school, I never missed any camp. They were fun, educative, and most important they taught us survival and independence skills that have stayed with me to date. We learnt to live in the wild with the bare minimal and absolutely no glitz and glamour, no running water, electricity, or heating. We had to improvise by digging holes and lining them with leaves to create makeshift refrigerators to preserve food. We walked for miles to find streams of water for daily use, and when it came to keeping the whole camp warm in the night, at the tender age of 12, I already knew how to make the best bourn fire.

Although I transitioned from primary school to secondary school with these basic survival skills, it did not guarantee me a place in the camp with Rangers. The competition was stiff; every ranger wanted to go camping as they were on a higher level in the major cities. Being an introvert, I always stayed in the back of the room and let the ones at the front take all the limelight until one particular day at the age of 15 when I realized that one can only speak against injustice by stepping forward, one can only lead by standing up to be counted, and one can only take the front seat by asking for it.

That sunny spring afternoon, our Rangers Director called a meeting to inform us of the next Rangers' camp which was an international camp involving over 250 countries. Indeed, there was excitement as Kenya was hosting such a big gathering for the first time in the history of the Girl guides and Scouts movement. In the meeting, our director made it clear that it was only the rangers who always put efforts in our regular activities would travel to the capital city Nairobi for the international camp. Almost immediately, you could spot thumbs twiddling, faces dropping and heads turning because not many of the rangers were committed; therefore, in the

ideal world not many of them qualified to make this trip. Did I qualify? Yes, and more! But guess what, when the list of the people that had been picked was read out, my name was missing. I knew exactly why. One, for my dark skin complexion because our director was a man who always favored rangers that were lighter in complexion. If you are reading this part of my story and you are not black, you will not understand what I mean. So, I would like to simplify it to you and request that you to look up the word 'colourism', and that will explain it all. The other reason why my name was left out was because I was tiny and very thin for an African woman. This same man preferred what they called 'proper African woman' with curves to represent our school at the international level.

Having observed the proceedings at that meeting with our director, I did not waste time to step forward and asked loudly and clearly: "Sir, why is my name missing from this list? I want to go to the international camp. Not only do I want to go, I also want to represent the whole school as the leader of this group because I have done more for this organization than anyone on that list. I have led them even though I have never been appointed or elected by you to do so." By the time I finished expressing myself, there was complete silence in the room, followed by endless clapping. This brought shock waves through my spine as I did not expect that reaction, especially as I wasn't particularly polite with my choice of words. I said, 'I want' instead of 'I would like, or I would love."

Within seconds, a deep authoritative and sympathetic voice followed, "Your wish has been granted Pauline. I will see you later for strategy meeting for the trip. Everyone, meet your new leader," said the director in his address to the Rangers. The clapping continued; the whole group embraced me and more important they admired my courage. From that day, I have taken on several leadership mantles from diverse community levels to the world level, and with each level I continue to comprehend that leadership has

never been about being appointed, elected, or selected. One must put the first foot forward then the other one will automatically follow. You alone know your capabilities, you alone know your strength, and you alone know your hidden talent, and all this can only come out if you give them a chance to see light by asking for opportunities and then showing up for the opportunities.

With all the above in mind, I'm thrilled to reveal that I'm eyeing up the very top seat as the president of Kenya. With a great team around me, I look forward to showing up as a servant leader to serve with integrity and clarity 54 million Kenyans.

H.E Amb. Prof Dr Pauline Long FIIM

H.E Prof. Dr Pauline Long FIIM is a AUGP NOBEL PEACE PRIZE recipient. She is a multi-award winning serial entrepreneur, serial philanthropist, media mogul, public speaker, author, peace activist, mentor, TV/film producer and presenter who has been listed on Black Women In Europe Powerlist, named the most outstanding woman of the year (2016), Europe's most powerful woman for changing many lives through BEFFTA (2017) and global African Woman of the year (2022). She has also been honored in UK parliament as one of 100 most outstanding Africans.

The graceful humanitarian and peace activist is the most celebrated African woman in Europe with 18 Lifetime Achievement Awards and over 355 awards given to her for endless service to the society and selfless support she gives to charities and humanitarian projects around the world. She has been awarded a special Lifetime Achievement honor by the president of USA, H.E Joe Biden for being a strong advocate for human love committed to bringing communities together. Prof Long has been named by NELAs Academy awards as a phenomenal leader for 5 consecutive years, an honor she does not take lightly as a committed servant leader.

One of the most striking aspects about this phenomenal entrepreneur is that she works day and night to fund all the humanitarian initiatives she has established, she has done this for over 20 years.

Prof Pauline Long's status as a role model has earned her the highest African recognition honor and Heroic Award alongside Her Excellency, the former president of Malawi Dr Joyce Banda.

She is a global ambassador for Universal Peace Federation (UPF) and chief ambassador of Academy of Universal Global Peace based in New York. Prof. Long is also a governor of the American University USA and United Nations University. She is passionate about delivering leadership lectures. As an advocate for great leadership, Prof Pauline Long was appointed the African ambassador for the Nelson Mandela Book which was launched in UK Parliament.

Dr. Long is the owner and founder of Europe's biggest award ceremony for black and ethnic personalities entertainment, film, fashion, TV, Arts as well as leadership, business and philanthropy - BEFFTA (Black Entertainment Film Fashion Television & Arts Awards) where she has transformed thousands of lives. She also founded FEED THE STREET CHILDREN CAMPAIGN where she engaged her team to provide food to thousands of children who are homeless in Uganda, Kenya and Tanzania. Recently, she founded sanitary pads campaign called 4ME 4HER where she has so far distributed free sanitary pads in African villages to over 600 orphaned girls and those from underprivileged backgrounds who often skip school during menstruation and so by providing these free sanitary pads, she helps keep the girls in education.

Prof. Dr. Pauline Long is a popular TV presenter on Sky Channel 458 who has transformed lives through Pauline Long Show by giving platforms to the voiceless and fight global injustices such as abuse, extreme poverty,

bullying. She has interviewed over 4000 guests on the show from UK, Africa, Asia, Europe USA. Some of the guests she interviewed include football legend Didier Drogba, Oscar nominee and BAFTA winner Chiwetel Ejiofor, The Drifters, famous actress Jocelyn Dumas, Vice President Of Malawi Saulos Chiluba, veteran Nollywood actor Ramsey Nouah and more. The show also highlights on business and politics. Prof Long is the president of Pauline Long Entrepreneurship Foundation(PLEF) where she supplies sewing machines, food and agricultural products to women in different parts of Africa. Through the foundation she takes care of over 60 old and widowed women in Kenya and offers scholarships to 150 students in Malawi, Zambia, and Congo. She also founded Dr Pauline Long Super Cup Football tournament to empower youth from deprived backgrounds. She is currently building multi-purpose women and community centers in Malawi and Kenya. She mentors over 1000 youth through Pauline Long Empowerment and mentorship club both in UK and Africa. Her latest movement called YOUTH CAN TOO encourages the youth to become leaders in various sectors.

Her persistent and long-term support for women has led her to establish these three powerful projects:

GAWW(Global Africa Women's Week), WAW(Women Appreciating Women) and I AM A SUPERWOMAN CLUB. She is also the founder of Diaspora Commonwealth Community Leaders (DCCL), a program that brings community leaders from over 30 commonwealth countries to build stronger communities and offer lasting solutions to problems faced by those in the Diaspora. She also runs Dr Pauline Long Awards for humanitarians and Leaders.

Prof. Pauline Long is an ambassador and patron for over 20 charities and organizations.

Respected by her peers and seen as an inspiration by many, Dr Long sits in several boards. She is former chairperson of the multicultural global organization LOANI (Ladies Of All Nations International) A women's organization represented in over 70 countries which she gave a lot of her time and expertise. She has been appointed by several organizations as ambassador including African International Achievers Awards, SHAI Foundation – a Christian charity that educates orphans in Haiti, Girl Child Network Worldwide organization founded by CNN Hero Betty Makoni, a charity that supports girls who have been raped and abused women. She has also been patron and ambassador for 2 charities in Sierra Leone that support persons with disabilities and amputees, Melqosh Mission and Disabled international charity. She continues to support several charities as patron including Migrant Disability Network, AOS charity, Voice Of Hope Foundation, AAA Foundation, International Women of Power and many more. She was also appointed ambassador for Africa Nations Cup UK.

Dr Pauline Long sits in the executive board of Women Economic Forum and she is also the Chairperson of

Forum for Asian, African and Caribbean Women in Politics (FAWP). Her latest venture is I AM A

SUPERWOMAN CLUB AND AWARDS, an exclusive membership club bringing the most phenomenal women together from different parts of the world and career paths.

As an entrepreneur, Dr Long is a consultant, ghost writer, journalist and a contributor to various publications.

She runs a major film studio in London called East End Studios with a wide range of clients including BBC,

Walt Disney, Channel 4, Netflix, Amazon, Facebook, YouTube, Pepsi, Reebok, Adidas, Puma, Sony music,

Warner music and more. Some of the artists who have filmed at her studio include Leona Lewis, Girls Aloud, The Script, Wretch 32, Wiley, Burna Boy, Azelia Banks, Kelis and more. She continues to support many unsigned artists through the studio.

Dr Long is the chairperson of Institute of Information Management UK.

As a servant leader and politician, she is working towards becoming the future president of The Republic of Kenya, an ambition she's pursuing with a lot of passion to change lives.

It's all
About
Showing
Up

When You Realize You Have Been Showing Up and Asking Your Whole Life and the Path that Became Yours by Doing So

Dr. (h.c.) Regina Lundy

My name is Regina Lundy, and I am 68 years old. I spent most of my life trying to be the best me. I definitely wanted to please and try to be there for the people around me and my loved ones. I recently retired and lost my husband, in that order. I found myself facing a new chapter in life. I was asked by a dear friend to join her at a GSFE meeting, where she wanted me to meet her mentor, Robbie Motter. I had heard about Robbie for many years and was excited to go but really didn't think GSFE would be fit for me. After all, I was not an entrepreneur, but I thought, why not Show Up and give it a chance? At that time, I did not know that Showing Up and Asking was the whole motto behind this organization. I soon began to understand the meaning of these words and how powerful and empowering they were. I also started to put two and two together and realize how Showing Up had impacted me my entire life. I was also motivated to take another look at the new chapter of my life and how this motto of Showing Up and Asking could and would help me fulfill the years to come!

I was born in Covington, Kentucky, and grew up just north of Cincinnati, Ohio. My childhood was somewhat unconventional; my mom and dad divorced when I was five, and my mom remarried when I was eight. At that time, we moved to a lovely suburb, and my mom had a baby. Life was great!

But when I was eleven years old, my mom was killed in a car accident. I was surrounded by people who loved me, but losing my mother at that age was devastating. I made the decision to stay with my stepfather and help with my 18-month-old brother. My family let me make that choice, and even at that early age I realized I made a choice to Show Up! I did see my father and relatives on both sides of my family and always felt very loved.

My high school years were fun as I had a lot of friends and was involved in several extra-curricular activities. After high school, I went off to college, first at Eastern Kentucky and then to the University of Cincinnati. I racked up many units but didn't really know exactly where or what I was going to do with them. This was the early 1970's and some of those high school friends I spoke of decided to go to California. (One had relatives in Orange County)! So, I put on my bell bottom jeans and my red bandana and hopped in that Volkswagen van! I Showed Up, and little did I know, at the time, that this would definitely be a life changing experience for me.

Once I arrived in Southern California, I continued to take some classes at a Junior College and that is where I met the man I would marry. Certainly, one of those loves at first sight, and soon after I turned 21-years-old, we went to Vegas and got married. We lived in Costa Mesa, CA, and at the time. I worked at a semiconductor company and was a production control planner. I liked numbers and moved up the ladder pretty fast. But, at age twenty-six I had my first child, and within four and a half years I had three children---two girls and a boy.

While they were young, I stayed home with them and then started a daycare business. I was licensed by the state and had one employee. I knew that being home with my kids, not to mention the expense of daycare, was the best thing for my family, Again I Showed Up but not really knowing that was what I was doing.

By the time my second child was in school we made the move to Menifee, CA; it was 1991. I began working for Menifee Union School District as an instructional aide. Unfortunately, a recession hit, and after my husband lost a couple of jobs, I decided it was time for me to finish up that degree and get my teaching credential. I started looking for options and found a program, but I would have to drive to March Air Force Base in Moreno Valley two nights a week. At the time our family only had one car, and my kids were in elementary school and middle school. I also still had to work to help support the family. One day I decided to go over to the junior college right here in Menifee and try to get some information about continuing education. I walked into the front office, and as soon as I looked down on the counter, there was a brochure from Azusa Pacific University. They were advertising that they were starting a program for adults going back to school to get their teaching credential. You had to be over a certain age and have at least 75 college units to qualify. Well, I did not only meet those criteria, but the junior college was right across the street from where we lived so I could walk to my classes two nights a week. Again, another time that I Showed Up. It changed the direction of my life---not only my life but for my entire family.

I continued a career in Education and now have a comfortable retirement. This would not have happened if I had been persistent and showed up and asked pretty much against all odds. I went on the fast track and didn't stop until I finished my master's degree. I worked in public schools for 35 years (25 of them as a credentialed teacher). I taught kindergarten, first, and second grade, and during my years of teaching I took on many roles! I was voted Teacher of the Year in 2009/2010 for Val Verde Elementary School. From 2010 to 2021 I served as Grade Chair for my grade level and was on the Administrative Leadership Team. I assisted and taught many classes during District Professional Development days, which included Early

Reading Strategies. I also served several years on the Curriculum Council and assisted with developing online testing questions that aligned with CAAASP assessments which tested achievement and aptitude.

In 2014, I was diagnosed with breast cancer. I had a double mastectomy and 6 months of chemotherapy. It totally took me off guard because I had never really been sick. Going through that experience was most certainly the biggest growth and time of reflection that I had ever experienced! I for once, had to sit down or lie down and depend upon others. I was very used to being in control and doing it all. Lying down and having someone bring me tea and food was a new experience. But I decided from the beginning that I was going to Show Up and do everything that I could to do (follow Doctor's directions) and beat this dreaded disease. It definitely was a rough couple of years, but I am now eight years with no evidence of cancer! In remission!

I retired from teaching in June of 2021 after teaching the last year and a half online zooming! Again, this was a huge learning curve. My technology skills were not nearly as accomplished as my younger peers. But I certainly Showed Up and ASKED for help. I spent so many hours just learning how to set up a digital classroom and communicate with parents via emails and texting programs.

Just three weeks after I retired my husband of 46 years passed away. We knew he was ill, and that is the main reason I DID RETIRE....so I could take care of him. But God had other plans. The family gathered, and we gave him the military sendoff that he so deserved. I then started soul searching for what was to come next in this new chapter of life. It certainly had not turned out as planned. I knew I would be busy helping with my seven grandchildren but also knew I would want and need more!

My dear friend Deborah Irish invited me to a GSFE meeting in October of

2021. I did not know if that would be a good fit for me, but I immediately felt a bond with Robbie Motter (the founder of the organization) and many of the women that were there. In January of 2022 I became a member of Menifee's GSFE Chapter. (Global Society for Female Entrepreneurs) I was not an entrepreneur; I was a retired educator and recently widowed. What could I offer these extraordinary women of all walks of life? I soon learned that some of these women had organized nonprofit organizations that needed support. There is ALWAYS room for more volunteers and more help. So, I thought this is perfect...here I have a chance for me to Ask and Show Up! This past year I have met some amazing women and volunteered with a couple of non-profit organizations. One of which is Milvet, started by Raven Hilden. It is a 501(C)(3) nonprofit that supports veterans and active military and their families! It was exactly what I was looking for. My husband was a veteran that served two tours in Vietnam and was 100% disabled when he passed away. We spent so many weeks, months, and years trying to get him the benefits that he deserved. Had I only known about Milvet and their services, it would have relieved my husband of so much stress. We finally got the VA services for him and his 100 % disability, three months before he died. By Showing Up at that first GSFE meeting in October 2021, I realized what a help it would have been had we only had known of Raven and her organization, but now because I Showed Up, I do know! And I plan to help others that are in similar situations that we were.

This past November I received the GSFE World Kindness Award in recognition of my volunteering and support of GSFE, and just this past week (January 2023) I was asked to take over the Directorship of the Menifee Chapter. I feel so honored and so blessed. I will be traveling to Atlanta this spring with several of my GSFE sisters to receive an Honorary Doctoral Certificate in Humanitarianism---something that I think I have spent a lifetime working toward but never in a million years thought I would receive. Again, this would have never been possible if I had not SHOWED UP at age 66, after retiring and losing my husband, to a meeting where I thought I did not really belong. I look forward to this new beginning and I am sooo glad that I SHOWED UP! I had heard about Robbie and GSFE for many years, and now I realize I have been Showing Up my entire life but not realizing the impact that it has had on the path that this life had in store for me! I now know that this next chapter holds many exciting new paths... and I will continue to keep Showing Up and Asking! And remember age is just a number...it is NEVER too late to Show Up and Ask!

It's all
About
Showing
Up

"How Do You Show Up for Yourself in Challenging Times??"

Dr. (h.c.) Sara Lypps

To start from the beginning of my story, in this case, I need to give you some recent history. At the young age of 38, I was tragically widowed with four small children; they were 13, 11, 4, and 2. However, you can either choose to turn the page now or see how I chose to "Show Up" to set an example for my children, be an inspiration to others, and prove to myself just what I was made of.

From as long as I can remember as a little girl, I was taught from my mother that to think of oneself or do something for yourself is selfish. I loved to read books every day and excelled all throughout school, but always felt like somehow, I never really fit it. I was extremely shy and often at times it seemed as if I was just floating in a bubble going about my days as an awkward adolescent and then a teenager. These years were uncomfortable, and I couldn't wait for high school to be over. It wasn't until I started junior college that something finally clicked for me. The professors really didn't care if I showed up to class nor did I have to worry about being sent to the principal's office for cutting class or sticking up for myself in front of authority figures. I had arrived at a crossroad in my life where it was just about me and finding my own moral compass. I don't ever remember missing a day of class nor turning in an assignment late. I passed on going to parties and social events at times, to study for an exam because my education was just that important to me. Why am I telling you all of this? Because how you do anything is how you do everything. This story is about how I "Showed Up" for myself!

I graduated from college with honors, got married, and started a family---not necessarily in that order. My last semester before receiving my Bachelor of Arts degree was my first trimester of pregnancy. Not the best combination in life! I remember telling my professors if I go running quickly out of the classroom during their lecture, it wasn't because their teachings were awful, it was rather that I had horrible morning sickness and had to book it to the nearest restroom or trash receptacle. Did I mention that I was taking 21 units that semester; 12 is considered full time? I was determined to get my college degree before that baby came and my school only offered spring graduation at that time. I finished all my required courses in December; however, we didn't officially walk with our graduating class in our gowns until May. My son was born in the middle of June. Needless to say, I was packing a small beach ball under my cute little gold crocheted summer dress, gown, and cap. But what else was I packing? I had a new sense of accomplishment and self-worth that would change the entire trajectory of my life.

Why was school so important to me? For the first time in my life, I truly felt empowered and powerful. Getting an education was something that mattered to me and no one else. I never remembered getting the talk from my parents about "the birds and the bees", nor why "getting an education" was so important to my future. Maybe school was just a way for me to rebel against the world. I thought, "No one is going to tell me what I can or cannot do, I will become whatever I put my mind to in this life". Four years after getting my BA and two children later, I had an identity crisis. I knew who I was as a young mother, a wife, a small business owner, a daughter, a sister,

a good friend, and so on. But who was I as a woman? What is my personal identity? I clearly remember the day that I thought I had lost myself forever. I was at the grocery store alone in the cereal aisle. Now, keep in mind that my two toddlers were two and four and both at preschool that day. There I am, all by myself, and I start humming a catchy tune. Then, I started singing to myself, and before I knew it, I was even doing a little dance to go along with it. What was the song you're probably asking? I grew up with amazing bands like The Rolling Stones, Beatles, Billy Joel, and Elton John. Nope, it was not a song by one of the greats. Have you ever sung a song that you just couldn't get out of your head? Why of all the places on all the days, when I was alone, why did this particular song pop into my mind? Now, I'll tell you, it was a catchy tune all right. I'm embarrassed to say, but it was something I grew up on when my young mind was at a critical developmental time. It was one of the theme songs to Sesame Street; I could tell you which one, but you know how the saying goes. It was right then and there that I knew without a doubt that I had truly lost my identity. Sometimes we need to lose ourselves before we can be found. I needed to find a way back to me, and quickly. But how? Buy a sportscar, get a tattoo, take up a crazy hobby? The answer was clear, me and my mushy toddler brain are going back to school; I applied for the Master of Business Administration program at a local California State University the very next day.

At 29 years of age at the time, I had the burning sensation in my belly that this was an opportunity for me to "Show Up" for myself. I immediately set up an appointment with the college Dean at the CSU and was prepared to turn in all of my necessary paperwork in order to officially sign up for the MBA program. The process was not easy by any means. But, at this point in my life, I was absolutely not going to take "NO" for an answer. This was something that my inner self was telling me was a "do or die" moment. I knew this wasn't going to be easy, but I was up for the challenge. Criteria

for this program was pretty serious: 2 letters of recommendation from prestigious people, 2 essays that thoroughly demonstrated your character, and a 3.5 GPA or better from your undergraduate degree. Fortunately, for me, I had all three in the bag, so to speak. Letters of recommendation from two local and successful doctors that knew me professionally; CHECK, two amazing essays that demonstrated my self-discipline; CHECK, and transcripts that showed I had a 3.8 GPA; CHECK and double CHECK. I was feeling confident that I would be accepted into the program; and remember, "NO" was not an option for me; I needed this opportunity to prove to myself that I could do whatever I set my mind to.

I handed my application to the Dean, and he immediately said without even looking at it, "Why should we allow you to come into this program?"

I responded without hesitation, "Because you need me more than I need you!" My justifiable passion behind this response, "I am here to better myself and am not waiting for nor expecting a promotion after I am done. You sir, need to represent the hard-working small businesses and entrepreneurs of our communities!"

He sighed, looked at me with a very strange gaze in his eyes, and said, "We will let you know."

My next three years would be anything but easy. Since I didn't minor in business, I needed 5 undergraduate courses in order to be officially inducted into the MBA program. It took me two semesters; keep in mind that I had two toddlers, and I was running my husband's granite slab business behind the scenes. During this time, the only classes that I needed in order to meet this undergraduate criterion and that made sense were taking night courses.

So, with my husband's support, I was away from the family two to three nights a week at night school. "What time do you need me to be home?" My husband would humbly ask, "By 5:00 pm dear?"

I would politely respond, "By 4:45pm." I would see his little white, beat up, flat-bead, 20-year-old Toyota work truck speeding up the driveway to relieve me of my mommy duties so I could put my "student" hat on for a few hours. Although my late husband wasn't much of a scholar, he never questioned my intentions and was always there to support me on my mission to complete a higher education; for that I am eternally grateful. Once the main part of the program began, I had two choices to complete the requirements in the two-year allotment: night school three days a week or all-day Saturday school with three, three hour classes back to back. I opted to take Saturday school as the best course of action---the least amount of time sitting in traffic and the least cumulative time away from my small family. These next two years were truly a test of how I was going to "Show Up" for myself and be there for my family.

Students in my university's cohort of 43 people came from a wide variety of backgrounds, but just as I had anticipated when I got a little sassy with the Dean, I was the only small business owner in the MBA program. They came from all over Corporate America! For example: we had a vice president of Wells Fargo Bank, a police sergeant, an engineer from the municipal water district, an engineer from Caterpillar Turbines, and a female engineer from Barona Casino. Everyone in my class was there because someone else was paying for them to achieve a higher education and receive advancement in their careers. I was so angry at them and so proud of myself at the same time. Who is looking out for the underdogs, the "Mom and Pop Shops", and the solo and entrepreneurs? We all deserve to have the same opportunities, and I questioned how we could be so out of balance in our educational system. However, I was determined to stay on course and complete what

my spirit, my soul, and my intuition had set out to do... get my master's degree. So, I kept "Showing Up" for myself and kept pushing forward.

On the day of my graduation(s), all my family came out proudly to cheer me on. But I often wondered, where were you when I was going through this entire process? Again, keep in mind, my parents never once encouraged me to go to college. I enrolled in junior college at 17 years of age and throughout the years never got any emotional nor financial support from my family. I was living on my own and financially on my own at 18, worked full-time and then began going to school full-time. So why ten years later would I expect things to be any different? My parents never paid for a single unit of school, a single textbook, nor even a parking pass. Is it possible to be resentful and grateful at the same time? I was so resentful towards my parents that just expected me to figure things out on my own, but I was so proud of myself for "Showing Up" and figuring things out on my own. Perhaps this was simply a blessing in disguise that would later help to shape my life's true core values and the trajectory of my future.

As planned, I received my Master's in Business Administration, with honors. My daughter was just about to start kindergarten and my son would begin second grade. I pondered what I would do after achieving my goal of getting an MBA. Join the masses in corporate America, start my own business, focus on being a mom? Why not have it all... with the exception of the corporate America part. I decided to start my own business. I immediately after graduation studied and received my Broker's license in real estate, my insurance license, and became a notary public. I was, a "One Stop Shop". I loved what I did and thoroughly enjoyed helping others, especially first-time home buyers. I learned a lot about several different financial industries and thought this is where I truly can relocate my self-identity. Little did I know that my maternal clock had other plans for my immediate future. I had leased an office for two years, only a couple of blocks

from my children's elementary school and could literally hear the bell when it was time to pick them up. However, when their little brother was on the way, I really needed to prioritize my life. With some resistance, I decided to focus on my growing family while growing my small financial business. Little did I know that God decided that my family of three children needed to be a family of four... twenty-three months after having our third, we were blessed with a fourth. I was so exceptionally grateful to be a mom, support my husband in our small granite slab business, but still found a way to "Show Up" and be there for myself.

Unfortunately, only two years after my youngest was born, my husband died suddenly in a very tragic accident. I wasn't sure how I could "Show Up" for myself, let alone anyone else. After spending a year in a complete state of nothingness, on autopilot, and utter numbness, I decided to get my contractor's license and become, "The Goddess of Granite." I continued my late husband's legacy as a granite slab contractor while continuing to build my financial advising business and raise our four small children. It wasn't easy all the time and it wasn't pretty most of the time. I was a woman doing a man's job in construction while being a woman in the financial world 90% dominated by men. The odds were stacked against me, but somehow, I just found the strength to push through, one day at a time. Needless to say, I excelled as a granite slab contractor, but that was my late husband's dream, not mine. My passion and purpose is to educate, empower, and encourage women to take control of their finances. Twelve years later, I am still here, "Showing Up" daily as a single mom. I "Show Up" at my boys' soccer and water polo games every week, I show up to support local fundraisers and charities every month, but I must always remind myself; show up for yourself daily because you are worth it, you matter, and your strength will inevitably help change the world.

I am extremely passionate about educating, empowering, & encouraging woman and their families to get their finances in order. I am a Comprehensive Financial Advisor offering a wide variety of services to meet all of your retirement planning needs. I take a 360° approach to looking at your current plan and determining where there may be gaps that need filling in or areas that require attention or improvement. There is no such thing as a "one size fits all" method when it comes to your financial future; every client gets a custom financial plan as well as a customized course of action. There are many cares and concerns that we will address, leaving you with a better overall understanding of where you are now and where to go from here which offers you a greater peace of mind.

My ultimate goal is to provide my clients with freedom from doubt, worries, and anxieties around all of their finances and their financial future.

WHY ME?? Because I've been there. I lost my husband tragically at a very young age and wasn't prepared. I'm a mom raising 4 children on my own and I get it. There are a lot of financial advisors giving you advice that sounds good to them, but many are looking out for their own skin. I am proud to say that being a Fiduciary for my clients allows me to serve them with utmost integrity and I always put the needs of my clients first. I little more about me: I also have an extensive real estate and construction background which gives me a very unique edge over my competition. I'm a numbers girl who knows how to get the job done, is passionate about people, leads from the heart, and always goes the extra mile to do the right thing for my clients.

WHAT'S NEXT? I'm creating three programs for financial literacy for young people. The first is for adolescence, the second is for teenagers, and finally a program for young adults. I believe it's important to learn the skills to pay the bills and save from a young age, and our school system simply hasn't

caught up yet to suit their educational needs. I'm also working on two books myself, one that's a quick guide to your finances and the other that dives deep into my personal story, triumph from tragedy. I was nominated by Dr. Robbie Motter to receive an honorary doctorate this summer which will be taking place in Atlanta, GA. Stay tuned, I'm really going places.

#Let'sTalk About It Foundation
Suku Moyo-Mackenzie

Suku is a survivor of child abuse and a fierce champion for raising awareness of its effects and mental health. She, unfortunately, never received any support or counselling and was hence diagnosed was PTSD as a result of the historical abuse. This led to Suku realizing that most people of ethnic minority go through abuse but don't report or speak out for fear of being shunned or silenced. The same is indeed true with Mental Health illness.

Suku was inspired to start groups to encourage people to speak out, and the response has been overwhelming. This led to the founding of Let's Talk About It: a platform which exists to support survivors of abuse and raise awareness to stump out stigma attached to both mental health and abuse. She has been to The House Commons to speak on Housing and Mental Health.

Suku self-funds any travelling she does to talk to groups and all events she runs. As a result of her passion and commitment, countless individuals are seeking support and finding freedom.

My foundation and pages Let's Talk About It are based on my life story.

As per the name, I felt led to encourage people to talk about matters that our society seems to avoid talking about but brushed under the carpet instead.

Growing up the name "sex" was a taboo. You wouldn't mention such and get away with it.

Which brings me to the reason why most and myself never reported any cases of sexual violence.

Raped at a young age as 12 in Africa by known relatives destroyed my life. It happened again in 15 years and when I was 16.yes, at 16 he was caught red-handed which is why it was reported to the police at last.

Abuse destroys lives.

From high school I chose to be there for other students not on sexual context but bullying. I became the "voice" and confronted the bullies, but I was still that broken girl hurting inside from abuse I never dared talk about. But still I had told myself when I grow up, I will make sure I talk about it and name them.

Also, I had this vision of helping other victims.

So, when I got to this country at age 24, I wanted to work and build a safe house back home to help others who were abused like me which by God's grace I managed to but still couldn't talk about it.

To cut a long story short when I decided to do a campaign/awareness on child sexual abuse, the person I trusted with my deep secret on abuse, who at that time had no clue was a journalist, decided to publish that on a Zimbabwean newspaper which then went viral on social media including Facebook.

That was painful, but instead I choose to turn it for good.

So, I told my story and the effects of abuse on the same platform I was judged and had all hurt full comments passed on.

From those videos people started to contact me and open up about the abuse they went through, and in turn I listened and advised them where to get help. This went on until I was invited on TV to tell my story and how my dream of being "the voice of the voiceless " was coming to pass.

I continued and never stopped. I even spoke about abuse and mental health at the House of Commons.

"The Test that changed to a testimony "

Now I am a founder of a registered foundation Let's Talk About It… self-funded but rendering my services for free.

I am also now a speaker invited to many places to talk about mental health. Abuse, and more.

Because It's a God appointed vision When I support others going through What I went through, God gives me strength to do so.

I am now working with the youth, too, to support and give them the voice.

The Journey wasn't easy, but I was called to serve.

My main reason for coming to the UK was to study nursing. However, it didn't happen as early as I thought. Caring for others was a calling for me, but my journey had its own problems.

After finally deciding to leave my marriage, I told my aunt about my wish to study nursing and how I needed to get away from all the abuse, and yes, she came through for me!

My aunt just sent me an invitation letter from Birmingham.

I was excited and without thinking twice I took my proceeds from the selling of our house with my ex-husband and started the preparations. I

remember my mother being worried about me travelling alone, but I was on a mission. It turns out one of the neighbors and colleague of hers was planning the same journey so now I wasn't going to travel alone after all. The lady told me to go through the South African airport. I would need to have Rands worth a thousand pounds with me so she arranged to go days before me to secure the Rands, and we would meet there to board so obviously I gave her the money.

It turns out the woman didn't even have any and had planned to scam me and travel without me! Remember we had already gotten the tickets and everything ready so on the day when I tried to call her, she ignored and switched off her phone.

"Determination!" Considering I was on a mission, I just told myself I wouldn't give up and would continue with the journey so at the airport I just produced the invitation letter and because God was with me, they didn't even ask for proof of funds but just allowed me to go through even wishing me a safe journey. Meanwhile the woman was already seated in the plane with my seat next to her vacant so you can imagine the shock when she saw me come in to sit next to her .The whole journey she was telling me how embarrassed she was and asking for forgiveness as much as I had already told her, I forgave her, and we just needed to continue with the journey.

I showed up!

When we arrived at the Birmingham Airport, I was a bit anxious on what to expect, but once again everything went smoothly. I even handed the authorities the letter without them asking.

As per instruction I got a taxi to my aunt's, and that evening I prayed and thanked God for his love.

I was finally here and was on a mission. I never worked from the time I got married at 21. I was just a housewife as instructed. Now, I was ready to follow my dreams and sent in my nursing application.

My first job was a cleaner at a disability center for 3 hours. I was on a mission. I wasn't going to start choosing no matter my qualifications, and as in every task I gave it my all. Little did I know that from thar agency job I would unlock another step to my mission. The manager at that place had a child with autism, and sometimes they would drop him off just before we left so I used to wave and greet him so as days went by the woman said, "Sue, I love your character, and it seems you have an admirer, too" meaning her son. As you have it from just a wave now the boy was looking forward to seeing me, and we would both have a few minutes of laughter together. That's my character. The manager invited me to one of the fundraising events they had for the center, and when I SHOWED UP, he introduced me to a man who had a care agency, and they both felt I was more suited in the care field and invited me to meet him the next Monday. That was the beginning of my long-awaited job/calling in the health field. I worked with the elderly attended training and started working as a support worker with people living with learning disability. I loved and enjoyed the job because to me care was not just a job but a calling the same as nursing. Granted I wasn't close on building that safe house, but I was making donations every month without fail and meanwhile doing voluntary work at a youth center and working with the youth at the church which means I shared and raised awareness the same way I would do at the safe house. Basically, as time went on, I was the "go to auntie" when the youth needed advice.

In 2004, I got admission at JMU University for mental health nursing! I was over the moon finally things were coming together.

I put my all in and at every placement I had glowing compliments when the time ended. I remember in my second year; my placement was at a residential nursing home. This lovely elderly client refused to have anyone help her until I resumed, and the saddest part was on the last day of placement she put some clothes on her handbag and waited at the gate saying she's leaving with me. Leaving her behind broke my heart.

Unfortunately, on my third year 2007, I had a breakdown. I had not dealt with my traumas of gang rape and many others but was already struggling with PTSD "Post traumatic stress disorder " so working with and assessing people who were going through what I went through took its toll, and the PTSD got worse, and I eventually had a breakdown and got admitted.

As hard as that was, it was a blessing in disguise because that's when I started to get help and address the trauma. The Road to recovery was not easy, but God and my family supported me through it in as much as I pushed them away, especially now that I had to take a break from my course.

Fast forward I started making and sharing awareness videos on abuse more but still didn't want to talk much about the gang rape even with the counsellor.

And yes, many started calling me for advice even when I was still on my road to recovery.

It turns out due to pressure and focusing on others more than myself was another trigger.

I started getting severe physical pain, I couldn't stand for long, got headaches, had tingling and needle pain on my hands, and more now. I was struggling to even do personal care. After a while I was diagnosed with fibromyalgia which they call chronic pain; it has no cure.

Now statistics say it might be caused by childhood trauma.

I got angry, I was angry with the world, my abusers, my parents for not protecting me, and even God for allowing such to happen.

With time I accepted my fate, but that would be after going back to finish my course after 3 years, but of course things were never the same. I now had an open wound after speaking out about the trauma, and my placement was at a crisis team which is the depth of them all and in addition unwell physical relying on strong medication.

Unfortunately, that triggered the complex PTSD, and one night after one of the episodes I decided I didn't want to live anymore so I tried to end my life.

The next morning when I woke up to a doctor saying you are lucky; they found you in time or you wouldn't have made it, but please speak to someone. The look on my girls beside my bed and message from my son was an eye opener after realizing how I had hurt the people I loved.

That was my new chapter and second chance where I decided to do things differently!

I am very excited to see where GOD leads me. I am looking forward to the prosperity of my foundation and the lives it will help.

Showing up can enhance your life with the dynamic people you meet.

Prof. Dr. Caroline Makaka

Three years ago, I met one of the most beautiful women who has touched so many lives all over the world. Her name is Dr. Caroline Makaka, the founder of LOANI (Ladies of all nations international). I want to dedicate this page to her and all the work she does to make a difference in the world. She works tirelessly to help women of all ages and all nationalities and in all points of their lives to become stronger and to reach out and go for their dreams. She has one of the most positive attitudes no matter what of any person that I have met in my life. She is always there for everyone, and that is thousands of women days or night. She is the SHOW UP Queen for all and has opened many international doors for many of our GSFE members. She introduced me to Lady Dr. Lenora Peterson which offered me the opportunity in April 2021, to receive my Honorary Humanitarian Doctorate degree and last year presented me in London with a Lady title. The introduction to Lady Dr. Peterson also opened the door for me to nominate GSFE members for this Honorary degree and 26 received theirs in 2021 in London; 41 will be going to Atlanta in 2022 to receive theirs. She shows up all over the world touching lives and making the world a better place. She was instrumental in helping us start a London GSFE (Global Society for Female Entrepreneurs) network in London.

Below are just a few of her accomplishments. We at GSFE are honored to know this dynamic woman who gives from her heart to everyone and works tirelessly to make the world a better place. She shows up in every country and touches thousands of lives every day. She certainly has touched my life. We are dedicating this page to this beautiful individual.

Dr. Caroline Makaka, President /CEO of LOANI - Ladies of All Nations, International & Creator of We Are the Change World Movement, was just recently selected as Top Global Chairperson of the Year by the International Association of Top Professionals (IAOTP) for her outstanding leadership and contribution to her industry. The organization she founded and is CEO of LOANI which operates worldwide chiefly to bring in together different nationalities with a mission of connecting various cultures and the uniting together of Nations around the World. Every language, every tribe, every clan, every culture, all diversities, and every individual coming together to help, educate and support each other. LOANI also honors and celebrates survivors as heroines and empowers them to move out of the positions of victims. It is also dedicated to Empower the younger generation by giving them the tools and adequately equipping them with resources to become leaders of tomorrow. LOANI is comprised of Beautiful Survivors, Galaxy of Stars, LOANI Spirit of sisterhood, International Sisterhood of Strength, Men's Movement, and LOANI Global Book Club.

Dr. Caroline is a Global Goodwill Ambassador, International Human Rights and Traffic Control Global Ambassador, The International Chairperson of The Global International Alliance based in USA. Dr. Caroline is also an International Advisor for International Youth Society, philanthropist, a community leader, an advisory board member for several organizations and Academies around the world, World Peace Ambassador, Global Change Maker, Chief operating officer of Women Changing the World and Diversity and Inclusion Ambassador.

She has also been selected as a recipient of Global dreams and making a change special award. Dr. Caroline Makaka has been selected as one of the top 50 most inspirational black women in the United Kingdom and received a special recognition for Global Leadership of Humanity for Uplifting the Underprivileged and Empowering Survivors. She was also selected as the Finalist for the Female Civility Award and inducted in The Global Library of Female Authors. During the pandemic she was selected as one of the recipients to receive a special recognition towards the contribution of the world development and raising awareness. Some of the few Awards she has received in recognition of her work include: Philanthropist Award by Waterfront Awards in Canada, Women of Excellence Award at the House of Parliament in the UK , 100 Successful Woman in Business in USA, Inspiring Indian Women Special Recognition Award at The House of Parliament for supporting the Indian communities across the globe, Dr. Sarvepalli Radhakrishnan Award of Honour by Mentorx Global Women Who Care Award in Malaysia, MTM special recognition Award and also the Global Iconic Women Creating a better world for All. Dr. Caroline Makaka is also the Editor in Chief and Founder of LOANI International Magazine and Founded Worldwide leaders Association.

We send her love. Anyone that has the opportunity to meet this caring and dynamic woman is very lucky as she is a rare, beautiful jewel with a magnificent heart and soul. Thank you, Dr. Caroline Makaka for being in my life and the lives of everyone you touch.

Show Up!

Dr. (h.c.) Kara Lynne Maldonado

Showing up is essential to achieving your goals and leading a successful life. When you show up, it demonstrates that you care about yourself, your work, and your relationships. It sets you up for success and helps you to stay motivated. Showing up regularly helps to build trust, as it shows that you can be counted on and that you're reliable. It also helps to create strong relationships and build strong networks.

When Covid shut the world down in March of 2020, I decided to Show up for my clients by learning how to Pivot. I closed my two clinic locations so that I could reopen in my new residence. Prior to Covid, I lived in Ladera Ranch. I had been in business for nearly two years with one clinic in Laguna Niguel, South Orange County, CA and a newly opened location in San Clemente, CA, also in South Orange County, CA. The thought of not being able to serve my clients was not an option for me.

When the CDC, local and state officials told us to work from home and use Zoom to hold meetings, networking, etc. That suggestion was not going to work for me. The problem was that I needed to touch my clients with my "Magic Wand." Cryo-cell therapy is a technique that I use to assist in permanent fat removal, lymphatic drainage, rebuilding muscle and cell regeneration. I am the Founder-CEO of the Real Bodies Period, and an expert in pain management and holistic weight loss. I developed an effective, comprehensive approach to attaining maximum health and strength.

Because I can relate to the feeling of despair. I used to be right there. I took care of everybody else but me. By everybody else, I mean, my boss, my customers, my family, and my friends. By the time I married the father of my children, I had no idea who I was. I lacked self-worth, no Purpose other than the one my mother and siblings made for me. All I knew was I wanted to be loved and I wanted the pain to stop, so I married what was familiar! I married a Narcissist because to me that was love! I stayed in a toxic marriage for over 17 years until I could not hide from the humility any longer.

My life changed when I lost my sister to cancer. I was very close to her and took care of her when she came down with the cancer that killed her. I lost my grandmother who raised me a few months later. My biological mother passed away 2 years later. I had a tough time dealing with losing them, and I made a life changing decision at that time. I decided to leave my successful 27-year career in senior-level management of commercial/residential property development and started my own business.

You cannot even imagine how vulnerable I was. I found myself in my second toxic relationship with a charismatic and handsome man. I fell in love with him and believed that he loved me too. When he continued to hurt me emotionally and physically year after year, I made excuses for it and blamed myself. But I asked myself why did you stay in that relationship? I won't make excuses or sugar coat things like I used to. The truth is I didn't have self-worth. I didn't have self-worth because I was never taught to have self-worth. How many of us were taught how to love ourselves when we were little girls? I know my birth mom taught me to do as she said and not as she

did! The result is you lack self-love and courage!

After Five years in this extremely unhealthy relationship, I found out that I came down with cancer, then lupus, and fibromyalgia, all diseases that are caused primarily by stress. It is true that most autoimmune diseases are caused by prolonged high levels of stress. In my case, the stress was from enduring the emotional and physical abuse from the man who was supposed to love me and protect me. I found myself in financial ruin, he was physically violent with me, and caused legal issues that could have damaged my career. This relationship nearly destroyed my relationship between my children and me. His abuse and the mind games got so bad that I wished he would just leave me to die in peace. Instead, he kept me emotionally chained in his need to control and make my life even more miserable.

I know all too well how it feels to be physically and mentally unhealthy, alone and afraid! When I started chemo treatments because my body stopped producing red blood cells, I found myself completely lost! Now, I needed to be cared for by not only the 5 medical specialists, but my baby girl, only 25 years old at the time.

Now, telling you about my past is not easy for me. In fact, it is very painful to have to relive that part of my life, but I share my story because the more I share, the more I heal and in turn I help others find their voice and eventually heal. I blamed myself for others' bad behavior and felt like such a failure; I continued to attract the same types of personalities in friends and romantic relationships.

During that time, the only good news I found out was that my middle son was expecting a baby boy. You know I did not realize how hopeless my life had become until I realized that if I did not get well, I was not going to be here to meet my grandson. I wanted to live. I wanted to see my grandson and the route I was going I would not get to. I started seeking help from

therapists and medical specialists. All of which were so conceptual. I felt as if I was in a scripted interview at every appointment. Some of them simply wanted to put me on a whole bunch of prescription medications instead of getting to the root of my problems. So, I started searching for holistic modalities to help me get my life back. I came across cryo-cell therapy. Once I healed myself physically, I decided to Show up for myself and I began my journey to self-empowerment, starting with my Self-worth.

I welcomed my little grandson into the family and by changing lives internal and external through sharing my story, cryo-cell therapy, and transformational coaching. Today, I have been in remission and drug-free for over three years. I am healthier now in my 50's than I was in my 40's and my 30's. Now, my Mission is to help all women live to their maximum potential. I don't want to be redundant, but I believe that your view of your self-worth is going to determine your Net-worth!

I don't intend for this story to be a pity party for me. I am giving you background to help understand why I am so passionate about Showing Up! I can relate to the individuals that I help, especially women and children who have been subjected to domestic violence, both physical and emotional. Stress causes illnesses! When stress is ongoing and chronic, it can lead to stress-related illness. This has to do with the ongoing "fight-flight-freeze" response during stress. This leads to changes in hormones as well as changes in the brain. This is why I left my toxic relationships, including my over 30-year successful corporate career to become an entrepreneur so I can choose to help those who don't have the tools to help themselves.

The decision to Show up was easy for me. While the world was frozen with fear, I decided to take a leap of Faith! I wrote a quick business plan, which consisted of downsizing by permanently closing both clinic locations, moving my home centrally to better serve my clients. Since I had several seniors suffering from chronic illnesses which affected their Immune system, I moved to Laguna Niguel, South County, CA. I thought the move will make it convenient for my clients who were used to coming to my location in Laguna Niguel. Every decision I made was strategically thought out to ensure that I could still serve my clients and bring awareness about immune- health to everyone suffering through the pandemic.

I found an overpriced renovated condo with easy access and enough space to set up a spa-like setting. I negotiated a lower lease-term using the skills that I learned in my Sales and Business Development career. I converted half of my condo, so that I could continue to serve individuals in their body, mind, and soul transformations.

Many of my so-called colleagues, family, and friends said that I was out of my mind to risk my savings and to expect people to come into my home for such intimate services. People were so disturbed that I kept pushing forward that I was reported to the city for operating during Covid. I received a letter from the city of Laguna Niguel requesting information on my business, Real Bodies Period LLC. Once I showed them that my services help individuals permanently remove fat cells by releasing the toxic cells through the lymphatic system. We couple it with the Sea of Youth, Sea Moss Supplements which help rebuild and sustain your immune system. The City of Laguna Niguel deemed me an essential business. Next, I prayed that clients would come and trust the process.

I chose to step out on Faith, and I announced on social media that on July 1st, 2020, I was opening my doors to offer Immune System treatments, supplements, and transformational mindset coaching for those struggling with depression, anxiety and self-worth issues. I held my breath waiting to see if anyone would schedule an appointment during one of the worst pandemics in the history of the world. And boy did they come!

The Universe blessed me with 90% of my clients who returned to me through the pandemic and my referrals increased by 60% from word-of-mouth. I closed 2020 year-end, in the high six figures after only 5 months operating. Because my current clients chose to Show up, their referrals more than doubled my clientele. Not only do I know how to Pivot when obstacles get in my way, but my services helped maximize the overall physical, emotional, and spiritual wellbeing of many individuals not only in Orange County, but in Los Angeles County, Inland Empire, and San Diego County.

By choosing to Show up, I demonstrate courage and strength. It takes courage to put yourself out there and take risks, but it's also important to remember to be kind and gracious. Showing up with positivity, empathy, and understanding can create a more inclusive and supportive environment for everyone. I know that this is who I am. And that's why my clients trust me and support me and my business still to this day.

At my business, I Show up for individuals every day. I believe in the power of community and collaboration and strive to provide support, encouragement, and resources to help our individuals reach their goals. I am here to listen when they need advice, and to celebrate their successes. I strive to create an inclusive environment that fosters growth and development. When my clients, colleagues, and sisters show up, I show up right alongside them.

"Ultimately, showing up is about believing in yourself, having faith, and pushing yourself to do better. It's about not giving up and continuing to work hard towards your goals, no matter how difficult it might seem. Showing up is an important part of success and an essential part of living a meaningful and fulfilling life."

- Dr. Kara Lynne Maldonado

It's all
About
Showing
Up

Show up, even when life gives you lemons!

Lisa Mayer

My name is Lisa Mayer, my husband of 42 years and I relocated in 2018 from Newport Beach to a beautiful property in Fallbrook, CA. This property was also the home of a somewhat neglected Eureka Lemon Orchard. We will get back to that later. We lived in Newport Beach for 40 years. To say we were established would be an understatement. When we moved, of course, I missed my friends and family, but I tried to be open to new possibilities. When we lived in Orange County, I owned and operated a very successful Sewing School for Kids and Adults for 27 years. My husband was an elite Plumbing Contractor, which means he only worked on multi-million-dollar homes, of which there are many in Newport Beach. You would not hire just anyone to install your $2000.00 dollar faucet.

When we retired, we wanted to do something different but still creative. My sister told me about these cool people that were Painting silk scarves at the street fair the pier in Huntington Beach. My hubby and I went to visit to see what they were up to. Well, we were captivated and decided to take an extensive 80-hour workshop to learn the art of Turkish Marbling on 100% silk. We immediately started to do street fairs and farmers markets teaching people to paint on silk. Our workshops were very well received; however, both my husband and I found it very tiring, standing all day.

Then something happened, our magical moment. A friend of ours, who happens to be a framer, said to us, "Their silks are so beautiful; they should be hanging on a wall". So, we said let's give a whirl. The end product was amazing. My husband, Richard, who is a true engineer at heart designed a very large stainless-steel tray for us to create our artwork. Now we were able to paint very large pieces. Most of our work is approximately 3 x 5 ft., and they are then stretched on to canvas and are ready to hang and enjoy. At the present time, we have our own Gallery and are featured in several other galleries in San Diego and Orange County. We even have some Collectors. Again, another case of showing up. We showed up, out of curiosity, and ended up turning it into an art business. Listen to Lady Robbie Motter, Ladies. Just keep showing up!

The next part of my story is about taking a leap of faith. Our Art business is called Newport Art because we started it in Newport Beach. We were invited to come to an art show in Pauma Valley Country Club. I said to my friend that had invited us, "It is a long drive for us, would it be worth our while?". She assured me that it was a really great show and that we should definitely go participate. When we drove into Pauma Valley Country Club, we were amazed at how beautiful it was. If you have not been there, you should definitely check it out. It is said that Billy Graham was asked what he thought heaven looked like, and he said I hope it looks like Pauma Valley Country Club. The next week we were looking at property there. You see, even though I was as snug as a bug in a rug, my sweet husband really wanted to move to some place where he could have some land. That was not going to happen in Orange County, so we started looking in San Diego County. First in Pauma Valley, then in Valley Center. Our wise Realtor said if you let me show you Fallbrook, I think we can find what you are looking for. After looking at approximately 40 houses, we finally settled on a beautiful Property with a slightly sad Lemon Orchard. We moved in June 2018, and

Rick started to lovingly care for the Orchard. It is Amazing what water and fish oil will do. I don't think that I was really paying that much attention until we realized that we had brought it back to life. When Covid hit, our Art Business took a hit and went into a holding pattern. Even though we still had the Galleries, there were not many sales.

This next chapter of our lives began. We can call this one when Life gives you Lemons. We were in the middle of Covid lockdown with approximately 20 thousand Lemons in our Orchard. Not just any Lemons, we have completely organic Eureka Lemons, which are in my opinion, the best. I started searching the internet for lemon recipes. Rick started making everything Lemon. He made Lemon Jam, which is amazing. The reason you never see it for sale is that it is very labor intensive. Then we started to do flavor pairings. He made Lemon Ginger Jam and Orange Cardamon Jam which were so good. He did not want to share them with anyone and keep them all to himself. He made Lemon Ginger Syrup, and last but not least, our beautiful Lemon Sugar face and body polish. This exfoliating face and body scrub is made from all natural ingredients and comes in six different scents: The Citrus Group- Lemon, Grapefruit, Mint. The floral group- Gardenia, Jasmine, and Lavender. I spent hours researching the best and purest organic essential oils to enhance the experience of these wonderful scrubs. the Sugar Scrubs were very popular; however, Rick was getting restless to try something new. Rick started making Limoncello which if you don't know is a Lemon Liquor made from Lemon infused Vodka. After experimenting with every recipe out there, it looked like every Italian Celebrity had a recipe, and we tried them all. Rick is very specific about everything that he does, so we started buying every Limoncello available in the marketplace. Our daughter went to Italy and brought back Limoncello from the Amalfi Coast, which is where Limoncello originated, or so the rumor has it. I hate to brag, but none of them were as good as our Limoncello. The differences were unbelievable;

all the other ones that we tasted were super heavy on the alcohol taste. Because of the technique that Rick uses to make the Limoncello, our first flavor note is Lemon, not Vodka. This quality makes our Limoncello extremely enjoyable to drink. The Limoncello has become our signature product. Because I have trouble with sugar, I discovered a company that makes fermented sugar, which has no calories and no carbohydrates. There it was, Sugar free Limoncello. We started to taste test with friends and family, and it was a big hit. One Sunday morning, as I am pouring some of our lemon syrup, which we had put sparkle dust in to make it interesting, I had a thought. What would happen if we put the sparkle dust into our Limoncello? Well, that was the secret sauce. All of a sudden, we started selling Limoncello like crazy. Rick handles product development and I handle the sales and marketing.

At this time, we are applying for our state and federal licensing. We are creating our website. We are on our way to our new adventure.

Now that you have heard our story, my story. Don't be afraid to take a leap of faith, keep showing up, and be open to new ideas, and, of course, when life gives you, lemons make Limoncello!

In closing, just a few bits of wisdom.

Keep in mind that most small tragedies turn into a funny story later.

"When someone shows you who they are you can believe them" Maya Angelou

And last but not least, the sign I saw in a cute restaurant, "Everything's gonna be alright."

It's all
About
Showing
Up

What does it mean to show up for life?

Nicole Wild Merl

My name is Nicole Wild Merl, a native Australian. I have lived overseas since 1996. Currently, I am on move #6 and living in Atlanta with my husband, daughter, and our Vizsla dog, Oscar. I am inspired to share this story of showing up with a heart-filled with gratitude for all the women (people) in my life, who despite life's trials, intentionally understand that "showing up for life means showing up for other people, and showing up for people helps us show up for life." To add some context, I come from rural Australia, the bush, and a small country town with heart, and at the same time a place where life challenges you from many perspectives and you learn adapt early on and to make the best of things. I was a shy bi-racial kid (half-Australian, half-Singaporean Chinese), outwardly confident, and yet, inwardly, I hid my pain tightly inside my chest as I struggled to fit in and find my way in life. My early childhood friends, Michelle Labahn and then Shelley Parker Griffith were my lifelines. I was deeply influenced by my beautiful mother and my charismatic and fearless father, ordinary people who were extraordinary, and the strong women in my life, many who struggled through the pain of loss, divorce, health concerns, economic and societal constraints and moreover lack of opportunities to advance and succeed with limited employment opportunities. However, as this

life's lessons go, they garnered respect as they were respectful and their accomplishments in life reflect this simple truth—they showed up and they were unconditional.

As a direct result of my early experiences and from those living around the world, I was instilled with a deep passion for service. From my time representing, my employer, ANZ Banking Group, in the Miss Australia Awards on the Gold Coast Australia (move #2), I was determined that no matter where I lived in the world I would always show up and make a difference. Upon landing in Miami Beach (move #3) in the late 1990's, I found my way to a grassroots nonprofit, Suited for Success co-founded by Sonia Jacobson and the late, Barbara Tifford. As the saying goes, "opposites attract" and these two remarkable women showed up to help women in need with business clothing for job interviews and workforce training. I was their first employee as Director of Special Events, and I was in awe of them both; they were stunning, perfectly groomed and with strong voices about everything, and it was my first understanding of how showing up helps us connect the dots in our own lives. It was then I met my lifelong friend, Robin Jackson, who was the then Board President, and who is unprecedented and always very close in my life as a sister and mentor. Being in the presence of empowered women is empowering; they are always in the moment, present, and ready for the "ask." Interestingly, as a passion driven fundraiser, I was never afraid to get in front of people to request charitable and philanthropic support (or anything) despite my fast-talking Australian accent and somewhat then limited experience. It allowed me to feel useful and know that I was making a difference. I was on my path. However, as a self-described introvert trained to be an extrovert, when it came to ask for myself, I was sometimes tongue tied and nervous, and this is still true today. So, as I am writing this submission, I decided to push through this feeling, and reached out to Sonia Jacobson

for a personal quote, and just as the power is in the asking teaches us, she just provided. "Nicole never takes no for an answer, incredible fundraiser, charming, magnetic and irresistible...a secret weapon for those that know her!" WOW, thank you, Sonia. When Suited for Success was a start-up, we had to be creative to get people to pay attention to us and our work. I remember when the nonprofit was selected as an opening charity for the opening of Bloomingdale's in Aventura and we needed a catch, Sonia said "We need a Harley-Davidson", and I prayed for the universe to deliver. Sure enough, Linda Peterson, Peterson's Harley-Davidson South and advocate was in my networking group "Women of Worth", and we had the right connection and sister help us get the Harley. As always, we needed money though, so I decided to write to Bill and Melinda Gates to see if they would consider co-chairing the event and ride in with the famed Harley-Davidson Drill Team parade. I am sure everyone thought I was "wild" except Sonia. Anyway, a week or two later I received the customary letter from the Gates' declining the invitation; however, another couple of weeks later I received a call from Microsoft Atlanta saying it was going to donate and be a major sponsor. Again, if I did not ask, this miracle would never have happened. It goes without saying, when Chuck Porter, Crispin Porter + Bogusky came on board as our ad partner, our fundraiser "Rebel for a Cause" was a huge success. I showed up to meet him on my wedding day!

As I further reflect, it was more than twenty years ago when I was put in the path of dynamic women leaders like Carol Evans, Subha Barry, Dr. Betty Spence, and Edie Fraser who were leading advancement and diversity initiatives in the United States and globally, and as I showed up at conferences and events, I was then afforded the opportunity to host silent auctions at all the major events and conferences for Working Mother Media (now Seramount) in my next role as Executive Director for The Women's Alliance, a national grassroots charity empowering women.

Then one day in New York at a women's conference, I met our now Lady Robbie Motter, and I felt that despite my progress to-date in life, I was only showing up part-time. So, it was in that moment, when I was put in the path of Sister Jeanne O'Laughlan of Barry University, I made the decision to close-the-gap and finish my bachelor's degree, which I accomplished. This moment ignited my passion for life-long learning. At the right time, synchronicity led me to Jody Rowe Staley, who was the then President of the Women's Chamber of Commerce of Miami-Dade County, and I found an incredibly gifted ordained minister and spiritual teacher to help me work on strengthening from the inside out. Continuously, I became aware of how we truly can be of service to ourselves and others, how to tap into and follow my intuitive guidance, and how to speak the unspoken and have a stronger voice as I worked to follow the stepping-stones of my life. It was an incredible time that brought forth my passion project all those years ago and opened my healing path. More to come on this later! Again, quoting our Lady Robbie Motter, she asks "What is your gift from God? Success doesn't come overnight, but you've worked hard to get where you are now. God has equipped you with the essential tools to achieve anything." I am adding, but you have to do the work and listen, and you need allies. Here, I want to mention the incredible leadership of Lisa Woll and Sheri Cole, past presidents of The Women's Alliance, two very different leaders dedicated to change and making the world a better place. Dynamic communications executive, author and speaker, Candace Sandy, showed up in my life early on during move #3 in Miami and is an inspiration, trusted advisor and is always showing up and delivering social impact and making a difference. It would not be right not to introduce Thomas Cook. We met at the offices of Susan Davis International, our PR firm for The Women's Alliance, and she pointed out the importance of men as allies to bring high level introductions, expertise, and resources to your cause and projects.

Moreover, profoundly showing up and speaking up are "two-birds with one stone" when I met Betty Baraud on the way to the Cayman Islands to find a place to live (move #3). I was sitting right opposite Betty in airport lounge. I had goose bumps, and I knew I had to meet her, and it took my daughter Izzy's ball to roll over to her for me to speak up. So, I said "You know what a French chef looks like?"

She looked at me with a big smile and said, "My ex-husband was a French chef...."

You see my husband had called me earlier and said to look out for the chef and his family on the same flight coming in for an interview. It was uncanny. Betty said to me "When you come to the island, find me. My name is Betty." From there on out I served with her on the Cayman Islands Olympic Fundraising Committee where we hosted many fundraising and community outreach events to support Caymanian athletes on the world stage, a special event to celebrate the 100-year anniversary of International Women's Day and participated in hosting the Guinness World Record for the World's Largest Bikini and Swim Wear Parades, and many more. We had so much fun being on purpose we opened our own boutique PR firm, Baraud and Wild, to formalize our mission. Later, I was one of Betty's honored guests at Buckingham Palace when she received her 'Most Excellent Order of the British Empire for community services to the Cayman Islands." While we live far from each other, we were still as close as ever.

Then the time came for the next move, Miami Beach return (move #4), and I was truly in the land of working motherhood. My husband was on the opening team of a major luxury hotel and post my experiences in the Cayman Islands and my early understanding of economics, I sought a different career and became the Brand Ambassador for Jimmy Choo USA at Saks Fifth Avenue, Bal Harbour. I was understanding luxury sales and how to navigate a high-level sales floor took showing up to a whole new level. I learned to put my "ducks in a row" before asking for anything and how to win. I nearly quit at least three times (and I am no-quitter) as I struggled to manage work life. If it was not for my husband and my dear mom's friend Shannon Rayman (of course Robin) and colleague Barbara Goldenberg, I don't think I would have made it. In the end, my experience in luxury retail sales was one of my most valuable as I learned to work in a very diverse and complex environment and win by being humble, kind, and continuously showing up.

When the day came for the next move, it was to Charlotte, NC, and we packed up and moved up to the south (move #5). Now, I knew this would be a big change. However, I underestimated how much of one. If I hadn't showed up at the pool in the first week and met my dear friend, Elizabeth Tanos-Priest, at her table on the rooftop, I am sure the outcome of this experience would have been much different. I write this with a very heavy heart as most recently we lost Elizabeth way too soon; she was one the most humble, smart, giving, and loyal women I have ever met. One of the first female Certified Financial Planners in the United States and Villanova alumna, she and I were fast friends. She showed me the ropes in Charlotte and introduced me to her tight community of Greek girlfriends led by Christina Melissaris, and we shared everything together (and with Patty Rainey). When it came time for me to tackle my master's degree at Northeastern in Communications, she was a constant mentor and supporter. A passionate writer herself, I am praying for her guidance in this moment, so I get this message across correctly. So here I go. She was saying "Life is too short to live in the shadows. You never know which day will be your last." Elizabeth spent her free time on a passion project to honor the legacy of her father, the late Mr. James D. Tanos, whose contributions as a Greek American were many and especially in support of youth leadership. I

remember going to Centennial Olympic Park in downtown Atlanta to find the engraved brick she adopted in his name. She was behind the scenes and very well connected and showed up "over and above the call of duty" for her clients, friends, and family, and in a life that was taken away so suddenly, she represents the very best of humankind. Her legacy is now with her twin sister, Ellaina D. Tanos and her aunt, Ms. Alexandra Papadopoulou, Her Excellency-the Ambassador from Greece to the United States. RIP "E" you will be very much missed. Memory eternal!

So, now we are back to move #6, and in Atlanta for the foreseeable future. Previously, I had hosted a conference for The Women's Alliance many years ago in the city, and I knew it was sprawling and diverse even then, and I wondered how I would fit in in this metropolis. With all these moves it takes time to get settled with work, school for our daughter, and life. Immediately, as a first step, when the Global Society for Female Entrepreneurs was formed, I joined to support Lady Robbie Motter and join the incredible "sisters" in this global network as a sharing of support and to keep connected. Personally, Atlanta was a challenge early on. I just didn't feel a sense of belonging. I was trying to contemplate my next career move and for the first time, really unsure of my next steps. Then my daughter's soccer dreams were put on hold with a knee injury, and so I consulted for nonprofits and startups, worked from home, and showed up for my daughter. I had to dig deep to find my next move and one that I could manage as a working mother. During the pandemic I set my goal on getting my real estate license, and now I am a Forever agent with Berkshire Hathaway Georgia Properties, Buckhead Atlanta office. As I completed the onboarding and wonderful training programs and from lessons learned from past experiences, I immediately set my sights on finding a mentor. I kept showing up and showing up, and then one day this wonderful gentleman, Harrison Rogers with a legacy in real estate and founding member of our

company came up to me and asked me to help him sell his home. I could not have asked for a better partner to learn this business from along with an incredible broker, Bill Murray, and a dedicated team. Moreover, I also want to point out as I kept putting myself out there and not feeling as if I really fit, I took a look around and realized other people were most likely doing the same. Why is that? I had always been able to find my next move before, and all I could feel was limitation. I was stuck. I really missed seeing my friends in person and having that connection in Atlanta, and then, Julie Moran, who I was thankfully introduced to by Thomas Cook because of her work empowering women, came into my life and a "Birthday Club" of other incredible women: Mary Blackmon, a serial entrepreneur and devoted to helping people LiveGrounded.com with wellness travel experiences and Alina Rierson, a mom of two beautiful children pioneering in the world of finance and technology. We meet up on each other's birthdays at Le Bilboquet to share and celebrate each other (Mary's idea). Always an admirer, I think I first really truly connected with Julie and her voice when I heard her speak at the most recent Coca-Cola Women's Summit and heard her keynote "You can have it all, just not all at the same time" and I realized the truth in those words. Julie had shown up in her career as the first female sportscaster on Wide World of Sports and co-host of Entertainment Tonight and then she wanted to become a mom. This came with many challenges which I will leave for her to share when you hear to her speak. However, then when she became a mom, she left Hollywood with her husband and moved back to Georgia, so her children could be raised in the south. Her story and faith not only resonated with me; she had an entire audience of women on their feet (including me). I was so honored to be in that room with her daughter and Alina (Mary was traveling somewhere fabulous). In writing this piece, what I realize is that while I was showing up and showing up. I was really not sharing and asking for the right things and being true to myself. From here on out to restate if "showing up for life

means showing up for other people, and showing up for people helps us show up for life", I am continuing on this path AND now it is time to show up for myself and share my sacred story and book that has been sitting in a box for more than 20 years. As I show up, I am asking for support from my sisters in the Global Society for Female Entrepreneurs and my "Birthday Club". I understand it's a two-way street. If anyone needs real estate in Atlanta (or anything else), please give me a ring...

No Matter What Happens, "Just Show Up"

Dr. (h.c.) Susie Mierzwik

Was there ever a time when your life course changed? I found that life can change on a dime. Just show up and see what opportunity awaits!!

It was my last week of my junior year in college at Chico State in northern California. I didn't have a date that Saturday night, so I decided to attend Church service.

It was held at the Newman student center on campus. As I entered the building and passed by the office, the girl sitting there asked me if I would watch the phones while she quickly took her dog for a short walk. I said, "yes", and minutes later, a tall good-looking guy entered the office. I found myself engaged in a conversation that quickly led to a first date. One week later, I confided in my roommate, "It seems hard to believe, but I just met the guy I'm going to marry!!" There was something magical about the way we quickly connected that later proved to be true. Two years later we walked down the aisle, and I began my life as a Navy wife.

The next year I was looking for a teaching job. It was the last week of August, and I hadn't gotten hired yet by any school district.

I decided to take matters into my own hands. So, I drove to the school where I was most interested in working and parked my car. I came armed with four trusty props; a spelling book, a dictionary, a pencil, and a pair of glasses so I would look like a teacher! I strode boldly into the front office and announced that I was here to see the principal about the teaching job. The secretary quickly told me that he wasn't available. "No problem" I said. I sat down and prepared to wait. Two long hours later, the door to his office creaked open and I jumped up and sprang into action. "Hi," I announced thrusting out my hand. "My name is Susie, and I'm here for the teaching job. I know school starts next week. If it's ok with you, I'd like to walk through the halls, explore the campus and locate my classroom." Before waiting to see his reaction, I turned and quickly exited his office. Actually, I had never done anything so bold before and I couldn't believe my audacious behavior. So, I walked around the campus and then drove home. I was sure I would never darken the halls of that school again. However, to my surprise the next day I got a phone call from the principal, and I was hired for my first teaching job! I learned then that we can speak something into being by showing up and taking action!

"Showing up" can also be valuable in life with events that may have negative outcomes as well. After three years teaching high school, I took a detour and completed my MBA degree and then got a job as a manager in training in the finance department of a large corporation. A year later I lost the job. I was completely unaware that this was about to happen. After I packed up my things, I asked to speak to the Vice President of Finance, the head of our division. She received me cordially, and I asked her about why I was losing my job. My supervisor had told me that they were merely eliminating my position. But the Vice President said something more important. She told me that if your boss doesn't like you, then it's best if you leave. I was able to understand that frank answer. It felt honest to me, and I was able to take it in stride. I didn't NEED to speak to the Vice President about the loss of my job, but I wanted to come to terms about what happened and not just settle for a stock answer.

"Showing up" continued to play a vital role in my life. When I was in my forties, I was suffering from chronic back pain as well as depression. I showed up at the doorsteps of a career counselor. She helped me to reassess my current career path from corporate finance back into teaching which led to twenty-three more satisfying years as an educator. I also showed up at a pain clinic which not only gave me strategies to deal with my physical pain but also provided psychological therapy to handle the depression I suffered in a stressful marriage.

Did it take courage on my part? Yes, and it was a skill that I would use again in the future. "Showing Up" means being fully present and engaged in the outcomes of life, not merely gliding along on autopilot tossed about by the changing tides.

In 1997, my troubled marriage of 24 years came to an end when my unfaithful husband handed me divorce papers. My life felt shattered, and I struggled to create a new life for myself and my two daughters. After a period of introspection, divorce therapy, and healing. I "showed up" again. I went to a New Year's Eve dance for Christian Singles that a friend had invited me to attend. This evening was another turning point in my life, where I met a man who enabled me to heal from the trauma of my former husband. I had a lot to learn emotionally, and I was moving into a new phase of my life by reading, journaling, and praying. I was able to learn how to "Show up" emotionally with my new partner who was a Christian. I was learning emotional skills I had not learned during my first marriage with the emotionally abusive spouse. Four years later I married my second husband. I was now an entirely different person because I "showed up" to go through several years of growing, learning, and healing. I was no longer

sleep walking through my life. I was emotionally present.

Many years later in 2011 after a long teaching career, my new school principal developed a strong antagonistic feeling toward me when she learned that I wouldn't go along with her plan to violate our union rules. She placed two probationary teachers in charge of our grade level, so I would no longer have a voice in the operations of my department. This was a position I had served in successfully for about twenty years through numerous different principals.

This rang a bell in my head, and I remembered the words of my VP of finance years earlier, "If your boss dislikes you, then you have to go." I didn't stress over her sabotaging my position. Instead, I saw the writing on the wall and what this meant for my future at the school. At this point I was eligible to retire with a golden parachute. I prayed for my young boss who I recognized was jockeying for power and the recognition that I had held in my school district, where I was awarded "Teacher of the Year" in 2000. I realized that God had another plan for me. I happily retired, ready, and prepared to "Show Up" for the Next Big opportunity of my life.

Opportunities keep knocking if our eyes are open. In 2009 I was finishing up the current school year when the parent of a former student changed my life again.

I had been suffering with a lot of pain in my hands, feet, and joints. I also had frequent bouts of allergies, bronchitis, and laryngitis. As I was working in my class at the end of the day, a mom entered and started to tell me that her son who was my former student was now graduating from high school. She looked at my hands which were all cramped up with swollen joints and asked me about my problem. I told her about my painful arthritis. She said that she had received tremendous pain relief herself from nondrug phototherapy which had eliminated a dozen prescriptions from her life and stopped her chronic pain. After checking out the product, I tried it myself. I always believe that solutions to our problems can be found if we are diligent to search for them.

Within one month of using the Lifewave nondrug technology, my joint pain went away along with decades of allergies. Again, the solution was BEING present, being open, and listening to the universe which was responding to my search for a solution.

What I discovered was not just a solution to MY CHRONIC Pain but also a business opportunity that now opened up to me. After I retired from my twenty-six-year teaching career, I asked God "What is next?" The answer I received was "Start your LifeWave business."

This was the beginning of my experience with Lifewave phototherapy technology which helped my body to recover from decades of pain. As my health continued to improve, I added additional members to my team. My loving husband was my business partner, and we were able to generate an additional stream of income. Within a few years we were able to set aside enough money to purchase our first rental property. Now we "Showed up" in a whole new role as landlords.

We continued to experience additional opportunities to show up in our rental property business. Within a few more years we had acquired ten rental properties. The secret was always being open to new situations which could enhance our lives.

Joining GSFE was another key component to developing as an entrepreneur. When I started my Lifewave business, a friend suggested that I attend a network group ran by Robbie Motter. I became a member of that group, and I showed up for meetings, training, and networking opportunities which increased my business.

I also continued to show up for additional personal development courses such as NLP (Neurolinguistic Programming), Sales training, and Empowerment workshops which increased my business skills.

Then Robbie Motter, my mentor, suggested that the members of her group write a chapter in her collaborative book. Unfortunately, I lacked the confidence to write a chapter in that book, which became a best seller. This was ONE TIME I did not show up for myself, and I regretted it!

The following year, however, I had the opportunity to be in three other collaborative books, and I seized these new opportunities. The books were: "Love Your Haters" with Angela Covany; "The Impact of One Voice" with Arvee Robinson; and "100 Successful Women around the World", with Maria Davila and Professor Caroline Makaka.

Now I was on fire with seeking new expanding opportunities. When Robbie Motter suggested I write my OWN book, I agreed immediately. During the year of Covid I spent every night on my computer writing my memoir. It was a painstaking undertaking as I had to dig through the bloody bones of my childhood and first marriage to uncover the source of my years of pain both physical and emotional. The outcome was self-publishing my own book called "Sow in Tears, Reap in Joy-A Transformational Journey". Then I realized that all the emotional growth I experienced in the past several years gave me the skills I needed to mentor others who were on the self-empowerment journey.

In the summer of 2022, Dr. Robbie Motter nominated me for an honorary doctorate in humanitarianism. At first, the "old me" felt intimidated by this lofty honor. However, upon reflection, I realized how far I had come in my personal, business, and philanthropic endeavors. I humbly accepted this honor. I "showed up" in London in December of 2022, with my esteemed colleagues. I received my honorary degree, so now I can add

Dr. Susie Mierzwik to my list of awards and accomplishments. Not only was I honored to receive my doctorate, but it was awe inspiring to meet with my colleagues from so many countries globally to learn about their philanthropic work.

Now that I had learned to appreciate the art of "Showing Up", I was able to increase my participation with the Samaritan's Purse Foundation by 500%. In addition, I invited others in my networking circle to contribute to this worthy cause which provides tangible gifts for children around the world.

I continue to seek out opportunities to "Show Up" since my book was published. I have been on several podcasts, and I continue to book new speaking opportunities where I offer three strategies for my readers to enhance their lives by tackling the challenges that we all encounter.

During the time of Covid I enrolled in an online class to learn Spanish. In our recent travel to Tenerife in the Canary Islands, I was happy to be able to converse with the locals in Spanish. Wherever we went, I spoke to fellow travelers and residents in their own language which fosters a greater connection with the people we meet.

In 2016, I was presented with an opportunity to go on a safari to Tanzania in Africa. This was the trip of a lifetime. We had intimate contact with local people everywhere we went. We saw and learned firsthand about the animals, habitat, and people of the country. It reminded me of teaching my students about the land and habitats of Africa during my many years of teaching. Now I "Showed up" to see it firsthand.

My showing up included the opportunity to acquire new clients in Africa for my Lifewave business. I was also able to visit and contribute directly to an Orphanage for Children.

In 2021 my husband and I decided to take our second safari to Tanzania.

Besides renewing my acquaintances from our first safari, I was able to meet and befriend the chief of the Masai tribe. We had visited his village on both of our safaris. I received a personal phone call from him on our return home. What a thrill it was to have this incredible outreach from across the globe!

Now reaching out when I travel is becoming second nature. Through my membership in the Global Society of Female Entrepreneurs (GSFE), I am connected with women throughout the country and abroad. Now I serve as the co-director for GSFE (the virtual chapter). I love this position because now I can invite new acquaintances to join our chapter, no matter where they live.

Through GSFE I met Laurie Davis, who has run personal empowerment workshops for thirty years. After completing many of her workshops, myself, I will now start to run my own empowerment workshops on an international scale.

So, as I reflect, "Showing up" has become the cornerstone of all the growth that has transpired in my adult life. Whenever I feel the nudge inside me to "show up", I have uncovered immense riches professionally as well as physically, emotionally, and spiritually. In this current phase of my life, I will continue to "show up" to assist my clients to heal physically through my Lifewave business and to heal emotionally through my empowerment workshops and the encouragement they find in my writing.

It's all About Showing Up

From Parks to City Council

Councilwoman Bridgette Moore

In 1998, my family and I moved to Wildomar, California. At that time, Wildomar was part of Riverside County and identified as an unincorporated community. One of the reasons we purchased the house that we did was because the elementary school and a community park were in our housing tract. Unfortunately, a year after we moved in, the community park was closed. In 2000, I decided to attend a Municipal Advisory Council (MAC) meeting and inquire about the parks closing. I asked what I could do to help in getting our parks reopened.

I learned that when you ask certain questions, you are also volunteering, or as I say "voluntold," to assist in that said task. I volunteered by organizing meetings, park events, and fundraisers. I never would have fathomed that it would take seven years, but it did and finally our parks were reopened in 2007.

Meanwhile, our community was discussing the possible idea of incorporating into a city. Remember that we were an unincorporated community, and we had no local governance. I, again, asked what I could do to help with the Wildomar Incorporation Now (WIN) committee. I joined WIN and assisted with many tasks, including raising over $50,000

for incorporation. Our 12-member board led the incorporation effort all the way to election day. On February 5, 2008, the residents of Wildomar and SEDCO Hills voted to incorporate and become our own city. On the same ballot were 14 residents running for the first ever Wildomar City Council, including myself. The top five residents with the highest number of votes were the first city council. The top vote-getter was Bob Cashman who became the first Mayor of Wildomar. Since, I was second top vote-getter, I was named Mayor Pro Tem (Vice-Mayor). On July 1, 2008, we held the inauguration ceremony at Elsinore High School in Wildomar.

Fast forward to today and I am still serving as a councilmember. In 2010, I was the first woman Mayor for the City of Wildomar. I was meant to serve our community. I take this role seriously and work tirelessly to improve the quality of life for our community. I have successfully been re-elected three times and currently serving in my fourth term.

It has now been 23 years since my first 'ask' about parks. Parks led to incorporation which in turn led to city council. What if I never went to ask about parks? I am sure glad that I did go ask!

It's all
About
Showing
Up

Getting Individuals to SHOW UP and ASK around the world is my Mission

Lady Dr. (h.c.) Robbie Motter

Showing UP is like a treasure map, you never know what treasure you will find. I know for me, over the years there have been thousands of treasures, and the women members of my Global Society for Female Entrepreneurs GSFE (501 c3 nonprofit) are doing this every day. They too are seeing how it can open their world up and change their lives.

Did you know that your postings on social media can also open doors for you? It certainly has for me so it's important to really look at what you are posting because people do look at it.

A few examples: last year I was asked by two different chambers in two different cities to be a speaker and when they called me and asked me to speak, I said, "I would love to!" Then, I asked them, "Do you need my bio?"

They responded, "No, we already looked at your social media and know everything about you."

\Wow! I was surprised I did not need to send them anything. I spoke to large crowds both times and made lots of new friends and even got new members for GSFE. This never would have happened if I had not SHOWN UP.

Another example is when I got a text from the US Ambassador for Peace for the United Nations in Washington, DC, telling me she was nominating me for the California Global Ambassador of Peace Award. She told me many people had told her about me as well as seeing social media postings about me. I was blown away and I learned that the next step would be to go through a vetting process. I had never heard that word before, but when I filled out the paperwork, I found out that they only wanted all the social media places I'm listed. It was not like when I worked for the government. In order to get a top-secret clearance for the government they needed to know everywhere I lived, all names I ever used, etc. All the Ambassador of Peace people needed was my social media stuff. That made me see again how important what we do on social media can be. I'm going through the vetting process now and it's a long process, sometimes as long as 6 to 8 months.

I've received over 186 awards in my lifetime for my work including many "Call to Service" awards from 4 Presidents of the United States, but I would say to be the Ambassador of Peace for California would be one of the most honored ones I could receive along with two I just received in London. One was a Lady title and the other an award in Parliament. I never dreamed any of this would happen, but when one SHOWS UP and lives their passion, anything can happen. It would be such an honor to become the Ambassador of World Peace for California designation as I could certainly add world peace to our nonprofit as we already cultivate kindness and peace. Even if I don't get the designation, I am honored that I was nominated.

I've made so many connections in the United Kingdom and other countries. All of that happened because individuals saw postings I made, and postings others made about me on social media giving them reason to reach out and connect with me.

Ada Gartenmann from Chelsey London, who is a very successful businesswoman, author, and speaker reached out to me and nominated me for her She Inspires Me Award. She offered me the opportunity to be a co-author in her book, "Quarentina and Beyond" which was the first international book I became a co-author in. Since then, I've co-authored four other books. All because I SHOWED UP and met the right people. Ada came to California in 2022 along with others that I met on my first trip to London in 2021. We collaborated on her SIMA Gala. It was a sold out with people traveling from all over the world to be there. Since it was also an awards event, I was honored to have 80 of my GSFE women get awards. Everyone who SHOWED UP got to meet so many wonderful international women.

Ada introduced me to Dr. Caroline Makaka online, and we became friends. Dr. Makaka is the founder and CEO of Ladies of All Nations in 189 countries. Ada also introduced me to Professor Pauline Long who is also doing valuable work in many countries. All these women are incredible entrepreneurs and supporters of women. In fact, on my trip to London in 2022 we launched two GSFE networks, one that Ada leads and the other that Dr. Caroline leads. I met other women that want to do one in their countries.

Prior to Covid, GSFE had only live local networks in California, but when covid hit in order to keep going and helping our members we realized we had to do online meetings. Many of us never knew what Zoom was, but we SHOWED UP and found members who did know. They taught us how to expand our horizons via Zoom meetings. We realized with this new concept we could become Global. We reached out to become Global and increase the number of networks we have in other states. Canada was our first international chapter, and since then we have expanded so much. In 2022, we added 143 new members, and we are continuing to grow. Our mission is to EMPOWER, INSPIRE, MENTOR, EDUCATE, and TRAIN

women to be successful entrepreneurs. This new concept of live in CA with Zoom and Zoom in other states and internationally has helped us achieve great success. We are touching more lives of amazing women who are SHOWING UP and learning to ASK. One of the things we do at our live and online meetings is allow everyone to introduce themselves and to tell us what they do, but the greatest part is we tell them to tell us what they need (their ASK), so we can help them achieve it. It's been amazing to watch how many we can help with their ASK.

Through Ada and Dr. Caroline, I met Ambassador Dr. Imambay Kamara, and she is in the book. You can read her story. She's an amazing woman who leads an amazing life. She lives in England, but is from Sierra Leone, a country that she is a philanthropist and human rights activist for. Imambay is a woman who changes lives. She's even thinking of doing a GSFE network there.

Ada invited me to London in 2021, for my first trip, and I SHOWED UP. I stayed in her beautiful home and met so many unbelievable and dedicated women. I attended her SIMA Gala and was presented an award.

In 2022, all these dynamic women continued to introduce me to other fantastic women and I in turn started introducing them to my members.

In 2021, Dr. Caroline Makaka introduced me to Lady Dr. Lenore Peterson and her fantastic assistant Dr Tincie M Lynch. Dr. Caroline nominated me for an Honorary Doctor of Humanitarian degree for the college that Dr. Peterson runs. I wasn't able to attend the 2021 graduation in New York, but I did go to Atlanta in April 2021 to received it. What an honor! I never dreamed that would happen for me. When you SHOW UP, anything can happen.

Through my relationship with Lady Ambassador Dr. Peterson and Dr. Lynch I was able to nominate 26 of my dedicated and dynamic GSFE members to go to London and receive their Honorary Humanitarian Doctorate Degrees in December 2022. In June 2023, I have 41 of my GSFE members going to Atlanta to receive their Honorary Humanitarian Doctorate Degrees. The London trip for many was the first time they had ever been outside the US, and for some getting their first passport which was exciting. All of us got dressed up in gorgeous gowns and went to many Galas. We saw many other extraordinary places. We met people we never imagined we'd meet which was like a dream for many. This trip will forever stay in our minds. When you SHOW UP, magic happens!

My beautiful friend, Professor Pauline Long arranged for all of us to receive the prestigious Superwoman's Award and speak in Parliament. Each of us got to meet all the other dignitaries that were also present at the event. Who ever thought we'd get to parliament in England, let alone get an award and be able to speak in Parliament? Like I said, anything is possible when you SHOW UP. One of my members Gigi Mindreau Banks' husband is English and from England, and they live in CA now. He said to her, "I am English and from London, and I never got to go to Parliament or get an award. How lucky you are that you had that opportunity." There were so many "SHOW UP" opportunities for that trip, Galas for many other organizations that we were invited to and given awards at, it was like a dream, but it was real. We dressed up in different colored gowns for each event and felt like queens, and we were treated that way by the guests at each of the events we were at. We met beautiful people not only from London but from other countries as well.

What was also great was as my 26 GSFE members got together and showed up at the numerous events on our calendars, they built even deeper relationships and learned more about each other as many were in different

networks and really didn't know each other. The day they graduated and received their honorary degree they met women from other states and other nations something that would never have happened unless they SHOWED UP.

Through my connection with Dr. Caroline Makaka who does numerous events all over the world online, she has opened the door for me to invite members to be a part of each event she does and that has allowed those that are chosen to start to build their brand in other countries. They've had opportunities to be co-authors in many international books as well.

Who would have known all these opportunities start with SHOWING UP and then ASKING to be a part of things? If you see something you want to be a part of, all you need to do is ASK, and then SHOW UP. If I see something, I text or email that person and ask them if they need guests for their podcasts, speakers for their events, etc. I tell them I have amazing ladies who are exceptional speakers who would love to be guests. I've opened many doors for them to SHOW UP and become everything they thought they could be.

I'm not a technology expert. I'll be 87 on March 8, 2023. I'm not that great on social media, but I do post on Facebook once a day and have almost 5000 friends and followers and thousands on my LinkedIn but need to work at that more. So that's an area where I can SHOW UP more. I'm learning TikTok. My goal for 2023 is to build my network and double our size this year. I can do it by SHOWING UP more on social media and on Zoom (which is not my preferred way). I love face to face. It's the way the world is going, and if we want to grow, we need to step out of our comfort zones, and just SHOW UP.

Here's another SHOW UP story I must share. I get asked to attend many red-carpet events as a judge or just as a guest. I love dressing up, but like

each of us, I wasn't always in the mood to SHOW UP at these events. What I have learned is that when I do make the effort and SHOW UP, I'm always glad I did because I get to meet incredible people that become friends and hundreds have even become members of my GSFE nonprofit.

Several years ago, I showed up at a Red Carpet in Hollywood and met a dynamic, accomplished actress, and former stunt women. She is also a singer, song writer, and more. Her name is Marneen Lynne Fields, and she has worked with Clint Eastwood, Stanley Kramer, James Garner, and many more. Over the years of knowing her, I learned that she was producing a movie that she wrote from a script that has won numerous Best Screenplay Awards. Marneen read on social media that on my bucket list, I had always wanted to be an extra in a movie. She contacted me and said, "I'm going to do more than just cast you as an extra in my movie, I'd like to give you a speaking role after hearing what a great speaker you are." I was blown away, in addition I mentioned to her that if she needed more extras that I had lots of members that would love to be in a movie, especially hers. A true drama about saving her mentally ill and homeless mother titled, Who's Gonna Take Care of Me? She told me to send her their names as she needed lots of extras and would cast all of them in extra roles in the movie. As it turns out several are also getting speaking roles, a total of over 50 GSFE members will be in this movie. Once the film is completed it will be submitted to Academy Award qualifying film festivals. I believe the film will win an Academy Award. I not only play history teacher Helen Watson in the film, I'm also an associate producer, and head extras casting director on the production. The people in the movie are all great and so are my members who are going to be part of it. I never dreamed anything like this would happen for them. Marneen has already filmed my part and another member Chebra Dorsey "Ochea, who is a celebrity designer in San Diego also plays the role of Aunt Muggs in the film. The rest of my members will

film their roles this coming summer of 2023. Marneen has been an award-winning actress and stunt person for years and she is making her directorial debut with the film. You must read her story. Her amazing story in this book titled "Showing Up Takes Courage."

For me SHOWING UP as an actress was something I never thought would ever happen. I realized after filming my part (Marneen says I'm great in the role), that being an actress was not a passion of mine and that I loved helping my members get a part more than playing one myself. The role of talent agent is a better fit me because I love helping others and opening doors for them to dream big and soar high. In my talent agent part, I recommended 50 of my GSFE members and was surprised when I learned because of playing the role of Helen I got to have my own IMDB page. Here's the link so you can see it.

Robbie Motter - IMDb I'll also be listed as a casting director on the screen for the movie, and my beautiful house was a location site where a few scenes were filmed. Wow! who knew that would happen? When one SHOWS UP it's like a treasure chest and magical things can happen.

Also at these red-carpet events, I get to see and meet amazing live performers. Many of them I've contacted and asked them to perform for me at some of my fund-raising events. They've all said "YES" whenever I have ASKED. If I had not SHOWN UP, I would never have met any of them.

Many times, we get opportunities handed to us on a silver platter to us, and we look at them and do nothing. I look at every one of them as a treasure chest for me to explore, even those I see posted on social media. I evaluate each opportunity so I can share it with my GSFE members. Jump on them and share them! You must get in the habit of looking at everything as a possible SHOW UP AND ASK opportunity, I do.

In January 2023, an opportunity came in and it looked amazing for our nonprofit. There's a Consulting Institute that has it's MBA students pick companies and/or nonprofits to study for the year and then make recommendations on things the companies or nonprofits can do to make them better and grow. I read about this opportunity and immediately jumped on it. I saw it as an opportunity for my GSFE organization to learn to be better and grow with fresh eyes. I responded immediately to the senior professor who teaches at the school who posted the opportunity saying GSFE might be interested as it was a no cost opportunity, and I wanted to learn more. She called me about ½ hour later, and it turned out that she and I had met years ago when I was introduced to her by one of my Temecula GSFE members Shelly Rufin. This person Elisa Magill, Ph.D., used to be the Dean of that school and now works as a professor and consultant who recommends companies and nonprofits for them to be considered each year in the school program. On the call she asked me questions and filled out the referral form and sent it to Dr. Rick Johnson, the Director of the Consulting Institute. We are being considered to be selected to have the students work on GSFE as a project for 2023. How great is that? To have more knowledge on how we at GSFE can become better and reach out to serve more women and soar to greatness with the work we do. It's a no cost yearlong program to those selected, and at the end of the year on Zoom they will present their suggestions from their research and knowledge.

Another opportunity came from another member, Althea Ledford, who offered our members the opportunity to write articles to get published FREE of charge in her E Executive Global Magazine for Women. It's an amazing online and global magazine; many GSFE members took action. She also gave us a page for me to list our GSFE Networks and for me to feature a few members each edition along with me writing a column each edition

titled, From the Desk of Robbie Motter where I'll write about GSFE and all the wonderful things happening.

A good example of missing opportunities was when we did Book One, It's All About Showing Up, and the Power is in the Asking. An email went out to about 80 of my members and I asked them if they wanted to be in the book as a co-author to submit 2500 words, a short bio and their contact info with their photo at no cost to them as we picked up the cost. Everyone thought it was a fabulous idea, but only 45 came back and were co-authors in the book with me, (46 counting me.) The first day the book was published we made #1 Best Seller, and the second day we made #1 International Best Seller. We were online at Amazon, Barnes & Noble, the Walmart online bookstore, and bookstores all over the country that picked up the book. We received beautiful letters from all over the world telling us how the stories were changing their thinking and their lives. Not long after the book was published all those that didn't take action to be in the book said they were sorry they didn't do it. I told them, "Stop taking so much time to make a decision and always take action." By not taking action, you could totally be missing out.

We decided to publish this book volume Two, It's All About Showing Up and the Power is in the Asking because we know everyone has even more exciting stories of SHOWING UP and ASKING to share with the world. We know that these stories will change lives and make more people see the value of SHOW UP and ASKING. The reason we wanted it published on March 8, 2023, (International Women's Day), is because it's a fabulous day all over the world for women, and it is also my 87th birthday! We know this book is going to reach even more women globally, and we're honored. Our international co-authors said, "Yes!" For this book we charged a small fee of $300.00 to be in the book to cover editing, layout, and printing costs, and we know that buying the books from us at wholesale and reselling

them they easily all coauthors will get their investment back and more. The stories will reach millions around the globe touch more lives, and because the co-authors took the action to be in the book, they are a big part in changing lives with a publication they can be immensely proud of.

I love these great opportunities that come my way to share with my GSFE members. There are many valuable opportunities to take advantage of and capitalize on. So many times, we don't take action, and we miss out because we take too long to think about it instead of just doing it.

Asking is also hard for women so that has been another project of mine and I have found that the more you ASK the easier it becomes. I had a hard time ASKING until one day years ago one of my members said to me "Robbie, you get so much pleasure in helping others, don't you?"

I replied, "Yes, it fills my heart with joy when I see our members taking action and soaring to greater heights than they ever could have imagined."

Then she said to me, "Well, then why don't you let others have the same pleasure and get that same feeling you get, by helping you?" Wow, I'd never thought about it that way. So, I started to ASK, and it was amazing all the doors I could open for members and for GSFE just by ASKING. More and more of my members started asking too and they have found out that it does work. ASKING can help you so much if you just ASK.

I hope the many sensational stories in this book written by my team of amazing co-authors will inspire you to the max and help you achieve your dreams. Remember their contact information is here also, so why not reach out and connect with them.

Ms. O Keeps SHOWING UP!

Jean Olexa

Hello, I am Jean Olexa. I am known as "Gigi" or Ms "O". I have been an advocate for youth and women for years. Over the years in my various businesses, I have showed up and inspired youth of all ages to go to college and have helped many complete their college papers for scholarships. I continue to teach youth and women about being kind to one another and being organized as I am. As a professional organizer I teach them that being organized helps them mentally and also teaches responsibility and taking action.

We all raise our children by instilling great words of wisdom, but sometimes we really never know if they get it or not. Recently, my daughter Kimberly had a situation in which she explained to me she was going to do a "Gigi". That's what my grandchildren call me. So, what is that I ASKED? "Mom, you always stated when growing up never FEAR to ASK." I decided to ASK, I took ACTION, and the situation was resolved. Wow! I didn't realize the impact I had instilled in my daughter, but it touched my heart to hear her say this.

With that in mind I took a journey back into my life and discovered how my "SHOW UP" and "ASK" opened so many avenues.

So here goes....

The most rewarding one was when my children attended parochial schools, and I drove them each day to school. One day I saw a bus picking up children for school. So, I followed It for two weeks and asked myself "Why are they not picking up all the students." To my dismay, the bus only had a certain territory, but this was not fair. So, I took ACTION, wrote to the State's Department of Transportation, completed all the forms, and submitted my criteria. I constantly called to get an update. There was a lot of paperwork that I had to do. Many phone calls and more documentation. I had to be persistent and because I never gave up, a "Victory" happened. My request was approved, and my 3 children got picked up in front of our home to go to school as well as other students benefited as well.

Now, unbeknown to the parents that I took "ACTION" and did the "ASK" that when the announcement was made it was a "Jubilation." I received recognition for implementing this for the parochial school and received so much gratitude from all including from the diocesan for my strong persistent and criteria. It proves that one person can make a change if they never give up.

For me it was gratifying and rewarding that I was able to contribute to the school and community. The impact was an astonishing achievement.

Another ASK was my son's "Notre Dame Experience".

Being avid Notre Dame and Penn State Fans, one day I met someone who was above just being an avid fan. Our conversations were all about Notre Dame – the fighting Irish and the whole nine yards of the Notre Dame experience. Wow! I was in AWE. I stated I would love to have the experience with my son who was 11 years old. So, I "ASKED" how can I do all that for my son?

The individual replied," Well, to start, you need tickets for all the Notre Dame experiences, airfare, etc."

I responded, "No, I can't afford that. I am a single parent." Oh well to my dismay, I received a phone call, and the party had two tickets for the game since someone cancelled due to illness. I replied, "This is EPIC." So, the plans were on the agenda.

My son woke up for school and I said, "No school today. We are going to Notre Dame so go pack your bag." It was an amazing adventure; I could go on and on with the exposure we were exposed to. The memorable moment of the Notre Dame trip was when we went to the Cathedral. As we walked, it was incredible and my son stated, "This is the most beautiful house of GOD." The impact for my 11-year-old son was amazing.

We knelt, lit candles, prayed, and I thanked GOD for sending us on this amazing journey.

Next adventure was "My daughter's Notre Dame Experience."

I took my two daughters Kerrie and Kimberly for the Fightin' Irish Experience in November 1992: Notre Dame vs Penn State.

What a game! 25 seconds to go, and the Irish scored 17 – Penn State 16,

We all rushed out to the field wearing our Norte Dame gear for the incredible win. All the press was there, and we were on TV. Everyone saw us. Luckily a dear friend filmed it, and I have it in my archives. To add to the excitement, they were filming "Rudy" lights, camera, and action everywhere.

The Disney Institute

Disney was auditioning for internships in Florida. I encouraged my two

daughters to apply so they took the initiative and applied; they were ecstatic they were accepted. Kerrie was in her last months of her last year of college and was graduating and was hopeless because a conflict set it. So, I said "Just ASK the Dean.":

Sure enough her ASK was granted. They were on their way to Walt Disney World internship. This is an honor as Disney's criteria is very severe and strict. I am so proud of my two daughters to have had this experience in their lives. They made the best friendships and to this day 21 years later they have all remained the best friends.

Opportunity only knocks once – so I opened it.

I first met Lady Dr. Robbie Motter at the Menifee Lakes Country club as at that time I was new to the Menifee, CA area, and at that time I was living with my daughter. I had relocated from New Jersey to be closer to my two daughters and grandchildren. It was a difficult move as I had so many friends back in New Jersey. One day I said to myself, "Jean, you must go out and meet people in your area. So, I went. I heard the country club had an event that night and I SHOWED UP not knowing a soul. I arrived and I was appreciative and proud of myself that I took the effort to get out, but I was nervous. I entered the country club, and all the tables were marked reserved. I asked a beautiful lady, "Are they all reserved?"

She responded, "Yes but you are welcome to sit at my table", so I accepted. The Lady spoke of NAFE which later became another group called GSFE (Global Society for Female Entrepreneurs: when NAFE went another direction after Covid.) She invited me to the next meeting as a guest. I capitalized on it and went to the meeting and history was made.

I was intrigued by the members and the goals of NAFE and later GSFE and I decided to join. The perks were amazing, and I really felt as if I was part

of the Menifee community.

I volunteered many hours to the organization and always did all the baskets for the opportunity drawings for all their events. The rewards are captivating. For me, it is important that I feel that I am a part of the community and showing up and volunteering has been an asset to me throughout the years.

Lady Dr Robbie/s mantra is ASK and SHOW UP.

I SHOW UP!

You never know what can happen when you "SHOW UP". I had the excitement to be with the stars at the Emmy's, Grammies, and the Oscars, What glamourous events. I felt like my own a "STAR," Also another time at an event I showed up in Palm Springs, CA. I met the original poster guy for Marlboro. It was cool since I am a smoker needless to say.

Over time all the introductions I have personally met are astounding, so the bottom line, SHOWING UP is certainly a treasure map.

In your journey of life, you can review your posts and see how "SHOWING UP" led to exciting new avenues.

I never expected anything from doing my volunteer work, has been great to be recognized for my work.

Over the years I have received 3 lifetime Achievement Awards from 3 presidents, President Donald Trump, President Barrack Obama and recently from President Joe Bident. I was awarded the Women of Achievement by California Senator Mike Morrell. Awards from Mayors, Congressional Leaders, Riverside Board of Supervisors, The Institute of Global Professionals, and from GSFE award events as well as the international award from London "She Inspires me."

GSFE offers many opportunities to SHOW UP at collaboration events they do. One of these opportunities was a golf tournament in Orange County, California. I SHOWED UP at a NFL golf tournament in Orange County by hole one. NFL players were in golf carts and since I love football, I knew who most of them were. One such cart stopped, and the NFL player jumped out and came to me knelt and said, "Would you marry me" he placed three NFL rings on my one finger. I was in AWE as on a vision board I had done I put I wanted a ring on my finger. At that moment I felt I needed to be more definite on my vision board as to what I wanted. I took the rings off and said," Thank you but I have to give this more thought, but I appreciate the offer." I was stunned and did not know what else to say. It was an unplanned moment. I was stunned and at a loss of words. It did show me the significance of setting intentions with goals, the way a vision board does.

New Beginning

Years ago, going thru an acrimonious divorce and being a traditional wife and mom, I was devastated and said to myself, "What am I going to do? Where do I turn?

Prior to being a mom, I was an Administrative Assistant to the Academic Dean at Misericordia University in Pennsylvania. One day, my uncle and dear friend said, "Jean, why don't you pursue the job as a Nanny? You love children and are an incredible mom." That being said, All 3 children were in college, so I decided to embark on my uncle and best friend's idea. So, I SHOWED UP to being a Nanny.

This is when the ASK was rewarding. I saw an ad in the paper, responded,

and had an interview. I had no idea what my career would be. I was interviewed by the lady and her daughter. I stated, "I can make a difference in your children's lives. Please try me for 2 weeks; if not satisfied you owe me zero.

The lady responded, "When can you start?"

I said, "Tomorrow."

The lady said, "Great."

You have no idea what exposure I have had being a Nanny for "the privileged". When I applied, I did not know who these people were. As time went by, I learned they were the power breakers for New Jersey. I did not realize how lucky I was. They gave me the opportunity to be their nanny for their two children. All their other friends commented "Ms. O" is the best.

I am a grandmother of 8, 3 girls and 5 boys whose names are Jada, Ted, Xavier, Neil, Nate, Austin, Alana, and Allison, all 6 months apart, ages 16, 15, 13,13,13,11 and 10. Yes, there is a set of twins. my grandmother had two sets of twins, so when my daughter informed me, it was twins, I was ecstatic.

My world is my grandchildren. I am proud of who they are and love them oodles of noodles.

My legacy to all my grandchildren is as follows:

Keep God close.

If it doesn't seem right, it's not.

Follow the ten commandments.

Print on the line and even steven.

Never be afraid to ASK.

Be a reader and you'll be the leader.

Volunteer.

Smile at someone.

Give a compliment.

Always respect your mother and father.

Always believe to achieve.

Reach for the stars.

Always thank GOD at the end of the day and in the beginning.

Cooperate.

Being an organizer, I have instilled from "messy to marvelous" to all my beautiful and talented grandchildren, you are my loves forever.

So, to sum it up....

Oh, the places you will go, and I have gone and am still going to so many beautiful places because I SHOWED UP and ASKED.

So, my message to you is just ASK and SHOW UP!

It's all About Showing Up

GSFE Show Up & Ask to Building Relationships

Dr. (h.c.) Katherine Orho

Is there any correlation between doing business and community development? In his book "In Human Rights from Below", Jim Ife makes correlations between human rights and community development noting that in order to practice one or the other, they are both necessary to the process. His abstract notes that the people attempting to make change can bring about human rights principles much more readily when community development principles are employed. What Jim Ife was looking for was a tool kit for doing human rights. And while I thought this was fascinating, it got me to thinking that I am always looking for a tool kit to doing business and there might be a similarity.

I have to admit, first of all, that I have not yet read "In Human Right from Below", but it is on my reading list. I have read several summaries on Ife's work, and they have met my appetite for the book. As an alumnus of California State University, Fullerton, with a Humanities degree in Asian-American Studies, I have an authentic interest in Cultural Studies, Human Studies, and Globalization. I also have a minor in Criminal Justice. Going through school at that time, I had a very soft heart, and it was extremely hard to research and study atrocities and human rights violations. Since stepping into GSFE, I think my recent studies of business have thickened

my skin somewhat---not as to make me completely uncaring, but just to open my eyes to the fact that what people are looking for are solutions to their circumstances, and we are all a small cog in the machine that ultimately brings about resolutions or solutions for better or worse whether we intend to be or not.

So, getting back to Jim Ife: I was reading all of this about his book, and the thought flashed in my mind that no advocates, activists, workers, politicians, leaders, nor volunteers were going to affect successful change in either human rights or community development without building relationships unless they just bulldoze over the current populace and start repopulating the demographics. That may change human rights, but not for the better. How do I see a correlation to this and doing business? As business owners one of the most consistently solid tools we can wield is building relationships. In community development, there is an aspect of building a relationship with the community you are serving and uplifting. You must earn their trust. You must gain their confidence in your capabilities. As business owners we are doing the same but with clients, businesses partners, and employees. We must build their trust. We must let them know that we can work together to find solutions to problems and supply product. We must gain their confidence in our capabilities.

A Cog in the Machine

If we equate each business to a machine and the employees and leadership in that business to pieces or cogs in the machine, then three things are immediately obvious:

The cogs have to fit into place in the machine for the machine to run smoothly.

The cogs have to be capable of doing their job for the machine to run at all.

The cogs cannot compete with one another or function in an opposing fashion to the machine's main function.

Bringing this analogy back to business examples, employees, staff, volunteers, and leaders must fit into their roles within the business. It is not helping your business to give a staff member a role that you know they do not fit. Wouldn't that be sabotaging your own business?

Make sure that each person gets placed in roles that utilize their strengths and makes them a more productive part of the team. Don't be afraid to let them know that they are valued for what they bring to the organization.

Provide training where necessary. There are so many sources online where someone can learn skills (Alison.com, Udemy.com, Skillsshare, LinkedIn Learning, even the public library). Many of these resources are either free or low cost.

Encourage your employees to continue learning. With technology advancements, we can now "read a book" while we drive long distances. I do this all the time. eBooks that I can listen to have been an invaluable resource for me, as I don't have a lot of time to sit and turn pages. Audiobooks are a little more costly but accomplish the same thing. Traditional books will never go out of style (we hope). Encourage your people to cuddle up by the proverbial fire light with a good book pertaining to their skills. Recommend books. Have them recommend books to you as well because increasing knowledge, influence, and building trust goes both ways.

"We don't compete; we complete!" This motto of the Global Society for Female Entrepreneurs is frequently heard in events and meetings alike. Why? Because if you have a machine that has parts battling to be the dominant part or to function outside of the machine's initial duties, then

you do not have a working machine. Furthermore, it is a costly endeavor to fix said problem.

Sure, capitalism is based on competition, but an organization must be built on teamwork. There's a difference. Don't compete with the people you are trying to partner with. If they are an ally, they have to be someone you can work with and vice-versa.

You cannot motivate people with competition, either. This is not relationship building, it is relationship burning. Before you know it there are whispers flying around, then full blown gossip, followed by hurt feelings, words you can't take back and hopefully it stops before lasting damage sets in. All along, did it advance your project or bring success in product development or sales? Probably not. Competitive relationships reap destruction as a norm amongst teams. Don't confuse competition with motivation or inspiration.

Remember, our goal is to build relationships in business. Compliment your people and teach your employees to complement one another. Compliments are the world's sugary coffee. It gives the recipient the kind words they crave and encourages them to work harder and smarter. It is better to stay worthy of such kind accolades.

That also can apply if you think of that sugary flavored coffee as two great things coming together. Michael is the coffee because he is great at deadlines and works excellently in a fast-paced environment. Leslie is the sweet flavoring because she is great at presentations and communicating with other Stakeholders. Together, they are the most awesome caramel flavored coffee because they make a great team. Tell Michael he is really good at what he does. Tell Leslie she is really good at what she does. Let them know that is what makes them have such a great partnership.

One of the hardest parts of relationship building is making sure that the people you are working with know where your company is going? Do they know what your goal is for your own company? Do they just think you are only trying to make as much money as possible? In particularly with Board of Directors & CEOs this point should be really clear but with other members of the organization, as well. Communicating this to people can be exasperating at best. It may have to be repeated regularly to assure that the message gets through, but it is worth it.

Share your dreams with them. Share your goals with them. Your employees and partners should feel that as they play their part in your mission for the company, they are a relevant piece of the puzzle. It instills pride in the work they do and pride in the overall mission you're trying to achieve.

It must be a clear image that you are instilling in your team about what you are trying to achieve. If there is no clarity, is there really a mission? Make sure they understand that the overall mission is a must. They can go elsewhere if they cannot support it. I used to see this as blackmail or brainwashing, but as recently as 2016 my views on this have changed drastically. There is something to be said for unity and loyalty towards a goal. It breeds determination, persistence, and dedication for all involved. It even inspires us to want to be more, learn more, do better. It can inspire precision in design and development. Clarity of mission is a vital part of relationship building with your team for these reasons.

The Social Relationships We Must Build

From as early as 1978, I can remember Mama training her two remaining daughters to be sociable. My earliest memory of this was a Juneteenth parade in Denver, Colorado, that my sister and I marched in. My sister was

6 years older than me, and I was so little that my white Go-go boots with cute fringe cut trimming just swallowed my skinny little legs. There was a baton involved and some twirling. No bystanders were hurt in my march from start point to finish.

In the 1980s, Mama sort of went on a mad mission to make me girlie and social. Neither of which was agreeable with my temperament. My sister and I were in the Catholic organization, The Knights of Peter Claver. Of course, we were with the Ladies of Peter Claver to be precise. The junior group was run by a bunch of old ladies who loved to bicker amongst themselves and then tell us young girls what to say and how to act as if any of that mattered in my thick head. I learned how to second a motion, adjourn a meeting, and wear white dresses and white gloves for no apparent reason.

I was classically trained in piano. My teacher had hopes of me applying to Julliard. My specialties were Bach and Chopin with some pop pieces in for crowd pleasing. Every year, California State University in Dominguez Hills held piano competitions in the summer, and I participated. My piano teacher, Mrs. Bufford, was on staff at the college and made sure I applied every year. One year I took second place, and that was a big rush. I didn't appreciate it then, but strangers in the audience kept approaching me saying that I should have won first place. I was just glad that I won and that I didn't have to practice day in and day out anymore.

We didn't have Facebook, LinkedIn, Twitter, or Tik Tok. I sang with 3 different choirs in high school, in addition to the high school choir at St. Matthias Girls High. I acted at the Performing Arts camp at California State University Dominguez Hills and was in the drama club at school. Being in social media meant getting an announcement printed in the church or school newspaper on a recent achievement. Those papers were lucky to reach a couple of hundred readers at most. LinkedIn allows us to have a

maximum of 30,000 connections...each of which could possibly also have 30,000 connections. Imagine the potential reach. Mind blown!

As business professionals of today's world, we should not neglect our branding and social media. It's not good enough to play the piano in that competition anymore. No. The world is watching and expecting you to write an article about it, show attractive photos from the event, and possibly upload video of the performance so they can feel like they were there. 30,000 people are waiting to hear from you. Also, you must post regularly because consistency is the key. Society wants to get to know you. They want to chat with you. And after all that, if they deem you worthy, they will grant you a scheduled appointment to chat and consider doing business with you or doing a collaboration of some kind. Social media is not for the faint of heart. It is another way in which we show up and ask in building relationships in business.

In the book, "Developing Business Relationships", Les D. Crause says,

"'Build the dreams. Get them talking and sharing their goals and their dreams with one another.

...get them to talk about the things that excite them.'" (Crause, Les D. ; Chapter 5, Lulu Press, Inc.; https://play.google.com/store/books/details?id=oqzVDgAAQBAJ)

It is easier to win people over when you let them talk about the things that they are excited about, like their hobbies, their significant others, their families or their creations. There is a trick to this. You must listen to the other people. On average. Most people like to talk about themselves. It is human nature. Let them have that. The general purpose is to get people focused on good, positive, and healthy topics of conversation. By allowing your people to open up to others about their dreams for the future, it should

get them motivated and riled up enough to get back to work with a more enthusiastic outlook.

Finally, procrastination, fear, and anxiety kill relationships that we can't afford to lose. Here's how I figure that statement is true? When you think about it, not only are we at risk of losing relationships that are in progress due to procrastination and fear, but we lose relationships that never even got started. How many times has someone decided to stay home because they let their anxiety get the best of them. Or maybe the chance to compliment someone's talent passed you by due to fear. Speaking from experience, those are the best moments of my life when I push past the anxiety or fear and showed up regardless. That is also when I end up meeting the most unexpectedly profound and dynamic influences in my life.

A recent example was when I offered to pick up Tango dancer, Monica Orozco, in Los Angeles only to realize after hanging up the phone that I would have to be at LAX the next morning to pick up Jacob. This would not be a problem if I didn't live 57 miles away from LAX and about 60+ miles from Monica. I promised to drive my passenger to Menifee (some of you might know it as Sun City) which was 33 miles east of my home and about 90+ miles east of Monica's residence. After the event I took Monica home, and the next morning, bright eyed and bushy tailed, I drove to LAX and picked up Jacob on time without complications.

So, did I lose the thread of the discussion? Not at all. What I experienced that day was wonderful. I felt so blessed to have met such a wonderful and amazing woman like Monica Orozco. I listened to her stories about her adventures in Tango dancing. She has a fabulous story to tell, and I can't wait for her to put it in a book. Teaching Tango dancing has taken her all over the world, into the front lines of war zones and into universities to teach. Les D. Crause says let them talk; well, I did! The reward was great. By

the time we parted, we were cherished friends. It was so worth it to bypass the fear and anxiety and show up that night. I gained a treasure in meeting Monica Orozco.

So, don't let procrastination, fear, and anxiety steal your chance at building a relationship with a prospect, a friend, a client, a partner that you never would have met if you did not SHOW UP & ASK.

Reference

I hope that you enjoyed reading this as much as I enjoyed doing the research for it and writing it. I admit that a good chunk of this submission is simply book reviews on things I just happened to be reading or listening to at the time. I genuinely liked these books and this podcast. Take the time to enjoy their work, too:

▪ "In Human Rights from Below" by Jim Ife, ISBN:9780521711081, 0521711088; Publication: Cambridge, UK; New York: Cambridge University Press, 2010

▪ "Developing Business Relationships" by Les D. Crause, ISBN 9781365916373, Lulu Press, Inc.

[https://play.google.com/store/books/details?id=oqzVDgAAQBAJ]

▪ Naketa Ren Thigpen's podcast, Balance Boldly Podcast with Bobbie Foedsich

[Networking For Sales 101: Learning to Build a Connection with Everyone with Sales Leader and Innovator, Bobbie Foedsich

https://pdcn.co/e/https://pdst.fm/e/www.buzzsprout.
com/1058833/10676959-networking-for-sales-101-learning-to-build-a-
connection-with-everyone-with-sales-leader-and-innovator-bobbie-
foedsich.mp3

https://play.google.com/store/apps/details?id=com.castify]

☆ An absolutely fantastic podcast episode.

It's all
About
Showing
Up

How God showed Up
Carmelita Pittman

I arrived at the location of the building that my mother owned and was annoyed to see a car in the parking space that I used. I soon learned that the Reverend of the Church of God in Christ was the owner of the car. I recognized him right away and we engaged in nearly an hour-long conversation. Although Mother Griffin, a Deaconess and longtime member of the church who held regular Bible study and prayer meetings in her unit had made her transition, the Reverend still attended to the remaining family members.

Mother Griffin had been transported to the Rose Variety Arts Show in a white stretch limousine. She was accustomed to wearing white and blended right into the theme, "Parade of Angels." As Mother of the Year she received fresh roses and a Certificate of Appreciation from Mayor Villaraigosa.

The Reverend pulled out a small vial which still had some of the oil that he had used to anoint the forehead of Martin Luther King. He put some on my forehead and told me, "Now put on your seatbelt." He told me that God had great plans for me. So many blessings had already showed up in my life. My mother, Juanita Zara Espinosa Uddin, a multi-talented woman, gave me

the gift of unconditional love. On a secretary's salary, she sacrificed and put me through the University of Southern California. Following my mother's footsteps, I entered the world of art by four years of age. My art professors noticed and insisted that I attend the art exhibition at Fisher Art Gallery where I was surprised with the Ross, Spayne, Perry art scholarship. The rest of my education was financed by mom and a government loan which fortunately I was able to repay.

I let the Reverend know of the relationship of my husband, Jerry Pittman, to Martin Luther King. Now in our 47th year of marriage, it was unknown to me for nearly 30 years to whom I was married. His maternal grandmother, Edna Butts, married one of Daddy King's 7 brothers, John Oliver King, and the product was Hazel King who produced Jerry with Clarence Pittman. Looking back at my life, I have been connecting the dots to realize my place in the world. I've been grateful for all the blessings and lessons learned.

My mother, a product of the era of the Depression, was very frugal, saved her money, and managed to purchase real estate. Years ago, she and my stepfather purchased a home in the Berkeley Square area of Los Angeles. It was predominantly occupied by what I described as "Pink" people. However, it did not take long for them to fly away when they saw faces of color arrive. There was a home across from ours that was owned by 3 elderly sisters, however, who took a different view and invited all of the children regardless of their ethnicity to attend their Bible study classes. I enjoyed the way they presented the lessons and invited other youngsters to attend until the classes grew.

Eventually Marvin Gaye purchased a mansion in that neighborhood. Before he moved in, I used to skate around that block as a child. Sadly, much of that area has been demolished to give way to the 10 freeway. I

recall when it was in its prime. I used to play with the little girl who lived in the mansion down the block owned by a movie star that had a large pool.

Following the graduation of my mother from the earthly stage on November 16, 1997, when breast cancer cut her life short after her four year battle with it, I founded The Rose Breast Cancer Society, a 501 (c)(3) nonprofit organization 1998 as a "Living Memorial" to give back to the community in her memory. It has attracted special individuals such as Gloria Berlin, who became a member. She was also a valuable member of the Thalians founded by Debbie Reynolds and Ruda Lee. As a live-in girlfriend at Rancho Mirage, she helped Frank Sinatra overcome his grief after his breakup with Ava Gardner. She was also the Beverly Hills realtor who sold Michael Jackson Neverland Ranch. The Rose Breast Cancer Society sponsored her book signing at Elderberries health food restaurant in West Los Angeles. She graciously acknowledged the organization by mentioning it in her book.

According to the Bible, God created the world in 7 days. There are 7 letters in both the first and last name of Michael Jackson. He is the 7thchild of 10. He loved the spiritual significance of the number 7. The address of Elderberries had number 7 in it. There are 7 arches inside the restaurant where I placed my art exhibition. I also invited Senior Senator Pasqual Bettio FRPS to exhibit his art, and he submitted a crystal sculpture that happened to have the number 7 in it. I had recently attended a sermon by the Priest which had 7 sacraments in it. I do not believe in accidents and recognize mini miracles in daily life. Just before the event began, I needed someone to lay the red carpet, and there was a homeless man who appeared. I hired him on the spot, and he was a great help during the course of the evening.

Michael Jackson's celebrity interviewer April Sutton, co-host of Geraldo Rivera's TV show and my friend of several years, contributed to the event.

She invited Michael Jackson's publicist named Angel, and Gloria Berlin invited Michael's bodyguard and photographer. The event turned out to be an artistic smorgasbord. Dr. Burt Danet demonstrated how a special kind of water produced in a UCLA lab had helped save his life from cancer.

The Rose Breast Cancer Society has hosted numerous events, most notably at the Celebrity Centre in Hollywood, where health care experts in the waterfall area gave visitors the opportunity to receive personal attention. The gardens hosted the Art Expo where the artists exhibited beautiful landscapes.

As President of St. Paul's Catholic Church Parish Pastoral Council, I invited members of English, Spanish and Korean speaking choirs to join the choir of UP (Understanding Principles) led by Reverend Della Reese-Lett, co-star of TV series, "Touched by an Angel". The choirs assembled at the Renaissance restaurant and sang as they marched through the gardens up the stairs to the Glass Pavilion. The décor was white drapery on the windows and balloons which led up to the center of the ceiling to form a tent effect. On the stage and throughout the gardens were 10-foot Angel sculptures which I commissioned by Francisco Ramirez of Jalisco, Mexico. The band started up and played "When the Saints Go Marching In" as choirs entered the Glass Pavilion and sang walking up to the stage. The ambiance was complete with the audience also dressed in white.

Dr. Cherilyn Lee and Dr. Darren Clair of Vibrance, in Beverly Hills received awards, and both delivered memorable and lifesaving information. The Visual Art Expo, Performing Artists which included students at Inglewood High School who wore white capes by Sibella, who has designed for Dolly Parton, plus Wellness Expo all combined to form what I have coined as "EDU-tainment". One of the attendees later told me that one of the members of her family had received information that extended her life from

cancer. In addition, Dr. Lee and Dr. Clair both accepted certificates from The Rose Breast Cancer Society which gave discounts for Thermography exams which can detect the presence of cancer well in advance.

Over the years The Rose Breast Cancer Society, an arts-based organization, has had many themes, including the International Rainbow of Humanity representing all cultures during which volunteers created a mural on the spot led by noted Latino artist Oscar de Salcaja. A circus theme occurred with Sasha Fedortchev of Moscow and formerly of Cirque du Soleil who performed an amazing aerial ballet. At one event in Studio City, we provided the beautiful white horse Miss Daisy with a Cinderella round carriage used in the Rose parade to transport the mother of the Year.

Angel sculptures graced the altar of Saint Paul's Catholic Church when I produced the Intercultural Concert. All cultural communities were represented. The Azteca dancers, Scottish bag pipe musicians, Korean children in native attire, Angels dressed in white wedding gowns covered with white capes Pasqualized with his painting and small shisha mirrors entered and walked up to the altar where they divided into two sections when they returned down both side aisles. My cherished friend, Cantor Estherleon Schwartz, a Holocaust survivor in her gorgeous robe and cap, sang Gregorian chants on the altar. Her father had made a deal with God that if his child was spared from the Nazis that she would serve and do great things for humanity. Indeed, she has done just that.

The Intercultural Concert occurred on the anniversary of 9/11. It was the date that I noticed the American people joining together regardless of ethnicity to exhibit their patriotism and love of America. We all became ONE.

The Rose Breast Cancer Society has experienced many mini miracles over the years. It appears that each effort has been blessed and the door opened

to present the Rose Variety Arts Shows. The most epic one was held on 6½ acres on the grounds of the Virginia Robinson Gardens just North of the Beverly Hills Hotel. This was a mini miracle because at the time we did not know where the event would be held with only 4 weeks to produce it. Thanks to Jarvee Hutchinson, founder of the Multi-cultural Motion Picture Association, a meeting was set up where I was introduced to management. They were impressed with The Rose Breast Cancer Society and its track record. Over the years the organization has been recognized by Civic and State leaders including Mayor James Hahn, Mayor Villaraigosa, and Councilmember Tom LaBonge who steadfastly supported it over the years. Former Congresswoman Diane E. Watson has been both an Honorary member and supporter. Her mother, Dorothy Watson, was honored as Mother of the Year. A white stretch limousine transported them to the event where fresh roses and a Certificate of Appreciation from the Mayor was presented. I believe in giving folks their flowers while they can still smell them.

An oversized check received via Elliot Handler, creator of the Ken doll whose wife, Ruth Handler creator of the Barbie doll, was presented to development officer P. Hosch and Yvonne Villalobos who was the rep for Michael Press, a leading cancer researcher at USC Comprehensive Cancer Center. At one time I took members of The Rose Breast Cancer Society to visit his lab.

Our huge angel sculptures were used throughout Olvera center at the Anniversary of the 200th birthday of Los Angeles, the "Creative Capital of the World". Honorary chairperson Mayor Villaraigosa and Councilwoman Jan Perry were part of the committee.

Jaime Alesandre, a former top model of England, advised me in her thick English accent to consider wearing a pink suit with a long skirt to the

14th Rose Variety Arts Show at Virginia Robinson Gardens. I could see that elegant outfit in my head. One day when I was out looking for a stove with my handy man, we went to Crenshaw Mall. As we were about to pass by a boutique window, there it was! There were only two of a kind in the entire shop. I tried one on, and it fit like a glove. On the way out of the shop I looked up, and there on the shelf was the wide brimmed pink hat which had a large rose in the middle of it. Another little mini miracle that let me know that I was being guided by special favor.

After meeting with management of the Virginia Rose Gardens, the event was placed on the tennis court located across from the rose garden that the original Charlie Chaplin used to play on. Our Audrey Ruttan, a longtime member and one of the best Charlie Chaplin tribute artists around, ventured in from Palm Springs to participate once again as Silent Master of Ceremonies. The organization was named The Rose Breast Cancer Society because of my mother's love of roses. She was married to Shiraj Uddin of Pakistan, whose name Uddin means "of the Light". I believe that The Rose Breast Cancer Society has been shedding light by empowering people with education. Knowledge is power. I also believe that the arts are healing.

Currently the mural project, "Gardens of Life/ Alley –O-Graphy" , has brought joy to the Mid-Wilshire neighborhood which has guarded it since 2015 when artist Katherine Arion of Romania first initiated it. It is located along the rear wall of Longwood Manor Convalescent Hospital. Patients came out to photograph her as she painted on the mural and offered her food and beverage. As a fine artist, I received a similar response. Little children in the neighborhood were fascinated when Senior Senator Pasqual Bettio FRPS and fine artist, former trustee of several years for the Hollywood Arts Council, added his touch of East Indian shisha mirrors to the mural. He is also an Honorary member of The Rose Breast Cancer Society and co-

founder with Debora Gillman of ARTery USA which has an interest in this project. The Dept of Cultural Affairs has lent support.

International artist Emmy Lu of Uganda whose murals have graced hotels in Japan, Hawaii and Las Vegas plus artist Armand Michael Sears, Jr. have also lent their touch.

There is scientific evidence that the happy hormones and endorphins, taken into the consciousness, boost good health. The Rose Breast Cancer Society is currently seeking sponsorship to continue the video documentation of the progress of the mural and to cover the costs incurred to obtain art supplies and compensate the artists. More information can be obtained by visiting www.rosebreastcancersociety.org Although the website is still a work in progress, it is recommended that the brief six-minute video on the home page be viewed.

Celebrities over the years which have supported our efforts include Lord Randal Malone, President of the Southern California Motion Picture Council of which I am a lifelong member, and the legendary Margaret O'Brien who has four stars on the Hollywood Walk of Fame. Raul Rodriguez who has created over 500 floats for the Rose Parade received The Rose Breast Cancer Society Lifetime Achievement Award. Carol Connors co-composer of the "Rocky" theme song has also received this award. I recently received President Biden's Lifetime Achievement Award via Sharon Doyle thanks to GSFE (Global Society of Female Entrepreneurs) founded by Robbie Motter of which I am a member.

Beginning in 2016 Carmelita's Corner Radio Show began and continues to this date. I recently received the Shea Vaughn Worldwide Impact Legend Award which contributed to feeding hungry children in Africa. Carmelita's Corner is heard Mondays after 10:20 a.m. pst following RBL on www. ezwayradio.com, Spotify, Amazon Music, Player FM, Blog talk, Speaker

By the way the large rose ring in the photo was given to me by Marlynn Northcutt, one of the main members of The Rose Breast Cancer Society, and I use it as a symbol of the organization. Marly has since made her transition, but she helped establish the 501 (c)(3) nonprofit status and her dog, Margarita, a beautiful Golden Retriever, Wolf and German Shephard attended the meetings and was also a guest on a TV show with our members, was the product of a German Shepherd who had breast cancer. Margarita became our four-legged good will ambassador, and she has gone on to doggy heaven.

Through
The Art of Sacrifice, Courage, and Resilience
Dr. Catherine Grace Pope

Let me begin my personal story with something the elders in my family would say whenever we shared our stories at home, "It's All in The Blood". They were referring to the impact that our history has on our lives. So, we must begin with the past to positively impact the present and the future. Keeping my ancestors in mind, I will begin my story with my grandfather, Dr. D. W. Gooden, the year 1927. Because of his activism and the activism of several other Black doctors, there were hospitals started for African Americans in Omaha.

I was raised in the projects. The projects were a legacy of a horrible summer in Omaha in 1919. The Omaha race riot. That race riot led to the creation in 1930 of housing projects that later became home to hundreds of African Americans in the 1940s. Like now, some people had money to move, and many didn't. However, my mother Juanita Pope addressed the mostly all-white male panel of the Logan Fontenelle Housing Authority in 1936. She told them that they must consider the needs of poor people. She also told them that she lost two children---the result of a fire due to living under poor housing conditions.

That story, her story, was told in the Omaha World Herald. Demolition began that fall. I'd like to think that through her bravery and the bravery of the other community members who were present and by using their voices, the Logan Fontenelle Housing Authority made sure that whenever changes were made, and people had to move, they would try to aid in their relocation both logistically and financially. Now there are all types of homes through various programs for Omaha residents---all because a young African American mother had the audacity to share her story.

During the Civil Rights Movement of the 1960s, policies that kept blacks out of public housing began to change. Even though this was before my time, eventually I benefited, and other poor people across the city benefited as well.

These are the historical stories and family stories that change the trajectory of our lives whether we are aware of it or not.

For me, one of the most memorable occasions was one of civil disobedience. It involved my entire family along with the black community. It occurred over a series of months at a local controversial amusement park, Peony Park. It was the Amateur Athletic Union Swimming Meet held in August 1955. I was about six years old. All of us in the family wanted to attend, along with many people in our community. Upon our arrival, we could see people waving signs, and there were shouts of "BLANK go home! This is our park!" We had come to see my cousin Leonard Hawkins to compete along with another Negro boy. They were not allowed to participate, not because there was anything wrong with their paperwork, but because they were black. My cousin Leonard and the other registered black swimmer were both turned away and were barred from the pool area.

With the encouragement and insistence of the entire black community, including the churches, the Omaha Star, the Urban League, and the National Association for the Advancement of Colored People (NAACP), the State of Nebraska took the park to district court. The suit was titled Nebraska v.

Peony Park. We won! I could barely hold up my sign as I marched, "This is My Park, My Pool".

Because of our actions several youth organizations and activists were instrumental in changing the color barrier restrictions through protests. The Neighborhood Community Action Council was soon formed. Out of that council Mrs. Rose Mary Pope-Moore and other members of the community formed the Hamilton-Lake Community Council (H-LCC). It started in May 1966 when I was finishing my junior year of high school. We requested aid in organizing our community into a structure powerful enough to begin meeting and solving our problems.

I participated in many community meetings that summer. I began to solicit the aid of high-school students from Tech and Central, college students from Creighton, Duchesne, and St. John's Seminary, and they began working with our membership. We canvassed the areas in and outside of our community to encourage black residents to register and vote. On December 10, 1966, the community center's grand opening was held. Now we were on our way.

We had several accomplishments. The Hamilton-Lake Community Center leased a facility in September 1966. The following year, on February 14, 1967, we opened a Head-Start preschool program. We develop three vacant lots into basketball courts, playgrounds for tots, and softball fields. We formed two Girls' Club troops.

In addition to Head Start, was the Sunshine Cultural Center. It was the only local school and youth cultural center dedicated to the performing arts.

By November 1967, I was volunteering at the Sunshine Cultural Center and seeing to the day-to-day operations. Artists came from all over the

city to volunteer, and the school even had artists-in-residence, something that most programs in the city probably heard very little about or had little access to. Children were allowed to write, direct, and make their voices heard. More importantly, they were given every opportunity to tell their stories.

In the aftermath of so many of the events of 1968 and 1969, the unrest, the riots, the on-going Viet-Nam War, were complaints of police brutality. I decided to participate in peaceful protests and yes, I was at the George Wallace Convention in 1968 held in my hometown, Omaha. He was seeking the Presidential nomination. He didn't want White and Black people to attend school together among other things. This occurred during my first run for the title, Miss Omaha 1968.

Of course, things got out of hand. Police appeared out of nowhere and began charging up the center aisles of the large auditorium. They began swinging their batons, forcing us to run into each other. I was falling into people as I tried to stay on my feet. Fists were flailing violently and angrily in the air. My mother and I were sprayed with mace by police officers while dodging blows. Mom cried out and fell to the floor. My sisters Joyce Pope-Goodwin and Rose Mary Pope-Moore were also there along with the Omaha community.

I'm often asked why I went –I went to use my voice.

Have you ever heard of THE NATIONAL PANEL of AMERICAN WOMEN? I hadn't either until they showed up at my home for a meeting. There were at least nine women, and they wanted me to run for Miss Omaha, Nebraska.

Little did I know that I would be asked to use my voice in this way. If I won the national contest, I would be the first African American to enter and

win the Miss America Pageant. After giving their request serious thought I decided to run.

During my run for Miss Omaha in 1968-69 and Miss Nebraska in 1969, people who didn't want to see me participate in this contest made attempts to discourage me.

I'll never forget the morning that my brother John and my father took a noose down from its low-hanging branch in our back yard while several of us looked on. That large, thick rope, tightly knotted and secured on a limb, was meant as a message—threats—to me, just like the noose that was rumored hanging in the university.

I was now in college and Miss Omaha, 1969, a part of the Miss America Franchise. On Friday, November 7, at 1:30 p.m. my college organization Black Liberators for Action on Campus, (BLAC) held a news conference in the Milo Bail Student Center with the University of Nebraska at Omaha (UNO's) President, Dr. Kirk E. Naylor in his office to present a list of demands to him in person. Two of the main ones were:

1. A voice in finding and selecting black instructors and speakers along with programming of the black studies curriculum.

2. A Black History Department and Program where you can obtain a degree in Black Studies.

A little after 1:00, members of the Omaha Police Department arrived in the Administration Building. Their numbers grew quickly. I could hear their tall boots pounding the ground in unison outside as they swiftly left their cars, wagons, and vans. Their large guns rattled as they got closer.

We were asked three times to leave peacefully, but nobody moved. Now I was asked! "Miss Pope, would you like to leave? I refused. I stood my

ground. I was led out the door with the other students and placed into a police car. Now in 2023, this program remains one of the few Black Studies Departments that exist today in the United States, 50 Years Later. I now understood that if something is worth anything at all, it must be worth fighting for.

When I was given a platform to speak or asked for my opinion on what was happening in my city, I spoke about the injustices in the workplace and in the schools. I spoke about the lack of jobs and poor housing conditions in the projects and the lack of housing for the black working class and the homeless. I spoke about bank loans and red lining. I voiced my concerns for women's rights and equal pay, health care, and family leave. I spoke about mental health in children, family leave, and police violence. I never got the killing of Vivian Strong out of my head. She was 14. I was 18, and I showed up in support of her and her programs for ending violence against youth. It happened during my reign as Miss Omaha.

Of course, my activism made some people uncomfortable and uneasy, even downright angry and it still does. I knew that it was up to me to walk in my own truth whenever possible and wherever it leads me. My ancestors demand no less of me!

While on my personal journey to discover the truth about my beginning, I found myself like most at times at the crossroads of discovering my biggest truth: There is more to a person than their outer self or their desire to be acknowledged or accepted by others as a beautiful woman on the outside.

In 1969, I could have been the first Miss America of my race, but I chose to become a fighter for truth and justice for my people, a role that I was always destined for. Still unknowingly I took my place in history as the first African American woman of color to become a title winner in the Miss America franchise in 1969, Miss Omaha, Nebraska.

Someone said of me:

My beauty cannot be tarnished by my dedication to my people or my ongoing fight---for justice. It can only be enhanced.

A reporter once wrote of me:

-That I stood my ground under difficult circumstances throughout my life and that I dared to challenge an unjust system during the Civil Rights Movement as a member of the Omaha 54.

- And that I became a dedicated Advocate and Mentor for women's rights and spoke out when I saw an injustice being committed always using my voice, unwavering.

When I opened my eyes wide, I found myself soon separated from my mother. I struggled to survive. Later I was moved to an orphanage where I spent the first six to eight months of my infant life. This part of my life was unknown to me, a secret for over 40 years. As a child I spent most of my days in pain fighting to survive. By three I was walking with steel braces on my legs the result of severe rickets at birth. By five I was attending school without them and by middle school I was preforming in dance recitals. Some of that pain inside and out has lasted throughout my life and so I find myself on a journey of healing.

To heal trauma, we must go back. Where you ask? Well, that depends on how far you want to go back and how deep the trauma is. We have all had trauma in our life, things that affect us emotionally and on a psychological level. The question is are we ready to face the reality of hurt and pain, disappointment, shame and at times regret? Yes, we all have trauma, and so I decided to go home and make a documentary about certain moments of the past experiences, and events in my life.

I found that I could change the trajectory of my life by using my voice and sharing my stories. I fed the homeless, gave out boxes of food during the pandemic. I used my skills as a Supervised Visitation Monitor to bring families together, uniting children with their parents. As a school principal I offered special programs at my school to help children catch up in their classes and enjoy extracurricular programs at the Joan Kroc Center learning art, dance, learning to play instruments, use technology and participate in sports. I went before the city council and used my voice for an underserved community. Within a year we were celebrating the opening of a new park--the second in the city of San Diego that carries the name of its African American citizens.

I was once told that history will always remember the first. That is why the first must always be remembered in history, a very difficult place to be. It brings with it struggles, pain, heartache, and, of course, a great deal of responsibility. The truth is it is never an easy road to travel. While searching I discovered that all women are much more than the sum of their parts. They must not allow others to define them, diminish them, or silence them.

I have several sayings that I want to share-

"Begin wherever you are. See yourself as an agent of change. Now is the time to be the positive change that you would like to see.

USE YOUR VOICE-

Then go out inspire and empower other women to do the same."

"You will never wear your crown with dignity if you're not willing to recognize that it may need a cleaning now and then."

Dr. Catherine Grace Pope, 2023

Without question, I am not done yet!

The Bridge To A New Life
Madeline Plate

Who would have thought...who would have thought that a bridge could change your life!

Not just any bridge, the Coronado Bridge in San Diego. But first, the back story leading up to the bridge experience.

I was raised by a 27-year marine, that knew how to raise marine troops better than he knew how to raise children. My father set an example of always striving to be the very best you can be. Never let up, take no rest, always a man of honor and a warrior. Later in life, I realized the discipline and demand for perfection was all part of my "schooling" to later achieve the levels of success in my business.

Being a dedicated career marine, my father was away on deployments during my teenage years more than he was home. Upon his receiving orders to serve in the Vietnam war our family home was immediately forced to relocate off the military installation. In the urgency of the change, no time to discover many options and finances being a consideration, our home was moved into a drug-infested troubled neighborhood that was circled in red for high alert by the Vista police and fire department.

As a 13-year-old girl, I was vulnerable to the street and behaviors of the culture that surrounded me. The top drug dealer soon snatched me up into his world. It was drug partying every weekend with every form of drugs imaginable and easily available.

Criminal behavior was rampant all over the neighborhood. As vulnerable as I was, today I cringe thinking I am fortunate to have survived without permanent damage to my life such as a criminal record or drug or alcohol addiction.

My world was so small. All I knew that existed was my neighborhood in Vista, and I assumed that was the way the rest of the world lived. I'm the girl from Vista and that's my fate, so I thought.

Once your vision is expanded, it can never return to its' former reality.

It was on a trip to downtown San Diego one evening that I first saw the bridge. It was all lit up like a jewel, sparkling on the bay against the star lit sky. I couldn't take my eyes off the site of the bridge. It was beautiful and alluring. And then the transforming thought came to me...there must be more to life than my life in the neighborhood in Vista, and I've got to find a way out!

I didn't know how, but someone said that once your vision is expanded, it can never go back to its' original place. As I look back, this became my transforming moment. That day I found my burning desire to live a different life.

All because of a bridge, its magnitude lit my imagination on fire, there must be more. That day I found my burning desire. I knew at that moment there was more to life, more adventure to live, and a larger world to be explored and experienced.

With that impression embedded in my mind, I became filled with determination. I was going to find a way to seek and discover this other world, I've got to find it. I made a commitment and the relentless desire that I would never raise my children in an environment that lacked integrity or core values.

So, at age 16, I took to heart the responsibility to live differently. I strove to push up against the culture I lived in. I stopped attending parties, stopped drinking and stopped taking drugs even though I still was living a life of brokenness.

I discovered a love for fashion and design and was encouraged by one of my high school Home Economics teachers. She took me under her wing and further mentored my creative abilities. With her encouragement, it was decided I would do well to attend fashion design school in Los Angeles. The scholarship I earned was not sufficient to cover the needed tuition money. I nervously approached my father; he spoke with the intensity I had lived my entire childhood in, "I'm not going to waste my money on you because you're just going to get married and have babies!" I heard him saying, "you are not worthy". It was crushing emotionally, but I wasn't going to stop there. I started a career in retail with one of the major department stores in San Diego. I was determined to make an impression by out working everyone, getting special permission to come in early and staying late, daily. Whatever it took to get promoted and have advancement in my career. I was promised, with my hard work ethic, that a career path to become a buyer would be the reward for hard work. I was recognized for my ability to oversee and run departments within the department store.

Then, the axe fell. "But we can't promote you because you don't have a college degree needed to advance any further." The promises were broken.

Test fast, fail fast, adjust fast.

It's not how many times you fall; it's whether you get back up. So, off to a new field and new career in the banking industry I went. I quickly rose to a managers' position and again applied my work ethic to my new career. I vividly remember my manager rubbing my shoulders, telling me, some day, I may just have his position; be patient. Quite honestly, I thought, that's all there is. To end up where he is? That scared me to death. I did not find the details, the design, or rewards of that position attractive. I desired more and would seek more.

It was a Friday evening, closing the bank, and one of the tellers couldn't balance their drawer. We worked feverishly into the night, trying to find the error. Finally, I put it in error in question into suspense and decided to get a fresh look on Monday morning. When Monday morning came, the executive team deserted me, and I was severely questioned as to my making the decisions I made. Not one stepped up to express his/her confidence in my management abilities; no one had my back. That night as they ran the business cycle the error was resolved and discovered to be a computer program error.

That was when I realized I will always be expendable in corporate America. I was literally heartbroken. I started seeking other opportunities.

I got out of Vista. Now I had the awareness and burning desire to get out of Corporate America. I needed another Coronado Bridge experience.

So young, so little ability, I certainly was not living life intentionally, I did not even have the "know how". Today, I know it takes desire. It is the essence of the human soul, the secret of our existence. Every accomplishment starts with desire. The life I had was not the life I wanted to live; it was not the life I was created for. I believe God chose to plant the seed of burning desire in my heart and fuel it so I would search for the life He prized for me to live. Psalm 37:4.

A bridge to a dentists' chair? God works in mysterious ways, doesn't He? I became enlightened once again. A door opened for a potential option, I said "yes" to an "ask", I stepped through the threshold. I was in the dentist chair as the Dental Hygienist was telling about a new career she was pursuing. She asked me to attend an information session pertaining to the company she was involved with. I showed up.

Nobody wants a boss; everyone needs a coach.

I learned that the company was a company that coaches and educates middle American families on how money works. I ended up attending an initial orientation meeting, thinking since I'm in banking, what could they teach me? They introduced me to principles that I was shocked that I didn't know, such as "The rule of 72", "The magic of compound interest" and other simple money concepts. Here I am in the banking industry, and I never heard of these principles or concepts. How could that be?

Since the company would allow people to start part time and not jeopardize their present job, I thought, I'm going to start part time just so I can become better educated in finance and learn how to better prepare, better understand, and have confidence in the world of money, buying a car or a home or saving for my future.

My past experiences had lowered my self-confidence, and I had come to feel as if I had no star qualities. My Father's telling me I wasn't worthy for attending college and earning a degree and my two former occupations never delivering the promises I had worked so hard to earn topped the reasons. I moved slowly, hesitantly, only absorbing information with tremendous doubt, very little belief in my becoming successful.

What I found was that I was in an environment of encouragement and positive thinkers. I didn't need a degree to pursue this or even a background in finance. They assumed I knew nothing.

Today, I look back and appreciate the company's willingness to have an open-door acceptance and recruiting policy. They mentored me rather than bossed me and encouraged me every time I did something right.

Just keep showing up.

Now going on 42 years with this company, reflecting back, one of the keys is that I kept showing up. If they had training, I was there like a sponge, absorbing all that I could learn.

If they had a social event, I was there. They told me, just show up, be coachable, and have a work ethic. Since I didn't think I had star quality, I knew, at least, I could show up. Even during times, I was challenged, and my burning desire helped me to push through any discouragement I faced. You might say I kept pushing through and showing up to my future even though at the time I didn't know it.

The real Madeline that was deep inside me started to grow and blossom. My confidence grew, I started to see great results, and I was coachable! There were no "gotchas" about being promoted. They told me exactly what I needed to do for the next promotion. I flew through promotions, and within a few of years, was promoted to Vice President.

The way to riches is to enrich the lives of others.

There I met my future husband, Glenn, who was also a Vice President with the company, and we not only married, but we also merged! Before long, we qualified for full ownership of our block of business that projected us into the 7 figures. We were doing something that we passionately believe

in, becoming a "financial rescue mission" for hundreds of families. Someone once said, "The way to riches is to enrich the lives of others!"

That is what we were doing. We have built lasting relationships with 1000's of clients by coaching and teaching simple concepts, strategies and providing the best solutions for the family to become financially secure and sustainable.

Survival, or success, or significance?

Most of all, my life went first from survival to success. Then we went from success to significance. I learned that success is what happens to you; significance is when you impact others, by helping them succeed.

In hindsight, I shudder with fear. What if I hadn't had the courage to JUST SHOW UP?

My life, my family's lives, the lives of 1000's of client would be different, not good.

Changing your family's legacy

Glenn and I have 4 children combined. We've lived in support of our children, their desires, being available and involved emotionally and financially. We supported the cost of colleges, provided travel experiences, purchased vehicles, and created a lifestyle that they mirror to their children. All are extremely successful. We have a son that is a professor at an Ivy League college in upstate New York, another son that is an attorney, a daughter with her master's in journalism, and our other daughter who is a successful hard worker and an entrepreneur.

In our hard work to build a business and pursue, our desires we have built a successful company within our parent company. Our children will inherit

our business, which will generate a continued income source for each of their families. We created a legacy.

Glenn and I continue to stay focused on our business purpose.

We develop teams that go into the communities we live in to help educate families. We teach simple rules of money and on how to win the money game. We believe that helping one family at a time we can change the economic infrastructure of a city. We challenge the traditional financial institutions high priced low valued products and the method of depriving a huge profit at the demise of the middle-class family. Our company's business model does not allow us to make one cent unless we help a family. We are proud of who we are and what we do. Our desire to not only achieve success but to live a life of significance.

Making an impact to bring change.

We've helped raise money to support building orphanages in India, paid for a school in Kenya, we help to eradicate sex trafficking and given to our church. We have fundraised for homeless organizations in our community and Semper Fi Fund that supports veterans, participated in programs for school age children and any other need that God impresses upon us.

Today, we seek individuals who have a relentless desire to live a better life and are willing to have the courage to JUST SHOW UP! We will work alongside individuals to help coach and develop their abilities to a high level of success within my company.

The greatest legacy is empowering other leaders.

My greatest happiness is in mentoring other women in our business, seeing the hope and confidence in them grow and watching them achieve levels of success they never thought would happen. Like me, they are seeking

equity, equality, fairness, respect and the ability to keep their family's needs as their priority. Women make up 58% of the individuals who come to work for our company. Forbes has recognized our company for diversity, equality, and Inclusion.

Four consecutive years in a row, Forbes has named our company, "One of the Best Employers for Women". Someone said the greatest legacy is the leaders that you mentor and leave in your place.

I'm no longer, "The girl from Vista". I'm a child of the King.

Today, our mantra is "Life on our terms!"

Was it the bridge? Or was it just an instrument that God used as a promise of His future blessings?

"For I know the plans I have for you, plans to prosper you and not to harm you, plans to give you hope and a future." *Jeremiah 29:11*

It's My Life!

Dr. (h.c.) Cherie Reynolds

Showing up always opens doors for me!

Today I am living on a Golf course in Oceanside, CA. It's about 10 minutes from the beach. I am Cheri Reynolds, and I have lived my life by design.

I have had a Superpower from the day I was born. First, I was number one of six! When I was graduating from High School in Bitburg, Germany, I was the Colonel's daughter! We will define Superpower as you read on.

I was a Military Brat which means I moved a lot. Every three years I was in a different state and a different house, and I had an opportunity to meet New Friends and face different Challenges---compliments of the Colonel and the USAF. I have seen a lot of the USA and some of Europe. I did not have to ask, but it was my privilege to experience a life of building relationships and living in different cultures like the South, the Midwest, Germany, and mostly California.

My maternal grandmother lived in Manhattan Beach, California, not far from where I was born. Her Home was my home base! She was extremely influential in my life. When I was there, I was learning lessons and mostly cleaning! My reward was to go to the beach... it has not changed! I still love

the beach and no surprise. Several years later I was the Owner and Founder of Executive Housekeeping and Janitorial Services. Clean is a word that predominantly ran through my life! Here is where the Ask was used a lot! I built the Company from Scratch knocking on doors in neighborhoods at first, and I transitioned to Commercial Contracts, making a million in sales by the 25th year. When I was awarded a contract, I showed up with my Crew to supervise, and then I hired Supervisors so I could market the Company and Ask for more Contracts. I will mention this again in my timeline.

I always strived to be better. The Colonel and I had different Ideas about my life. He wanted me to be the Girl in the Kitchen with Mom, and I wanted to travel and live life to the fullest. From the moment we landed in Germany, I was enrolling in my Senior year in High School, My Calendar started filling up! I was elected Cheerleader in the first week and later was involved in my school events and a boyfriend took up some of my time! I spent some time in the Kitchen with Mom cooking dinner and baking for her Women events during my Senior year! I did a little traveling with the basketball and football teams as their cheer support! That was where I learned most about German Culture. We were in homes local to our events where we broke bread and slept. We were in a foreign country and had to act as grateful Guests. I look back now and feel so grateful for the experience which added to my knowledge and values.

My Experience after High School was enriched when I learned to drop the Rebel Attitude and become a Lady. My mom and dad wanted me to become a debutante to be presented to Society, so I did. I was taught table manners, how to walk and put on makeup, and went to numerous fittings for my gown for the Event. I went to proper settings with the other girls who were also being groomed for the "Coming Out" like Teas and Greeting the Cadets from Notre Dame who were sent to escort us. I made my dad

proud and had a moment of accomplishment to have the Colonel's complete attention, there is a photo to prove it!   Respect your mom and dad!

So after the Cinderella experience, I went to London with a Friend and saw some English culture! We went to London on a Ferry and saw the Changing of the Guards. We actually saw some quite spectacular sites. Later a Girlfriend and I went to Spain and met a band called the Kingpins on the beach. Her boyfriend brought his motorcycle and transported us one by one from the train station to the Beach. We went to the clubs where the Band played and sang with them in an Officers Club. Dad did not know! No Regrets! Fun experience but late hours for me.

I wanted to parachute from an airplane (Dad was a Pilot). I wanted to tour Europe with my friends, and I wanted to Race in the Desert. I Did!! But since Dad was opposed to most of my ideas, I organically developed my Superpower... I asked questions about how to do these things and then found people who would help me. Sort of Going around Dad ...He didn't like it, but I have a hard time accepting which developed my superpower of just finding a way around a 'NO'. Anything is Possible. I found a way to borrow my dad's ID number to arrange for me and 13 of my friends to travel to Berlin on a Free train, stay in a Youth hostel for .25 a night and take a bus to the east Berlin to see what it looked like on the other side of the Wall. Things were a little weird, especially when I decided to take a photo with my camera! The Scene was a little bare, the windows were whitewashed, and no one was in the streets except a motorcycle with two men. The one in the back had a machine gun, and as soon as I snapped the photo, the guard on the bus snatched my camera from me! No discussion and it was best that I did not use the ASK.

I did go to college at the University of Maryland in Munich, so it was easy to travel on Weekends. After my first year Dad actually sent me back to

California to live with my grandmother... The explanation will be in the next book! I proceeded to clean at my grandmother's and graduated from Fullerton College with an AA Degree in Psychology. I then married and had two little Girls. About 5 years after that I studied to become a hairdresser. I had a talent and my childhood dream had come true also I used my degree as an underpaid Psychologist while I did hair. I listened to the clients' stories and told mine! I think the Ask of "how did that turn out" ensured their return. People don't care about what you know but they do care how you make them feel. That lasted about 3 years.

My Marriage was rocky, and I was growing. My partner was not amused by my direction, and he was non-supportive. I was performing my beautification talents on Women on Stage and working late to accommodate my clients. We divorced and I had to find a way to provide for my Girls that would allow me to be home at bedtime.

I started a job with a friend that gave me access to jobs available. I interviewed people for employment and talked to Employers who were looking for manpower. I did this for a short time and then found the Fun Job! Dreyer's Ice Cream was looking for a Sales Representative. I interviewed with Peter and Steve, and I Sold them on Me! I told them I would do whatever it takes! I was fortunate to enjoy meeting new people and asking questions and sharing the best Ice Cream in the Marketplace! That was my Job. My kids loved the Bubble Gum Ice Cream, and I was a hero to all their friends, too! I really put my all into that job. I helped Ice Cream Parlors Set up their Shop. I found a Baskin Robbins on base and told the manager that I needed to learn how to sell Ice Cream! (She knew my dad TA-DA Superpower) We copied the handbook, and I taught people how to scoop the Ice cream and hooked them up with my Friend at Coke; they got Ice Cream Storage and coke fountain equipment. We found Signage and they were in business! I ended up going to Oakland to Ice Cream University. Really!!! I completely

and earned my certificate. I put Dreyer's in every chain store and Mom and Pop stores in the Riverside and San Bernardino Counties. I also took Ice Cream connections to the Orange County Fair for the Octoberfest. My girls and babysitter and family came and dressed up in German Outfits, and we introduce our Mud Pie! That lasted about 3 years.

I was fired from my position! I was devastated! The reason was not valid nor is it pertinent to our conversation. The Event was a catalyst to my next Level! I Never Regret what I did prior to the End of a Relationship! Thank You, Jesus! What I gained was a blessing of experience, tools to add to my tool belt, and an edit to what's next! So, my contact at Coke reached out to me when he found out I left Dreyer's and connected me to Scotsman Ice Machines!

I was hired, and I was the only Woman on the Sales Team. It was a great season in my Life. I am very competitive and won a contest selling Ice Machine Dispensers to Hotels. I visited all Hotels under construction and sold 30 Machines in the period we had to compete. The runner up sold 8 machines and the prize was a dual Refrigerator and Ice maker to plug into my Office. I know there is always another story that is waiting for me. I always believe in what I do because I research the integrity of the Product and the People and the Company! I am all in from the beginning and work diligently to complete my Goals that I set for myself! A Lesson I learned early on is not to hold back but give it all you Got and Yes, Show up in Life!

Three years in and I was approached by Hobart Corporation. I was pretty impressed with myself, and I knew I was ready for National Accounts management. I worked with Arco and all national accounts in Southern California. I worked with Arco on their project in the Convenience Stores developing a Model to serve the Hamburger and Hot Dog Venue. My quota was set by Hobart at 1.2 million, and on my Annual Review I had met that

and surpassed it at 1.5 percent of that quota. The tricky thing about this was after I was recognized by the President of Hobart, I saw a change of attitude from my superiors. It was as if I was competing with my own team. I saw them try to discredit me and ignore me when I needed an answer for my customer. The "Corporate Life" was now my enemy, and I resigned after 3 years. If you have had this happen, you know exactly what I am talking about!

This was when I decided to become an entrepreneur. This was not a decision because it was easy, but because I needed to make my own decisions and design my life with purpose and integrity. If I was representing myself to a client, I wanted to do it as a genuine problem solver. I mentioned earlier that I opened a cleaning Service which engulfed 25 years of my life. I was dedicated to my business and rarely took a vacation. I did buy a Motorhome and had some time off with Family and friends. I drove from Riverside where I lived to Napa with my mom to watch my granddaughter graduate. Creating memories must be a part of the formula to a better life. I parked my Motorhome near 2 of my friends and their rigs at Lake Hemet! I always got excited when Friday came along because it meant a 30-minute drive to Nature and my friends dancing around the fire like no-one was watching! The agenda was letting go of the Stress on Friday, walking around the Lake, Games on Saturday, and preparing to leave and get back on Sunday...for 3 years!

2008 - 2009 was a huge lesson in Life for me. My Company was servicing a Homebuilder in every aspect of their business. Most of my Eggs were in their basket and when they closed the Models and stopped building and they also closed their corporate Office, I was no longer in the position to pay my employees and workers comp. The whole platform I had built crumbled with the demise of the economy. My health deteriorated, and I struggled for a couple of years to keep my precious business open. I was

maintaining my accounts and finally came to the realization that I needed to let go. I learned that I needed to spread the eggs around and diversify. Kudos to those who survived that Season.

I was approached by my office assistant about a Healthy Protein Shake that was a Meal Replacement. When I learned that I had a life-threatening disease, I asked everyone what it was and how I could make it better. My Office assistant brought me a nutritional Shake that changed my life for the better! Here I learned about a New Clean. Eating clean and wholesome foods, minimizing sugar and carbs, and working out was my new lifestyle. The old style plus Stress had created a condition called Diverticulitis. By drinking 2 shakes a day I was a Product of the Product and got my energy back! I lost weight and competed in the 5k at the LA Marathon. I encouraged others to take charge of their life and was able to help one client lose 100 pounds. If you don't have your health, you really are without energy and strength to take on any other challenges.

It took over 10 years to be ready for my next adventure. During that time, I had a partnership in a Travel Company called Liv. We traveled in a Group taking advantage of a fabulous discount to enjoy experiences in places we could never afford to go to on our own. I had lots of fun experiences like Cancun with 400 of my closest friends. The highlight on that trip was when we were transported to our private Island at sunset in 5 Catamarans. On the Island we were greeted by Islanders with champagne and fire and music. We enjoyed fabulous cuisine in a relaxed atmosphere while we were entertained by amazing fire dancers. As we left the Island, we left our desires we had expressed in the waves on biodegradable paper. Dreams do come True!! Later We did Hollywood like an Academy Award winner. It was also therapeutic! I love having fun and traveling. Did you know that Traveling makes you Rich?

In 2021 a friend introduced me to a renewable energy platform that would provide Clean Energy for the residential homeowner! About 15 years ago, I helped the Cal Poly Engineering team get Sponsors for their Solar Car in a race from Michigan to Disney world. The car was reliant on the Sun for its Fuel. I was hooked. Since I am all about Clean Energy from a health standpoint, I really became excited about the potential of a world where we have the possibility to energize Family homes with Energy of the Sun. The Resources of the Earth are running out, and the best answer to save the environment is to switch to Renewable Energy! This is a big problem to solve, and I am proud to be with a Company who cares. We can do this job from our computer, but I still have energy to go to meetings and networking events to accelerate the adoption of Renewable Energy. I have a team to help me accelerate the adoption of Solar and we are adding members all the time. The cool part about this is I am able to earn while I learn; so far, the adventure has been rewarding! The company rewards the Core of their company, the consultant, with 70 percent of the profits! With so many people losing their jobs this is an opportunity with perfect timing to offer an additional stream of income.

We are attracting those who are in the business of working with Homeowners especially Realtors and Lenders as well a pool guys, handymen, and Hvac companies. I have joined a tribe of Women in this industry, and we have the Powur! There is no wonder that this solar platform called Powur is the fastest growing in the industry! I love that we can help our friends in 32 states and project growth Globally. So, when I show up to an event and have an ASK which is really a gift, I request the homeowners Utility bill so I can provide the Free Energy Report. So far it seems that every meeting with the GSFE that I have been able to provide assistance for one of our members. As a matter of fact, we are now on the road in the installation process for a friend of Someone who just visited one

of our meetings. Nancy signed up as an ambassador and will receive $1000 at Install completion! The potential of this Opportunity is limitless.

My great grandson was born 2 months ago, and he as well as my 5 other grandchildren are my WHY! I want a clean environment, not a toxic environment that includes fossil fuels, where they can grow up and for their children and so on. I am energized daily to reach out and accelerate the adoption of Clean Energy.

I am grateful to review my life through writing this book. I am so grateful to Robbie Motter, CEO and founder of Global society of Female Entrepreneurs. The Show up and Ask is Key to an enriched life. I hope I have added value to your life and wish you blessings and success in your endeavors. Remember your Now does not define you! Go and be Great or Start Again ...It's your life!

Ask, And It Shall Be Given to You!
Matthew 7:7

Dr. (h.c.) Kathleen Ronald

I'm sure that if you asked a million people in the world if they had heard of that famous bible verse Matthew 7:7 Ask, And It Shall Be Given You, 90% would have replied "yes" that they had heard it. Or they may resonate with, "Ask, and you shall receive."

I'm curious, why do we have so many challenges regarding asking?

I've spent my entire career as a keynote speaker, trainer, and consultant, working with my clients, students, and audiences, helping them to get to the root cause of what prevents them from mastering their Askability factor. The ability to ASK, regardless of the context of the ask, is the one skill that will change your life and business.

As a young girl, I wasn't always able to ask. My father, Bob, was my first and most significant mentor, and he would always say, "Kathleen, if you don't ask, you don't get it!" He would then say, "What do you have now?"

I would reply, "Nothing."

He would respond, "if you ask, you could still have nothing, or you could get what you need by asking so why are you so afraid to ask?"

I responded, "Do you want the short or the long list?"

Can any of you relate?

I remember when I was working at Nordstrom in my late 20s as the manager of the Personal Touch (they did your wardrobe) department. I had to master the art of ASKing as I was NOT qualified to hold that position, based on my current experience. However, as my longtime friend and Earth Angel Robbie Motter always stated, "It is ALL about Showing Up!" So, I did show up for the application process for a job I was not qualified for ~ who does that? Not many. I knew nothing about the skills one should possess to work in that department. At that time, I couldn't shake the fear of being a disappointment to the store manager who had entrusted me with the job. Luckily, I've always been competitive and resourceful, and thanks to my father's lessons, I had the askability factor going for me in this situation.

To assemble a top team, I had to Show Up and Ask many questions daily. I walked through what felt like a steel door of fear most days. I was on a crash course to get a stylist and manager's degree. I hired a team, opened a store, ran a department, and created the training and client list.

In reflection, I had to put aside my pride, ego, limiting beliefs, and stories. In each case, I faced the fear and did it anyway. Those things, if entertained, will steal every one of our dreams...... EVERY time!

I love this quote, which is a reminder to this day to keep me walking when I want to run,

"The activity you're most avoiding contains your biggest opportunity!"

~ Robin S. Shanna

At this age, I'm old enough to know that anything is possible if you face your fears. If you had told me we would create the #1 department in all of

Nordstrom's within six months of opening that store, I would have called you crazy!

In that scenario, I had NO issues with asking; I would have failed big time if I did. That was not an option for me. Now, you would think if I could do all the asking needed in that scenario, I would have mastered the art of asking ... NO, that was just not the case. As I said, each situation will allow us to ask easily or land us in the ocean of fear! Then we cannot move forward based on what we think and speak about that situation.

In this next scenario, my askability felt broken.

As we all know, many things are easy to ask for.

My favorite easy ask is "Do you have cookie dough ice cream?"

A much harder ask would be "Can I borrow 25,000?"

Right?

So, the goal is to be able to ask regardless of the context of the question we are asking!

During my time at Nordstrom, I took over a client named Yvonne who was unhappy with her consultant for various reasons. I overheard her sharing her frustration from the back office. I went to see how I could help, and she spilled her issues and needs. The best thing about working at Nordstrom is that the Nordstrom family always gave us the tools to ensure every customer experience was great!

So, I listened to her story, told her I would take her appointment, and sent her upstairs for a free lunch. That gave me plenty of time to pull her wardrobe. She was with me for over three hours and was so thrilled and impressed with my customer service that she wrote a three-page letter

to the store manager. I tell you this story because she was the key person responsible for me getting the connection for my future dream job.

I feel everything is connected and serves as a piece of our life's road map. Imagine if I hadn't shown up for that job interview and had never asked thousands of questions to gain the needed knowledge. I would have never met Yvonne, who gave me the key to unlock my next dream job.

I didn't share earlier that I had many Apple clients while working for Nordstrom. They would share how amazing it was to work at Apple. Who wouldn't want to have significant raises every six months, big Friday beer bashes, free food, and more? I wanted to work there!

After I met Yvonne, it was almost a year later that I came across her name again. I was clearing out my customer files for the transition and discovered that Yvonne was married to the man running the creative department at Apple. WHAT? No way? I felt as if I had won the lottery with this discovery.

At that time, I did not have a computer, and my spelling and grammar were that of a ten-year-old. I am not one to read manuals. I wasn't a developer or programmer, but I thought the one thing I am, is creative! I asked Yvonne if I could meet her husband for an informational interview. It was nearly impossible to get on his calendar, so we did a workaround. I interviewed him while doing his birthday wardrobe in San Francisco at Nordstrom downtown! During our chat, they both came up with an idea as to how I might be able to get an interview at Apple even though I had almost zero skills to work there!

Yvonne said, "You need to know our friend Amy Bonetti."

I replied, "Who is she?"

Yvonne responded, "She works for John Sculley."

I replied, "Who is he?"

She responded, "He is the CEO of Apple."

I responded, "I guess that is a good place to start."

This is where my fear gripped me like a straitjacket! I couldn't make that call to Amy for the life of me. I wasn't showing up and clearly could not move forward with the next ask.

Yvonne was shocked and encouraged me to call.

Why did I have so much fear about making this call?

Again, do you want the short or the long list of reasons?

Being a small-town girl from Aberdeen, WA, I had NO idea of the gravity of Amy Bonetti's position or, for that matter, John Scully's position. Ignorance is bliss - if I had fully understood who I was calling, I'm not sure I could have ever made that call.

I'll never forget that day as the call lasted about 30 minutes which apparently was 25 minutes longer than 99.9% of her calls. Again, ignorance is bliss. Amy and I discovered she lived right down the street from my apartment in Los Gatos, CA. She was maybe five houses around the corner. We agreed to meet at her home after that call.

As we began to get to know each other, she asked me where I was born and raised. When I told her I was from Aberdeen, WA. she asked if I knew the Bowers. I answered, "Yes, they are our next-door neighbors." Talk about a small world, I was stunned to hear they were her aunt and uncle, and she would spend summers with them.

She next asked, "Do you know Rick Ronald?"

I responded, "He is my brother! How do you know my brother?" She shared they used to sneak out at night and smoke cigarettes in Sam Bend Park, just a few blocks from our house. It's a crazy small world!

We had a great visit and loads of laughs and found even more things in common. As I was leaving, Amy told me that she was going to Asia with John Sculley, the CEO of Apple, and we should connect when she got back. I only got that job in that office because I moved through the fear, picked up the phone, and ASKED some questions. This led to the next meeting and the care package I sent to arrive when she returned home.

I was thrilled to hear she showed the letter and the package around the executive floor and ended up bringing me in as a temp. That job was one of the highlights of my career! Beyond the position is what I learned, who I became, the friends I gained, and more.

That first gig led to working for another executive and finally landing my full-time job with Morris Terradalsky, the VP of IST and Customer Service. I went on to fill in for other presidents within other divisions during my time at Apple. While I was working with the president of Apple Pacific for nine weeks, I met the president of a top marketing firm, and that led to my next job, which led to my next job - you get the idea!

Showing up and asking is so worth walking through the fear!

That ONE ask changed the course of my life.

There are NO coincidences, so pay attention to the clues that present themselves all day, every day, especially if we are in the moment! We must see them, follow them, and Show Up and Ask!

The moral of the story!

Show Up to every opportunity even when you are not qualified!

Ask, and YOU Shall Receive!

Every Single Time!

I'd love to hear from my readers, be able to connect, and be a resource if needed.

Thank you for taking the time to buy the book and read my chapter, amongst many others.

I pray you gained some gems, inspiration, and the spark you may have needed to step up your Show Up and Ask dance!

If you have issues with Showing Up and Asking due to being stuck in the dance of limiting beliefs, stories, or excuses, I feel you! Life is funny like that. It is a constant learning experience. Even when we think we've mastered the art of showing up and asking in every situation, it is not always the case.

I would love to share a free training with you that will help you learn how to clear those pesky items that keep you from moving forward with your goals and dreams.

We cannot move forward until we clear the limiting beliefs, stories, and excuses that steal our dreams.

Once you clear the root cause of what prevents you from Showing Up and Asking, The Sky Is the Limit!

Stories of the Power in showing up:
90% of Success in life is just showing up.

Dr. (h.c.) Shelly Rufin

Shelly Rufin, Founder/Owner of EDFIN College Planning believes in the power of an education, having fun while learning as it expands our prefrontal cortex, and most importantly expands showing up. Shelly was interviewed about how in her forties she went from being a Director of Financial Aid & Scholarships for fifteen years to an Educational Consultant at EDFIN College Planning, showing up and opening her own practice in 2008 to receiving her business degree at Harvard Business School. Now, Shelly after 30 years in the business, as an Educational Consultant Shelly shares her insights on breaking into a new industry in 2008 during an economic downturn and finding comfort in the uncomfortable.

The risks of giving up her comfortable job, 401K, full benefits package, to venture into the unknown world of entrepreneurship; she showed up every day, she did it. This is how her story of showing up began and unfolded. In 2008, she made the biggest decision that would change her life and everyone around her. Showing up and opening her 1st college planning business. She returned to college for her second master's degree in Clinical Counseling Neuroscience, with late nights and early mornings, and showed up in her communities, business, and in leadership opportunities. She continued to show up and educate parents and the community on the importance

of early college prep, college planning. Shelly believes in "Success is the sum of small efforts, repeated day in and day out". Shelly says Showing up is the difference from being comfortable to uncomfortable, impossible to possible, and doing what it takes; She likes challenging and stretching herself out of her comfort zone.

Now, thirty years later, as Founder, Owner, and Educational Consultant at EDFIN College Prep, College Planning, she serves the best and brightest kids in the world. As her story unfolds, she continued to show up at local college fairs, high schools and community outreach platform. Shelly has met some of the best and brightest college bound students (first generation students) who shared their stories of how their dreams to attend Harvard, MIT, Cornell, Stanford, UC San Diego, or UC Berkeley that didn't know where to get started.

Story #1 His name is Diego, 10th grade student, Mexican American, 1st generation, immigrated from Mexico to the United States. His hard earned 4.0 GPA all through middle school while living in Mexico, and 4.3 GPA through high school, (adjusting to U.S. customs) with dreams of attending MIT in Aerospace Engineer.

As an eighth grader, Diego started college planning early, showing up for every college planning session eager to learn, writing essay after essay, meeting all requirements to apply for his dream schools for the Fall 2023. He earned high scores in Advance Placement classes all throughout high school while maintaining a 4.3 GPA and met all other admissions requirements. Diego applied to his 10 top colleges in the United States i.e., Georgia Tech, MIT, Cornell University, Harvard, University of Michigan, University of Pennsylvania, University of California Los Angeles, Cal Poly San Luis Obispo, University of California Irvine, and University of California Berkeley and currently offered interviews to Harvard and Cornell while

waiting on admissions & financial aid acceptance offers. Diego's story of showing up, doing what is takes, at times being uncomfortable, didn't deter this young man, and he has an exceptional bright future ahead.

Diego has trademarked himself with the mark of excellence. He's grasped the opportunity of "showing up" to make each day exceptional. Only the exceptional paths bring exceptional glories!

"Excellence is the jet engine, that pushes you faster and higher to success."

There is a saying that goes 90% of success in life is just showing up. Diego had done just that. Showing up has led him to success and to reach his fullest potential. Just because Diego made the choice to show up. It's a powerful habit that serves everyone; everyday, showing up, you'll achieve your goals and live a happier life.

Story #2: This next story is going to surprise you. This young girl, Rula, a senior with a 3.2 GPA and her mom was referred by . . .

She shows up in my office with her mom. She provided her academic transcript and goes on to say, "My high school counselor said, 'you won't get into a university'." Her counselor said, "You haven't met the requirements to apply for admissions consideration." This was devastating news to hear what this counselor had said to this this aspiring young student with dreams to follow in her mom's footsteps of becoming a nurse. According to published author, Shelly Rufin in "Nine Key Decisions to Better College, Better Life: Making College DREAMS a Reality," Rula had to first meet the A-G requirements:

Rula had a lot of showing up ahead of her, to meet at least the following number of credits in subjects specified:

a. Four years of courses in English

b. Three years of math including an algebra course, at least one mathematic course or a combination of the two mathematics courses algebra one A and algebra one B required for completion in grades nine through 12 to meet or exceed state academic content standards for algebra one. Completion of algebra course work in grades 7 and eight do not exempt a student from the requirements to complete three mathematics courses in grades 9th through 12th grades. (Education Code 51224.5)

c. Three and 1/2 years of courses in history, social studies, including one semester of world geography; one year of world, history, culture, and geography; one year of United States, history, and geography; one semester course in American government, and civics; and one semester course in economics. (Education Code 51225.3).

d. Three years of courses in science, including one year of physical science; and one-year of biological science. (Education Code 51225.3)

e. Two years of courses in PE to include JROTC and marching band programs for PE credit unless the student has been exempted pursuant to (Education code 51241).

f. One year of courses in either visual or performing arts, foreign language, American Sign Language or photography (Education code 51225.3).

g. One semester of health

After determining Rula had in fact met all A-G requirements, she was still concerned with the following top four (4) reasons why High school student relate they don't go to college:

1. Neither I, nor my family, can afford it.

2. My grades aren't what they should be.

3. I'm not sure what I want to do for a career.

4. My parents didn't attend college and they did well, so why should I bother?

Does this sound familiar? Your high school student is confused and overwhelmed? Not sure of what they want to be when they grow up? What college is the best fit for them or even if they want to go to college?

Rula with the support of her mom and an Educational Consultant completed her A-G requirements, admissions requirements, and essays for college using the Nine Steps to prepare for college including writing winning essays over the next few months:

1. Decision #1: Roadmap for College Success

2. Decision #2: Dream, Big — Career Choices

3. decision #3: Be Yourself— Find your path to success.

4. Decision #4: SAT/ACT Practice, Practice, Practice

5. Decision #5: Building & Writing Winning Essays

6. Decision #6: Recommendation Letters

7. Decision #7: Personal Statements

8. Decision #8: Best Fit for College Admissions

9. Decision #9: Financial Aid Package

Next, "How to write her winning essay" using the nine steps in "Nine Key Decisions in Better College Planning, Better Life."

Step 1: Make sure her essay fits the theme.

Step 2: Answer the underlying question.

Step 3: Share a slice of life.

Step 4: Show passion in her writing.

Step 5: Be Specific.

Step 6: Have a thesis statement.

Step 7: Build on her accomplishments.

Step 8: Avoid the sob story.

Step 9: Show positive energy.

Step 10: Find people to read your essays.

After completing essay writing and meeting admissions and financial aid requirements, Rula in on track with her major and minor as statically students change their major three to five times within the first year or two of college; this was part of Rula's individual college plan, to complete a three-part assessment, i.e., Pre-Assessment, Personality and Career Assessments. Students who change their majors three to five times, causing students to not graduate on time, pursuing the wrong career field or taking unnecessary classes, causing students to take unnecessary additional semesters costing students more money to finish an undergraduate program that could've been finished within four years. ("Nine Key Decisions to Better College Planning, Better Life: Making college dreams a reality pg. ix).

An aspiring future nursing student, Rula, is on course to follow in her family's path of nurses, despite being told by her high school counselor that she didn't have the grade point average to apply for admissions consideration.

As the days unfolded and Rula showing up to her appointments, together, she completed all admissions requirements to four universities and offered admissions to California Baptist University and California State University San Marcos. She still awaits admissions offers from Cal State Fullerton.

Shelly's ability to support and empower the best and brightest kids all over the world as well as create success and fulfillment is in being present in more than one way. It's about appearing consistently for things that matter. This means showing up focusing on the key areas where they need the most guidance, i.e., essay building, increasing their SAT scores for scholarships or meeting IVY league requirements, In-State and/or Out-of-State universities. Showing up in the different phases of their individual college planning beginning as early as 6th grade through 12th grade and again 1st year in college throughout their undergraduate program. In other words, her focus on professionalism, doing the job, taking the right steps, showing up, helping students to define their goals, and taking the necessary actions to accomplish it.

"Leaders become great, not because of their power, but because of their ability to empowers other." ~ John Maxwell

Story #3 This next story is going to inspire you. It was her senior year of high school for Heather. She had a 4.3 GPA and searched for every scholarship she could apply for since 9th grade. In showing up to Team Network, a mom explained that her stepdaughter is accepted to UC Davis, and she's trying to help her daughter with financial aid, with no results. This mom didn't know that to do. They had been paying another College Advisor to help Heather find funding but with no results. Read Heather's kind words of her college planning experience with Shelly.

Testimonial from Heather Dodson

University of California Davis

I have so many wonderful things to say about Shelly! She entirely changed my life and made my dream of going to University of California Davis a reality. In my four years of studying at Davis I have not paid a single penny out of pocket AND Shelly also found every grant, scholarship. and aid that I qualified for. Now UC Davis actually pays me to study neuroscience as an undergraduate. In my four years as an undergraduate my total tuition cost $90,292, but let's be real- NOBODY has that kind of money. Shelly worked her magic and earned me $126,292 in financial aid, scholarships and grants. I am now a fully funded student AND the extra $36,000 went straight into my pocket to pay for housing and books so I could focus more on my career and stress less about a temporary job.

I would not be graduating with a degree in Neurobiology, Physiology and Behavior from one of the top ten ranked schools in California without Shelly. Now I am heading into a PhD program for Psychobiology with zero debt from my undergraduate career and Shelly is still helping me every step of the way. Shelly and her team are some of the most amazing people I have ever worked with, and they truly make dreams a reality.

"Success is no accident. It is hard work, perseverance, learning, studying, sacrifices, and most of all, love of what you are doing.

- Pele

Showing up is key for Nicole Farnum, Manager of Community and Corporate Relations at Bradman University, she elaborated how college planning is crucial for college bound students. Putting together a solid plan can save families tons of time, money, and can result in a successful educational journey. Without a plan, students can find themselves buried in debt and in some cases, they don't finish college.

To sum it all up, 'showing up' is 'work hard' or 'put in the effort' — and so by pushing hard, you are increasing your chances of success. As you continue to show up, the more you put action in your life, the more your native talents and skills, spontaneity, and brilliance will show themselves. So, keep showing up for you, your business, family, and communities.

NO Way!!

Adella Sanchez

When Robbie asked us to think about getting in her next book, my first thought was NO Way!!

I thought to myself, gosh, I don't have anything to share. I've not been super successful in many years in my endeavors. What could I possibly share? I read some of the stories in Robbie's' first book and thought I have nothing! I let the negative thoughts take over, and I said 'NO' to myself and GSFE, that I wouldn't step up and share anything in Robbie's book. Then on Jan. 18th we made Vision boards at the Cherry Hills golf club. It was a fun and delightful day. Robbie expressed to us to just let the pictures and words speak to us, and then you will see how it's all going to come together.

Susan Mierzwik and I shared a table; we were both sharing our life experiences. We laughed, we cried, and we talked about our lives. She said to me, "Adella, you need to share your story in a book." Again, my thought was 'NO'. When I finished my Vision Board, it did speak to me. It's about showing up for life. In fact, the center of my board reads "COME TO LIFE" in big letters. Boy, if that didn't speak to me. Then I Showed Up at Joan Wakeland's GSFE Chapter meeting and of course, Robbie spoke of her book again. So, upon leaving the restaurant that night, I stepped out and asked Robbie if there was still time. I told her that I would like to be in her book. She said, "YES."

So, I will be speaking from my heart and how God has pulled me out of so much loss but also has given me much joy. I guess that would be showing up for life!

2017 was a wakeup call to me and my beautiful family. My first born, my 54-year-old son Rick was diagnosed with Gliobastoma Multiforme (GBM), a fast-growing and aggressive brain tumor. The news was shattering to me and his family. I remember at the hospital refusing to accept this news as a death sentence for my son. I immediately went to prayer and asked God to heal my son. I really believed he would be healed. A friend said to me that no matter what Rick would be healed even if he went home to be with Jesus. For non-believers that might be hard to understand, but I knew what he meant. I kept reading God's word and stood on the Bible verse Mark 5;36 Be not afraid only believe, until he passed.

The next two years, during all of Rick's Chemo treatments, different experimental drugs, and procedures I kept praying and believing that he would be healed and survive this ugly cancer.

I stopped doing my business with Premier Designs Jewelry. My thinking at the time was that I had a hard enough time motivating myself, less long trying to motivate my girls on my team. When I told Rick I had quit, he was upset. He said I should keep doing the business; that I was a good motivator to my girls and should keep working. However, during this time Premier Designs was also going through lots of changes as well; in fact, it closed its doors in 2020.

I believe God gave me the time off from working to spend more time with Rick and my family.

Unfortunately, Rick lost his battle to GBM on Dec 1st, 2019.

We were fortunate that we had Rick that long. Most patients don't even have a year.

I hold onto the memories of my son, especially the last two years of his life. He showed us all that we could be strong if we hold onto Jesus's Love. He preached to us that Family was everything and having faith is what mattered. He wrote in his journal daily about God's love for us.

He would cross his fingers, in the good luck form and say, "Don't worry me and Jesus are like this". He left us a video that he secretly made for us where he is singing "If I could only Imagine". It was played at his memorial and had us all in tears.

I was no stranger to this type of grief, but losing Rick was the higher mountain I had to climb. You see, after Rick was born in 1965, we had a daughter born on May 23,1967. We named her Maria Adella. Unfortunately, she had what they called Anencephaly, whereby babies live just a couple of hours. Part of the skull is not formed, and the nervous system doesn't fully develop. This was very hard for a 20-year-old to go through. We had everything ready at home for a new baby---bottles, diapers, clothes, everything. The roughest time was that they did not even let me hold my baby and we had to go home to an empty bassinet and all. I was numb all over. I thought God was punishing me, for what I don't know. Doctors said it was a freak thing and for us to try again, and we did. The next year Oct. 3, 1968, our Son Alexander Ruben was born, a big 9 lbs. 1 1/2 oz. and 22 inches long. A big happy baby boy. I remembered looking him over good, making sure he had all his fingers and toes. So once again we were happy with our two boys. Then in 1972 we thought it was time to try for a girl again. However, once again tragedy hit. We had a baby boy, Edward Anthony, who also was born with Anencephaly. He lived just an hour, and once again they didn't let me

hold or see my baby boy. Back then they thought it best for mothers not to see or hold their babies. Now it's different, thank God. Once again, I was numb and couldn't understand why.

After Edwards' death, I was really depressed. I was thankful for my two boys, but it was hard losing for the second time a full-term baby. My sister saw how I was and invited me to get out of the house and go to a Princess House Rally. I remember Showing Up and seeing all these women having fun, winning awards, and being so enthusiastic with such positive attitudes, I told my sister yes, that I would join her in this venture of sales. I had never sold anything before. I was very shy, but for some reason I excelled at Princess House. It was like being in college with a bunch of Sorority Sisters. I won many major awards, prizes, and went on to become an Area Manager. However, my most precious awards were the Major Trips that I won---Majorca, Spain, twice; Paris, France, with dinner on the Eiffel Tower (which was amazing); Costa del Sol, Spain, where we took a Hydrofoil boat to Tangiers, Morocco. We passed right by the Rock of Gibraltar. I went to Hawaii two times, Canada, Boston, Texas, and many more.

So, now that I was feeling better, we decided in 1973 to adopt a baby girl. It was hard because of the abortion law. There were not many babies up for adoption. In 1974, I rededicated my life to Jesus. I learned that he knows me inside and out and that he has plans for my life and knows my life from beginning to the end.

For I know the plans I have for you "Declares the Lord,"

plans to prosper you and not harm you, plans to give you hope and a future "

Jeremiah 9:11

God answered our prayers. On Sept. 6,1974 the adoption agency called and said they had a baby girl and asked if we could go to the office and see if we

liked her and wanted to adopt her.

What's there not to like, she was adorable. We adopted our daughter Tina Marie, one of the happiest days of our lives. She was such a joy, and the boys loved their little sister. We were all happy.

So, you see, the Lord had a plan for me. One day I was at a Bible study, and the pastor was talking about how God knows the past, present, and future. We are seeing only the past and present. One thing that has always stood out to me was that when we went to have Edward buried in 1972, we asked the mortician if we could have him buried near Maria's grave. He was adamant that there were no open gravesites in that area, and that there was a new baby section. I was so thankful to my mother-in-law because she insisted that he keep looking for a spot. He almost fell off his chair because there was one unused grave; and you know where that was? At the foot of Maria's grave. A coincidence, I don't think so.

Why is this so significant to me? It's because after I became a Christian GOD has always shown me that my heavenly father knows my past, present, and future, and that He loves me.

God has helped me go through many rough times in life, having one of my son's friends in 1981 get hurt in our garage and die a week later. That was super hard. My 22-year marriage ended in divorce in 1987 and now even in losing Rick, God has a plan.

In 1988 I Showed Up for a Dinner party which I did not want to go to, but my sister Rita said that Mom and Dad would be there, so I said yes. It was so funny because that night my dad said to me, "Oh, honey, one day God will send you another husband."

I remember laughing telling him, "No way! I was going to move to lake Elsinore with Tina because I didn't want another man." But, once again

God had other plans for me. Little did I know that I would meet this tall, dark handsome man, Daniel Sanchez, who swept me off my feet and who by the way lived in Fall Brook, just about 30 minutes away from Lake Elsinore.

You can guess the rest. We were married in 1990. We celebrate our thirty-third anniversary this May 26th.

God in his grace has shown me love and endurance and shown me that He is always there for me.

Now, what does this loss and grief have to do with Showing up and asking?

After Rick's death I shut down for a year. This time the mountain seemed too hard to climb. I was just existing. Grief had overcome me. Grief is hard on everyone; I hurt from the loss of my son; I hurt seeing his beautiful wife Tina go through losing her one and only love; I hurt seeing his children and his grandchildren hurt. It was a long year of grieving, (However, there really is no timeline to grief.) Then one day I picked up an old favorite book of mine,

"Hinds Feet in High Places" is an allegory of a girl named Much Afraid who goes through the difficult times of her spiritual journey of life. It's all about the journey of life and seeking the Good Shepherd, being God. It's about how we have to go through the valleys of life to also enjoy the highlights of life.

There is Sorrow and Suffering, but there is also Joy and Peace. By showing up and taking action in your life. Once again, the Lord picked me up.

The Lord God is my strength, and he will make my feet like hinds' feet,

and he will make me to walk upon my high places.

Habakkuk 3:19

So, around May of 2020, I decided to Step Out. Robbie calls it Showing up! (Which I didn't know at the time). I remember laughing and telling my family and friends that I was stepping out, that I was going to do something and do more with my life.

All my life I have been in direct sales, so I reached out to my friend Sandy VanDyken, who BTW was one of my girls in Princess House Crystal. Even though the years went by, we always kept in touch.

Sandy had been posting on FB how her new business with Rodan and Fields Skin care line was so successful. Her pictures of Before and Afters were amazing. So, in May of 2020 I became a consultant for Rodan & Fields. The products are amazing, but what was even better is the fact that I was out and about and working with my good friend Sandy again.

I reached out to Denise Gregory and joined GSFE and in Oct. of 2021, I am now Co-director. I am feeling more like my old self again when I used to work on affirmations, dreams, goals, and uplifting others. Making my vision board last week with Robbie and my GSFE sisters was amazing.

I want to do more in my life, touch others, and let them know first and utmost that our heavenly Father loves us. I want to do good. I believe we are to be all that we can be to give Him the Glory.

So, I guess, I've been showing up all along!

I want to thank Susan Mierzwik for the encouragement she gave to me. She really helped me see that I needed to share my story. I especially want to thank Robbie Motter for being the amazing woman that she is, helping women of all races grow to their full potential in life.

Thank you, Robbie, for being so inspirational to all of us and showing us how important it is to Show Up.

I'm learning that Sorrow and Suffering is part of life, but that Joy and Peace are there for us, too, if we just keep showing up.

Isaiah 40:31

But those who hope in the Lord will renew their strength. 'They will soar on wings like eagles; they will run and not grow weary; they will walk and not faint.

God has blessed me with a beautiful family of 11 grandchildren and 9 great grandchildren.

It's all
About
Showing
Up

Journey of Entrepreneurship
Secret Ingredient - Showing Up and ASK

Dr. (h.c.) Jaya Sajnani

The idea of entrepreneurship is beautiful. You wake up each day believing you're in control of your life and can spend that day doing whatever you want. All the while, your business is generating income taking away the stress of financial pressures. You are creating something that lets you live life on your terms and make an impact in the life of others. The income and other opportunities are a fun bonus. However, the everyday reality doesn't always equal the dream or the idea we have in our mind. Depending on what stats you believe, there are entrepreneurs quitting their businesses as fast as others are starting one. Entrepreneurship can be a hard and lonely journey at times, and the issues are compounded when not enough income is being generated from the business.

Everywhere you look, you see a course being offered that promises the "one thing" or some secret strategy to unlock wealth and opportunity. Thousands of frustrated entrepreneurs buy into this fantasy because they hope it's the missing link. Successful entrepreneurs understand that there is no 'one thing'. They know that there are 100 things and steps to accomplish any major achievement. Successful entrepreneurs understand that challenges are lessons and opportunities for greater growth.

There are programs, courses, and coaches you can hire that will help you speed up the process. They can help you with strategies and tactics to make moves quicker. However, there is no substitute for putting in the work. Apart from your hard work, if there is anything you need in particular to make your enterprise successful, that is the right attitude. That means the attitude of **Showing Up** and **ASK** when it needed.

Power of Showing Up:

Successful entrepreneurs show up every day ready to do that work. You become successful when you wake up every day focused on what will help you grow and just show up wherever you have been needed. After all, if you don't show up, you won't be able to complete any of the tasks in front of you. Bear in mind, of course, that showing up is not all it takes to achieve your goals. It's always important to perform our jobs well. If showing up is half the battle, you certainly want to show up prepared. There is a saying "80% of success in life is just showing up". Showing up can lead to success by enabling you to reach your fullest potential.

So what happens if you don't Show Up? Say you wake up one morning, and you don't quite feel 100%. Maybe you are going through drama at home, or maybe you just feel blah. You decide that instead of going to a meeting, you are going to take the day off. So, you call in and tell your client or delegates that you can't make it. Your absence may end up costing you the future prospect. The client or delegate may go to someone else to complete the tasks or meet the need.

Of course, there are times when calling off meetings is justified. If you find yourself calling in sick because you just don't feel like it or don't feel emotionally up to it, you are making trouble for both yourself, in personal life and your business. Now, take a few minutes to analyze why you do not feel 100% or is this an excuse you are giving to yourself? Sometimes, we do

not know exactly what the reason is and why we behave the way we do. If you look closely, it could be the fear or the feeling not confident enough or something else. Whatever it is, being an entrepreneur or business owner, this has the high cost to pay. As a businessperson, when you're growing a business, or even planning to grow, it's so important to show up at every place where you are needed. It also means fighting our negative self-belief or dealing with them.

We've all been in a situation where we made plans with someone and then the day of the event arrives, and you no longer want to go. In the past, you'd have to either call someone's landline and cancel over the phone or stand them up. Both options put a lot more pressure on you. With a phone call you hear the disappointment in the person's voice, and if you stand someone up, you're going to make someone pretty angry.

Now, thanks to the tech, you can simply send a quick text message or WhatsApp dipping out of plans with seemingly little consequence. You don't have to see or hear the person's disappointment, and you can give a fake excuse knowing full well both parties are aware of the lie. This will not only create a bad habit in you to cancel the plans every time if it does not fit your convenience but also gives an impression to others that you are not a reliable person. When it comes to the entrepreneurship, you are the business, and your impression is your business impression.

Therefore, every time you show up to create a new habit, you cast a vote towards your identity and who you want to be. For example, if you want to grow your business, every time you send an email or make a call, you vote towards becoming a better businessperson. James Clear, the Author of Atomic Habits, says "To create new habits, you need to start by working on your identity."

Showing Up is a powerful habit that will serve you; you'll achieve your goals and live a happier life. Showing up really means to be present in more than one way. It's about appearing consistently for things that matter. This can be showing up at work by making an effort to grow, showing up for your family by listening to them, and showing up for yourself by pursuing your goals.

The key is not to be perfect but to simply **show up**. When you take even the smallest step towards building a new habit, you can shape your life. The next time you think about skipping an online webinar, show up by participating in the session even for a little while. This way, you reduce your resistance to building new habits over time, and the new habit becomes part of what you do and who you are.

Showing Up also means being present by living in the moment. You take things one day at a time. The idea is that it's better to take the smallest step you can than taking no step at all.

Power of ASK:

I consider myself a businesswoman. To be one, one of the keys is realizing I don't always have all the answers. Often in business — and in life — people are not comfortable with asking. Asking for help is another strength which helps entrepreneurs to grow faster and sustain their business. It is not a weakness; it is a strength. If we perceive that asking for help will help our performance, we are more likely to ask for help. However, if we perceive that asking for help will mean someone will view us as needy, not well equipped to do a task, or incompetent, we aren't likely to dip our toes into the help-seeking waters.

It doesn't matter what age or level of ability a person has when asking for help. What matters is the intent. There are so many examples of the

power of asking. Here is one example from my own experience. In the height of the COVID pandemic in the UK, I was merely sitting at home as my primary business - YG Travel, the name suggests, we do transport solutions and tours of the United Kingdom and Europe countries - was completely shut. During that time, I had all the resources, vehicles, drivers as I cannot let them go just because business was shut down in the interim period. Being an entrepreneur, you have not only responsibility of your own finance but also the people who are working for you. I feel it is ultimately my responsibility to provide them pay as they are relying financially on my business to sustain. However, I had no work, no income, but set expenses for the business. So, I wrote an email to our local council to **ask** if they need any help from us to support our borough council. This email went to the strategic level of senior managers and resulted in giving me some compensation to provide services to the vulnerable adult and children to ride to the hospitals and deliver their medications, necessary foods, and other shopping to their home. I only asked to help. I was not expecting to get any reward or monetary compensation; however, the council decided to hire our services instead. This was the biggest example of how the things got turned around when all other transport operator were sitting at home and struggling for money. My business was able to survive through the pandemic and throughout the lock down---just because I cared to **ASK**.

When asking for help, the key is to be solution focused. Make sure your ask will solve a problem of yourself, your work, or your agenda. Most importantly, remember that most people want to help. They will be excited to see you succeed.

Here's are some tips for you to take away:

1. **Frame your ask.** If you frame your need as helping you to improve your performance or do something productive, this will help you ask for help.

That is because you aren't viewing yourself as needy or incompetent. You are, instead, looking to solve a problem or improve yourself or your situation. This is an important distinction to make. You want to see yourself as proactive. This provides a potential helper something specific to help you with.

2. People like to help people who ask for help. In most cases, people are eager to help others. This is why volunteering, mentoring, and philanthropy endeavors are so popular. The adage "tis better to give than to receive" is actually true. Giving to others is especially worthwhile when there is meaning and productivity attached to it.

3. Help others. When you help others, it gives you perspective on how it feels to give to others. Take note of how much enjoyment you get from helping a person solve a problem. Allow yourself to see "the other side" so you can see that you aren't a burden, incompetent, or needy. You will likely be much better at asking if you've had the chance to give.

Business is the word traditionally attached to make profit and earn money. However, we have moved far away from the way we used to do the business in the past. Today, Business is not only a tool to make money but also to serve the society by providing employment, providing the service/product which solve the issue, or making people's lives more comfortable. To do that, we must remember that we are alone, are not enough for anything. We are a part of this society, and when you **ASK**, you create a network of trust among everyone.

The reputation of a business in the surrounding community, among other businesses, and for individual investors is paramount in determining whether a company is a worthwhile investment. If a company is perceived to be not open to the market, investors are less inclined to buy stock or otherwise support its operations. A business that promotes open an

environment to feel comfortable to ASK in its management and operations creates an investment-friendly environment. Investors like putting their money where they are sure it is safe.

It's also important to realize that millennials are the next generation of talent entering the professional world and they're the ones dictating what's important for companies. According to a Bentley University study, 86 percent of millennials consider it a main priority to work for a business that creates an open and friendly environment for their stakeholder to perform their duties, an environment where they do not feel judged by asking the questions, where there is a trust among the team members, and it promotes the ASK behavior in the team. In fact, most millennials would be willing to take a considerable pay cut to work for such a business.

The bottom line:

People can't help you if they don't know what you need, but it's hard to ask for help -- so you usually wind up just doing the job yourself.

Showing up encompasses the philosophy of acceptance. When you commit to showing up in life, whether it's by writing a post for your blog or making a call to a client, you accept any outcome that happens. In other words, you focus on doing the job and taking the right steps towards your goal. You remain open and accepting of the result of your actions and just do the best work you can. When you show up to the event, place, or any situation, it shows that you are open to the future and when you are open to the future and to the universe, it serves you and then miracles begin. It also represents Power; showing up means you show up, you stand up, and you are a leader.

As an entrepreneur the hardest part is keeping the finances in line. If you want your business to succeed, you need to exercise the courage to ask the difficult questions. Often this can be about something as simple as payment.

Be upfront about payment terms when speaking to your clients and do not be afraid to ask for better terms because if you do not ask, then the answer is always 'no'. Never let pride or fear stop you from asking something that might lead to better opportunities or smarter deals for your business.

Never leave the opportunity of repeat business in the hands of fate. After a successful project with a client, ask them for one good lead that you can get in contact with for more work. Don't wait or hope passively that they will do it for you.

Employees who love their jobs, enjoy their coworkers, and look forward to the workday are more likely to do whatever they can to help the company thrive. A positive workplace culture affirms the value, dignity and worth of each employee which benefits the individual and the organization.

It's all
About
Showing
Up

For Such A Time As This

Dr. (h.c.) Nephetina L. Serrano

For if you remain silent at this time, relief and deliverance for the Jews will arise from another place, but you and your father's family will perish. And who knows but that you have come to your royal position for such a time as this?

Esther, 4:14, NIV

In this famous passage of scripture, Queen Esther is being advised by her wise uncle Mordecai to courageously risk it all in order to save an entire nation of people. It is in this moment that Esther, a woman of influence and beauty, has the realization that her encounter with the king, her husband, could at chance, result in either the purging or salvation of her people. It was in this pivotal moment of epiphany that Queen Esther had to make the decision to show up for her people as their future hung in the balance of her presence or lack thereof. Esther's showing up was an encounter of destiny that etched her presence forever in the chronicles of time and turmoil, defining her legacy and future for generations to come.

It's amazing how encounters like this can totally change the trajectory of life as we know it. I have had my personal brush with destiny upon meeting

the incomparable Robbie Motter. I remember it like it was yesterday. I had boarded the luxurious Queen Mary ship after being chosen to be a lead speaker in the California Woman of Achievement Pageant that would be held on the ship. This event was an exclusive gathering, hosted by Marlena Martin, the Founder of Woman of Achievement Pageant. As I prepared to check into my room, suitcases in tow, my eye caught a vision of an intriguing woman coming from the dining room with what looked to be a colleague. She was truly a vision, donning a wide-striped black and white jumpsuit with her blond tresses perfectly positioned under a matching wide-brimmed hat. Her accessories perfectly accented her look, very much giving Rodeo Drive glamour. She was tall in stature and made an entrance in the room, crossing the dining area to the promenade. Wow, I thought, what an amazing beauty. Her presence spoke volumes of her grace, elegance, wisdom and intelligence, without her ever saying a word. "I would love to meet with her," I said to myself. "As a matter of fact, I am going to meet her," I thoughtfully whispered to myself before proceeding to check into my room and get situated for the evening.

The next morning as I prepared to address my message for the audience, I was delighted to see that the same woman that I had spotted the day before was present, and was also a speaker, the keynote in fact. I learned that her name was Robbie Motter. I made a note of it and continued to focus on my speech for the day's event. After I delivered a stirring message about the power of one and the necessity to pursue purpose, there wasn't one dry eye in the room. Although I didn't share it with the group at the time, I was going through a trying situation in which a close family member was undergoing major surgery after being unjustly injured, and I believe the emotion from my experience was conveyed through my speech by the power of God.

As the morning event culminated, Robbie Motter and her entourage graciously greeted me before we broke for lunch. I decided I would eat on the ship at one of the exclusive restaurant on board the ship. Upon my arrival, to my surprise, Robbie was there sitting at one of the tables and when she spotted me, she invited me to come over to dine with her and her party. With eyes sparkling bright, she exclaimed, "We were just sitting here, talking about you!"

"Really?" I said, humbled and flattered. She went on to say that she and her colleague were buzzing about how deeply impressed they were by me. She noted that one of the greatest takeaways of the event was my speech, mentioning that it was anointed and excellent. I graciously thanked her for her kind words but inside, I was so excited that I was speaking with this woman who just one day earlier I had been taken aback by, remembering that I had spoken into existence our meeting. She formally introduced herself and her organization, GSFE which stands for Global Society of Female Entrepreneurs and asked to know more about me. We continued to learn more about each other as we ate our meal and prepared for the second half of the day's activities.

Later that weekend during the course of the event, my roommate and I were going to breakfast and we saw Robbie again. She bid for us to dine with her at her table with her friends. And that was the start of an amazing relationship, friendship and partnership with her. Who knew that choice encounter would initiate a life-changing course of events in my life?

Fast forward, I am now a soon-to-be Director for GSFE. When Robbie had initially introduced me to the elite organization five years ago, it had 100 members, and is now an international organization of over 400 members with ten directors. It is one of the largest networking organizations of which I am affiliated with, to date. Indeed, my encounter with Robbie truly

changed the trajectory of my life. Since meeting her, I have met so many amazing people, both nationally and internationally. I have procured many speaking opportunities as a result of connections I have made with other dynamic women of influence within the organization. And now five years after our initial introduction, I have been chosen and crowned as Woman of Achievement Legacy Queen, a position of prestige, honor and influence to make a great impact on a chosen social cause that impacts the world.

As I reflect on the impact of my relationship with Robbie, I can not help but think that I never would have had that choice encounter had I not made the decision to show up despite life's hardships. I kept my commitment as my family member underwent surgery and did a hard thing in a hard time. If I had not shown up in spite of the turmoil, I would have never met a woman whose connection would provide me with the opportunity to impact thousands of women worldwide through my work with the organization.

Along with showing up, I also spoke into existence my meeting with her, as I sensed that the excellence and elegance that she emanated would complement my person and life. I was not afraid to vocalize "my, ask" to speak what I wanted into existence. Had I saw her and been somehow intimidated by what she carried, I would have allowed insecurity to rob me of a great opportunity. Similarly, if I would have let an arrogant ego take center stage, I might have tried to compete with her in a negative spirit of pride rather than collaborate with her in the spirit of sisterhood and community.

And what if I would have allowed a spirit of fear to cause me to lose out on a mutually beneficial partnership? If so, then I would have never become a part of GSFE. I also may not have never gathered the courage to compete and win upon my first-time entry in the Woman of Achievement Pageant 2021-2022. I would have then never been asked to become the first

African American in the history of the pageant to be a Legacy Queen. All those opportunities would have been lost. I understand that in this life the choices we make not only affect us but many people around us and even those whom we may not have met yet. We must step over the fear of what can't happen and step into the possibility of what can. Imagine if the late Martin Luther King, Jr. would not have stepped over fear and marched for freedom. What if, Harriet Tubman did not overcome her fear and escape to freedom, what if she had waited on someone else to do what she was born to do, hundreds of slaves would not have seen freedom. What about the 44th president of the United States of America former president Barack Obama who made history as the first African American president of the United States, serving two terms from 2009 to 2017. These three mentioned all were born with purpose and destiny. They each had to be "the one" by leading themselves first and then leading others.

What are you not doing that might be hindering you or holding you back from reaching your fullest potential? Rise up from the ashes of fear, hesitation, procrastination, and self doubt. Know that you matter and there is POWER in one.

For Ester the first step of destiny was in showing up. But the power was in the ASK. Do not be afraid to ASK because if you want change, it begins with you. You just might be the change someone is looking for. Tomorrow is not promised so do not put off for tomorrow what you can do today. Timing is everything. Show up, for you first then be willing to help someone else along the way.

You must grasp the moments of your life that are pregnant with divinely appointed opportunity. And like Queen Esther, it is important for you to be in the right place, at the right time, doing the right thing. Do not allow insecurity, intimidation, pride or fear to steal your moment of destiny.

Be in your moment and grasp it. Timing is quintessential to pivot your opportunities to success stories.

I thank God for every open door and season which I have embarked on to become the women of destiny that God has purposed me to be. I pray that He continues to empower me with His strength and determination to show up so that the people connected to my purpose are positively impacted and encouraged to reach their full potential. Much like what was inquired of Queen Esther, we must further ask ourselves if God has indeed positioned us to show up and ask for the things that propel us into purpose for *such a time as this.*

It's all
About
Showing
Up

Nothing is impossible when you Show Up!

Katherine Setzer

I may look like a pretty normal person; my family may look pretty normal before you know our story. My name is Katherine Setzer. I am a Navy wife, mother to two children, a small business owner, and now a semi disabled homemaker and homeschooler. I wanted to share with you my journey in the hopes that it might inspire you, or let you know you're not alone, or maybe give you some new insight to homeschooling or children on the spectrum. I hope that after you have read my story, it will provide you a call to action to face things that may seem like an uphill battle or impossible to achieve. Like my favorite actress Audrey Hepburn once said, "Nothing is impossible; the word itself says I'm possible." Nothing placed before you is something you cannot handle. It just may need you to view it from a new perspective.

All the possibilities and paths that are presented before us at our feet each and every day is a glimpse of a possible future. One that if we embark on it by taking that first step can change our future for good or bad. The hardest part of the journey is trusting the path and process that will lead you to the future you want.

The road that led me to homeschooling my two special needs children has not been without its struggles. In fact, it's been many struggles and

stumbles. It has required testing, changing ideas, plans, and schedules to find a perfect balance: a routine that is right for us. It took adapting to medical limitations, acceptance of educational levels, and flexibility.

This is a story of overcoming health issues, fighting for basic needs my children needed, and losing my independence and in turn gave me wings to fly and become the mom I always wanted to be. It is very humbling, and you get better at asking for help and support when you have no ability to walk or drive. It provides wonderful clarity that the universe moves things in alignment even if it doesn't make much sense at the time. You will be called to your calling sometimes in the rockiest way that you do not think you would make it through. But just that one small step propels you forward.

The story of how I became a homeschooling mom started back long before I was in elementary school. When I was 9 months old, I contracted spinal meningitis after receiving a vaccine for it. I was rushed to the hospital 6 hours afterwards I developed a fever and seizures and underwent brain surgery. I suffered several seizures and many delays of normal milestones over the years.

When I was in school, I always dealt with mean kids. It wasn't until I was in 2nd grade that I experienced the start of the worst three years of torment from my peers. I had two boys cut my hair in class and tip my chair over causing me to fall on a pencil that one of the boys was holding. I still have that piece of lead in my leg to this day.

My mom moved me to another school to hopefully help the bullying stop, but no, at this school two girls in my class were ruthless going as far as throwing rocks at me on the playground, and constantly tormenting me, even once in front of my mom. She changed my school again. When nothing was done by the school during this time. You can see that I've had a lot of changes and roads that have shaped my life. I had a wonderful insight and

education in what I did not want for my children.

Fast forward now to 2014 when I had my daughter Evelyn. I had her at a military base. The team that delivered her were mainly interns. I was subjected to seven failed attempts at placing the epidural before they finally got an actual doctor to place it. I spent 5 hours of non-stop contractions and pushing before they realized something was wrong. Evelyn was stuck with her hand up by her cheek and required forceps to get her out. I couldn't walk for three days after her birth. I was also torn badly and when they stitched me up, they did it causing a large amount of scar tissue resulting in me needing to go in for a correction surgery. When I requested that the doctor do the procedure, not an intern, they told me they would. When I woke up after surgery, I discovered that they allowed the intern to do the surgery against my wishes.

Even with all these bumps in the road I was so excited to be a mom but also nervous for her to go off one day to school. When I went back to work, and she went to daycare I started to see the patterns of bullying even with a young age group of children. She was diagnosed at three years old with ADHD and sensory processing disorder. Then in December 2019 my daughter was diagnosed with Autism and Pathological Demand Avoidance. Evelyn has a verbal stereotypy where she literally cannot stop talking, she tends to overshare personal information and trusts strangers. This has been one of the scariest parts of her diagnosis for me. Teaching her the safety component that doesn't come naturally to her has been a struggle, but every day I see her improvement.

I had to work to help support our family so I knew that unfortunately my daughter would have to continue in a similar path that I had during school. The public school system.

In 2017 I was pregnant with my second child. During this time, I was under an extreme amount of stress not only from losing a baby two months before, strains in my marriage, dealing with being basically a single parent with a military husband who was gone most of the time, and dealing with a bully at work. She had managed to take my position, had me demoted when I told my boss I was pregnant, and was constantly rude and disrespectful towards me.

I was depressed, full of fear and suffering from PTSD and anxiety. I remember constantly thinking and saying to my mom when I would speak to her, "I can't stand any of this anymore! I just cannot stand it anymore." Then one day shortly there afterwards I literally couldn't stand. What we put out into this world does come to pass. I was injured after moving some boxes at work and then picking up my daughter from her crib at 17 weeks pregnant I felt a waterfall effect of pain near where you would have an epidural. I dropped my 2-year-old Evelyn and couldn't feel my lower body from the waist down. I spent the rest of my pregnancy and many months after that on bed rest and in a wheelchair. I was also in and out of the hospital.

My son tried to come early starting at 27 weeks. The doctors ended up giving me shots to stop the labor. I had to fight for him and my own health with doctors. When I was close to my scheduled c-section, Graysen decided to come early, coming at 38 weeks. The hospital didn't believe me that I was in labor and so I was forced to sit in the waiting room until they finally checked me and found that yes, in fact, I was in labor and needed to be admitted.

During this whole time, I was on disability leave from my job. When I was 27 weeks actually the day I was released from the hospital after having my labor stopped, my boss fired me. Our landlord gave us notice that they sold the house we were renting. It was a dark scary time.

In all reality even with all the blows after blows, it was a blessing. I know reading everything I just wrote you think I have lost my mind, just hear me out. All these setbacks were really setups and things in the universe shifting to put me in alignment for what the future held for me and my children.

When my son Graysen was finally born via emergency C-section, he had major health issues. As he grew, we noticed more and more things that were cause for concern. He wasn't making the milestones even slightly late like his older sister did. He was not eating by mouth, and when we tried to put food in his mouth, he would immediately projectile vomit.

But the final moment that I decided I needed to have him medically evaluated was after his first birthday party when he touched his cake and vomited everywhere. At 13-months-old he was diagnosed with autism spectrum disorder, nonverbal, failure to thrive, sensory processing disorder, and global developmental delay.

I have had a huge education in the way the medical system works from fighting for my son to have the care he needs. From nursing care to his blood transfusions, major dental surgery, and g-tube surgery. I have had to fight doctors who told me that making a home blended diet and goats milk formula would kill my son. When, in fact, it made him so strong and healthy he went from being 24 pounds a weight he was for a year in 2018, to weighing 44 pounds at his last check up in January 2023.

During all these scary times I was able to homeschool my kids and focus on their strengths and weaknesses. Graysen being nonverbal has been the biggest sign that I made the correct choice in homeschooling him. If he were in a traditional school, I wouldn't really ever know what was actually going on with other children. There would be a lot of uneasy feelings. I couldn't be his advocate to the degree my mom was with me because he can't tell me of things going on. He also is at higher risk of injury due to his g-tube so the

best outcome for his success and growth is at home with me as his teacher working at his pace and knowing his limits and stress tell signs.

I now have a third grader and a kindergartener. We are able to do hands-on learning and exploring. This fall 2023 we are taking a two-and-a-half-week trip and will be doing studies on the state parks in Montana and Colorado while we camp there. I hope one day to take a trip and spend a month or two in Europe with them. I also have been able to create my own business, something I really did not think I would be able to do. Graysen has made so many leaps and bounds over the past few years. He went from not speaking any words only growling and yelling to using short sentences and his AAC device. He went from not walking to running around playing. So many huge wins. He has finally begun to eat some foods by mouth. With our help he has worked through so many textures and has begun to explore eating. Every day he and his sister are meeting goals that were near impossible. They are blossoming in their strengths and slowly making strides in their weaknesses. Being home with them and working one on one with them has been such a wonderful blessing, one I wish more parents were able to do.

But all the "bad" things that happened to me at the time turned out to be the catalyst I asked for all those years ago to be home with my kids. I am grateful for the road of darkness and hardships; it gave me courage, strength, and grace to face all the challenges that present themselves with being a mom to children with special needs.

It also led me to many great things in my career. I went from the bottom to the top. So, when you are getting hit with overpowering waves after waves stop and let the process happen, listen to your inner voice and just take that first step... You really could be on the way to a wonderful and fulfilling adventure. The biggest obstacle is that you don't fight the changes; let them

lead you, and once you've passed the "bad" you will have a wonderful and exciting new path to follow.

It's All About Showing Up And Asking

Kaye Sheffield

When I was **Asked** to **Show Up** at a friend's house to hear a dynamic speaker and a woman who I really admired, I showed up. She is a well-known health care provider in the community, who has her own business. I showed up to hear how this woman had almost died several years before. A couple of big well-known hospitals had given up on their ability to help her in any way, to get better. She was unable to move around or to eat. She had to wear a diaper all day, and she crawled out of bed in the morning and laid on the couch all day as she was unable to move and in so much pain. She was unable to function as a homemaker or to take care of her home or family. This woman was young in mid-life and had young children. She was scheduled to have surgery to remove much of her inner digestive parts. She was then given some capsules by a neighbor who suggested that she try them. "They are fruits and vegetables in a capsule," the neighbor told her, and they should not cause any complications with the medications that she was on. She decided to try them, and miraculously, she began getting better within a short time. She was able to move, eat, do some of the household chores and be with her family. I was very moved by her story and decided to try these capsules with just Fruits and Vegetables in them.

As a Speech Therapist in the school system, and a single Mom of three young children, I was always getting sick. Every school year, I would get the first bug that came around in the fall and then would be sick or on the verge of getting sick again, the rest of the winter months. I began taking the fruit, vegetable, and berry capsules, and a year later I realized that I had not been sick, not for a long time. After realizing that I had not been sick for about a year, and then asking myself "what happened"? I finally realized that I had been putting those fruits, vegetables, and berries in my body, and maybe that was causing me to be well and building up my immune system.

I also noticed that I was now cancer free from two bouts of cancer, two years apart. That is now 22 years ago, and I am cancer free. I am very thankful that I showed up at that meeting and asked about the capsules that I now take daily.

I also Asked what can I do to get these capsules and shakes at a better price and to help others to be healthier as well. My leader was really surprised that I "asked" to promote these capsules, and she was really delighted that I had asked.

There are many times that we just show up and ask. I think of when my children were little and just by showing up at soccer events, swim meets, recitals and concerts, or basketball practice or games, you may have the opportunity to ask if you can simply be of help.

On another occasion, I decided to attend the annual virtual GSFE (Global Society for Female Entrepreneurs) event. While signing up to come to the event, I asked if I could make a donation to the event to help others be able to attend GSFE events. I had second thoughts about it and wondered if I had enough money to give to the sponsorship but felt lead to attend and donate. As Eric Worre says, "Say "Yes"; then figure it out." I had not figured out how to obtain the money to make this larger donation but felt that

God was saying to me, just say "Yes." So, I showed up with the donation and attended. At the beginning of the event, they raffled off some prizes. I ended up winning the first two prize drawings; both were Amazon gift cards. They were giving me prizes for the exact amount that I had donated to GSFE, when I just said "yes". I ended up using that money to purchase three Dr. Sears new books on Cancer and giving them to two friends who had recently been diagnosed with cancer. I Love how that works out when we just show up, and ask, and there is a wonderful response...but sometimes it is not what we expect. Sometimes it is a chance to give to others.

There are many times that I have shown up and asked and received a negative response or what appears at the time to be a negative response, and it was really a "wait" or "wait and see" or a "learn from this experience" response. There is always something to be learned when you receive a negative response from others. Sometimes at a later date, that response is turned into a positive response or a learning experience. Sometimes people need to think about an idea, or an "ask" before they make a positive response and agree to something new. Out of the blue, I have just been asked to take on a job doing my speech therapy (SLP) work with children, parents, and teachers and to supervise a speech therapy assistant (SLPA). I will need to decide if I want to give up retirement and show up for this part time job for the rest of the school year.

There are times when the ask comes first, then the show up comes. As in what just happened to me while writing this.

It may be a cyclical event. You show up, you ask; they show up, and they ask. It is a very positive continuous outcome, watching the cycle happen over and over. That is what we really love to see, the continuous positive cycle of showing up and asking. One time in the fall, I decided to just show up and love on people. I would keep them in my client folder, and as their

name came up, I would call and/or text them and let them know that I cared about them and how they were doing. Later I began to ask if they would be interested in trying my product, the fruits, vegetables, and berries in capsules, or seeing a video. They often said "yes" to the asking, which moved me up on the rankings for my business, and they then began to show up and ask. That was a big lesson for me. Consistency in just showing up is so important.

I have seen that when we show up and ask to help or donate/give to people that God gives that back to us. It can be in the order of money, recognition, time, or maybe a ride.

At a recent GSFE event, four of us agreed to present on Wellness and health. As I showed up, I told one of the panel members that I had been trying to find a ride on an upcoming flight so that I could see my daughter and family in a state on the other side of the US, Michigan. He suggested that I just ask the GSFE group in attendance for help in finding a ride. I asked for that ride during our self-introductions, and two people offered to drive me to the airport. Yahoo, just ask! As it turned out, a friend texted me, the next day, who lives closer to me than the two offers at the GSFE meeting and asked if I had found a ride. She asked to take me to the airport. That was a surprise "ask" for me.

I have heard it said: "Eighty to Ninety percent of success is just Showing Up"

And "If you don't ask, you don't get." Mahatma Gandhi

From one of my favorite people, Zig Ziglar: "Positive thinking won't allow you to do anything, but it will allow you to do everything better..."

Action Steps: Show Up!

Be Here

Be there.

Be Involved

Be Positive

And Ask!!

Ask to help.

Ask how things work, to develop.

Ask to Learn

Ask for what you want or need.

Showing Up makes magic happen!
Dr. (h.c.) Charmaine Summers

Today I am a golf Pro and also love to sing and help others achieve.

This started at a young age with my father Patrick. I constantly showed up when he played golf and because he saw my interest, he made me show up at lessons. He also loved music, so I was always around singing and dancing, so I started showing up singing, taking piano and guitar lessons. My love of music was expanded. I love singing and have sung for women's conferences and today for different organizations.

In 2022 I also was introduced to the women of achievement which is an international pageant based on what women achieve with their programs and what they have done in their lives. I stepped out of my comfort zone and entered one of the categories and was shocked when I won the title of Queen in my category. I won because I showed up, I met so many dynamic women changing the world as my passion is also to help to change the world and make a difference.

As a mother I was always encouraging my daughter Crystal to SHOWUP and ASK, and today my daughter Crystal is an International professional Tennis player and mother who is setting examples for her daughter like I did for Crystal.

As a golf pro my love is helping the youth. It's so inspiring to me to know that years ago when started teaching the youth at the Orange County Golf Academy and that they SHOWED UP to see me and tell how their lives have changed because of golf and the time that I took teaching thousands of youths.

As the manager of the local golf club, I also love to help organizations with their fund raising so I show up at their meetings and offer them the use of the space to promote their projects. Also, because I love helping people, I showed up at a new GSFE network in Lake Arrowhead, CA, that was recently launched and currently serve as the co-director. In March I will step into the director slot as the mission of this organization is to serve women is exactly one of my passions.

Also, I am a boss of the Golf Course with a staff. I encourage my staff to SHOW UP and ASK, and I am there to help learn so they can advance their careers as well.

What I have learned is that many life-changing events make you a stronger person, and as you succeed and deal with all the things that life brings, you learn that is part of life 101 on the road to greater success than even better than you dreamed. I have learned in SHOWING up that when things are not going right to not dwell on that but look at the things that our going right and it immediately shifts me back to positive. I also know that we have to be true to ourselves and be who we are not what others want us to be. We need to lead by example, and we can be the role models for future generations.

I did not think when I moved to Sun City, I would join another women's organization as I thought I was done in joining organization's and then someone invited me to GSFE (Global Society for Female Entrepreneurs) a 501 (c)(3) nonprofit and hearing their mission, I immediately became a

member and now show up at my network meetings monthly but also other GSFE meetings as well as they all have dynamic speakers. I have learned a lot from their wisdom. They inspired me to step out of my comfort zone and show Up and do things I never thought I would do, like I was an author in a best-selling book last year "Love Your Haters" and now am doing a chapter in this book and next will be in 2024, I will start writing of my own book. Showing up at GSFE constantly reminds me that anything is possible.

I am excited to be the director of Lake Arrowhead GSFE and plan to reach out to the local women to inspire and mentor them to network with each other and to reach out to others in their community and to learn to ASK.

I moved to Sun City 6 years ago and have been reaching out every day to make difference. In December 2022, I was honored by the City Council as "Citizen of the Year", and they talked about the work that I have done for the community.

This December was the second year I put together the decorated golf cart parade and gifts for local senior living places which each year gets bigger, and it's such a wonderful feeling to see the smiles on the senior faces as we drive by wishing them a Merry Christmas and giving them their gifts from the heart.

This year I showed up and put together a fund-raising chili cook-off which benefited two charities and was a big success and encouraged others to SHOW UP and those that did thanked me for doing the event and including them.

All the years prior I lived in Orange County, and I showed up everywhere, I was the owner of Orange County Golf Academy, and during those years had the privilege of teaching many men women and juniors to play golf.

Because Cherry Hills Golf course is very important to me and the City of Menifee, CA, I wanted it to be beautiful, and it needed some work so I made many efforts and attended numerous meetings to get them to approve a beautification program which also will save the golf course money on water and save the environment. This was not an easy task, but I am a determined woman that never gives up. This is going to happen in early 2023, and it will make all who see it so happy because it's going to be a masterpiece.

I love when I do events decorating everything as the beauty of the event brings smiles to the people's faces. Around Christmas time we had four decorated Christmas trees, and everyone loved them as some people are not able to decorate anymore, and they could come and enjoy the beauty.

I also allow the space to be used for Celebration of Life celebrations, as our town does not have many places to select from and this has a beautiful room and a beautiful view. Hearing how great the space is, others are coming to do Birthday Parties, Baby Showers, Weddings, and even a Prom event where the youth are given free Prom gowns.

Family is first for me. I have an amazing mother who is always there for me and such a lady. She is kind to everyone. She was widowed 7 years ago. I also have a sister who is strong and a great example who does not let anything hold her back and two brothers who are always there when needed. My husband Freddy and I showed up and rescued a Siberian Husky named Paris who is the love of our life.

I also host many fundraisers for organizations to help them with their causes as my passion is reaching out to help others and making a difference is something I have done all of my life.

Asking has been hard for me, but I am learning how powerful that can be, and I am stepping out of my comfort zone to do it more.

Because I am stepping out more, I am meeting more dynamic individuals that are opening more doors to help me do my passion of golf as well as helping others.

Some my goals for the coming year are the following:

To start a Cherry Hills Golf Academy for the Youth, DO training to help the seniors better as I have an expert who will open their, minds to things they need to know. I am reaching out to help women grow their business and learn how to ASK and to SHOW UP.

To be open for individuals to feel comfortable to share ideas and thoughts and even issues with so that together we can find solutions.

To take time also for me and my husband Freddy to have time for vacations, golf, and all the things we love to do and inspire others that first we need to take time for ourselves than we can help others and also have a more successful business. I want to share the power of showing up and asking as those are the two greatest tools one can use.

I love SHOWING UP and helping a community know the power of what they can do together and learn that we do not compete we complete each other.

I started Line Dancing on Monday and Karaoke on Tuesday to continue to grow as prior to starting this with the experts there was no place for the community to do this.

Because of starting the Karaoke one couple met each other and got married and another is engaged and more seem to be less stressed and happier. My showing up has not only helped them, but it has filled my heart with joy knowing that I have the ability to make a difference.

When I first took over the Golf Club 2020, it was owned by different owners and was facing much difficulty in staying open. I have worked hard picking the right staff, training them, and filling myself where needed, and I am happy to say we never had to close, and its membership is growing. I know that 2023 we will all work together to make it double in size.

I regrouped the women's golf when I took over as golf pro and manager as it had dropped to 6 players, so I ASKED and was able to build it up with dynamic learning to increase their golf skills, have fun, and meet other dynamic women.

I also was able to put some events together to help the local lions club not only make money but get exposure to build their local group.

I have co-sponsored many GSFE events in 2022 and already have many planned for 2023 which helps women grow which is one of my passions.

I make a point to SHOW UP at many of the town's activities done by the city, the Core, and others and also do many sponsorships.

We also did a golf tournament at San Jacinto College to make a difference in the community.

My method of teaching golf has proven to be infectious, and I believe that I keep it fun, keep it simple, Show Up, and say "let's play." Those that thought they could never play golf are amazed at how this system that I have put together makes it so easy. They have learned they can also do business on the course and get exercise as well as stay healthy and enjoy the beautiful surroundings.

My future plans include a trip to Pennsylvania to show up and spend time with my daughter and grandchildren.

I want to expand the events that I do at the clubhouse to include dancing

one night a week as in our town. Currently, there is no place for Seniors to go dancing.

I also want to have a Sunday Brunch with entertainment as bringing people together I find keeps them younger and happier, and it makes me happy knowing that I am able to do this. These events provide a safe environment for all to attend, and I love that I can keep the cost affordable.

Startup Cherry Hills Golf Academy.

Play Nine and Dine.

Cherry Hills Women's League expansion.

Golf Tournaments.

One of my other goals is to take part of the land I encouraged my golf course owners to set aside for a park for the city and make that happen in 2023.

Together we can change the world, and I certainly am going to continue to do my part to be the change in the community.

The Power of Showing Up

Josie Torres

As I look back, it's as if my entire life was one synchronicity after another. I might not have noticed it for what it was at the time, but I was always on the lookout for signs with a silent prayer asking, what to do? From an early age I had to try to find solutions to problems like, where am I going to live at 15 years old? My childhood was unstable and dysfunctional.

I used to read a lot of fiction growing up. It was my escape from the chaos around me. I would borrow books from the school library. I also enjoyed writing in my journal. I would ask questions like, why was this my life and why me? I always felt the answer was that it was all serving a deeper purpose and would make sense in time.

Although I felt hopeful it was still too difficult to imagine the simple things like having a home, I didn't want to run away from steady meals and family who didn't make me feel as if I was just a burden. I was on survival mode, and I didn't have time or space to be creative. I didn't know how it could get better, but somewhere deep inside I knew this will not be forever, and although I had no clue how it would change, I believed it would.

I had an innate belief that magical things happened like in my books, and it all works out in the end. I also believed in miracles in a spiritual way, that

our ancestors, angels, spiritual guides, or GOD played a hand in guiding us where we needed to be. I would always talk to myself and examine my situation and ask to the universe "ok what should I do now, what are my options"? I trusted there was a plan for me as there is for all of us.

I wasn't brought up religious like going to church on Sundays. We never went to church except maybe for a baptism. Even funerals were held at funeral parlors and if anyone did happen to get married it was at city hall. I can't count how many funerals I have been to. Yet in the mix of it all you don't realize the difference or compare it to others. Most of my family all had similar stories and there wasn't internet or much tv. The only comparing or outside view I had was from my books where I developed the belief that it would all work out and it will all be worth it one day.

Now I see how silly that is to wait around for life to just work out in your favor. The real magic happened when I learned we create our life with our thoughts, and I decided to show up. I decided what I want in life and to go after it. I knew the universe, God, and Angels would align those who can support my focus at the right time. I also decided to help whomever I can when I can along the way. I was going to make something of myself and be proud of who I am. I accept my past, live in my present, and create my future.

My first change occurred when I was about 19 years old. I was staying with a friend and her mother, but they were moving to a smaller apartment and made it clear I was not able to join them. I appreciated them allowing me to stay for whatever time they did and held no bitter feelings as they had no obligation towards me, but it had meant I had nowhere to live.

I didn't have a permanent job but was cleaning houses with another friend of mine. There was a van that picked us up and took us to a nice area across the bridge in NJ and we all chipped in to pay the driver. One day during my

15-minute lunch break, I was quickly eating my burger. I looked around at the neighborhood with all its beautiful trees, grass, lack of sirens blaring, and this calm energy that I was experiencing and thought "I would love to get away from it all and move to an area like this", but of course I didn't believe it could happen to me because I had no money. I barely made enough to meet my basic needs and was soon to be homeless. I dismissed it and went about my day.

I reached out to my father's sister in desperation. I had to swallow my pride asking for help. I didn't want to as we were estranged, and I had not spoken to her in years. She sent me some cash which was appreciated and asked for a phone number she could reach me at. Not long after my cousin called me. I was shocked as we have had our share of disagreements and were not on the best terms. My aunt told her about my situation, and she wanted to help. It felt good talking to family, and she sounded to genuinely care.

She was in the army reserves and was currently living in NJ. She was renting a room in her boyfriend's grandmothers' attic and was willing to share it with me. She offered to help me get a job at a daycare that she worked for it and was within walking distance since we didn't have a car. This sounded like a blessing although I was a bit hesitant given the past, but I didn't have many options.

She came to pick me up with her boyfriend and his friend. I didn't have many belongings and it all fit into a medium sized cardboard box that we stuffed into his small trunk. That was the last day I ever lived in the ghetto. It was the day I took control of my life and didn't feel like a victim anymore. Even though living in an attic working for minimum wage was nowhere near glamorous. I felt more independent. The little money we earned left us broke after paying rent. We went hungry quite often. Nothing I wasn't

used to. Somehow it didn't feel as bad as before. It was more about being young and in the struggle not just desolate and feeling less than.

My first day working at the day care center during my lunchbreak I was walking to find something to eat, and I saw Burger King. I couldn't believe it; yes, you guessed it, the same burger king. I'm living in the neighborhood I thought would be impossible not so long ago. We get so caught up in the "how" that we think it isn't for us. In the not thinking it was possible I dismissed it but nevertheless launched a missile into my asking and the universe delivered.

I will never forget that feeling like I can do anything from nothing. I didn't know where I was going to live but was presented with an answer. Life felt great, and I was dating someone who I was over the moon with. He actually ended up being a jerk but at the time he was a great guy.

My cousin enlisted into the army full time, and I had to move again, but it was ok I had a job and got a second job at a nearby supermarket. I found another room to rent. I was going to school for my associates degree at the local community college.

While working the night shift in the supermarket, this older man came in. He was very friendly, maybe too friendly because he asked a lot of personal questions. He kept coming into my line, and the other cashiers would tease how my future boyfriend walked in. One night while he was making small talk, I blurted out "I have a boyfriend, and you're way too old for me."

He laughed and said, "I wasn't hitting on you; I'm just being nice and want to help you. You're working the late shift, and you seem too smart to be here. I looked at him suspicious and with a lot of attitude, I said, "I don't believe you. Help me how? and what do you want in return?"

He looked me in my eyes and said, "Give me your resume, and I will give it to the HR department where I work to get you a better job. I want nothing from you but maybe your friendship and by the way I have a girlfriend". I still didn't believe him but thought it couldn't hurt and so I gave it to him. He did just what he said and became a good friend. The most he asked of me was to babysit his kids which he paid me for.

We worked at the well-known company for 8 years, and I earned several promotions and even made Employee of the Year. Eventually it was bought out and I broke up with that jerk boyfriend who could not be faithful to save his life not that he claimed differently, still I thought he might just for me. Stupid I know but we live and learn.

A few years later I met my husband. At first, I wasn't going to give him a chance but eventually he won me over with his humor and intelligence. We were both getting over heartaches, and he proved to be someone who cared about me and made me feel safe. I could be myself around him and he didn't judge me. We enjoyed each other's company and now we have two kids living in Queens. I never thought I would move back to NYC, but it is home.

After staying home with the kids a few years and feeling the urge to get back to who I am other than a mom and wife because I felt lost and out of touch with that part of me. I joined an online group looking for some direction. One of the participants was talking about her experience as a healer and I found it fascinating. I went online looking for everything that had to do with healing. It led to another like, law of attraction, manifestation, and nutrition. I found a school called IIN Institute of Integrative Nutrition that taught health coaching which I attended and graduated from.

Starting over was difficult along with going back to school. I learned about social media, technology, and marketing while being a wife and a mom. I knew starting a business was not going to be easy as I supported my

husband while he started his, but this was beyond that. This was bringing up some emotional stuff that I thought I had worked out already. I struggled with feelings of not being good enough, feeling ashamed, and dealing with some serious imposter syndrome.

Still, I couldn't quit as it was bigger than me; it fueled and lit me like nothing before. I had to follow my own advice by working on my nutrition, a fitness plan, a meditation practice, journaling. I started a creative hobby and met new people who inspired me. I had to care how I felt and how I talked to myself, have compassion and understanding the same way I showed it to others.

One thing led to another and now I have an awesome team of women who I am working with who make it all seem so easy and worth it. I began an online virtual retreat center. I'm staying focused on why I'm doing this which is to do what I love and help others. I love to share my knowledge and passion about nutrition, motivation, living intentionally and help by empowering moms find joy and purpose to get out of living on autopilot and feeling stuck. Because these are lessons that I have learned, I feel it's my calling!

I came across a comment on Facebook and decided to respond to it. It was by Verlaine Crawford. Immediately I was drawn to her. We began messaging and then emailing. We spoke on the phone. She sent her books to me and even signed one which I treasure. She is a wonderful writer and person. It's funny because on paper we have little in common as in total opposites with culture, education, age and live on the opposite sides of America but I feel it was destined for us to meet. She introduced me to GSFE and Robbie Motter. I am looking forward to continuing to show up and ask and see where else it will lead.

I now love to read non-fiction books and learn about the energetic change

the Earth is currently experiencing and we are all transitioning into. Intuitively I believe in what is being said especially from all the different sources. I'd like to assist those who are struggling with this transition to vibrate at a higher level due to karma or being stuck somewhere on their journey. The universe gives us guidance all the time. We just overlook it because we think it has to be a huge sign with lights and arrows pointed to it. Its subtle clues and nudges to keep you on your path, but it's your freewill to choose to follow it. We need hope and strength to put your fear on a shelf, show up and ask. We are all connected and aren't meant to do anything alone.

Susan Vanderburgh - Host

Finding my Table
Susan Vanderburgh

On Wednesday, November 2, 2022, I awakened to 40-degree weather in my spacious bedroom around 6:30 in the morning. It was still dark, and I had only gone to bed around 2:30 in the morning. I had a commitment to be at a virtual meeting with my Entrepreneurs Toastmasters Club at 7:00 a.m. and I wanted to be presentable. There is no excuse for not showing up just because I did not look good enough. I logged into the meeting with my cell phone and my camera off as I made myself presentable.

Bond Wang, one of the speakers was talking about mahjong, a Chinese gambling game, which I had previously thought was like dominoes. One thing that Bond said that stood out to me was that you would not win much money when sitting at a table with small chips. Bond said if you are "sitting at a table with players far beyond your level, you will be crushed in no time." If you are at a table with high enough stakes, that is worth your time, and you still have a chance to win. Choosing the right table is relevant in life because the table sets boundaries or limits, so choose the right table wisely. Oftentimes, people would have to change tables to win some of the pot of money.

My experience with Chinese movies as I grew up was, I would see men gathering at mahjong tables, having a good time, and then all of a sudden slamming the tiles on the table with a fight erupting. What Bond pointed out was that to win, you need to change tables when you find yourself playing at a table with smaller chips. This analogy really stuck with me because life is like a table, and I never really belonged to any table in life, at work or at social settings. When I do find myself at a table, likely a table with smaller chips, I often needed to find a table with bigger chips or more skilled players very soon. Perhaps that was my biggest challenge during my entire life -- finding the right table. I shared my sentiment with the group that morning, and I told the group that now I understand I have been sitting at the smaller tables and the boundaries were too small, so I had to quickly change tables. Prior to joining the group, all I knew we had in common was that we were entrepreneurs. I did not know this was a more advanced Toastmasters group, so I felt privileged to be socializing and learning from highly qualified and expert public speakers – this was my group and I felt quite at home. So, I said, "like the Green Arrow, I have become someone else."

I did not realize how similar I was to the Green Arrow, until I watched the television series. At the beginning of each episode, the main character Oliver Queen would recite something like "I had become someone else. I would become something else." For some peculiar reason, I, like Oliver Queen, have become something else and someone else. But the "someone else" has always been within me. It's just that I did not know at the time.

When writing this chapter, I had to consider when I "showed up and asked" for anything. When it was time to show up in school, I showed up, but did people know I was there? While I was growing up, I did show up and had excellent grades, but I did not ask for anything. I was not taught to ask for anything. As the years went by, I learned that the world would see me for what I presented. My teachers in middle school made comments about me "choosing the path less traveled" and that I "should speak up in class

so others can learn" from me because I "sit and watch like a wise owl", but unless I spoke up and share knowledge, no one else would know that I was there or had something to contribute. It was unsolicited advice from the teachers. Being a youngster in the Chinese culture, I was taught to listen to the elders and the teachers were the elders. So, anytime a teacher said anything to me, I would listen and not question but reflect on what was said to me and do better next time.

I did start speaking up in class, especially when people described me as "shy", and one day I realized that being "shy" was not really a good thing. Instead, it made me a target for bullies. And if I did not stand up and speak up for myself, no one could come to my rescue quick enough.

So, in sixth grade, to prove to everyone that I was not "shy," I did what most people thought was scary -- public speaking. I remember taking my spot in the Spelling Bee, which is a form of public speaking, having to appear in front of an audience observing us, the spellers, as we each spell a word given to us. I did what I could and won first place which took me to the districtwide Spelling Bee where I competed with other champion spellers in San Francisco.

Also in 6th grade, I ran for student body government. I did not believe I was popular enough for any votes to win anything, but I signed up anyway. I created my posters, asked everyone to vote for me, and made my speech during the assemblies. For 6th grade, my first election ever, I ran for Student Body Secretary and lost. Oh well. I showed up for myself and that mattered.

For 7th grade, I also took part in the Spelling Bee and won first place again and represented the school in the districtwide Spelling Bee in San Francisco. In 7th grade, my second election, I ran for Student Body Vice

President and lost. I showed up and did my best. No one can be a winner all the time, right?

For 8th grade, I took part in the Spelling Bee and made it to the final round. I decided to give the winning spot to another eighth grader because he was often nice to me, and he had not won for the three years that we competed in the Spelling Bee. So, he took first place – yay. I was sort of tired of winning, and it was becoming boring without having a good challenge. For 8th grade, my third election for student body government, I ran for President and lost. I thought maybe I was just not destined for politics -- not "this shy Chinese girl." "It's okay. I did my best," I consoled myself and prepared myself for graduation. A few weeks after the election, the elected student body president got expelled from the school indefinitely, so guess who became president? Me! Wow, I could not believe it. As a result, for graduation, I had to prepare a speech because I was also Valedictorian for my graduating class. I guess other people wanted the Valedictorian position, but because I was so studious, and I took part in sports and I really kept myself busy with studies, I was excelling in all my classwork and was far ahead of others in my graduating class.

On graduation day, it was sort of hectic because I did not know if my parents would be able to attend graduation. My father arrived at the graduation, and we took a couple of pictures and then he rushed back to work or take care of another sibling.

Because of my excellent grades, I was chosen to attend summer camp during my middle school years at Summerbridge which was held at University High School, a prestigious private high school. Perhaps that was when I realized the world was bigger than just my neighborhood and my school. And because I had to compete for the camp, and got in, I felt as if I better not waste that opportunity, and for once I felt as if money was not a struggle

anymore. I also volunteered and was on sports teams. My academics and extracurricular activities got me quickly accepted into Lowell High School, which is a well-regarded public high school in San Francisco. The admissions process was rigorous, and I took it for granted; perhaps it was too easy for me. I delayed my response to accept my admission letter, by applying to three other lower-rated high schools. The other lower-rated high schools rejected me, stating that the population was over impacted. I spoke with Mr. Beltran, one of my teachers, and told him that Lowell High School accepted me, and I thought of not attending that school. Mr. Beltran was silent for about a minute. I thought he did not hear me so I repeated what I told him, and he said, "Why would you decide not to attend Lowell High School? That is the best school in San Francisco! Do you know how many people want to go there? You will do great there."

I took Mr. Beltran's advice and attended Lowell High School. The four years were not easy because as you could imagine, I was competing with the crème de la crème of all students admitted to this high school. Many of them attended private schools most of their lives and were well-equipped with private tutors, had amazing sports skills and vacations. Although my education was not that bad, I was transitioning from a lower socioeconomic population into one that was a little bit higher. On the first day of school, we were told that we were all competing with each other even though we could be friends. At the end of it all, we are all competing for top positions at top universities and the school would do its best to equip us for that challenge.

I was no longer that special. Most people I met were also Valedictorians or won some type of award or had done something wonderful outside of school.

Even so, I ran for student government the first year of high school, second year, third year and fourth year. I lost each year, but during every election, I did my very best with my posters, impromptu announcements in all my classes about running for a student body government position and asked people to vote for me. I did not win a student body government position. It is likely that I was not popular enough, but at least I showed up and asked.

I also applied to be on the prom committee. But for whatever reason, I was excluded from that committee. I have not regretted asking.

So, high school was not completely successful, but I did graduate. I showed up for all the good and terrible days and I graduated. I am glad I did because I was the first one in my family to graduate from a high school in the United States. I was the eldest of five children, so even though high school was challenging, I still made it through. Perhaps that helped my younger brothers and sisters make it through as well because those were very tough years. In fact, it was so tough. One of my younger brothers got in trouble at his high school, and my two younger sisters were being bullied and were being attacked by gang members. By the time I was graduating from high school, I really wanted to run away from the chaotic lifestyle at home. I was also clinically depressed and was hiding the depression so well by keeping busy, learning multiple languages, learning new skills, being on sports teams, participating in many school clubs, and volunteering. Volunteering at Laguna Honda Hospital contributed to saving my life. I later realized that because I showed up for "Oliver", a blind bedridden quadriplegic veteran, as Oliver's hospital buddy, and as a special events buddy for the seniors, I was making a difference for someone else. At the same time, I was also selfishly curing myself of my depression.

When my younger sisters got in trouble with the gang members, my parents ran out of ideas. I was also pestering them about going to college because

everybody from high school was going to college, so why shouldn't I? The problem was we had no money. My mother said to me in Cantonese, "You only need to learn one thing in life and that one thing will feed you for life." She said that I had enough education, and it was okay if I did not get to college. I thought that was not right, simply because we didn't have the money does not mean I can't find a job, save, and go to college. There were five children. I was the oldest. And when the next one graduated from high school, then there is another college tuition to take care of.

My parents were going to send one of my sisters away to complete high school, and I was assigned to accompany her to make sure she does not get into more trouble. My mother said by enrolling into the program, I would get two years of free college. Well, that was a silver lining. I was happy to go. What was even better was that we would get paid to go to school. I couldn't believe it!

We ended up going to Job Corps in Reno, Nevada, which was funded by the Department of Labor. My sister and I were in the same dorm, and we shared an adjoining bathroom. We were in one of the nicer dormitories. I thought the recruiter did very well for us, and I reported to my mother how happy we were. I did what I could to watch my sister. Because of her hot headedness and temper, she got into a few physical fights in the dorm. Apparently, fights are usual, especially when a bunch of teenage girls are living in the same place and trying to share a television, telephone, and chores. I learned a lot and I also taught my sister how to communicate with people. I believe she learned that on her own as well. I would like to believe that because I showed up. I made a difference.

I was told that my business program would take three years to complete. I refused to believe that program would take three years. I was determined to complete that self-paced program in one year. Within my one year at

Job Corps, I excelled in student government and leadership classes, won first place in a writing contest, and completed my business program at the highest level -- all because I showed up for the challenge to complete the Business program in one year and asked myself to stick to that goal.

Fast forward to June 2016, we visited San Francisco to celebrate Father's Day weekend with my parents, brothers, sisters, and in-laws. My husband developed a cough about three weeks before we went to San Francisco. By the time we were driving up to San Francisco, his cough did not go away. We stayed the night at my sister's house and the next morning. She asked if Erik (my husband) was okay because he sounded as if he was dying. She works in the medical field so I guess she would know what someone dying would sound like, so I said, "I hope so. If the cough does not go away tonight, I am taking him to ER tomorrow morning."

My sister rolled her eyes at me and said, "Okay, he kept all of us awake last night with his cough." I apologized and said that kept me awake, too.

That afternoon, I told Erik, "If your cough is not gone by the morning, I am taking you to ER. Don't give me any objections." He nodded as he coughed. Erik's cough worsened that night. At 5:30 in the morning, I woke him up and said, "Okay, we're going. I am taking you to ER." My sister was already awake, not surprisingly. I told her, "I need you to watch our kids because I'm taking him to the ER. We should be back in about 3 hours." Within an hour of getting to the Emergency Room, the doctor had given the diagnosis that Erik has End Stage Renal Disease, and his kidney was in active failure by the test results; he had pneumonia, and he would need to be hospitalized. Erik insisted that I leave him and the children so that I could return to work on time. Erik was in no condition to drive 550 miles from San Francisco to home. Essentially, I showed up for my husband. That trip was supposed to be a weekend trip, but I ended up having to

take a week and a half of unpaid time off from work so I could coordinate insurance payments and medical appointments and take care of our five young children.

Erik decided to wait until 2017 to start dialysis for his kidney failure so we could use my medical insurance benefits to help pay for medication and dialysis which cost upwards of $300,000 per year. In 2017, I was working multiple jobs, and completing my master's degree. When I decided to do something for myself, I joined business groups. One such group was National Association for Female Executives (NAFE), and I managed to attend one meeting because of the hectic work schedule and the distance. During that one meeting, I met amazing women and learned that we needed to show up and ask. I remember saying that I had no problem asking for what I needed, so my ask for that night was for a kidney donor, which I knew was a huge ask. I showed up and asked anyway. I only started to look around and started asking, but I did not really know how to ask. Robbie Motter (the founder of Global Society for Female Entrepreneurs) believed in me and was a stranger who extended her kindness to write and publish an article about us. This act of kindness gave me the confidence and the nudge that I needed to move forward. I was also speaking with other leaders in the kidney transplant community. Jim Myers, Karol Franks, Bunny Vreeland, and others were critical in helping me move the "1 in a 1,000,000" campaign for a living kidney donor for Erik. The theory behind the one in a million idea was that if I tried hard enough and if I asked enough people, likely if I asked a million people, there would be one person who would be willing and able and be a good match to donate a kidney to Erik.

I was not afraid to ask. I ran donation campaigns and events and literally asked for cash from colleagues and strangers because my family depended on me to pay all the bills and be there for them.

I remember showing up at each Denny's restaurant location as scheduled and telling people about our kidney campaign for Erik. People reached into their pockets and gave me $20 bills; something I did not expect. But looking back, what would one expect when approached by someone in the restaurant with a story like mine? There were people who ignored me, but that was okay because I had a job -- show up and ask -- that is what Robbie kept saying at every meeting and every email. Even though I could not attend the meetings, I still showed up by reading the emails.

One week, I was so desperate when my husband kept getting sick, I was getting more depressed. I really needed to do something different. I decided maybe I should go to medical school, and that might lead me to a kidney donor. I accepted an invitation to a dinner meeting that introduced me to a medical school and the admissions process. During this dinner, I met the professors who were medical doctors, and I met one professor who was a nephrologist. I discussed the kidney transplant and the electronic kidney research with this famous nephrologist. The nephrologist said to me that the funding for the electronic kidney research was pulled. I thought, "Wow, it was a good thing I showed up because I would not have known that." And here, I was listening and hearing this from a professor who has first-hand knowledge of that. When I got home that night, I told my husband that earlier in the day I received a phone call from the UCLA Hospital confirming that he was on the waiting list and the wait time for a kidney is seven years. I also told Erik that I spoke with a famous nephrologist at dinner who told me there was no funding for the electronic kidney and asked him if he still wanted to wait especially with the condition that he was in at the time and dialysis was minimally effective.

By the last quarter of 2019, I almost gave up with my one in a million campaign because I felt as if I had no support. If I did not send any messages, publish articles, or make appearances on social media, there was no activity. When

I almost decided to quit, I thought I would send one more message. I logged into a Facebook group, and I saw a message from Donna Moore, a woman who seemed extremely upset because she had already gone through the first segment of tests to become a kidney donor for someone, and the intended recipient had another kidney donor come through quicker. I took a chance and asked Donna if she would consider donating to Erik. I thought at the least, that was showing up and asking. I did not know what to expect. It could be "no", but at least I gave it a good try as this was my last try. Donna wrote back "yes" she would. I could not believe it when I read that. It was almost feeling as if I were a man proposing to a woman to marry me and the woman said yes. I guess that's the best way to describe that feeling when someone says "yes". Wow, I could not believe it! I had to contain my excitement and hope this was really going to save, not only Erik's life, but my life and the lives of our five children.

After Donna said yes, I said "yes" to Jared Brown and Steven Belcher (in New York) who interviewed me and Erik on air because we were looking for a living kidney donor. Because I said "yes" to Jared and Steven, it created a chain reaction of appearing on a show a few days after Donna said "yes". Since Donna and her husband, Dean, in South Carolina were able to see us (in California) on the show broadcast live worldwide, Donna and Dean said that was what solidified their decision to donate to Erik. In a way, I was relieved. But I was not sure what would happen if it was not a good match. But I had to show up and ask anyway. Even though Donna had said "yes" I still had to show up for the television show and ask for support and a backup donor for Erik and for people to consider being a kidney donor for others.

Looking back, I learned that I cannot cancel on myself even when other people do cancel an appointment with me or if something happened to cause us not to meet. When I make a commitment to do something, I must

show up. If I need something, I need to ask. My mother once said, "We don't know where you're itching if you don't tell us" which is similar to "show up and ask". People cannot help you unless you ask. Oftentimes, people are willing to help if they are able to. And that's what I found with the power of showing up and asking. When you are in the right crowd, you show up, and if you ask, you will get an answer.

When reflecting on Bond's speech about choosing a table in life, I see how my life's story is coming together, and it makes more sense now. I could have slept in on November 2, 2022, because it was so early, especially only having slept for 3.5 hours, and I was not due to start work for another 4 hours. I could have "slept in" like most "normal" people on a cold winter morning. I am glad I showed up because I was seeking inspiration to write this chapter and was not sure how to tie together so many opportunities for me to show up and ask or show up and make a difference.

At birth, I was assigned a nice table, but circumstances changed for my entire family, and we had to change to survive. I became skilled at adapting to change and working with change. I also became something else by showing up and asking and then achieving. At the time of writing this chapter, only fragments of my past remain – the immigrant Chinese girl who did not speak English until she was nine years old. I have transformed from impoverished and living in fear to someone who achieved higher education, created, and followed her dreams of owning and operating multiple businesses, investments and becoming a director of a nonprofit organization, American Society of Community Benefits and gained support from the community and 15 Board Members. I have also won many awards and am holding other Board Members positions with organizations that continue to make a difference. Overall, I chose a table, and when one was not being enough, I created a table where boundaries continue to expand

with me. Only the people with a similar drive and mindset will continue to grow with me.

Follow Your Heart

Dr. (h.c.) Marie Waite

"Follow Your Heart" is a mantra that has been a guiding light for me throughout my life and career. Through countless learning experiences and challenges, it has kept me on track to being the best I can possibly be and helped me to achieve my life's ever-expanding goals.

I actually began my career in the healthcare industry, but after 15 years in the field, I made the life changing decision to transition into real estate. It all started during the early 90s when I was living in Albuquerque, New Mexico. An opportunity presented itself through the VA (Veterans Administration) programs that allowed me the possibility to buy a house with a surprisingly low down- payment, and this eventually grew to ownership of several real estate properties in the area. After a short period managing these properties, I reached a point where I needed to sell in preparation for a move to California.

The one big mistake I made was hiring and trusting a real estate agent without the knowledge to properly vet his work ethic and character. I was naive and had little experience selling properties. What I hoped would be a profitable return on my investment didn't materialize, leaving me feeling taken advantage of and unsatisfied with the outcome. I was confused, and

a voice in my head told me that this agent had not looked out for my best interest, and that if I continued on with little knowledge of the process of selling properties, this would happen to me again in the future. Suffice it to say, I wasn't about to let that happen!

Learning About Real Estate

After my negative experience selling my first properties, I was firmly dedicated to going back to school and learning all there was to know about the real estate industry and putting control back in my own hands. I studied incessantly, took all the related classes, and in 2005 became a licensed real estate agent. This led to me starting a real estate brokerage firm, my first big step as a new agent in California. My unwavering determination for getting things done had paid off!

My next goal was to recruit real estate agents for the brokerage deals, which was a challenge for a budding new firm. We had competitors in the market who were always ready to outdo us, and competition was fierce. Despite these hurdles, I was able to recruit 50 agents through a local networking group. Throughout my journey of running my own brokerage my belief in myself and my mantra "Follow Your Heart" led me to make the most of my experience with the company, and I discovered a knack for creating effective marketing programs for real estate professionals.

Being willing to take such a life changing leap allowed me to create a network of amazing professionals, opened doors of opportunities to create new projects within the community, and culminated with a charity focused business expo attended by more than 100 companies. The charity funds raised were donated to a high school in the City of Temecula, California. The project was such a success it motivated us to start a 501(c)(3) nonprofit

organization called the IVBCF (Inland Valley Business and Community Foundation).

My Journey with the Inland Valley Business and Community Foundation

The IVBCF quickly grew to become an organization hosting several yearly business expos and fashion shows in the City of Temecula and Murrieta, bringing many from the fashion industry to visit the community. It was astounding to me to see the work put into the branding of the participants and the opportunities that came my way as producer and organizer of these events.

Invitations started flowing in from all directions. I made many new connections with famous photographers and international fashion designers and was invited to major fashion industry events from Los Angeles to Paris, surrounded by Hollywood stars and prominent business figures. These events exposed my name to the industry, and I soon realized that I was creating a brand for myself, both in real estate and fashion.

Starting a real estate brokerage business and a non-profit organization proved to be a good combination for me. I followed my heart in helping business professionals during the recession, which led me to bring many people together and expand their exposure and mine. The experience provided me with highly effective branding, a concept that was previously unfamiliar to me, and made me a respected business leader in the community.

My Valuable Connection with Robbie Motter

One of the most fruitful relationships that the IVBCF blessed me with was the one I developed with Robbie Motter. Upon meeting, she and I immediately collaborated without hesitation. She proved to be a great influence in my life, and even now she keeps blessing me with so many great connections and opportunities. I believe my relationship with Robbie played an important role in who I am today.

I was interested in joining Robbie's GSFE (Global Society for Female Entrepreneurs) group and was looking into the San Diego chapters. After talking to several chapter leaders, I decided to go out on a creative limb and ask if she was willing to allow me to create a new chapter. It was a big step, but it was one I was ready to take. Robbie was extremely supportive and put her trust in me to lead the new group. Her belief in my leadership skills allowed me the possibility to connect with so many amazing women in San Diego, and she continually blessed me with more opportunities that I would never have known about if I hadn't joined her group.

Robbie Motter is in her 80s and she is such an inspiring person, I sometimes wonder where she gets so much energy to always be present and active in so many events. I admire her love for helping us become successful. She is not only smart but incredibly creative. I like being creative, and when I see her ways of collaboration, I realize she is a master at it. She absolutely follows her heart, and that's where I believe she gets her energy and passion for GSFE.

Recently Robbie nominated me to receive the honorary doctorate award for humanitarianism in London. This was a great surprise! I am grateful for this opportunity and consider it a notable accomplishment in my professional journey. I flew to London and met so many amazing women from GSFE and also from the Ladies of All Nations International. My visit to London was an

amazing business experience as it gave me the opportunity to collaborate with many businesswomen. They are all very talented and enthusiastic women who are eager to achieve their goals, and together we celebrated our group. I look forward to meeting them once again.

Looking back through the years that I have known Robbie, I'm reminded of all the support and opportunities that she's shared with me, and most of all, her generosity. She never fails to want the best for us and to cultivate great connections, opportunities, and collaborations. She is my inspiration, whether it's in business or in my personal life. I will always be grateful to Robbie for believing in me!

The Importance of Presence and Professionalism

Showing up is the first step to being visible. When meeting new people, they will always have that first impression of you, so make it a good one! When you are joining a group like the GSFE and being led by an inspiring leader like Robbie Motter, be sure to align yourself accordingly with their professionalism. Whether you are in a business or casual setting, maintaining respectability is a must. You cannot build a brand within a group like GSFE if you lack professionalism, regardless of how skilled you are at your work. People will continually observe your behavior and take note of how you present yourself, and judge whether or not you might be a good fit for their business and branding, so be professional and make sure to leave a powerful first impression!

I have seen people behave and dress unprofessionally, forgetting when they are in a business setting working with a professional organization. They could be losing great opportunities because of their behavior. They could be losing an opportunity that might turn out to be a game-changer for them. There are opportunities that can alter the entire structure of one's life and these moments do not come around often enough to waste them. I wouldn't have benefited from so many connections with the GSFE if I had turned out to be unprofessional at our first meeting.

Being a professional means being someone who is dedicated to maintaining their branding and image around other people. I myself have a high standard for bringing people into my business world. I can see who I would be interested in connecting with based on how they communicate and present themselves. If I see that they are acting wild and communicating with no consideration for others, they will not be a good fit for my business.

Gauging Communication is Key

Some women are very open in terms of talking about emotions and personal matters. I personally prefer to maintain a level of discretion when discussing or expressing my emotions. Not all women are comfortable with that level of communication. While I do believe it is okay to show emotions, there are certain situations where you need to act professionally, especially in a group setting where your behavior reflects upon you.

Everyone has his/her own unique personality. Some people are quite open with their feelings while others are more reserved. I am one of those people that does not want to share problems openly in a group setting. I dislike expressing my concerns in front of everyone. If I have a message for someone, I like to deliver it one-on-one. It is how I am built, but it does not mean others have to be the same way.

Building Your Brand and Network

As a business branding strategist, I believe that consistency and commitment to building your brand will be a requirement to becoming successful in your career. By consistently presenting a cohesive and aligned brand image to your audience and staying committed to the branding process, you can establish trust and credibility, which are essential for building successful business relations.

Ultimately, building good business relationships involves being considerate of others, showing concern for their needs and interests, and finding a balance between dependence and independence. By striking this balance, you can establish strong and productive connections that are mutually beneficial for everyone involved.

When I see someone who takes the time to plan ahead, it shows me that this person is proactive and is taking responsibility for his/her actions. I value and appreciate being in the company of individuals who show consideration for others and do not take them for granted. Building a relationship with someone who demonstrates this kind of behavior is important to me because it helps to foster a positive and respectful dynamic between us.

Here are a few things that I believe can help you build strong business relationships:

Good communication is key to any relationship, and this is especially true in business. Make sure you are clear and concise in your messaging and listen actively to what others have to say.

Show others that they can count on you by meeting deadlines and following through on your commitments.

Respect the schedules and commitments of others and try to minimize unnecessary meetings or interruptions.

Show appreciation for the work of others, and make sure to thank those who help you or go above and beyond.

Take the time to understand the perspectives and needs of others and try to find common ground and mutually beneficial solutions.

Developing Business Leadership

Developing your leadership skills while surrounded by varied groups of people is fundamental to your leadership growth. When someone is put in an awkward situation, their behavior can tell you so much about how they are in business. Some will appear to be patient while others are easily angered. Some are polite while others are putting themselves first. Some are quiet and smiling but unhappy, and some are often just too loud! Others are very enthusiastic but never sincere with their commitments or careful with their words.

Being a leader requires a healthy combination of social characteristics, a solid business foundation, and good moral values. Great leaders are focused on serving and inspiring people. They understand that leadership is not about gaining power or control over others, but rather about serving and supporting others in their development and growth. They maintain a harmonious relationship with people and help them succeed. They are there to support, teach, train, and share good examples of working with each other. Having a good perspective on situations that might seem negative to some people can help turn the situation around. Addressing a stressful interaction in a positive manner will not only help everyone to be better in their interaction but will inspire others.

In Conclusion

As we wrap up, it is important to understand that following your heart might not be the solution for everyone. However, as we have seen, it has the potential to greatly improve our lives and the world around us. The challenge now is to take the ideas presented here and put them into action. We've seen how I started my journey by trusting a real estate agent who did not look out for my best interests. I could have just accepted the feeling of regret and not done anything about it, but I chose to use the experience to motivate me to go back to school and learn the ins and outs of real estate so I could prevent it from happening again.

The challenges I have faced along the way have ultimately contributed to my current success as a well-known real estate professional and a strong business leader in California, and I am honored to have received a doctorate award for my contributions to society. I have made friends throughout my journey that are very close to my heart, and none of it would have been possible if I had not gone back to school. I indeed believe that going back to school, starting everything from the bottom and reaching the top, was the turning point in my life. I chose to follow my heart, and it led me to the doors of success.

As a female entrepreneur, I have learned the importance of consistently demonstrating professionalism, cultivating creativity and independence, and building strong communication skills. These qualities are essential for powerful branding and success in both your personal and professional life. My advice to all young entrepreneurs, women in business, and other business leaders out there is to always follow your heart. It will lead you to the success and fulfillment that you deserve in your life!

Enjoy your journey, Suit up, Show up! Live in the moment, why stay home and wait to die!

Dr. (h.c.) Joan Wakeland

I got a call from my friend Lady Robbie to join her at the Cherry Hills Golf Club. She said, "I am going to support Nicole, she is playing there tonight ". I did not feel like going anywhere that evening. However, I always felt that I needed to support my GSFE Sisters. The venue was close to home, so I thought I would show up for a few minutes.

Start time was six o'clock. I got there on time. Lady Robbie was on her phone. She raised her head up and indicated that I should sit in the vacant chair to her left. I did! Beside me was a gentleman so I acknowledged him by saying "Hello". Lady Robbie then introduced me to Charlie. He indicated that this was his first visit to the golf club. He wanted to meet more people. He was just checking out the place because one of his neighbors told him he could meet active Seniors here. I told him that he was in the right place; if he met Lady Robbie, he would meet many more people. I could guarantee that because in 2001 when I came to Menifee. I knew no one who lived here. It has been 21 years, and I have wonderful relationships with many people who were introduced to me by her. Lady Robbie is a connector! She opens the door; the rest is up to you.

Later that evening, another friend Angela who wanted to speak to Lady Robbie showed up. I gave my seat to her and sat in the chair on the other side of Charlie. We all sat there listening to Karaoke and watching people line dance. When Nicole changed the tempo, she played an Elvis song "Wise Men say …" I started swaying along; it is one of my favorite songs. Charlie noticed my expression and asked if I was a fan of Elvis. That simple question opened a conversation. I told him that I loved his gospel music, his rock and roll music, and his stage presence. I also mentioned that I never missed an Elvis movie when I was young. All the girls loved Elvis the pelvis moves. I was indeed a fan of Elvis!

With all the information given to Charlie, he not only asked me to dance but also accompany him to an Elvis movie when we went back to our seats. He was not certain which theatre was showing Elvis's life story; he would call to find out if it was showing at a nearby theatre. I said yes, wrote my number in his phone, but did not save it. Smart lady?

A week passed and I was in Orange County at a GSFE meeting when I got a call from my friend Charmaine. She said, "There is a gentleman here by the name of Charlie that is looking for you. Is it okay to give him your number? I told her to go ahead. Later that evening, I got a call. We confirmed what was the first of many other dates.

We had dinner before going to the movies, conversation was based on "getting to know you, getting to know all about you." Charlie said he was a shy guy! Since I was not born yesterday, I told him that I am forced to believe everything he says now until I can prove it to be different. I found out that he has a good sense of humor. I like that, and the time spent with him was enjoyable. Charlie asked me to go to dinner with him after a few days. We spoke briefly about ourselves. There were many similarities even though we were functioning in different worlds.

What's happening in your world? Think about what I am asking. I don't want the answer, I don't need to know the answer. What I need from you is to be honest with yourself. To thine own self be true!

Be Real!

Are you single? How is that working for you? I have been single for 40 years! If you went to Sunday school, you may remember that was the time Moses spent with the Israelites in the desert! He was taking credit for the good things that God was doing for the people. The Glory belongs to God. Moses died before reaching the Promised Land. Being single worked well for me for many years! I will share some of my benefits.

Benefit number 1:

After my divorce, I wanted to be a good mother to my child. He did not ask to be in this world. He was a gift from the Lord to his parents. However, when shift happens in life, you have to pray to make the right decisions when you realize that you alone will have to take care of your child. You have to pray that your child makes the right choices! Single parents can raise children when they make a lot of sacrifices. Adjustments have to be made. It is not easy, but it can be done. Many of us have been mothers and fathers to our children, we need a special day! What do you think?! If you are a Single Mom reading this, please let me know what your thoughts are.

Benefit number 2:

I could make my own decisions taking responsibility for the outcome. I learned from my mistakes.

Benefit number 3:

I could wear what I wanted, long pants or shorts, long, knee high, or miniskirts. I could use makeup or no makeup the choice was mine!

Benefit number 4:

Are you lonely? Why? You have the privilege to serve your community! First, be a friend and build your own friendship circle! You have the privilege to go where you want to go without being asked where are you going? Who is going with you? What time will you be back?

Benefit number 5:

I can stretch out on my bed vertically or horizontally if I want. I can adjust the room temperature to please me!

Benefit number 6:

I can snore without worrying if the person beside me can't sleep.

Benefit number 7:

I can enjoy all beans, garlic, onions, and cruciferous vegetables without thinking about malodorous backward jet propulsion that may get trapped under the sheets! No longer do I have to say excuse me, for a perfectly normal body function. Ha! Ha! There is no one there!

Benefit number 8:

I cook sometimes when I remember the house has a kitchen! I cook because I want to, not because have to!

Are you looking for a companion? Why? Why not? What are you willing to give up?

When you are not looking to find a companion, strange things can happen. You may not be looking, but he may be looking! When you least expect it damsel, your knight may just show up in shining armor! That's what happened to me. Charlie is now my fiancé. At my age, I never thought I

would fall in love again! I have reversed the number 81 to 18. I feel loved like never before. I give out love like never before. We live in the present! We enjoy each day that we are blessed with, tomorrow is not promised!

I worked in a corporation for many years. I loved my job. I sold products that made a difference in people's lives! I had several mentors who helped me. It is great to have more than one mentor. This exposes you to many options, allowing you to make your vision happen.

Along your journey, you will find people who make it happen, watch it happening, or wonder what happened!

Time Management is important! Prioritizing is important!

Dream Stealers will waste your time and railroad you into the "Quit Station!" They will derail you from achieving your dreams. My parents told me to ostracize Gossipers because they don't have your dreams or aspirations! They are usually people with low or no self-esteem who will use whatever deceptive means to ride on the coattails of others and dare to call themselves their friends. They thrive on chopping down the people who are doing their purpose. They bring news so that they can carry news! If you don't participate in their vitriolic schemes, there is nothing for them to carry! You should remember this, when people talk about you positively, you are important! When they talk about you negatively, you are important! Could it be that they are just jealous of your accomplishments? Don't let anybody steal your dreams!

Stay focused and be passionate about achieving your dreams! Ask God specifically for what you want, write down your vision and keep your eyes on the Prize!

I would like to share these fundamental keys that worked for me! This is not intended for advice.

No.1

Attitude

Your good attitude can get you through a door that will be closed to others that are obnoxious! A smile doesn't cost you money, yet the rewards are often worth more than the effort it took!

No. 2

Good Communication

Keep your message clear and concise!

No. 3

Be a good Listener!

This is a skill, develop it! If not plan to leave money on the table or break relationships that took you years to build.

No.4

Building Strong Relationships can catapult you into places or positions you desire to reach!

No.5

Credibility

You don't have to be the Expert!

If you don't know the answer to a question, say so; offer to find the answer and get back in a timely manner.

This way you won't lose your credibility.

No. 6

Salesmanship

Everyone can sell something. The child sells Mommy when she/he wants a cookie.

Ask for the business after you earn it. Know when to close! Avoid overselling!

The customer is ready to buy; you decide to keep talking about your wonderful product/service. Suddenly the customer changes his/ her mind. Why? What happened? Could it be that you like to hear yourself talking, so you lost the sale!

No. 7

Respect!

Make people feel special! Don't Gossip! You may have behaved like that in the past! Control your tongue!

No. 8

Be Authentic and Honest.

When you lose your integrity, you lose your credibility!

No. 9

Value

What do you bring to the table! Sell to the customer needs! Being Pushy is a turn off.

If you are offering a product/ service and your customer sees the value, they will purchase.

No.10

Good Customer Service.

It is great for referrals and repeat business. It is better to under promise and over deliver.

The customer is always right; that's what everyone in sales is accustomed to hearing. However, we all know darn well that there are some difficult people out there that thrive on creating drama!

It is amazing how one can do everything possible, everything right and rarely hear "Thank you". The first time you make one mistake, you may get "shouted out, chewed out, or a demand to see your boss!" The dissatisfied customer can download all the frustrations experienced into Yelp! Why

waste time talking about the problems to the offender? They don't have a solution, and they don't care! Therefore, the dissatisfied customers get satisfaction by yelling to Yelp!

I have experienced unkindness, harsh words, mean spirited people as well as those who are kind, generous and hospitable. I am sure you have too! I interviewed a few people to get a response about how they felt when they were put down. Most just said, "Forgive them!"

One said, "Frankly I don't care. I am not hurting anyone."

Second person said, "They don't know me, I don't know them, so it doesn't matter. I live my life in a way that people see me and would like to know how I got there. These are the people I want to serve; these are the people that I hope to impact their lives so that they can and will help others in their journey.

The third person said, "Oh, let them talk! Let them waste their time. They have absolutely nothing productive or good to do. I feel sorry for them as they need to get a grip on their lives!"

If you have the gift of gab, a gift for entertaining use it positively by showing up at a place that could benefit others when you share your gift. All of us have a gift!

Recently, one of my GSFE colleagues Pamela shared her gift with me. She is an expert in branding. I showed up at the Menifee chapter meeting where she was presenting. At the end of her presentation, we were able to comment or ask questions.

I wanted to make T shirts with the Positive One name after leaving the Corporation I worked for in the early 1990's. I was discouraged from doing that as a business. Later in 2022 when I was ready and determined to

do so, the name was already taken. I tried tweaking it to Positeev One. I asked Lady Robbie for her input, she said "you spelled positive wrong." I knew that would not work. I explained to Pamela what I was trying to accomplish. I wanted to make T shirts with positive sayings written on them using the business name "Positive One". Immediately, Pamela said use "Positivl". In that meeting Jeanette got the Positivl domains in .com, .org and .net!! I registered Positivl as a business! Marcy created the logo! Lesson learned here is to be careful with whom you share your idea. In this meeting I got a new start from my GSFE sisters. Never listen to someone who does not have your vision! I had a "Be Kind" T shirt and Cups done for our Kindness Day Award Ceremony. I felt good seeing all those women who chose to support me wearing a Pink T shirt! My friends helped me to complete my dream! I am very grateful to the persons who have helped me along my journey! I am starting an Online store with my "The Run for Freedom" book, shirts, cups and adding more items when I can. I contribute to The Helping Hands Orphanage, and I will always need your help with this project!

My success was not achieved just by myself, it was a gift from God. HE sent many people in my path to help me, to guide me, and to protect me!

When I think "I got this" HE smiles! HE says, "She is confident, I blessed her!" When I am in the Driver's Seat and in the fast lane thinking I am fine, HE slows me down, saying "Stay humble!" When I sleep at the wheel or about to make a stupid decision HE says, "Wake up, I got your back." HE is always in control! Remember HE is always in control!

It's all
About
Showing
Up

You Are the Difference

Dr. (h.c.) Tomesha D. Walker

You ask me to show up. You ask me to stand tall in a world full of those who sit down. I hear the call. I feel the need. I wonder how to achieve this. Who teaches you to stand out in a crowd when going with the crowd is considered normal and easy to do?

Being alone is downright scary. Standing out is counter to cultural teaching. We are told to blend in, keep our head down, blend in, and be silent---never obstructing the flow or undermining the established routine.

I have had to face this many times. Yet, showing up, stating the truth, and sharing love have continued to guide me and produce positive results. This scared little girl learned how to stand tall, be heard, and change lives.

I learned from the women around me like my Mother Evangelist Patricia L. Henderson-Elam, Lady Dr. Robbie Motter, Gail Reese, and so many more. I watched the example and absorbed their concepts to shift me internally. I realized I had purpose and meaning. My thoughts began to shift.

The change that started within me began a realization. Once I learned that my life made a difference, I was able to share that difference with others. There was no more hiding though occasionally second guessing myself. My

change became the catalyst for more development in me and then the world around me. To answer the question of who teaches us to stand out in a crowd, I decided to share what has been my process of learning and growth.

When searching for wisdom and understanding, here are a few of the revelations and steps that helped me show up, stand out, and be the difference:

Selflessness and Sovereignty
Honor
Observe
Win
Understand What's Underneath
Pace

and

Align
Sacrifice, Be
Kind

Selflessness and sovereignty are some things I had to come to terms with. I realized I was the change, but I could not do it all on my own. There was a level of control and ownership I could wield, but God had all the rest. I had to make what I did about others and not only about myself.

How I perfected this relationship was through prayer and study. Just like friendships we must spend time building and honoring the other person. It is the same with God. When we choose a relationship with Him, we must take the time to meet, learn, and interact with Him regularly to gain a stronger and more connected relationship. As Jeremiah 29:11 NIV states,

"For I know the plans I have for you," declares the Lord, "plans to prosper you and not to harm you, plans to give you hope and a future." (https://jeremiah.bible/jeremiah-29-11) To learn of the plan God has for you, a relationship is necessary. The benefits of welcoming a relationship with God are innumerable, and the main thing that has changed my life.

Observe that our lives are continually shifting, an ever-evolving point of reference for all that are watching. When you show up, there are many ways in which you benefit. We can want what is best for our lives. We must stand tall to receive what is best for our lives. Presenting yourself at events, showing up in your child's life and taking time for yourself are ways this is achieved. Pay attention to what is happening and take note. Use the change to push you and move you into your mission and purpose in life.

We win as we show up by standing tall; those around us watch our transformation are given a unique opportunity. They gain enlightened permission to do the same and stand tall as well. A domino effect has begun. No longer is there a need to take a step back, yet a step forward towards your ultimate goal. Your goal becomes more achievable, and it becomes easier to believe that you will accomplish it.

Underneath the exterior you portray there may still be fear and at times dismay. When we ask for what is needed, we begin to change inside. The areas that no one sees are growing and healing. Know that you are amazing and up to the challenge. No matter what faces you, you do not have to do it alone. You are chosen by God and picked for a purpose beyond what you can imagine. Trust and believe in the process you are journeying through right now.

Pacing yourself and believing what God says concerning you will help you to get to the finish line. Trying to take on too many things at one time can cause you to be extremely fatigued and not be able to focus on the tasks to

complete them well. Choose your journey wisely and decide how best to focus your time. Pacing allows you to be in charge of what you do and how you do it and the amount of peace that you have while completing it.

Align with your God-given talent and calling to maximize your potential. When we live outside of our calling, we are stunted and unable to reach the heights available to us. Think back to a moment of leadership that you did not listen to. Only to find out later that it was in your best interest. Had you only listened you would have been further along and in a better place than you are now. Accept the truth, learn from the past, choose to make better choices, and listen to the leaders that have gone before you.

Sacrifice your desires for what God wants for you. We have all been presented with various opportunities, yet as we focus and submit our plans to God, there is a level of clarity and understanding that is revealed. Be comfortable walking without the things you think you need. Be safe in the knowledge that God has what is best for you. There is no need to grasp tightly to what you want; only keep your palms open. Release and receive what is for you.

Kindness through the love of Christ shown for our lives is paramount. The Bible says love is the most important thing. Spreading the love of the Lord is what we can do to ultimately change the world for the best it can ever be. We bring with us what is missing for so many. The gospel of Christ and love of the Lord are wanted by so many. We will stand up and share it, providing what is needed when people ask and the Lord leads.

I believe in you and your ability to strive for greatness. You naturally stand out; do not push yourself down to fit in with others. Stand up and stand out by showing up. Asking for what you need, giving to others and completing your call.

You are important.

You are a difference maker.

You are needed.

Show up and ask!

Navigating My Life by Learning How to Show Up and Ask

Janet Walters

When I was a young girl, I believed everything my parents told me. My dad called me dumb, stupid, uncoordinated, dizzy, and addlepated. Those names stuck with me for many years.

My mother said I was average. I didn't speak until I was four years old.

She took me to doctor after doctor because I wasn't speaking. She thought I was autistic, mentally ill, or had hearing problems. I was extremely shy.

As it happened, I didn't have any illness or disabilities. However, I bought into the belief I was below average.

During my years in school, I was a C and D grade student. I left my report card on the kitchen table. My parents never looked at our report cards. Mother signed them and told us to give them to the teacher.

When I was 13, I wanted to make some extra money. I asked Mother if I could help her wash her dogs to make some extra money. She said yes and gave me our old miniature schnauzer Cindy to bathe.

Mother barked, "You did a terrible job." She threw 2 quarters at me and said, "You will never wash my dogs again."

At 15, I wanted to live with my friend Jackie and her mom. Everyone called Jackie's mom, Mom.

Mom was cool. Although we were in the 70's, Mom dressed as if she was in the 60's, wearing pedal pushers and sleeveless tops with poofy auburn hair in a high ponytail.

We partied on beer and cigarettes with the girls and guys at Mom and Jackie's house. We partied at the beach, in the mountains, and at people's places where the grownups and the "kids" smoked pot and took tequila and vodka shots.

One day, I told Mom, the one with poofy hair, about my mother and family.

Mom said, "Come live with me and Jackie. You're safe with us."

When I got home from Jackie's, I said, "Mother, Mom said I could live with her and Jackie. I'm moving in tomorrow."

Mother snapped back, "You will not live with Jackie and her mom." She air quoted, "Mom."

17 Years Old - Time to Grow Up

On a Sunday around 6 p.m., I got home from spending the day at Santa Monica beach with my friends.

Mother opened the from door to inform me that I will no longer be living in her house.

She planted her fists on her hips and said, "You're having too much fun at the beach."

"I am?" I asked.

"Don't get smart with me." She was about to slap me, but she lowered her

hand down. Mother continued, "All you do is goof around. Now get out of my house and get a job."

I packed up and left the next day.

The next day, Mother changed the locks.

I left the nonsense behind, but I took the negative beliefs and resentment with me.

Anxiety overtook me. I never spoke up or spoke out. I was too scared to make a mistake or be put down. I did everything I could do to make others like me. Trying to win other people's approval exhausted me.

Later on, I decided to earn my bachelor's degree. I'll show my family, I told myself. At the time, I didn't realize I was showing up for myself. Rather, I saw it as a way to get back at my family.

Yet I was thrilled to be the first and only child in my immediate family to go to college. I invited my family to attend my graduation. No one came.

On the bright side, I earned a degree. Soon I realized holding a bachelor's degree did not solve my problems nor limiting beliefs.

Later In Life - The Corporate Chapter

I saw many growth opportunities at my job. However, I avoided talking to people. I never spoke up even though I wanted to contribute to the discussions.

I dummied down because I didn't want to stand out and speak about anything as I feared being criticized by others.

I was tired of lying low in the background. I felt ill-equipped. Yet I heard the voice in my head tell me, you're made for so much more. Do something different. Do something new.

I smiled and mentally said, "I'm going to get my master's degree!"

Fast Forward Six Months

My professor told us we were going to give a 15-minute presentation in three weeks about our future-selves five years from now.

What?! Speak in front of my professor and peers? I was ready to bolt out of the classroom, but I stayed. I showed up by not running away from my biggest fear, public speaking.

After class, I spoke with my professor telling her about my fear of public speaking.

Professor Harris said, "Janet, the only way you will ever get over the fear of public speaking is to speak in public."

"Dr. Harris, how about I do an extra credit assignment instead?" I said.

She shook her head no and said, "If you want to pass this class, you must give a presentation." She added, "I'm also going to give you an extra credit assignment."

Here's the extra credit assignment Dr. Harris gave me:

Go visit a Toastmasters club this week. The following week, give a one-to-three-minute speech in class about what you learned about public speaking.

Meanwhile

I continued working on my communication/public speaking skills.

While I didn't realize it at first, I was developing my leadership skills, too.

I began verbally and mentally participating at meetings at work. I became more assertive with my colleagues. I spoke more truthfully with others.

Everyone feared this top executive, Preston, a tall thin man with white stubbly hair.

He marched into the front office where I was working. He pressed his hands on the front desk counter and leaned in towards me.

I propelled backwards on my office chair with wheels.

Preston asked, "Why didn't Esther (my boss) send her report to me?" She was already three days late. Esther was always late.

In the past, I would have crumbled and stammered...." I don't know. Uhhhh...I'll remind her."

This time I said, "She's in Indonesia. You approved Esther's business trip, correct?"

He said, "Oh yeah. I did, didn't I?"

I asked Preston if he'd like me to email my boss to remind her to send her status report.

"Never mind," he said. "I need to talk to her anyway." He turned on his heel and left.

My colleague Shirley saw the conversation. She said, "Janet, how did you talk to the Big Boss like that?!"

"I've been working on my leadership and speaking skills in Toastmasters." I asked, "Want to go a meeting with me?"

I showed up by being assertive and polite when I spoke to Preston. I was factual and succinct with him. I also offered to assist him.

Showing Up as a Leader at Work

At my job I volunteered to set up workshops and organize events.

I made phone calls to the community and those who needed help. I attended off hours' events.

When I saw my colleagues who were in deadline mode, I helped them by making copies, preparing invoices, and packages to be shipped, Fed-Ex and Overnighted packages.

I began giving presentations. I admit it was intimidating to speak in front of certain people--especially when they glared at you or when they're working on their Blackberries. Do you remember the Blackberry?

Sidenote: The BlackBerry came out in March1984 and officially phased out on January 4, 2022.

While I was learning and growing at my job, I also was learning and growing in Toastmasters. I was presented a growth opportunity.

The top leader of our organization asked if I would be interested in serving in directorship.

I said, "Yes!"

What I didn't know was that I would be continually embarking unknown territory and stepping out of my comfort zone.

I worked through the fear and did it anyway. I gained self-confidence, and

I continued to grow.

As a Toastmaster, working professional, businesswoman and entrepreneur, I've learned and still continue to learn and improve by showing up to:

Be a better speaker.

Step out of my comfort zone.

Sharpen my critical thinking skills.

Think on my feet with ease and

Be a better time manager.

* * *

Showing Up to End Ageism

When I was 42, I asked my boss for a promotion, and he said, "Janet, I appreciate your enthusiasm. Enthusiasm doesn't cut it."

My heart sank. I felt shame, rejection, and feelings of not being enough.

Six years later, I never got that promotion. Instead, at the age of 50, thousands of us lost our jobs. I started search for a new job.

When I was 51, I met two recruiters who were in their mid-20s. I'll call them Blonde and Brunette. When I met them, they both looked me up and down. I felt frumpy next to them. They started the interview. Blonde asked why I thought I was qualified to be an office manager. I gave her my response.

The interview went on for another 15 minutes. Brunette looked at me with a smirk and asked, "Do you know how to use a computer?" The interview ended abruptly.

I acted confident. I squared my shoulders back and walked out of the office. Angry heat seethed out of my pores. As soon as I drove out of the parking lot, I screamed as loud as I could to release the pent-up anger and frustration.

At 53, I interviewed for a nonprofit job. I sat in the waiting room with five or six other people. They were in their early 20s, and I was at least 30 years older than them.

I met the 40-something Interviewer. We shook hands. I pulled out my padfolio, and the woman hissed at me saying, "Don't take notes. Taking notes in an interview is so entry-level."

She scanned my resume and said, "Your numbers are too low." The interviewer concluded, "You're too slow for this job."

She stereotyped me as slow because of my age. At the same time, I was relieved that I saw her real self at the interview.

I became even more discouraged. I thought to myself, why are corporate people so ageist?

I stopped believing that I could get a corporate job again. I continued looking for all kinds of work.

When I was 56, I applied to everything from retail to favorite cool places to work like Trader Joes, Wholefoods and Hobby Lobby. I applied to sales jobs. I applied for office temp work. I received no return calls nor rejection emails.

At 57, I got an interview for a sales job at a med spa in Downtown LA.

I walked into the glitzy reception where I saw the employees and salespeople in their late 20s to 30s with perfectly sculpted faces, plump cheeks, and strong jawlines. Their Eyebrows and eyelashes were strategically placed.

I looked down at myself. And I thought, oh no. I wore a suit and business flats. Cleary I was too businesslike for this culture. The truth was I didn't fit into their youth-oriented demographic.

The perfectly gorgeous red head interviewer said, "If you work with us, you'll be working in the back office." I understood that to mean the beautiful people work in the front.

We exchanged fake goodbyes as I walked out of the office. I got in my car as fast as I could. I wanted to burst into tears, but there were a few guards around. As soon as I turned the corner, I parked in the red zone and turned on my hazards. I cried. Hot tears and black mascara dripped off my nose onto my lap. I crumpled over the steering wheel and muttered, "What use am I?"

I wanted to crawl into my bed and hide under the sheets for a long time.

Later that year, I noticed my thumbs started to hurt when I used them. I went to see a doctor. She spoke slowly and loudly, "You have os-teo-arth-ri-tis. It's known as wear and tear arthritis, and it is very common for people your age."

I bought into what people were saying, "You get old and fall apart in your 50s." I felt, looked, and acted old. I complained how unfair life was and continually griping about pain.

The judgment I felt was taking a toll on me. I became depressed.

My once limber body became stiff. My balance disappeared over time. I consumed plenty of Ibuprofen and stopped exercising. I overate and disliked myself.

At 59, I showed up when I asked myself the question, "What am I going to do about this? Do I continue to a victim and allow others, society, social media, or myself--limit my future?

I knew I was being complacent by not standing up for myself. I allowed culture, social media, well-meaning and not so well-meaning people dictate my self-worth.

I began to research age discrimination. I learned it was my responsibility to educate myself and share what I've learned with others. I realized that I had to stop the ageist talk.

I took ownership in changing my own narrative by reading, boosting my mindset, and incorporating exercise and balance work into my daily routine.

By remaining committed, I turned my life around from allowing circumstances, other people's opinions, and judgement to define me to taking responsibility for my mindset, self-worth and wellbeing.

In the same year, I showed up again by embracing my age and ensuring my 6th decade of life will be (and is) an amazing one.

I started my online company, Janet Walters Consulting, helping women over 40 to Redefine Ageism in their lives.

Redefining Ageism means we overcome this often overlooked "ism." We stop our ageist attitudes and be more aware of our thoughts, communications, and behaviors towards others and ourselves. Ultimately, we embrace our age and be confident in our own skin.

I became a certified coach, trainer, and speaker with the John Maxwell Team. We each have the power to strengthen our confidence and

self-esteem. Together, we can end ageism through education, awareness, and building empowering communities.

Think about it. We have tech geniuses, artists, athletes, and celebrities in their third trimester of life who are showing up every day. They don't let their age define what they can achieve. Let's show up and help end ageism towards ourselves and others.

I'm showing up help people and myself break the age barriers.

I am asking all of us to make the effort to continue to learn, daring ourselves to try new things like starting or joining an inter-generational group, learn a new language, or finish writing that book we've been meaning to publish.

Let's push ourselves to get to know other people who are younger or older than us and spend time with them.

Most importantly affirm as many times as you like, "I am my authentic self and I embrace my age."

#Wegotthis

Azhur wa Atawasal
(Showing Up and Asking)

Dr. Randi D. Ward

Growing up as a shy but intelligent girl in a small town in West Virginia, I was always too afraid to let anyone even my family and friends discover who I truly was. I would "SHOW UP" in many places because of my never-ending curiosity and desire to explore and learn about new things, but I would always remain silent in the shadows of others. I only observed; I never "asked" for anything in return, but I did acquire valuable knowledge.

It wasn't until I met my late husband Bill when I began graduate school at Marshall University that I began to learn it was not only important to "show up" but also to "ask" for what I needed or wanted. Even with this realization, it was still difficult for me to "ask". Being extremely independent in my mindset and often stubborn at times, I believed I could achieve whatever I needed by myself and needed no one else to achieve them. I do not believe I am perfect; no one is that. I just wanted to do things my way; I also just did not want to bother other people if I could do what I needed to do by myself. Of course, living the first sixty years of my life like this caused unnecessary stress, more work, and wasted time that could have been spent in more pleasurable activities.

So, when did I FINALLY have to change this insane mindset, lose my silly pride, and admit I did not have the skills and knowledge I needed for EVERYTHING? When did I FINALLY have to ASK for help? When did ASKING become essential for my survival? It happened when I put myself in a situation totally foreign to me---literally.

On November 3, 2011, I traveled to Cairo, Egypt, to teach English as a second language to university students and graduates at a center called Spread Your English (SYE). I had no idea what was ahead of me. I just knew in my heart I was meant to do this. I felt as if this teaching experience was something God also wanted me to do. It was my greatest desire to do something to help Egyptian students in some small way to become more fluent in English and possibly to help them to be able to acquire international jobs. In May 2011 I had also visited Cairo as a tourist and visited SYE. I observed some classes being taught by non-native English speakers and humbly believed I could offer more creative lessons. In 2008 I had retired from teaching English, Language Arts, journalism, drama, public speaking, and a gifted education program for 37 years in public schools in West Virginia and Georgia, USA, in grades 7 thru 12. I was a confident, experienced educator, but I was not prepared for my life changing experience in Egypt. I "SHOWED UP" to teach and was prepared to do that, but what I was not prepared for was all the "ASKING" that would be essential to survive during the next three months. I had to also become a "Student", ASK for help, and "surrender" my "fabricated" belief I needed no one to survive.

I am an international traveler and have visited 61 countries. I can easily adapt to most cultures successfully now. However, before my Egyptian experience, the majority of my travels were arranged by tour companies. Thus, the trips were carefully and conveniently planned---hotels, meals, transportation, city tours, etc. All this was also conducted in English. I knew things would not be as convenient when I went to Egypt to live

and teach, but I did tremendously underestimate just how difficult it truly would be. I would be "thrust" so to speak into this alien culture and be expected to live as a local. I assumed I would receive assistance from the owners of SYE, but they turned out NOT to be helpful once they moved me into my flat. I was basically on my own. I am a strong woman, but my strength was not enough. I did not understand or read Arabic; I did not understand Islam at this time; I did not understand their cultural practices. I had much to learn.

To add to these problems, one week after my arrival, the second revolution for Egypt's democracy began, and my flat was three blocks from Tahrir Square. This square would become the main area for the violent protests that would occur during my stay. Also, there would be days when violent protesting would occur on my street Saad Zaghloul. I would listen to people get injured and sadly die. The first revolution had ended on January 25, 2011, with the overthrow of Dictator/President Mubarak. Things had been calm since then even though no new government had been established. My family was upset I was going to Egypt, but I honestly felt no fear. As I have stated earlier, I felt God wanted me to do this. I believed I would be safe. I never imagined the violence I would hear, see, and personally encounter.

My "ASKING" began on Day 2 after my arrival. I DESPERATELY NEEDED HELP! The "ASKINGS" were numerous:

How can I get a taxi, use the metro?

How can I buy food not understanding Arabic and their alien number system?

How can I successfully shop for supplies I need in stores?

How can I get internet and phone service?

How do I renew my Egyptian Visa in Cairo which would expire after 30 days?

How can I get medical assistance if needed? (In January I got a bad cold, so this became necessary to know.)

How can I stay safe?

And so many more questions. Ultimately, I needed to learn how to become an Egyptian woman. I had no other choice. I had to develop many plans to survive with the help of others, of course.

My first major task was learning how to get a taxi or use the metro to get to SYE. During my three months of teaching, SYE was located in two different buildings. The first building required a taxi to get there. The first day my boss got me there, but after that, I relied on my students for assistance and occasionally it was necessary to request the help from strangers on the street. I would find young people I felt might understand English. Thank God, this always worked. Egyptians were usually so kind to me. I did experience one horrendous day with a taxi driver though. Protesting had occurred in several places, and the military police had shut down roads that led to my school. The driver got so angry he made me get out of the car in the middle of a vacant street. I had no idea where I was, but I had no time to cry or panic. I had to find a way to get safely to SYE. A young man drove by me and then stopped. After we talked, I felt comfortable enough to "ASK" him to drive me to the school. He happily "rescued" me. Another day during an unusually busy rush hour, no taxi would stop for me. Two male university students volunteered to walk me to the school, which took 30 minutes. I "ASKED" for their support, and they "SHOWED UP" for me. Also, there were days some of my students would drive me home. Such a blessing! In the middle of December SYE moved to a beautiful building in el Dokki, an upscale area of Cairo. A metro stop was just a short walk from

SYE now. Friends taught me how to use the metro---much faster, much easier, more reliable---but very crowded. In Egypt, there are metro cars for men only and for women only. I tried to ride with the women, but for some reason the women were mean to me. A Coptic Christian lady pulled me off the train one day and told me to ride on the men's cars, so crazy American "me" did that from now on. Surprisingly, the men accepted me with smiles. I finally became very skilled at using the metro and stopped using taxis.

The second issue was how to buy food. I needed to eat. If the canned food or bottle did not have a photo on it or it was not obvious what was inside, I avoided it or once again I "ASKED" someone to tell me the content inside. Fresh vegetables, fruit, cheese, bread, and similar items were obviously easy to recognize, but purchasing chicken and meat was a challenge. No one in this department at the store where I shopped ever understood my English. Also, since the metric system is used, I had to learn how much to buy. Prices were in their numeric system, so I asked my students to convert it into mine. I needed this since I was living on a budget---my school salary only. Foolishly, I always overbought since I only food shopped once a week. I taught six days a week. I was so busy. My flat was 8 long blocks from the supermarket, and I had to walk to get home. There was no metro connecting the two places. So carrying 5 to 6 heavy bags on each arm, I was exhausted, and my arms were red and burning in pain by the time I was halfway home. Feeling foolish, I was forced to "ASK" for someone to carry some of my bags to my flat (or abandon some bags on the sidewalk---not what I wanted to do). No one ever refused me. I must have looked so pitiful to the high school boys, the college students, and the elderly lady who followed me home. None of them ever accepted any Egyptian pounds for their service. This warmed my heart deeply. I "ASKED", and they "answered" with their generosity and kind hearts.

I was so blessed to befriend my students as well as some former Facebook friends I knew before my stay there. With their face-to-face connections, they "SHOWED" me how to negotiate prices in the street markets and how to effectively purchase items in the stores where they shopped. My flat was supposed to be fully equipped, but it was not. It was necessary to buy some additional kitchen and bathroom supplies. They took me to the appropriate stores to buy these items at great prices when I "ASKED" them.

My dear friend Moustafa Abou Hussein (Saf) took me to purchase a phone and to Vodafone to set up internet and service for my phone and my laptop. He also took me to the government office to renew my visa---an insane experience because of the lack of any normalcy in the government during this revolutionary period. It took 7 hours standing in various lines with dozens of other frustrated, tired, and angry people to get my new visa. This was truly a nightmare experience and might not have resulted in an updated visa if not for Saf. He was my blessing that day.

The weather turned unseasonably cold for Cairo in January. I caught a really miserable cold. I continued to teach since there was no substitute teacher to replace me. My flat also had no heating system---only window air conditioners which obviously could not be used. These situations prolonged my recovery for several weeks. I found a pharmacy near me and "ASKED" the pharmacist for medication. In Egypt, pharmacists can prescribe medicine without a doctor prescription for some pills. Luckily, I had a friend who was a doctor. I "ASKED" him to recommend medicine and to write me prescriptions. This medication eventually healed me.

Keeping myself safe was left up to me. I was tear gassed, surrounded by protesters, and exposed to violence often, but I learned quickly how to avoid the worst of it. When I left Cairo on February 6, 2012, I had "SHOWN UP" in Egypt to achieve my main goal---to teach English to

young Egyptian adults. I was proud of what I had accomplished. But that pride was only a small part of what I gained during those three months. I had been born again. I discovered an even more independent Randi. I had made unimaginable friendships that I hope will last for a lifetime. I adapted to a foreign environment and became successfully submerged into this alluring Egyptian culture and language. I learned to embrace two very unfamiliar religions to me: Coptic Christianity and Islam---once so alien and mysterious to me but now so familiar and often inspiring. I became more appreciative of being an American. I no longer took for granted all the luxuries I have in the USA. My life is Egypt was far from easy. There were many days I missed all the conveniences I have in my home in Georgia: my car, central heating system, English, my shopping centers, peace of mind from violence, etc. Living in Egypt, I proved to myself I could survive without all these comforts, keep myself safe, and still be happy most of the time by "SHOWING UP" and "ASKING" when needed, but I must admit I was happy to return to my American lifestyle and to my husband and my dog.

One year later in January 2012, I "SHOWED UP" again in Cairo. This time I brought my memoir Because I Believed in Me (My Egyptian Fantasy Came True) with me to launch as well as to open my first English-German language center called Rise Up with two Egyptian partners (former students) followed by my nursery school 6 October Nursery two years later. "SHOWING UP" to teach in 2011 created two new careers: author and entrepreneur. I now write in all genres, except drama, and am an International Best-Selling Author in 5 books and appear in many others. Although the schools are closed now, I have no regrets. I learned much about owning businesses which will help me with my new business RM Infinite---OneStop Possibilities with my fiancé. My experience in Egypt has brought me recognition globally. I am humbly a multi-award recipient.

"SHOWING UP" has also been influenced because of my life philosophy: Believe! Don't dream big; dream BIGGER! The sky is the limit so reach for the stars!

It's all
About
Showing
Up

Change Your Mindset To Flow!

Dr. (h.c.) Violet Williams

It's interesting how life happens for you. I always wanted to be successful in my life, and when I was on a path of doing so, I was in a car accident leaving work one day and was broadsided. From that accident I sustained multiple injuries, there was one that was diagnosed four years after the accident which was a TBI a traumatic brain injury. It's interesting how that injury helped guide me to living my life on purpose. I knew that I would have to think a certain way, be a certain way, and act a certain way to get over this big trauma that had taken place in my life. I knew that I would have to ask and show up in my life, and that is exactly what I committed to do.

As I aligned mindset with my passion and my mission in life, things began to flow, and each time things happened I became stronger. I pray that these stories will help guide you in fulfilling your mission and your purpose in life and knowing these, you will show up and ask for the things that you desire in your life as well.

It is often said that you know well God did that for you, God did that, and yes, God will do it, but God can only do what we act on. The word says now faith is the substance of things hoped for---the evidence of things not seen; you have to have faith. Faith without works is dead.

If you do not have works or if you do not have actions behind it, then nothing happens. So therefore, you have to open your mouth, you have to ask, you have to seek, and you have to find. You have to show up. That is the part that can become the work. It's only asking if it is showing up as in the faith, as in taking action, as in moving forward; that's how you move forward in life!

With my student loan (I had taken out loans to complete my masters and even though you always say you're not going to take out as much money, that's exactly what happened), the money that I took out equaled almost 90 K. Due to the accident I was sick. I sustained injuries and with the head trauma, I could not return to work. I had made attempts to return to work and actually got a job, but due to my brain trauma injury I could not perform the job (I constantly had to leave work to get treatment). Then I became aware of a loan discharge program by watching a minister speak on a show--a sermon he was giving. He shared a story of another woman and how she was in financial debt due to loans she had, and her loan was discharged. I can't remember all the details, but I just thought to myself wow if she can get her loan discharged, then maybe I can, too. So, I decided to make a call to the loan company and ask. At the time I knew not what I was asking for; I just asked if there was some way that I could get my loan discharged? When I explained to them my situation about the car accident and my traumatic brain injury, they gave me another number to call and said, "this is the company that you need to call". I called the company, and they said, "yes". I could get my loan discharged through getting the proper medical forms filled out by my doctor indicating my injury. So, when I went to my doctor's appointment, at first, I was afraid to ASK, but I was determined to make it happen, so I asked my doctor. Much to my surprise, he asked me "What do you want me to say?" Wow, it was a green light. I was so happy that I was jumping up and down inside. He put my injury down and signed

the paperwork. I submitted it, and three years later I'm 90 K debt free from my student loan.

Through the course of healing from my injury, in the process I heard God tell me that in spite of my injuries I had to take care of my mother who was ill. I was also working at the time and knew of the hardships that I was facing to care for my mother and did not at that time have adequate caretakers, so the burden was all on me. Caring for my mother and having adequate caretakers for her and the means and resources to get additional care for her were difficult. It became a reality that I also needed to find resources to help me. Through ASKING, I found someone gracious enough to share a resource to help me find caretakers and help my mother mainly for her care. The resource was able to help me get help for my mother on a whole new level, and it was much needed. She was able to help execute the process and have it expedited. Even though it was hard, I am so grateful that I had this opportunity. It has been a great journey of learning and love with my mother. My prayer is that she sees her 90th birthday and many more.

After high school it took me 10 years for me to get my bachelor's degree which I received in San Diego state, and then after that it took many years, but I did complete my master's. After completing my master's, I have just always had a desire for a doctorate. Maybe it was a little bit before, but I always thought that I would just have a doctorate degree. I don't know. I just love education and love knowledge. I love learning. My dream was always to have a doctor before my name. Wow, that was just something that I felt I would feel so thrilled to have.

I was starting to write my book "Create a Life You Love", and during the process of completing this book an organizations leader, said to me: "Violet, when you complete your book, I am going to open the door for you to receive an Honorary Doctorate of Humanitarian degree in London, England." She had no idea, not even to this day that that was a huge desire of mine. In this chapter of this book, I am so grateful to tell the story because it has all to do with why I cannot share the story in the process of the asking and showing up because this happened when I did not ask. I may have asked my spirit but not vocally; however, I did show up.

By Showing up in my life and for the things that I desired to do, I became a transformational coach. By showing up to the meetings and living out my passion and mission, and having that burning desire to become an author it opened the doors for me to receiving a Doctorate Humanitarian degree in London. I also was a special guest and got to go to parliament, There I received an award for being a superwoman, and got to speak. How magnificent is that. I'm so elated, and it doesn't stop there. You see I used to dance professionally as a little girl, and I loved to sing and did sing in a choir. Would you know I took my books to a luncheon and was asked to sing a song for an upcoming event this group was having? I was just elated and joyful, and my heart is full of such gratitude as I love to sing. The power of asking and showing up is the greatest gift that we can have, and we should all practice it every day as it works.

How blessed I am to be able to have my book published and to sing at an event on International Women's Day this year. The song I've chosen is "Living My Life Like It's Golden". Life is golden when you show up and ask.

It's all
About
Showing
Up

NO Coincidences

Katherine Zacharius

I went to bed on New Year's Eve 2013 an only child. I woke up on New Year's Day 2014 the oldest of 9 children! OMG!!!

I was born in January 1970 as Laurie A DeMello Graham. That is funny in itself because when I was young, I loved the name Laurie but only spelled Laurie, not Lori! NO coincidences. In April of 1970 I became Katherine Sai Wichmann. My whole life I had struggled with identity, always wondering who I was and where I came from; it was not fun. I also spent my whole life telling myself stories and making up stuff in my head wondering why I was given up and wondering who and where were my real family.

Jan 17, 2014, I'm nervously talking to my birth mom for the first time on the phone. She asks me if I am sitting down. Of course, I am sitting down!! I am in shock and awe and have a huge bottle of wine sitting in front of me. She notifies me that not only does she have 4 kids but that she was forced to talk to my birth father for the first time in over 40 years, and he has 4 kids as well and the youngest is 10! OMG! Crazy but now I finally have an identity! She also told me my dad was going to be getting married again and to someone my age. It's so funny because at first, I thought OMG! Now I love my stepmom, and it's been an even more special relationship because

she was meeting her birth family too at the same time. She is definitely my sister from another Mister.

I had tried 2 or 3 previous times in my life to find my birth family. Once when I was 18 and again in my 20s. When I didn't find them, then I figured it was not meant to be, and I was OK with that even though my adopted Tiger Mom and I didn't get along. We couldn't be in a room together for more than 5 minutes without a fight starting. It was very sad. I joke that she was the woman in the book Tiger Mom but 1000x gnarlier. But that's for another story and possibly another book. I digress.

Then I met my now husband in 2001, and he encouraged me to look again, especially after he met my parents and saw that I was NOTHING like them. He kind of tricked me, but I find it amusing now, and I am glad I did it. He said if were getting married, we might have kids in the future, and don't you want to know about your medical history just in case? Wow! I had gone over 30 years answering medical questions on forms with my adopted parents' info!! That was NOT my medical info. So, I said yes, and we went down the path to start finding my birth family again. This was very funny, since when I met him, I knew right away the first day I was going to marry him. I gave him heads up that I wasn't going to have kids because I was deathly afraid to give birth. Plus, since I was adopted, I wanted to pay it forward and possibly adopt a child IF I ever wanted to have kids, but at that time I did not!

Within a few years I found two adoption angels online who started to look for my birth family for me. I also filled out the paperwork with LA County for non-identifying birth information. I was on the phone with the person who worked with LA County when she informed me that as soon as she hit enter on the computer it might actually match with my birth family immediately. She asked if I was ready for that. OMG NO!! I had no idea

that it would happen or could happen that fast. Thankfully, I got brave, and she hit enter and it did not happen then. But after she did that, I received my information, and it was very fascinating when I received it. There were soooooo many commonalities in the paperwork, like my birth family loved being outdoors and they loved football and hockey. So do I!! The whole nature vs. nurture thing is REAL! I am definitely more of a nature girl than a nurture.

My new hashtag on social media is #nocoincidences. Every day it seems for the first few years I was learning something new, but a birth family member and there were all non-coincidences. They were all born in Hawaii except for me! Ever since I was able to walk, people in Los Angeles would ask me if I was from Hawaii. I would say "No, but I wish I was". Then for the next 15 years I would be asked the same question. I would give the same answer. Who knew I was actually from there even though I was born in LA. I was born there because my birth mom was forced to leave Hawaii to give birth to me and then went back to Hawaii after she put me up for adoption.

I got married in Hawaii in 2003 to my amazing husband and best friend. We have no idea to this day why we picked Hawaii, but we did, and we chose the big island, which is where my birth mom raised my 4 siblings. NO coincidences! The only Hawaiian vacation my adopted parents took me on was to Kona, HI too. VERY Odd! Especially since they hated to travel. I also went on a trip to Oahu for my high school graduation present. I also won a trip to Hawaii on Twitter to Oahu in 2010 and was looking for my birth family then as well. We found out years later when I met them in 2014 that the place where we were looking and staying that year was exactly where my birth father's office was as well as where a lot of his family members live currently and grew up. NO coincidences. I also learned that my father was a famous Roller Derby Star. He even had groupies, lol! I have LOVED to skate my whole life, both roller and ice. When I was a kid,

I won every roller-skating contest I ever entered. So amazing! Again, No coincidences.

My brother on my birth father's side also pointed out once that we are all entrepreneurs on his side and that most of us deal in the subject of finance. NO coincidences. My adopted parents never asked me about my business. My birth family always does and so does my father-in-law who was also an entrepreneur his whole life. That warms my heart.

I will also never forget the first time I saw my siblings on Facebook. My adoption angel first found one brother on my mom's side and then another. But the one that Got me was my sister Nat on my birth father's side. She was riding her bike in NYC in the photo that I saw when my adoption angel sent me her name and info. I FINALLY saw someone that looked like me for the first time in 44 years! Incredible!

Also, my birth family always say to each other, "I love you" just like my husband's family. My adopted parents never did until they were on their death beds. That also warms my heart and makes me happy because I have been told many times that I am on earth to spread love. And I now believe that. I remember when I first heard people say that to each other so often I thought it was so odd.

I spent 11 months of 2014 meeting my birth family both on my mom's side as well as my dad's, and my dad's side and I have so much in common; its surreal. It's been 8 years since I met them all, and I am still in awe and still wake up some days thinking I'm still in a dream. When I was meeting everyone in 2014, especially once during a wedding in Washington state, why DID I do that!!!! I felt as if I was in a movie playing someone else role. Since I had been an actress in college, it felt very familiar but also so foreign and SO surreal.

2014 was a very crazy and surreal year for me, extremely stressful and overwhelming, but I am so glad I did it, and I am so happy that I was fearless! Today I still have a great relationship with all of them, and I talk to my dad's side of the family weekly. I Love it and them. I have NO regrets!! I am so glad I showed up, and yes, it has opened many new doors for me! I took the risk, and it has given me so much joy and given me new opportunities including writing this book and others in the future. Thank you for reading my story and letting me share it with you. This was very risky for me.

It's all
About
Showing
Up

ACKNOWLEDGEMENTS

Today, is International Women's Day and also my 87th Birthday. This book is dedicated to you wherever you are in the world. I also want to dedicate the book to my son, Ed Burtnette, Daughters, Lori Ann Soltas, and Lisa Gritzner and Grandchildren. Heather Burtnette, Amber Burtnette, Joe Soltas and Jessie Soltas and to all our GSFE Board Members, Directors, Co-Directors and GSFE sisters and also our GSFE Men Ambassadors in the US and International as well.

It is so exciting since we did Book 1 in 2021, that now more and more women are starting to SHOW UP and ASK.

We received lots of letters from individuals all over the US and International that told us that they loved the stories, and it gave them the courage to start ASKING and that they could now see the power of what SHOWING UP meant.

Book 2 is a continued gift to the many people who have joined me on this journey called life, you are all my greatest joy.

I want to thank our 64 co-authors, all of whom are GSFE sisters for each of the beautiful stories they have written for this collaboration. As you read them you will feel their messages are coming from their heart.

A big thank you also to Lady Dr. Lenora Peterson who wrote the foreword in the book and to all who also wrote the beautiful testimonies.

I also want to dedicate this book to you our readers who, I hope will continue to apply and share this little-known secret to success. Just SHOW UP and

ASK. You will be rewarded with friendships and opportunities that you wouldn't otherwise have known.

To our Editor Dr Randi Ward, our Formatter Marcy Decato, and our Publisher Angela Covany who also worked on the original cover design and published not only our first book but this book as well. Her company Havana Book Group LLC also published many GSFE members books, I am most grateful to all three of these dynamic women who are making this book happen.

This book just like book volume one will change lives around the world as each story will impact them and let them know that others have gone through some of the same journeys' they may be experiencing.

Thank you also to all that purchase the E book to help us get to #1 US and International by purchasing the book when it comes out. I also appreciate individuals who write a testimony about the book on Amazon for us.

I wish for each of you Health, Happiness, and great success. I know these stories will touch your life. I would love to hear from you. I can be reached at 951-255-9200. My email is Rmotter@aol.com. Check out our GSFE website.

GSFEUS.com

We would love for you to consider being a member and one of our GSFE sisters. We are global so no matter where you live you can join us. My personal website is robbiemotter.com. I am also on Facebook and Linkedin as Robbie Motter.

With love and appreciation,

Robbie Motter

It's all
About
Showing
Up

CONTRIBUTING AUTHORS DIRECTORY

MARY AURTREY
m.aurtrey@hotmail.com
317-894-9421
712 Creston Point Circle,
Indianapolis IN 462

MARY MOBILEMARY BARNETT
mary@anotherbrilliantidea.com

DR. BARBARA A. BERG
barbara@barbaraberg.com

DR. ALESHEIA RANDOLPH BUSH
ladyalesheia1@yahoo.com
alesheia.r.randolph@gmail.com
Facebook and IG: LadyAlesheia

DR. (h.c.) ANGELE CADE
acade@execonthego.com

TINA CASEN
tinacasen@gmail.com

LADY DR. (h.c.) AMANDA COLEMA
ladyamandaspeaks@gmail.com
407-775-0850
Website: ascenterprise.acnibo.com
IG: @LadyAmandaSpeaks

DR. (h.c.) ANGELA COVANY
angelawcovany@yahoo.com
havanabookgroup@mail.com
www.havanabookgroup.com
www.howtoloveyourhaters.com

DR. (h.c.) VERLAINE CRAWFORD
verlainecrawford@gmail.com

DR. (h.c.) LAURIE DAVIS
thelauriedavisshow@gmail.com
www.lauriehdavis.com

DR. (h.c.) YOLANDA DAVIS
contactyolanda@yahoo.com

DR. (h.c.) CHEBRA O'CHEA DORSEY
ocheafashion1@gmail.com
619-985-3804

DR. (h.c.) VIOLA EDWARD
info@violaedward.com
WhatsApp +357 99675094
www.gritacademy.co
www.violaedward.com
www.creativewomen.co
www.rgmentores.org
www.ugivme.com

DHARLENE MARIE FAHL
dharlenemarie@gmail.com
My books can be found here: Dharlene
Marie Fahl on Amazon

NICOLE FARRELL
nicolefarrell123@hotmail.com

DR. (h.c.) STONE LOVE FAURE
stonelovesays@gmail.com
510.972.0528
Union City, CA 94587
www.decisiontimestonelove.com

MARNEEN L. FIELD
heavenlywaterfallproductions@yahoo.com
www.imdb.me/marneenfields

ADA GARTENMANN
info@sheinspiremeawards.org
IG: @ADAGATERTENMANN

JACKIE GOLDBERG PINK LADY
pinklady7@earthlink.net

MARY GREENE
mary@gwwn.org
gwwenet@gwwn.org
director@gwwn.org
gwwnsocial@gmail.com
202-580-8884
GWWN
P.O. Box 65532, Washington, DC 20035
www.gwwn.org

DENISE GREGORY
densjems@aol.com

LYNDA J. BERGH HERRING
ocladypi@gmail.com

DR. (h.c.) LAURYN HUNTER
hunterarttherapy@gmail.com

DR. (h.c.) DEBORAH IRISH
artuncorkedpaintnsip@gmail.com
Deborah.A.Irish@gmail.com
951.536.3580
DeborahIrish.com
Facebook Deborah Irish Fine Art
Instagram @deborahIrish

JAYNE JORDEN
ladyjj2u@gmail.com
Onmyheartbyjayne@gmail.com

AMBASSADOR DR. IMAMBAY KAMARA
imankadie@live.com
Telephone +447926893992
WhatsApp 07926893992
www.difsil.org
Facebook: Imambay karama

ANNMARIE KELLY
annmarie@annmariekelly.com
https://FiveYearMarriage.com

DR. (h.c.) LYNNETTE LAROCHE
libre.lynnette@gmail.com

DR. CHERILYN LEE
drlee@nuwellnesshealthcare.com

DR. (h.c.) JEANNETTE LEHOULLIER
jeannette.lehoullier@gmail.com
Fb-profile: https://www.facebook.com/
jeannette.lehoullier/
Fb (JEANNETTE'S JOY): https://www.
facebook.com/jeannettesjoydj/
Fb (Business Group - JEANNETTE'S
JOY): https://www.facebook.com/
groups/243486807876689
Fb (DJ's Virtual Management/Senior Tech
Tutor): https://www.facebook.com/
djsvirtualmanagement/
Fb (JEANNETTE'S JOY SHARED
RECIPES): https://www.facebook.com/
JeannettesJoy/
BLOG (JEANNETTE'S JOY): https://
jeannettesjoy.blogspot.com/

WEBSITE: https://www. djsvirtualmanagement.com/
YOUTUBE: https://www.youtube.com/channel/UCZD7OvGN_GfvuluFT_MOLUQ/videos
LINKEDIN: https://www.linkedin.com/in/jeannettelehoullier
INSTAGRAM: https://www.instagram.com/djsvirtualmanagement

H.E. AMBASSADOR PROF. DR. PAULINE LONG
admin@paulinelong.com

DR. (h.c.) REGINA LUNDY
reginalundy54@gmail.com

DR. (h.c.) SARA LYPPS
saralypps@icloud.com

SUKU MOYO-MACKENZIE
smoyo8@yahoo.co.uk
#let'sTalk About It Foundation

PROF. DR. CAROLINE MAKAKA
contact@loaniglobal.org
Loaniglobal.org

DR. (h.c.) KARA LYNNE MALDONADO
info@realbodiesperiod.com
949-438-6111 Mess.
949-607-1339 eFax
Real Bodies Period, LLC
Dana Point, CA
https://dr-kara-maldonado.now.site
https://squareup.com/appointments/book/D165DGQNVF189
https://outlook.office.com/bookwithme/me

www.realbodiesperiod.com
www.instagram.com/realbodiesperiod
www.facebook.com/Kara.maldonadol

LISA ANN MAYER
lisaannmayer@gmail.com

NICOLE WILD MERL
nicolewildmerl@gmail.com

DR. (h.c.) SUSIE MIERZWIK
kinderkat9@gmail.com

COUNCILWOMAN BRIDGETTE MOORE
bridgettemoore2012@gmail.com

LADY DR. (h.c.) ROBBIE MOTTER
rmotter@aol.com
27701 Murrieta Road #216, Menifee, CA 92586
www.robbiemotter.com
http://www.blogtalkradio.com/diva-weekly-strategies-for-success

JEAN OLEXA
gigi8247@gmail.com
O2Borganized.com

DR. (h.c.) KATHERINE ORHO
katherineorho@gmail.com
Korho.vips@gmail.com

CARMELITA PITTMAN
therosebcs@sbcglobal.net
http://www.rosebreastcancersociety.org
Carmelita's Corner podcast airs Mondays after 10:20 a.m. pst on eZWay Broadcasting following RBL. www.ezwayradio.com

iHeartradio
Spotify
Amazon Music
Player FM
Blog Talk

MADELINE PLATE
mad_plate@yahoo.com
858-335-2517
www.primerica.com/nsdglennplate

DR. CATHERINE GRACE POPE
cpope7@cox.net
YouTube: Dr. Catherine Grace Pope
Twitter: @n3acts
Instagram: Catherine_Grace_Pope
Facebook: Catherine Grace Pope
In Search of the Crown

DR. (h.c.) CHERIE REYNOLDS
cherischallenge@gmail.com
858 223-6677
@I_lovemotherearth
https://www.facebook.com/cherirey
@cherisenergy
linktr.ee/Cherirey

DR. (h.c.) KATHLEEN RONALD
kathleen@speaktacular.com

DR. (h.c.) SHELLY RUFIN
shelly@edfin.net
shelly@edfincollegeplanningexperts.com
CALL/TEXT SHOW UP to (951) 375-6125
Office: (951) 261-9799
www.edfincollegeplanningexperts.com

ADELLA SANCHEZ
adndsanchez@hotmail.com
adellasanchez.myrandf.com

DR. (h.c.) JAYA SAJNANI
sales@ygtravel.co.uk
jayasajnani@yahoo.com
+447808 522157
www.ygtravel.co.uk

DR. (h.c.) NEPHETINA L. SERRANO
drnephetinaserrano@gmail.com
www.DrSerranos360.com

KATHERINE SETZER
katherinethegreat.sales@gmail.com
www.etsy.com/shop/katherinethegreatart
Instagram @katherinethegreatdesigns

KAYE SHEFFIELD
kaye_slp@msn.com

DR. (h.c.) CHARMAINE SUMMERS
charmaine@orangecountygolf.com
text or call: 714-350-3626

JOSIE TORRES
jhloayza@gmail.com
https://www.facebook.com/home.php

SUSAN VANDERBURGH
talk2susan@gmail.com

DR. (h.c.) MARIE WAITE
marie@finestwomeninrealestate.com

DR. (h.c.) JOAN E WAKELAND
joanewakeland@gmail.com

DR. (h.c.) TOMESHA D. WALKER
thewalkergroupcle@gmail.com

JANET WALTERS
toastmasterjanet@gmail.com

DR. RANDI D. WARD
randiteach@yahoo.com

DR. (h.c.) VIOLET WILLIAMS
yourbestspirit@gmail.com

KATHERINE ZACHARIUS
katherine@fiveringsfinancial.com

www.ingramcontent.com/pod-product-compliance
Lightning Source LLC
Chambersburg PA
CBHW062108020426
42335CB00013B/889